EXCEPTIONAL
Violence

Deborah A. Thomas

EXCEPTIONAL
Violence

Embodied Citizenship in Transnational Jamaica

Duke University Press

Durham and London 2011

© 2011 Duke University Press

All rights reserved

Printed in the United States of America on acid-free paper ♾

Designed by Heather Hensley

Typeset in Arno Pro by Tseng Information Systems, Inc.

Library of Congress Cataloging-in-Publication Data appear
on the last printed page of this book.

for Vinny
AND ALL WHO LOVED HIM

Contents

Acknowledgments

This project began as my first book, *Modern Blackness*, was being launched in late 2004. On the morning of my first public reading, I glanced through the *Jamaica Observer*—one of Jamaica's daily newspapers—and saw the first article about the gang war that was taking over the community in which I had done the research that animated *Modern Blackness*. What I was to discuss that evening suddenly seemed hopelessly out of date, and although I had been hearing about several small "incidents" that were occurring in the community from friends, the escalation into full-scale war took many by surprise. Including me. I returned immediately to my field notes. What had I missed? How did I not see this coming? Were there indications of things to come that I had noticed but had not processed or analyzed? I found nothing—or, at least, nothing that seemed instantly relevant—so I began further investigations. Of course, as I would come to see in the process of research and writing, there were things I had noticed, but they did not speak explicitly to how the war started or the forms it would take. Ultimately, however, these were things that would help me understand how the war was organized, and thus I was launched on a much longer and more involved project than I had originally envisioned. This means, of course, that there are many, many people to thank.

First, I acknowledge the financial support of the University of

Pennsylvania, Duke University (the Duke–University of North Carolina Consortium for Latin American and Caribbean Studies, the Department of Cultural Anthropology, the Program in African and African-American Studies, the Josiah C. Trent Memorial Foundation, and the Arts and Sciences Research Council), and the Center for the Americas at Wesleyan University. The Wenner-Gren Foundation for Anthropological Research (#6063) provided funding for the dissertation research on which sections of this book are also based. Earlier versions of sections of what follows were previously published as "The Violence of Diaspora: Governmentality, Class Cultures, and Circulations," *Radical History Review* 103 (2009): 83–104 (the discussion of the "culture of violence" that appears in chapter 2); "Development, 'Culture,' and the Promise of Modern Progress," *Social and Economic Studies* 54(3) (2005): 97–125, "Governance, Institutions and Economic Growth: Reflections on Arthur Lewis' Theory of Economic Growth" special issue (the discussion of Jamaica's cultural policy that appears in chapter 3); "Blackness across Borders: Jamaican Diasporas and New Politics of Citizenship," *Identities* 14(1–2) (2007): 111–33 (the discussion of the film *Belly* that appears in chapter 4); and "Public Bodies: Virginity Testing, Redemption Songs, and Racial Respect in Jamaica," *Journal of Latin American Anthropology* 11(1) (2006): 1–31 (the discussion of the "Redemption Song" statue that appears in chapter 4).

I also thank Ken Wissoker for being so open and encouraging and for working collaboratively with me on this and other projects. My appreciation also goes to Aisha Khan, who graciously identified herself as one of the reviewers of the manuscript for the Press, as well as to the other anonymous reviewer for their engagement and helpful comments.

Colleagues at the various institutional spaces I have inhabited have been critical interlocutors for this research, and I especially thank Anne Allison, Tina Campt, Charlie Piot, and Orin Starn at Duke who, at an early stage, urged me to push aspects of my analysis further or in new directions. I am grateful for the intellectual camaraderie that has been generated in various spaces at the University of Pennsylvania, especially the Race and Empire faculty working group and the Ethnohistory Seminar. I have benefited from close readings and commentaries on several chapters by a number of colleagues in these spaces and beyond, including Philippe Bourgois, Ezekiel Dixon-Roman, David Eng, Ann Farnsworth-Alvear, Damon Freeman, Toorjo Ghose, David Grazian, Laurie Hart, Tsitsi Jaji, David Kazanjian,

Suvir Kaul, Ania Loomba, Christopher Nichols, Nate Roberts, Peggy Sanday, Salamishah Tillet, Bob Vitalis, and Tamara Walker. Of course, my students (especially my graduate students) inspire me and challenge me, and I especially thank Attiya Ahmad, Giles Harrison-Conwill, Tami Navarro, Bianca Robinson, and Kaifa Roland for being such a critical part of my intellectual growth at Duke and beyond. The stars aligned for my "Race, Nation, Empire" graduate seminar at Penn in 2009 — what an impressive array of talent, kindness, and engagement!

A number of people beyond my home institutions have also played active roles in this project, either by making important interventions or by offering ongoing comradeship. Audiences at Yale University; the University of Chicago; Swarthmore College; the University of California, Irvine; the University of Puerto Rico, Rio Piedras; the University of the West Indies, Mona; Brown University; Cornell University; the University of Oregon; Rutgers University; and the University of Toronto were engaged and generous contributors, as were those at various meetings of the American Anthropological Association, the American Historical Association, the Caribbean Studies Association, and the Association for the Study of the Worldwide African Diaspora. I especially thank Tony Bogues, Yarimar Bonilla, Chris Charles, Barry Chevannes, Manuela da Cunha, Miguel Diaz-Barriga, Margaret Dorsey, Kesha Fikes, Jorge Giovanetti, Isar Godreau, Barnor Hesse, Percy Hintzen, Niklas Hultin, Yanique Hume, Rivke Jaffe, Joe Masco, Bill Maurer, Will Mazzarella, Wayne Modest, Stephan Palmié, Jean Rahier, Michael Ralph, Danilyn Rutherford, David Scott, Michael Silverstein, Sonjah Stanley-Niaah, and Roxanne Varzi. I should note that in some cases, I have had significant differences of opinion or emphasis with these interlocutors — most notably, with Christopher Charles, who makes compelling arguments about why we might think about violence in terms of a "subculture" or, at least, in terms of a series of crime patterns that are unique to Jamaica. I have genuinely enjoyed being pushed in our conversations and take responsibility for my own shortcomings and my occasional intellectual hardheadedness. Special thanks also go to Tony Harriott for encouraging me to do this research and for trusting me with his daughter; to Pat Northover for asking me to take a look at Jamaica's revised cultural policy and to offer my thoughts about it on a plenary panel at the Sir Arthur Lewis Institute of Social and Economic Studies (SALISES) conference in honor of Arthur Lewis; and to Jake Homiak, who generously offered commentary on several drafts of chapter 5, as well as his own and Carole Yawney's many influential papers. Librarians at the University of the West Indies and the National Library of Jamaica facilitated my research in important ways, and I especially thank Onanie Christie and Beverley Lothian at the Documents Center of SALISES.

I owe a special debt to Icient Iyah, Ras Kanaka, Ras Junior Manning, Empress Enid Steele, and Edward "First Man" Wray for allowing me to learn and write about what they are trying to accomplish. In particular, I thank Junior Manning, who passed on in March 2010, for involving us in his efforts to document the aftermath of the Coral Gardens incident and for trusting us to represent these efforts within the space of documentary film. Respect.

I also give singular appreciation to Hazel Carby for inviting me to Yale on several occasions to present aspects of this research and for the generous support she always offers. My crew of Caribbeanists has also put in significant time helping me to think through the issues that permeate this book. They are Belinda Edmondson, Honor Ford-Smith, Rhonda Frederick, Harvey Neptune, Annie Paul, Shalini Puri, Lara Putnam, Pat Saunders, Faith Smith, Michelle Stephens, and Alissa Trotz. Michelle in particular read drafts of several chapters and spent many long hours helping me to clarify my evidence and crystallize my arguments. Honor, of course, inspires by her example and her scholarship, and I thank her for twisting my arm to attend the Hemispheric Institute of Performance and Politics conference in Bogotá. And Alissa, my fellow traveler, provides support in countless ways and on numerous dimensions.

My friendship with Sharon Craddock has spanned several relocations, and I thank her for trusting me to tell Vinny's story properly. Vanessa Spence remains my favorite storyteller and travel buddy. Julian and Tricia Spence provided car seats, meals, and kiddie romps, and I am grateful to them for including me within their family circle. Carol Lawes has opened her home and her world to me on innumerable occasions and has become a sort of surrogate mother and grandmother. Many, many thanks are due to Annie Paul, who always provides me with a home away from home— literally and figuratively—and who is constantly ready for adventure. Tina Campt, Dawn Crossland, Angela Mitchell, and Lotti Silber continue to keep me sane, despite everything, and Shelley Smith's weekly presence at Sunday dinner has made Philadelphia an infinitely more compelling place to live. Connie Sutton, with Antonio Lauria, remains one of my most important interlocutors, my most constant mentor, my friend, and the children's "grandma Connie," spice of the Dragon! And thanks beyond measure go to Junior "Gabu" Wedderburn for always having an open mind, open hands, and an open heart. I thank him for traipsing around the country with me, for his sense of adventure and discovery, for his commitment to following the story where it leads, and for agreeing to become a filmmaker.

Although I consider several of the people I have already mentioned family, it is my "real" family that shoulders the main burden of projects like this, and that should be celebrated as they come to completion. My parents, Delroy and Doris Thomas, are my biggest fans. Their support comes in diverse forms: they paint our house, repair everything from droopy hemlines to electrical wiring, entertain the children in hotels during conferences, help us navigate the world of mortgage refinancing, and accompany us to zoos around the country. I appreciate all of it more than I ever remember to say. Ethlyn Roberts, Arlene Roberts-Scurry and Malik Scurry, Jason Roberts and Lakresha Stanford, and, finally, Jayon Stewart and "Baby Jade" have shared Thanksgiving dinners and breakfasts of "small-island" saltfish, New Year's Day football, Fourth of July spades tournaments, and choir concerts and in doing so have made my life fuller and richer. John Jackson makes everything possible, and he makes it look so easy. I aspire to be more like him every minute of every day. He is astonishingly generous and supportive, and I am lucky to have had the good sense to marry him. He reminds me that the sum total of who we are only has meaning in relation to what we build together, and for this I am grateful. And, of course, this brings me to the two small people who were both born in the middle of this project. It would be trivial and incomplete to say that Oliver and Marleigh have changed the world for me. The transformations in work, life, love, and personhood that are brought about by infancy and toddlerdom — the joys and frustrations, laughter and temper tantrums, tickle fights and trips to the emergency room — are impossible to measure. I thank them for initiating my education all over again. I love the whirlwind that is our foursome. It always gives more energy than it takes away.

Moving Bodies

RELUCTANT WITNESSING

I have tried *not* to write about violence. It is an old cliché of anthropological area studies that if one wants to study kinship and political systems, one goes to Africa; hierarchy, to India; exchange, to Melanesia, and so on. Within the Caribbean, if one wants to study violence, one goes to Jamaica. I did not, however, go to Jamaica to study violence. I went to Jamaica for other reasons—some personal and familial, and some intellectual. I went to Jamaica because in my previous professional life as a dancer, I became interested in the ways artists could have a role in social transformation, the ways dancers could project a politics (as well as an aesthetic) on stage. Because the company I danced with had been working in communities with grassroots organizations to use dance and music as media through which broader kinds of sociopolitical change might occur, I wanted to see whether this could be possible at the level of the nation-state. Conveniently for me (as someone with Jamaican familial background and having spent some years of my early childhood there), Jamaican dancers had been involved in—in fact, fundamental to—just such a project. I spent several years working with dance companies, arts organizations, community groups, and other individuals and families who were involved in various ways with these nation-building projects—as well as with many who were not—because I wanted to assess the effects of this kind of cultural politics and to think through the ways particular socioeconomic and political contexts influenced these effects. I had written about this at length in a number of venues, but nowhere had I discussed violence.[1]

Yet despite the fact that violence was generally absent within the community where I lived and worked (an absence often apprehended as unique among community members and outsiders), violence surrounded me and everyone else in and around Kingston. It defined where we went and when; it structured the degree to which we followed laws, such as stopping at red traffic lights in certain areas after dark; it generated a particular kind of alertness throughout the long nights, a sort of sleeping with one eye perpetually open. Even so, I, like many Jamaicans and some anthropologists, have attempted to foreground other aspects of social life in an effort to destabilize media stereotypes: this one of Jamaicans as violent psychopaths, and another of Jamaicans as ganja-smoking, reggae-producing beach dwellers.[2] This has been part of a related pursuit—that of legitimating the Caribbean as a serious research location, dispelling the notion that what an anthropologist might do on a typical research day is lazily smoke weed on the beach while drinking rum from a coconut.[3]

In spite of my efforts at avoidance, however, this is a book about violence, a topic that has, in recent years, become the number one preoccupation of both Caribbean governments and citizens. The region as a whole has a murder rate higher than any other region in the world, and instances of assault throughout the Caribbean are significantly above the world's average, with kidnapping a growing phenomenon, especially in Guyana and Trinidad and Tobago. Violent-crime statistics for the Caribbean are so high, in fact, that in 2007 the United Nations Office on Drugs and Crime and the World Bank issued a joint report identifying crime and violence as development issues, documenting how violence undermines growth, threatens human welfare, and impedes social development. Jamaica, with a per capita murder rate that is rivaled only by those of Colombia and South Africa, is usually singled out within the region as an exceptional case (Abrahams-Clivio 2005). Most commentators attribute this high rate—in 2009, 61.4 per 100,000 people (Strangeways 2010)—to two dimensions of Jamaica's social worlds. The first has to do with the various failures of the Jamaican economy. In 2009, services (mainly tourism) accounted for more than 60 percent of the gross domestic product, while remittances provided an additional 20 percent (Central Intelligence Agency 2010). The country's debt burden is the fourth highest per capita in the world, and although the overall unemployment rate for 2009 was 14.5 percent, men and women in their early productive years experienced unemployment rates as high as 32.9 percent and 43.7 percent, respectively (Statistical Institute of Jamaica 2009). The second, and related, cause of Jamaica's high murder rates has to do with the ways democratic political nationalism was forged in the mid-twentieth century and the various political gangs that were established (and supported by prominent politicians) in and around downtown Kingston. These gangs, and the so-called garrison communities that they originally represented, have been the source not only of some of the most spectacularly violent murders in Jamaica over the past four decades, but also of the various public scandals surrounding particular government representatives, including the most recent regarding the government's attempt to block the extradition order from the U.S. government of Christopher "Dudus" Coke. Jamaica's reputation as the most violent Caribbean nation has also been trafficked transnationally both through the diasporic scattering of these gangs during the 1980s and the subsequent emergence of the "posses" that infiltrated the underground economies of New York and Miami, and through more general contemporary migratory circuits and popular cultural representations that bounce between Jamaica and the United States.

While I will discuss gangs, murder, and spectacle in these pages, this is really a book about the particular forms of violence that are foundational to the development and deployment of ideologies regarding citizenship. It is a book that uses a discussion of violence to rethink the postcolony from the perspective of an earlier imperial moment: that moment of New World expansion that led to the establishment of what we now know as the Caribbean. And it is a book that seeks to explore how notions of citizenship within the Caribbean are being transformed by the contemporary dominance of neoliberalism. In other words, it is a book about the fraught process of state formation, specifically within the context of postcolonial Jamaica. But because this is a book about violence in Jamaica that circulates beyond Jamaica's shores, it is also a book about diaspora and transnationalism. Finally, it is a book about social change and how people envision justice, which necessarily means it is concerned with space and time, with the ways violence not only destroys but also generates—in this case, new senses of dimension, new ideas about community and citizenship, and new notions of participation and organization. And while the spatiality of violence has to do with neighborhoods as much as transnational public spheres, statecraft as much as diasporic mobilizations, its temporality requires that we approach repeating waves of violence in relation to changing political economies of labor and development, religion and representation.

Exceptional Violence therefore attempts to think through the repertoires and cyclical histories that expand to incorporate and accommodate the new while always giving us the sense that we have somehow seen this before. Two related sets of themes are repeated throughout. One has to do with "culture" and its relationship to history, to violence, and to notions and practices of citizenship. The other has to do with "culture" and its relationship to representation, debates about the appropriateness and availability of representations, notions of who has the power to create representations, and the relationships between representation and economic development. I have placed "culture" in scare quotes here to also make a point about anthropology and its object(s). Much has been written recently about how we, as anthropologists, conceptualize our contribution to an understanding of the world, given that scholars working in other fields seem to have poached both our subject matter and our methodological claim to fame (Comaroff 2009; Rabinow 2008). This project is itself a cyclical one — and one that marks a peculiar level of anxiety regarding our place within both the institution of the academy and the politics of knowledge production. It occurs to me, however, that our greatest unfinished business, and therefore potentially our greatest contribution, lies in reorienting the focus on "culture" away from the rubric of comparison and explanation and toward a deeper engagement with history, political economy, and practice. In other words, we must complete the liberation of American anthropology from those aspects of its history that privileged a focus on diffusion, traits, and personality (see Yelvington 2006a). My overarching agenda throughout these pages, then, is to present a variety of settings and mobilize a variety of methods of inquiry to parse the specifics of violence in Jamaica in order to demonstrate that violence generally is *not* a cultural phenomenon but an effect of class formation, a process that is immanently racialized and gendered.

To flesh out this argument, I mobilize a concept of reparations *as a framework for thinking*. The concept of reparations usually has been understood in relation to concrete collective claims for (monetary) redress for one or another experience of grave injustice. Within the world of activist reparations politics, claims are made, evidence is given, and injury is quantified, usually with the hope that descendants of those who were wronged will, in one way or another, feel strengthened by the recognition of responsibility. To make claims, give evidence, and quantify injury, however, hidden histories must be publicly acknowledged. Conspiracies are uncovered, lies are revealed, facades fall away, and suddenly what *everyone knew was true all along* is finally legitimated. I want to argue that if we take this approach to knowledge production, we will construct narratives that engage history in a way that is somewhat different from that which is usually expected within ethnographic work.

At the outset, we would be forced to always privilege the *interplay* of geopolitical scales rather than limiting analysis to the space of the nation-state. This has been the thrust of much of the recent Atlantic worlds scholarship and is instantiated by reparations activism related to transatlantic slavery. It is also nicely illustrated by a story I tell my students at the University of Pennsylvania about William Penn, the founder of Pennsylvania and an advocate of colonial unification, who stands majestically atop Philadelphia's City Hall. I will not go into all of the details (or the dramatic buildup) here but will merely mention that Penn, the Quaker who fought for religious freedom, only made it to the New World because he wanted to collect the outstanding debt the Crown owed his father for conquering Jamaica in 1655. As a "religious dissident" within staunchly Anglican England, Penn Jr. was given a land grant far away from the queen, and it was in this way that he came to found the Province of Pennsylvania in 1682. I tell the students this to get them thinking about how we are all implicated within *one* story and about how the Caribbean—which, unless they are from the region, seems to them to be small, far away, and relatively inconsequential as world regions go—is central to all of the processes that came to shape our understanding of modernity over the past five centuries. This is, of course, also the point of Susan Buck Morss's canonical essay "Hegel and Haiti" (2000): that the present in which we live has been built on a past for which imperialism and racial slavery were foundational—rather than incidental— elements of emergent notions of democracy throughout Europe and on both sides of the Atlantic (see also Gilroy 1993; Trouillot 1995). Yet this point is usually obscured, downplayed, and tempered on the grounds that a focus on these sorts of past relations might make people uncomfortable in the present.

Using reparations as a framework for thinking about contemporary problems also requires that we focus on structural, rather than cultural, lineages and inheritances. This is the most obvious thrust of reparations logic—that current structural inequalities have emerged and persist as a result of real and codified institutional discrimination rather than because of cultural "deviations" and "dysfunctions" that are passed from generation to generation. Nevertheless, this sort of analysis is one that is usually de-legitimized through a focus on those few extraordinary individuals who manage to succeed regardless of the countless barriers that structure their opportunities.

While in the first instance the mobilization of history helps draw a line between unlikely bedfellows, between far-flung constituencies and interests, and between then and now, in the second it draws a line between cause and effect, policies and populations. However, in neither of these examples are we mobilizing history for history's sake. This is because thinking about reparations as a framework for producing knowledge means that we are also, on some level, concerned not only with clarifying connections but also with accountability.

In other words, in different ways throughout this book I argue that reparations is not just about quantification of redress for past wrongs. It also provides an alternative to the liberal human rights framework that has become so dominant in our thinking about global inequalities today. Specifically for my purposes, I believe that using reparations as a framework for thinking compels us to refocus our notions of citizenship and sovereignty. Instead of thinking about citizenship in relation to existing notional rights, we might be moved to apprehend citizenship as a set of performances and practices directed at various state and non-state institutions or extraterritorial or extralegal networks—networks that are global, national, regional, and local—over time. This reorientation would require that we tease out the various ways in which the regulatory, disciplinary, biopolitical, and distributional practices of governments throughout the Americas (and beyond) have often been suffused with and enacted by extra-state, non-state, or quasi-legal entities. It might also, therefore, encourage us to publicly debate the extent to which we believe these entanglements are acceptable, as well as the degree to which particular individuals, corporations, and governments might be called to account for the contemporary effects of these pasts. Developing a better understanding of the complicated and contextually specific interrelationships of these different modes of governance, and entities would also likely compel us to make visible the creative and dynamic ways people make new worlds out of their own "bare life" instead of assuming that what marginalized citizens want is merely the extension of rights.

Using reparations as a framework for knowledge production might also move us to think through the centrality of slavery to the contemporary Americas in a somewhat different way. By this I mean to say that examining social and historical experience through the lens of reparations might allow connections to be made between phenomena that usually are not seen as related. My aim vis-à-vis this point is to be suggestive rather than exhaustive, thinking, for example, about how the common practice of providing slaves with provision grounds might have laid the groundwork for the patterns of authority that developed in the political sphere during the nationalist period (something I discuss in chapter 1); or about how arguments about the effects of slavery on family formation might have provided the scaffolding for culturalist notions of poverty and violence (my point in chapter 2); or about how spectacular forms of punishment and discipline during slavery might provide templates for the more performative dimensions of killing today (the topic of chapter 3). My ultimate argument here is that thinking through reparations could help to expose how and why biopolitical strategies of social control never fully eclipse disciplinary modes of power within postcolonial Atlantic worlds. Further, using reparations as a framework for thinking makes available a political project that other models of state formation and political transformation in the Caribbean and beyond—such as Marxist proletarian revolution—have not and so may provide us with a different register through which to make visible actual processes of social change.

At stake here are the broader questions of how we make and remake ourselves in the contemporary world. Nineteenth-century theorists provided us with certain blueprints—for Hegel, "man" produced "himself" through thought; for Marx, through labor. Hannah Arendt, writing in the post–Second World War context, believed that we produce ourselves through our engagement with the political, and during the height of anticolonial agitation, Frantz Fanon famously argued that colonized subjects could produce themselves only through violence. But what of today? How, in a postcolonial, post–Cold War context,[4] do we redefine citizenship so that it is a meaningful concept — politically, economically, and sociocul-turally — particularly for those who have been formally excluded from sig-nificant engagement? What forms of collectivity are possible today? What kinds of leadership might they engender? These are the vexing problems of our moment and the overarching issues that preoccupy this text.

ON VIOLENCE

Many scholars have suggested that neoliberalism has produced particular kinds of spatial effects that, while drawing inspiration from earlier patterns of hierarchy and inequality, have also mapped new geographies of belong-ing and exclusion. Here, I am thinking not only about those geographies with which we have come to be familiar — trade blocs or migration patterns, for example, or even those political federations or solidarity networks that cross territorial boundaries, creating supra-national communities. I am also thinking about the ways people transform space without necessarily going anywhere and in so doing alter hierarchies of status and influence in par-ticular localities. And though one of the vehicles through which this seems to be happening in the contemporary period is the proliferation of violence, violence itself has only relatively recently become a topic of explicit con-cern among anthropologists (Nagengast 1994; Starn 1991).

Over the past two decades, social scientists have begun to examine in earnest the connections among current processes of neoliberal globaliza-tion, various kinds of state collapse, and both spectacular and everyday forms of violence. Several scholars have explored the ways genocide and cycles of violence have been linked to patterns of colonialism and Zionism and how urban gangs have emerged within communities to take on vari-ous kinds of state functions. Others have looked at the ways state violence and mass killings have generated conditions whereby fear becomes a "way of life," death is greeted without surprise, suffering is the everyday state of things, and torture and fear are mapped onto reconfigured (individual and collective political) bodies, as well as onto living spaces and landscapes. They have explored communal violence in relation to the discourses of his-tory and nation that have undergirded the identity and political claims of groups marginalized from citizenship due to ethnic or religious differences, showing that these differences are always racialized and gendered and that violent acts against women's bodies are perpetrated and interpreted as threats to the whole communities these women are seen to represent. And they have thought through how human rights workers, among other interested parties, have grappled with classifying and coming to terms with violent events.[5]

Where anthropologists perhaps have been at their most effective has been in illuminating the structural violence that attends the neoliberal project and the ways this violence shapes symbolic, domestic, and intimate worlds for poor folk around the globe while publicly legitimizing social inequalities by obscuring their origination.[6] These scholars have highlighted the connections between spectacular (almost magical) violence and the intensification of ethnic and other conflicts in relation to what Thomas Hansen (2001: 222) has called a "wider anxiety regarding public order" or what Arjun Appadurai (2006) has identified as a sense of uncertainty that must be rectified through the production (and subsequent mobilization) of minor differences among populations.[7]

We see this especially when we look at the historical and anthropological literature on violence in Africa and South Asia (and with respect to the latter, particularly in India and Sri Lanka). The literature on Africa generally positions colonialism as the primary causal factor of genocidal violence, and emphasizes the ways both direct and indirect colonial rule agglomerated and segregated populations with the effect of creating (racialized) hierarchies of privilege within them, hierarchies that then provided the antagonistic camps for organized violence (see Malkki 1995; Mamdani 2001; Mbembe 2001). This sort of organized violence is thus both the cause and effect of struggles over the rights of citizenship within a context in which the previously taken-for-granted domains of the state—security, social order, justice—have evaporated or become privatized, either legitimately or informally (see Roitman 1998, 2005). The literature on South Asia has similarly stressed the production of religious and ethnic difference through a variety of colonial and postcolonial state policies and techniques like censuses, and has sought to elucidate how ethnicized groups then attempt to secure majority status by undermining the rights of groups designated as minorities (see, for example, Appadurai 2006; Daniel 1996; and Pandey

2006). In both cases, scholars have also examined how these identities are reproduced and sometimes intensified within diasporic settings, generating new sites for conflict.

Within Latin American and Caribbean contexts, however, the scholarly emphasis has been on the structural violence that has become part of the fabric of everyday life (Harrison 1997; Taussig 1986). Of crucial importance here has been a sense that the state, which should be protecting people from violence and providing social order and justice, has shattered—or, as Haitians among whom Nina Glick Schiller and Georges Fouron (2001) have conducted research would say, has become merely apparent rather than responsible.[8] Neoliberalism is the culprit here—shaping civil wars, legitimizing U.S. interventions, and generating gross social inequalities—and states (and those who lead them) have been partners in these processes. Jonathan Friedman (2003) has been among those anthropologists who have focused on sociocultural fragmentation, the proliferation of transnational criminal networks, the lumpen proletarianization of many urban zones worldwide, and the struggle for control over resources by privatized elites as causal factors for the new and resurgent incidents of spectacular violence that contribute to a general sense of insecurity, not only for Latin American and Caribbean populations within the region, but also for those who reside abroad. For these scholars, linking political or gang violence, for example, to patterns of structural violence remains an urgent concern.

For some scholars (and for many lay analysts), the violence that proliferates in, say, India, Sri Lanka, or the former Yugoslavia is different from the violence occurring in Haiti, Jamaica, or even Philadelphia, where I live. The former is seen as having some kind of logic that is associated with a sense of eternal subjectivity—in other words, it has to do with age-old religious strife or ethnic conflict—whereas the latter is seen as lacking any rationale other than violence itself (Scott 1997). Therefore, this type of violence must be deeply ingrained, and as a result, people's responses to violent events such as the murder of journalists, or of children, are framed in terms of "culture." That is, the perpetrators of such violence are seen as immutably bereft of moral responsibility or human empathy, and their behavior is seen to be patterned by a pathological culture that they cannot help but reproduce. While this is an argument I hope to thoroughly debunk throughout this book, it is also true that violence, like all forms of human expression, takes diverse cultural forms in particular locations, and it is critical to explore not only the histories that generate these forms (Whitehead 2004), but also the representational spheres through which these forms are aestheticized (Roach 1996). If we understand violence as a form of cultural expression that "expends a human surplus," especially within the Atlantic world, then, as Joseph Roach (1996: 125) has argued, we must see it as representing "a form of excess production and expenditure of social energy," as *exceptional* in both senses of the term.

The historical thus becomes both analytic category and method, a way to parse the place of the past in the present. This is something that is at the heart of Achille Mbembe's insightful analysis of sub-Saharan African postcoloniality. In his exploration of the relationships between colonialism and subjectivity, his notion of time is one of "entanglement" (Mbembe 2001:14). "As an age," he argues, "the postcolony encloses multiple *durées* made up of discontinuities, reversals, inertias, and swings that overlay one another, interpenetrate one another, and envelope one another" (Mbembe 2001:14). It is this layering of temporalities, not in any linear sense, that creates "an *interlocking* of presents, pasts, and futures that retain their depths of other presents, pasts, and futures, each age bearing, altering, and maintaining the previous ones" (Mbembe 2001:16). History in this context becomes so many stories that as we repeat them, sound vaguely familiar or so many experiences that as we confront them, feel like the same old same old, not unlike Antonio Benítez-Rojo's (1996) concept of repetition.

This sense of history also animates Jacqui Alexander's notion of the transnational. Like Mbembe, Alexander (2005: 190) argues that time is "neither vertically accumulated nor horizontally teleological." She deploys Ella Shohat's notion of palimpsestic time to evoke the image of "a parchment that has been inscribed two or three times, the previous text having been imperfectly erased and remaining therefore still partly visible" (Alexander 2005: 190). I will say more about this notion of time in chapter 3, but I have placed Mbembe in dialogue with Caribbeanists here to push our sense of time—and thus of colonialism as a particular modality of violence—backward to the fifteenth century, to that first period of exploration and imperial conquest that resulted in the elaboration of a notion of the modern West. After all, when Aimé Césaire (1972: 19–20) discussed imperialism as "thing-ification," the complete dehumanization of both colonizer and colonized, he was referring to the processes that generated Martinique—no less, Haiti—not Cameroon or Senegal. It is this first phase of imperialism and colonial slavery that saw violence deployed in the service of, among other things, the consolidation of both empires and nationalisms within Europe *and* the related development of the notions of difference that subsequently would be mobilized to serve the late-nineteenth-century project of indirect imperial rule (Holt 2000; Mignolo 2000; Taussig 1992a; Wynter 2003).⁹ This was a project that ultimately would result in the emergence of various strands of Social Darwinism in which the racially inferior "Other" would become biologized as the Native (Wynter 2003). Where "natives" could be the "raw material of government" (Mbembe 2001:33), however, slaves could not, and it would not be until after the labor rebellions throughout the West Indies in the 1930s that interventions would be instituted *at the level of government* that would initiate a concern with development and welfare and, therefore, with the biopolitical management of populations. These postcolonial Caribbean societies, therefore — or, at least, these formerly British Caribbean societies — share the palimpsests of colonial time but do so always with the sense that there are ancestral elsewheres, that the hybridities of Caribbean populations always exceed the boundaries of the nation (Puri 2004). They, too, are *exceptional*.

Despite these differences, however, Mbembe's notion of the ways the colonial state — and therefore also the postcolonial state — legitimized the reproduction of its own authority through the "miniaturization" of violence, the arbitrary and everyday forms of "micro-actions" that were designed to socialize the population into a constant state of fear and vulnerability (Mbembe 2001: 25–28) also holds true within the context of Jamaica, as I show in the chapters that follow. These are, of course, the issues that provoke more general reevaluations of the nature of the postcolonial Jamaican state during moments that are seen to represent a period of crisis or transition. M. G. Smith's (1965) plural society theory, for instance, arose during a time when analysts were attempting to understand the potential basis for national unity within the context of impending independence and, as Don Robotham (1980) has cogently argued, reflects Smith's disillusionment with a particular version of the Jamaican nationalist project. The current context is one in which exceptional violence has accompanied an intensification of Jamaica's integration — though on disadvantageous terms — within a globalized political economy, prompting more and more citizens to rethink the cultural and political dynamics of what it means to be Jamaican.

Obika Gray (2004: 5), for example, has offered a recent view of the post-colonial Jamaican state as both monopolistic and flexible, authoritarian and adaptive—in a word, contradictory. He argues that the Jamaican state is parasitic, a term he uses to describe a process of rule whereby the state maintains its dominance by "appropriating aspects of popular culture and blurring, even collapsing, the boundaries between antagonistic cultural forms of the poor and that [sic] of their nemesis in the class system." Parasitic rule, he states, is opportunistic; it incorporates norms and practices hostile to those that are publicly proclaimed as valuable, and it undermines democracy by making predation and state violence tacitly acceptable (Gray 2004:6). Because it draws on subaltern social and political forms of expression, Gray (2004: 8) insightfully points out, "Those over whom it rules typically experience it as culturally familiar, and even as representative of national-popular traditions." Gray makes these arguments about parasitism in part to counter the crisis discourse that is currently circulating more generally about how current processes of globalization have eroded the power of states throughout the Global South. He also identifies parasitism as the defining characteristic of the contemporary Jamaican state to underline the now common argument that, since the 1970s and especially since 1989, there has been a decline in the hegemony of the creole multiracial nationalism that characterized the mid-twentieth-century movement (Meeks 2000; Scott 1999; D. Thomas 2004), a decline that has coincided with the uptick in violent crime and homicide. Gray (2004: 6) suggests not that these shifts represent a situation of "turbulence-amidst-democracy" but, instead, that the democratic aspects of Jamaican statehood "have been supplanted by predatory, violent and illegal forms of rule," with the state engaging in extrajudicial violence, the violation of human rights, and corruption.

What I would contend is that these predatory, violent, and illegal forms of rule are the legacies of colonial state formation and plantation-based extraction and so could not but be incorporated within—indeed, were foundational to—postcolonial state formation in Jamaica. It is not, in other words, that we have incomplete, imperfect democracies, but that democracy in the Americas has been founded on a house of cards, as it were. In the formerly British West Indies, however, this has not led to the sorts of autocratic rule Mbembe (among others) has identified or the kinds of spectacular, though ultimately hollow, performances of state power Charles Piot (2010) has discussed in relation to Togo. In part, this is due to the sorts of practices Gray outlines—principally the incorporation of the cultural expressions and political modalities of working-class Jamaicans—as well as the Caribbean's more tangential connection to the support of dictatorships motivated by the Cold War that characterized European and U.S. relationships with Africa and Latin America until 1989.[10] I believe that the general lack of autocracy within the Caribbean is also the result of two additional dimensions of life with which formerly British West Indian governments have had to contend: the reconfiguration of relationships among family, sexuality, and national belonging, and long-term patterns of deterritorialized citizenship. As I attempt to demonstrate throughout this book, these are dimensions of life that are related in complicated ways, and understanding these relations is critical to a broader exegesis of postcolonial state formation.

Mbembe discusses sexuality primarily in relation to its disciplining, especially through forms of sexual violation. He is principally preoccupied with the vulgar, the workings of the belly, mouth, phallus, and anus. For example, mobilizing Bakhtin, he argues, "The grotesque and the obscene are two essential characteristics that identify postcolonial regimes of domination" (Mbembe 2001: 103), and, later, "The act of exercising command cannot be separated from the production of licentiousness" (Mbembe 2001:126); thus, the subsequent need to "rein in the abundant sexuality of the native" (Mbembe 2001:113). In a more recent essay in which he responds to critics of his work, he acknowledges that a more complete treatment of the deployment and management of sexuality in the postcolony would require "a genealogical analysis of the symbolic systems which in Africa have historically tied the social worlds of sexuality and of power to the phantasmal configurations of pleasure (*jouissance*) on the one hand, and to structures of subjection on the other hand" (Mbembe 2006: 162). Still, the examples he gives have to do with the body and the functions of its parts—vagina and penis, libertine sex and carnality, childbirth and domination. Where I would like to focus our gaze instead is on the ways the management of sexuality has been tied to sovereignty through the mobilization initially of a discourse of respectability and later, of "racial respect" that has been related to intensified transnationalism. This is a quintessentially Foucauldian project, to be sure (Foucault 1990), but one that seeks to recognize the simultaneity of processes of governmentality and disciplinary forces that continue to operate within postcolonial worlds saturated by a history of racial terror (Iton 2008; Mbembe 2001). In other words, it is a project that seeks to take into account not only how the social dimensions of sexuality in the Caribbean have been tied to notions of freedom, particularly in the post-emancipation and postcolonial periods (Miller 1991; Sheller forthcoming; Smith 2011), but also how anxieties about the transnational tend to be expressed through attempts to regulate the sexual.

Of course, several scholars within and beyond anthropology have interrogated the links among gender, state formation, and nationalism and have demonstrated that colonialism and anticolonial and postcolonial nationalisms are projects implemented through the production of "appropriate" gender relations and sexualities.[11] Two key insights have been generated by this kind of research. The first has to do with the assertion that gender norms are not merely effects of broader processes but actually constitute these processes in the first instance; and the second has to do with the recognition that gender norms are not static but, rather, change in relation to evolving labor needs and ideas about femininity and sexuality transnationally. We also know that gender does not stand on its own, but is intimately articulated with other social categories — especially race, class, and religion (see, for example, Brodkin 2000; Hall 2002; Mahmood 2004; Williams 1996) — and as such it always shapes more general struggles over the production of political, economic, and social subjectivities. These struggles ultimately have to do with the power to define the nation and cultural citizenship, and in Jamaica they have been indexed through the various binaries that mark the social, spatial, economic, and political distance between elites and non-elites — "upper class" versus "poorer class," uptown versus downtown, brown versus black, ladies versus women (Ulysse 1999). Ultimately, one of my aims in this book is to build on the work of scholars such as Hazel Carby, Jacqui Alexander, Ann Stoler, and Elizabeth Povinelli by showing how the classed and gendered dimensions of state projects in Jamaica have been entangled with anxieties about sexuality both at home and abroad, that the intensification of these anxieties is fueled by uncertainties and vulnerabilities related to the transnational situation, and that this entanglement is both reproduced by and reproduces culturalist-oriented scholarship, even in the face of transformed ways to organize global relatedness in economic and political spheres (see Carby 1998; Alexander 1991, 1994, 1997, 2005; Povinelli 2006; Stoler 2002).

The other dimension of life that is critical to a consideration of postcolonial state formation within formerly British West Indian societies has to do with de-territorialization, diaspora, and transnationalism. Of course, many Caribbeanists made early and insightful contributions to our understanding of these processes, but they have not necessarily been concerned about thinking through them directly in relation to state formation, except insofar as they have demonstrated that states have had to work hard to "catch up" with their populations.[12] This has also been true, to a degree, within interdisciplinary scholarship on the African diaspora, as questions regarding the state often drop out of the analytic frame (but see Patterson and Kelley 2000). This is not to say that there has not been a long history of diaspora scholarship that has taken the political economies of black folks' relations to particular states as its foundational rubric. I am thinking here not only of classic texts such as W. E. B. Du Bois's *Black Reconstruction* or *Philadelphia Negro*, for example, but also of canonical histories of black Marxisms and even contemporary explorations of particular sites of pan-Africanist or internationalist mobilization.[13] Of course, one of the points of using diaspora as a rubric for analysis is to get outside the limiting framework of nation-states for understanding modes of communication and the creation of political and cultural community. Yet what we miss if we do not think transnationalism and diaspora directly in relation to postcolonial state formation is a sense of the transnational—indeed, transimperial—dimensions of particular governmental projects.

I argue in these pages that a focus on modes of governmentality across space helps us (1) maintain a critical dialogue between the two registers in which we mobilize the term "diaspora"—both as an instantiation of a worldwide black community that is the result of the transatlantic slave trade and as the community formations resulting from transnational migrations; and (2) clarify how particular state projects have been imagined and developed transnationally. Again, these are objectives that, within the context of a commitment to reparations as a framework for knowledge production, also destabilize the continuing discourse that obscures the processes of colonial subjection that propelled European state formation and that generated seemingly new notions of freedom and participation (Taussig 1992b). A contemporary concern also animates this agenda, as state functions are being privatized to the sphere of nongovernmental organizations (NGOs) and other nominally non-state agencies, something James Ferguson and Akhil Gupta (2002: 990) have argued is "a key feature, not only of the operation of national states, but of an emerging system of transnational governmentality." As we will see, individuals and groups are also seeking to mobilize themselves through these very channels of transnational governmentality — such as the European Union or the United Nations — to support their efforts vis-à-vis the Jamaican state. We might position these maneuvers in relation to earlier pan-Africanist mobilizations, yet the neoliberal context that frames them presents problems as thorny as those that were the effects of mid-twentieth-century nationalist movements.

THE CHAPTERS

Each of the chapters that follow focuses on a different temporal and conceptual moment regarding the ways violence, citizenship, public representation, and counter-narratives have suffused the development of Jamaican subjectivities. Each also addresses particular aspects of the arguments about space and time, drawing attention to the various ways violent social processes are embodied in different ways over time. Francisco Ferrándiz (2009: 48) has suggested that "bodies may be used as analytical road maps, as entry- and exit-points to and from social, political and economic processes." My focus on embodiment, as each chapter title suggests, is similarly meant to evoke the ways that forms of corporality change (or are sometimes renewed or reinvented) in tandem with broader processes of social transformation. My interests in these questions have fairly traditional ethnographic beginnings, but like so much of contemporary anthropology, this book moves far beyond the space of community studies to explore the various ways violence — and notions of violence — circulate within and beyond Jamaica. Moreover, because my topic exceeds the conventional methods of anthropology, I have found myself compelled to deploy other disciplinary toolkits and more experimental narrative voices. For example, I have turned to literary criticism in some chapters, hoping that I might find some hints of how to deal with a notion of reference and citation that does not evoke the kind of literal tracking early anthropologists of the African diaspora attempted (and for which they are now roundly critiqued). Elsewhere, I have attempted to mine various sorts of archives to flesh out particular historical arguments. This has required a degree of retraining on my part — and more conventional historians or literary critics may no doubt find my efforts lacking — but ultimately I situate these sorts of methodological deployments as part and parcel of what ethnographic work can and should be. The chapters are thus meant to build on each other thematically, rather than chronologically, and this is my attempt to create the effect of "repeating islands" and "palimpsestic time" through the structuring of the text itself (Alexander 2005; Benítez-Rojo 1996).

To explore the preoccupations that animated this book, I begin with what to many observers of the region will be a familiar story—the development of a gang war within the neighborhood where I had concentrated my original doctoral fieldwork during the mid-1990s. This ethnographic story, however, has a twist because it represents a failed attempt to move already existing circuits of weapons, drugs, and political influence into new frontiers. I tell this story to illuminate the contemporary inconstancy of the Jamaican state's ability to govern, an ability that, in turn, is related to how early patterns of exploration and exploitation shaped the range of possibilities for postcolonial state formation in the Caribbean. In other words, in the first chapter I argue that the story of contemporary violence in Jamaica is one that has a longer history than that which is usually told. The silencing of this history masks the centrality of violence as an organizing principal of state formation in Jamaica. It does this by obscuring the effects of slavery and its various related modes of production on contemporary notions of political authority and by instead privileging the story of post–Second World War democratic political nationalism and its aspirational slogan privileging unity: "Out of Many, One People."

From these explorations, I move to a discussion of the common discourse that Jamaica can be characterized as having a "culture of violence." In the second chapter, I think through the proliferation of this discourse, arguing that its roots lie in the earlier mobilization of the "culture of poverty" trope. Both of these discourses emerge out of the culturalist approach to understanding inequality that gained speed after the Second World War and that identified "dysfunction" within the black working class as having its roots in a "deviant" family structure. I show that this approach to black families was a transnational one that has had particular but related effects among different diasporic (in the sense of worldwide black community) populations, and one that has also moved with people as they create diasporas (in the sense of transnational migrant communities). An investigation of these dynamics can give us insights into links that were made (and ultimately institutionalized) between the economy, family, and political participation for communities of African descent in a range of locations.

Broadly, therefore, the second chapter is concerned with black people's re-lationships to states across imperial and generational moments. Specifi-cally, I am interested in how the movement from a mid-twentieth-century emphasis on state-centered industrial modernization to the global neolib-eralism of the late twentieth century and early twenty-first century has the potential to generate new ideas about the relationships among black mas-culinity, black family formation, and modern development.

The third chapter is concerned with the spectacularity of violence in Jamaica. I propose that while most Jamaicans would casually root the proliferation of spectacularly performed murders in the consumption of (North) American films, spectacularity has actually been a constituent part of governance since the British took Jamaica from Spain in 1655. The popu-lar emphasis on American cultural influence reveals something about the ways Jamaicans experience the current postcolonial neoliberal moment and calls our attention to how more distant histories of imperialism and slavery are obscured. I argue in this chapter that these more distant histories, in fact, continue to inform the performative dimensions of local struggles, and that blaming "America" blinds us to the ways violence itself is orga-nized transnationally. When all that is harmful to a Jamaican cultural sensi-bility is located within the specter of U.S. influence, the inference is that the national space is threatened by what is ostensibly "outside." This empha-sis makes an appreciation of the multifaceted and intricate ways "outside" and "inside" have always been co-constitutive difficult and instead evokes a notion of "clash"—not the "sound clash" that characterizes dancehall cul-ture (Cooper 2004), but the *clash of civilizations*, here deployed at the level of both policy and the popular. To flesh out these arguments, I probe what might seem like a range of disparate sources: Jamaica's revised national cultural policy, historiography addressing slaves' punishment and death, material artifacts on display in a Great House outside Montego Bay, and popular music and myths, mining them for suggestions about how repre-sentations of bodily torture during the period of slavery may have created repertoires of spectacular violence, techniques of performance that have been developed over time and that are made available in various ways for improvisatory citation or reprisal.

In chapter 4, I explore the ways crisis talk is mapped onto black bodies in public space to think through anxieties about transnational circulations and the ways they have eroded regulatory norms related to gender, sexuality, and family. As I outline in chapter 2, these are norms that have under-girded notions of respectable citizenship in Jamaica. In chapter 4, I demonstrate that they also serve as the foundations for notions of racial respect that are deployed especially by Jamaicans living abroad. In other words, it is not only the Jamaican state but also its subjects who express apprehension regarding the effects of diaspora, transnationalism, and circulation, effects whose racialized dimensions are perhaps experienced most acutely by those Jamaicans living in North America and the United Kingdom. These apprehensions are reflected within both elite and popular cultural expressions, and I mine these expressions here.

First, I examine the hubbub that emerged in newspaper articles and commentaries about "Redemption Song," a statue whose very name makes reference to the oral iconography that for many around the world stands in for Jamaica. "Redemption Song" was commissioned by the government and unveiled on Emancipation Day in 2003 to commemorate the abolition of slavery. I show how the debates about the statue that appeared in the newspapers bring into relief ongoing struggles over the terms of cultural citizenship and public representations of Jamaicanness — struggles whose racial, gendered, and sexual dynamics are constituted transnationally. I place these discussions about citizenship in relation to those that suffuse popular cultural production and, in particular, to the gangster genre of popular fiction and film. I do this to argue that the various responses to both the "Redemption Song" statue and the fictional worlds of "Yardie" novels and gangster films suggestively map the disquiet related to both social and physical mobility in terms of the complicated ways class articulates with education, religion, generation, and notions of vulgarity. The intensification of transnational movement within the context of neoliberalism, in other words, has created a scenario in which both male and female bodies are publicly vulnerable in potentially new ways and in which Jamaicans at home and abroad are struggling to come to terms with the new gender norms that permeate this new, mobile, sense of vulnerability. I argue, finally, that this struggle has resulted in a convergence, across class and space regarding the ways sexuality marks the outer edge of authentic citizenship in transnational Jamaica, an edge that is often violently policed.

Finally, the last chapter of the book explores the changing relationships between Rastafari and the Jamaican state by examining how one instance of state violence against Rastafarians — what is now known euphemistically as the Coral Gardens "incident" of 1963—has been memorialized. If we agree that certain forms of violence are written out of nationalist narratives even as they define the terms of belonging, then we must understand the testimonies given at events like the annual commemoration of the events at Coral Gardens as an archive of counter-nationalist narratives. These sorts of counter-narratives do not merely fill in the blanks of an unfinished history, but also serve as performative building blocks through which community solidarity, authority, and futures are envisioned. These visions incorporate not only the immediate desire some have for compensation for wrongs done to particular individuals and families in 1963 but also the long-term project of seeing Rasta at the cutting edge of reorganizing our notions of both political and cultural citizenship for today's world. In this case, the cutting edge is occupied by a group of Rastafarians in western Jamaica who have been mobilizing themselves around issues of ownership and the legal protection of cultural heritage and practices—mobilization that necessarily has led to a greater engagement with the Jamaican government. On one hand, these initiatives seem to represent a capitulation to a neoliberal consumerist ethos whereby culture itself becomes a commodity to incorporate and consume. On the other hand, they mark an innovative reworking of a reparations framework. In this chapter, I address the complexity of these sorts of contemporary cultural processes, thinking through their implications for community empowerment and development. I elaborate on this discussion about reparations, justice, and social transformation in the coda, arguing that in this postcolonial moment, if we were to reorient our vision away from narratives of revolutionary social change, we might be able to see practices and projects of change that are already being realized.

The broader questions that move me through these chapters have to do with how people are envisioning their futures (as individuals and collectivities) and where and how these futures should transpire; the kinds of connections they make and dismantle to generate these futures, connections that are sometimes forged in relation to a conception of diaspora (both African and Caribbean); and how they understand themselves as transnational subjects who, even if they are staying put, carry with them particular kinds of racial baggage that is not only gendered, classed, and nationalized but also generationally specific. In other words, I seek to show how citizenship is both practiced and performed in a variety of modes and spaces, and I mobilize the notions of space and time in part to help bring these different levels of circuitry into conversation. It also seems to me that thinking about the ways particular circuits connect and disconnect locations at specific temporal junctures might be a way, on one hand, to avoid falling into the trap of culturalism, and on the other, to support actually existing social justice projects.

1

Dead Bodies, 2004–2005

Early in the morning on Good Friday in 2005, I received the phone call that Jamaicans — both those living "on the rock" and those overseas — dread. "Deborah, it's Winsome." Winsome was my closest friend in Jacks Hill during the longest period of my field-work in the mid-1990s. We have stayed in touch over the years as we have both traveled to and from Jamaica — she, for a couple of years, as a hotel worker contracted for six months a year at a family-run resort in Ogunquit, Maine, and I in my usual comings and goings for research and visiting friends and family. One of the hardest-working and focused people I know, Winsome is also brilliantly creative. The roots plays she wrote and produced in Jamaica hilariously and sympathetically represented the toils and triumphs of ordinary folk in Jamaica *to* ordinary folk in Jamaica, creating a space for public debate about community morality and the pitfalls of "progress." Most important for this story, however, is that Winsome was Selwyn's partner in crime, the mother of his children, his best friend and confidante for more than twenty years, and his wife for three and a half. Having moved to Atlanta earlier that year with her three youngest children, she was waiting out the U.S. government's residency requirement for her own citizenship and was counting the months until Selwyn's papers would come through and he could join her.

"Them shoot Selwyn," she whispered. "Them kill him."

After a long, silent pause, the questions came. When did they shoot him? An hour before, after they had finished speaking on the phone. Why? They came for his gun, a licensed firearm. Is everyone else OK? I don't know; I haven't been able to get through on the phone. What can I do? I don't know yet. I'll call you back.

I hung up the phone and burst into tears. Selwyn initially had been my mechanic (and pretty much everyone else's in Jacks Hill) but had become much more than that over the years. Most days, after taking the kids to school, he could be found in his garage tinkering with whatever car needed work, smoking herb, and reasoning with whomever stopped a while. A Rasta at heart (though he never let his hair lock), Selwyn was a self-made man who was not afraid to speak his mind but was gentle enough to be everybody's "uncle." A friend of mine used to say that when he laughed, he sounded like a goat, yet Selwyn was as serious as cancer.

After making a few frantic calls, the details began to sort themselves out. When he had finished speaking with Winsome on the phone, Selwyn went out with his grandnephew to pasture his goat. Gunmen met him at the gate — they were waiting for him — and told him they had come to kill him. "But yu cyaan do dat," he said, laughing incredulously. "What yu really come fah?" They lunged for him, pulled their guns and fired. Eight times. Selwyn may or may not have gotten his own shot off, but they did manage to take his gun, shoot him with it, and dump his body into the gully behind his garage. The police were called, but hours later, when Winsome did finally get back to me, she told me they had refused to do an extensive search for Selwyn's body. "The police are afraid," she said, "because those men are still hiding out in the bush, and the police don't know the bush." Ultimately, it was Selwyn's cousin and stepson who found his body and called the ambulance.

In Kingston, structural violence and violence related to politics or the drug trade are hallmarks of many "inner-city" areas. The rural hillside village of Jacks Hill, however — a community of just over a thousand people where I had concentrated my doctoral field research — had long been seen as existing outside these patterns, despite the fact that it is only six miles north of Kingston's corporate area. For those familiar with the logics of space, class, and politics in Kingston, "Jacks Hill" would typically evoke the upper-class hillside moving up from Barbican Square, inhabited by some of Jamaica's wealthiest families. However, "upper" Jacks Hill—the area in which my research has been concentrated—is the community that sits above this wealthy enclave. It is part of the East Rural St. Andrew electoral constituency that stretches above Sunset Avenue across the hilltop toward the (again) wealthy area of Skyline Drive. This part of Jacks Hill is *not* a depressed squatter pocket adjacent to an upper-class residential area, as so often happens in the urban Caribbean. Instead, it is a well-established community in which, during 1996 and 1997, about 5 percent of its approximately 1,400 residents were what one would identify as "middle class," part of the national stratum of brown urban professionals and civil servants. The remaining 95 percent called themselves the "poorer class of people" in relation to these middle-class residents. Some of their families' presence in the community dated to the nineteenth century, and many of them were either from or had family connections to neighboring rural communities. Despite the various conflicts that developed between and among community segments in Jacks Hill during the mid-1990s, in most ways it was a relatively progressive community in which middle-class and working-class families worked together for the betterment of the community as a whole. There is a long history to the forms of cross-class social action that were the norm in Jacks Hill. Norman Manley had been the member of Parliament (MP) for the community between 1949 and 1959, during which time he was able to encourage the National Water Commission to provide ninety-nine-year leases to community residents who had been living on their land without formal tenure (as the community is a designated watershed district), and the Community Council, established in 1978, was recognized in the early 1980s as one of the three most effective councils in Jamaica.[1] The dominant discourse by both community members and outsiders, until very recently, had been that Jacks Hill was a place where the relatively rich and the relatively poor "lived well together" and where supporters of the two political parties lived side by side without incident. During 1996 and 1997, people still spoke in shocked tones about a murder that had taken place in the community in the late 1980s—the last really violent crime event most community members remembered and one that was known to have been perpetrated by "outsiders."

However, what began as a few "isolated" incidents of violent crime in 2001—this time committed by community "insiders"—escalated furiously during the last six months of 2004. During that period, ten community members were murdered, several others were shot, and many women were raped. The intensely palpable fear and anxiety generated by these events resulted not only in a heightened discourse of violence, crime, and physical vulnerability. It also led to the overseas migration of several middle-class community members and the temporary abandonment of land and homes by roughly 80 percent of the poorer population. In a country of 2.7 million people that averages three to four murders per day (more than half of which occur in the Kingston–St. Andrew metropolitan area), this "outbreak" of violence in Jacks Hill may not seem unusual. It was, nonetheless, startling to people who prided themselves on bucking national trends in this regard. And like columnists' recountings of events in the two national daily newspapers, those of community members were framed in relation to the discourses of "crisis," the "failure" of the nationalist project, and the sense that there was diminished space for ordinary Jamaicans to "make a difference." In this chapter, I talk about how these discourses came to make sense to people as both explanation and analysis and about how we might think about violence and social transformation more generally.

Veena Das has recently suggested that we situate moments of extraordinary violence within the realm of the ordinary and in relation to "the routine violence of everyday life" (Das 2007: 136). She queries, "If violence, when it happens dramatically, bears some relation to what is happening repeatedly and unmelodramatically, then how does one tell this, not in a single narrative but in the form of a text that is being constantly revised, rewritten, and overlaid with commentary?" (Das 2007: 80). I want to attempt to take up Das's challenge—one that is about temporality as much as it is about scale—by exploring how violence in Jacks Hill remapped the material, ideological, and symbolic space of the community in three ways. First, I look at how the gang war mobilized—and by mobilizing, hardened—existing status distinctions among community members. Second, I aim to show how violence forces attention to the salient links between communities and the networks through which these links are forged, when these links are mobilized, and how they change over time. And finally, I seek to show how violence ties broader institutional structures—nationalist political parties, for example—into global circulations that are less often researched than migratory patterns or the circulation of cultural commodities (but see Nordstrom 2004; Roitman 2005). In other words, I am interested in looking at the spatial effects of violence at intra-community, inter-community, and transnational levels, as well as the temporal logics that shape these effects.

To do so, I lay out two different but related genealogies of the emergent violence in the community of Jacks Hill. This will not be a blow-by-blow recapitulation of events and memories. Instead, what I will offer will, on one hand, lead me to tell a familiar story about transformations in the role of the state and middle-class political leadership, given contemporary neo-liberal processes. On the other hand, it directs an attempt to think through what Anna Tsing (2005) has called the new "frontier cultures" created and then abandoned by those same processes. Ultimately, I argue that Jacks Hill represented a new frontier for the expansion of existing circuits of violence in Kingston. However, because the crisis generated by the violence in Jacks Hill led to a massive show of strength on the part of the Jamaican state, it was a frontier that was fairly quickly abandoned. In this case, the Jamaican state rallied. Yet the way in which it rallied exposed the unpredictability and arbitrariness that characterize its ongoing struggle for legitimacy and authority among Jamaicans negotiating dangerous terrain.

This struggle has a history, of course. As a result, we might most productively conceptualize frontiers not only in spatial terms but also as temporal constructs, themselves subject to (as well as reflecting) the vicissitudes of the state's ability to instantiate biopolitical power, an ability that, in turn, has something more generally to do with the ways early patterns of exploration and exploitation shaped the range of possibilities for postcolonial state formation in the Caribbean. In other words, the story of contemporary violence in Jamaica is one that stretches back further than is usually acknowledged (but see Bogues 2006), but it is one whose older structural underpinnings are often obscured by more recent pressing concerns about the development of democratic political participation after the Second World War. Moreover, as has also been the case in the United States, the mobilization of a nationalist aspirational slogan that privileges unity— "Out of Many, One People" — masks the centrality of violence as an organizing principle of state formation in Jamaica, both historically and in the post-colonial period. Selwyn's murder, and the broader conflict in Jacks Hill, gives us a window onto these more general discussions, and it is to that story that I now return.

Selwyn's death was only the latest in a series of murders that was rocking Jacks Hill, but because Selwyn was not involved in the gang war that was taking over the community, his death was surprising. People felt that "if they could kill Selwyn, they could kill anybody." The gang war itself was shocking, not only to a local community that had to deal with the immediate fallout, but also to a national community that did not understand how to read the violence in Jacks Hill in relation to the usual landscapes of crime and gang war in Jamaica. Ordinarily, murders of this sort tended to be concentrated in urban areas rather than rural outposts—though these two spatial frames are never as mutually exclusive as they are often purported to be, as people regularly circulate between Kingston neighborhoods and their family roots "in the country," a circulation that becomes especially clear during election periods.[2] Moreover, if they were not retributive killings, they usually had the consolidation of a drug route or political contracts as their motivation. Jacks Hill, however, unlike most rural communities, is a hillside community accessed only by two roads and a series of ancient paths that run through the foothills of the Blue Mountains; it therefore is not a significant vehicular throughway to other villages. Moreover, the community holds no history of either a sizable drug trade or partisan warfare, having elected Members of Parliament from both the People's National Party (PNP) and the Jamaica Labour Party (JLP) in relatively equal numbers over the years. As a result, what was going on in Jacks Hill did not *make sense* on the national map because it fell outside the usual terrains of violence. Furthermore, as I mentioned earlier, within most Jamaicans' social maps of Kingston, Jacks Hill refers to one of the most exclusive residential areas of the capital city. Indeed, the neighborhood has been canonized within the popular sphere of dancehall culture as *the* referent for wealth and power. (I am thinking, for example, of Lady Saw's "Man Haffi Mind Wi.") This means that newspaper reports of events in Jacks Hill needed also literally to put the community on the map. They did this by renaming the area "Jacks Hill Village" and describing it as "a depressed community sandwiched between Jacks Hill and Skyline Drive—two of St. Andrew's more affluent upper-class neighborhoods" (Walker 2004b).

Newspaper reporters, however, came onto the scene only after the particularly spectacular disinterment and (re-)shooting of the body of one of the gang leaders in June 2004 ("Dead 'Don' Dug Up, Shot" 2004). This was several years into the escalating violence, according to most community members, and only after "outsiders" had begun to make their way into the community. For Jacks Hill "insiders," genealogies of the conflict typically began with a fight that happened during a soccer match on the community's playing field in 2000. Although that fight centered on two individuals, it brought to life the status distinctions that sometimes divide members of the poorer population in Jacks Hill, mapping social distances between people who live "up the road" and those who live "down the road" and between people whose families have been in the community for generations and those who are more recent arrivals who tend to come with fewer resources. These distinctions are structured around the unequal distribution of resources such as education, the ability to migrate and develop legitimate and regular transnational networks, and a particular kind of relationship to the handful of socially conscious middle-class people who moved to the area during the 1950s and 1960s.

Let me clarify this last point. Some poor families within Jack's Hill—in particular, the families whose presence in the community dates to the late nineteenth century or early twentieth century—had tended to develop relationships that were not merely economically driven with local middle-class people who, beginning in the 1950s but intensifying into the late 1970s as the result of Prime Minister Michael Manley's emphasis on community-based problem solving and participatory development, worked to improve the community's infrastructure and its social cohesion. They did this by collaborating with middle-class community members to establish the Community Council and to build a community center that, with a few stops and starts over the years, was actively used for after-school programs, adult education and training, and communitywide events into the late 1990s and early 2000s. Those poor community members who arrived in Jacks Hill during the 1970s tended to come in with fewer resources—many of them were people who were escaping impoverishment in more remote rural areas, though others were seeking to remove themselves from the heat and escalating violent crime of Kingston. With few exceptions, they also tended not to develop significant relationships with the local middle-class families beyond (in some cases) working for them. The later arrivals sometimes felt that "the big families"—and by this, they meant that the poor families who were more established in the community—were "trying to run Jacks Hill."

Thus, a war developed between Jason (his real "alias" name),[3] a youth who was born and grew up "up the road" in Jacks Hill but whose immediate family arrived during the 1970s, and Macka (a pseudonym), a member of the more established Bradley family (also a pseudonym) "down the road," over local status and respect. Jason saw Macka as someone who had pretensions to leadership—to "donmanship." Unlike many communities in Kingston, even individual families themselves were politically split—without rancor—with one branch of the family supporting the PNP and the other supporting the JLP. Also unlike other Kingston communities, Jacks Hill has never had a "don"—the local term for an area leader—and by most accounts, Macka was more interested in status and style than in any kind of real "donmanship." Macka, however, *was* known to be a bit of a local playboy who, after his deportation from the United States, had his hands in a few questionably legal enterprises off the hill. He also was known to have a temper and was rumored to have been behind the killing of a young man who was disconnecting illegal cable hookups in the community, as well as the murder of an ex-girlfriend whose body was found burned and dumped in a gully close to his family home. And he was known to be behind a beating so severe it left a man who had challenged him on the soccer field unable to walk normally even after three months in the hospital. Moreover, he was accused of being responsible for the brutal chopping of a man who had intervened in a beating he saw Macka and his crew administering; the man had suggested that it was unfair for four men to beat up one youth. After he was released from the hospital, he and his girlfriend immediately moved out of the district. Beyond his temper, Macka was seen as someone who unfairly distributed resources. When money was allocated for road repair after Hurricane Ivan, for example, Macka was hired by the contractor to gather and supervise a group of men who would do the roadwork. Community members "up the road" complained that while he was supposed to pay every laborer 1,000 Jamaican dollars a day, he only gave this amount to his "down the road" cronies, paying the others 600 Jamaican dollars a day each and keeping the rest for himself.

Jason's crew therefore feared that Macka and his brother "Mophead" (his real alias) were consolidating power in the community and that ultimately this power would only benefit those who lived "down the road," leaving those "up the road" out of the loop. At the same time, Jason was said to have felt increasingly thwarted by middle-class community members, especially some of the women. He felt that even those people who worked actively with the Community Council were not doing it sincerely, that they were only involved because they did not want poorer community members to break into their houses. His sense was that they were all fighting against him, accusing him of things he did not do and working against the youth in the community more generally. At one point, he had established his own dry goods shop, and rumors developed that he was selling ganja. One of the middle-class women in the community began lobbying to move or close the shop and even called the police to search it. The police did not find anything during the search but kicked the shop over anyway, sending it careening into the gully below. For Jason, this was the last straw. Beginning in 2001 and sporadically through 2002 and 2003, a series of break-ins and rapes began to occur, all said to have been spurred by Jason's bringing "outsiders" into the community. Despite community members' trepidation about Macka and Mophead, these events turned general community support away from Jason and his "up the road" crew. "Jason was mad at everyone," a community member said, "but for a community to live with fear is a hell of a thing." A few people moved away at this time, though the mass exodus did not occur until later.

As a result of the increase in crime, police began to come regularly to Jacks Hill, so Macka and Mophead began to rally their crew against Jason's group. Then, in May 2004, Jason was killed, not in Jacks Hill but in Grant's Pen, a community near the bottom of the hill where Jason had friends and accomplices. Against the community's wishes, his body was brought up the hill to be buried on his family's plot of land. During the night of 30 May, his grave was dug up, and Jason's body was found the next morning with five new bullet holes in the forehead and several new shots pumped into his body, which was left outside his coffin. Community members were warned, in the tradition of Greek tragedy, that anybody who helped the police rebury the body would be killed.

Ryan (also his real alias), Jason's best friend and second in command, plotted to avenge the death of his friend. In fact, rumor had it that he had received funds from members of Jason's family who had migrated to England to place contracts on the lives of the three men whom he had been told had disinterred Jason's body. Three people were shot (two died) in retaliation, and two houses were burned down. At this point, the police were scrambling to find a way to contain the new gang war that continued to intensify in a series of tit-for-tat shootouts, including one at Jason's (posthumous) birthday dance "up the road" and another at Mophead's home "down bottom road."

In November, after a failed attempt on Macka's life during which he was shot but not killed, Mophead made it known that if Ryan were seen in the community, all of the members of his immediate family would be killed. Early in the morning on Thursday, 9 December, gunmen shot and killed Ryan's mother and her husband and set the home on fire, killing another man who was bedridden and unable to flee the burning house. As police responded to the emergency call, additional shots were fired in three separate locations "down the road" where Mophead's gang had connections. Another house and car were set on fire, and Mophead's girlfriend (who was eight months pregnant) was shot and injured. The police followed and were engaged in a twenty-minute gun battle *from which they had to retreat*. Such was the intensity of the firepower that had been amassed by gangs in a community where, a mere eight years earlier, only one or two people were known to own guns.

It was at this point that people began fleeing Jacks Hill. A once vibrant hillside community where everyone knew one another—indeed, almost everyone was related—had become a place full of strangers who walked openly on the road with high-powered guns; a place where people who once worked and socialized outdoors now sat behind closed doors and whispered, jumping to attention with every dog that barked or twig that snapped; where the post office, as well as the main shop and bar, that had been at the center of social life closed their doors, forcing community members to travel off the hill to buy daily provisions; where the school population dropped from ninety to just ten children; and where the tension in the air was so thick that just walking outside made you lose your breath.

One of the questions that kept haunting me as I listened to community members' genealogies was why now? Why, when Jacks Hill had remained outside the circuits of crime that had long encompassed other areas in or near Kingston, was the proliferation of this kind of violence so sudden? What had happened to create a situation in which gangs could develop and amass arms so quickly? What was it that could have changed the social and political geography of Jacks Hill so significantly?

In part, there was an economic dimension to the shift. With the closing of two local avenues for employment and a contraction of economic opportunities more generally, a sense existed among community members that it was more difficult to "get ahead" without migrating. Yet migration itself was a scarce resource that was structured along the same lines that otherwise divided the non-middle-class population of Jacks Hill and so contributed to the reproduction of local status distinctions. But there was also a significant social shift within the community. Several of the middle-class community members who had previously been actively involved in the establishment and governance of the Community Council had ceased to participate, in most cases because they had become too old or feeble to do so. In addition, newer middle-class community members seemed less interested in becoming part of village life or in committing their time and resources to working with poor people to improve the community as a whole. "They do not know the poorer families by name," one community member said. As a result, they had not typically involved themselves in the development of programming at the community center, the center itself had become generally less active, and the intimate ties between an activist middle class and poorer community members that had characterized social action and social support in Jacks Hill had weakened.

One of the results of this situation is that poorer residents of Jacks Hill now enjoy greater autonomy as the centrality of middle-class Jamaicans as social and political brokers for has diminished (Austin-Broos 1984). This is something I have written about elsewhere in relatively positive terms because it marks a dismantling of colonial hegemonic ideological structures that positioned "respectability" at the heart of nationalist development agendas, and that marginalized the social and economic strategies of poor, black Jamaicans (D. Thomas 2004). On one hand, the growing public strength of what I have called "modern blackness" within political, economic, and sociocultural realms has been an effect of significant structural transformation in which people have been able to reject the forms of class deference and paternalism they were previously (implicitly and customarily) forced to perform. On the other hand, modern blackness has nevertheless been experienced by many Jamaicans across class lines mainly in terms of an intensification of violence and incivility, as has also been the case in other sites around the world (see, for example, Holston 2008, 2009). While I am compelled to view these processes as a type of what James Holston (2008) has called "insurgent citizenships," forms of action that explicitly or implicitly challenge dominant paradigms of belonging that were rooted in colonial hierarchies and inequalities, the diminished role for a progressive middle class at the local level in Jacks Hill has also meant that poorer community members are left to fend for themselves without the benefit of the contacts or advocacy that had once been provided by community-minded middle-class people who, in many cases, were more integrally hooked into the structures of the nationalist state. Modern blackness, in other words, is not without its difficult complexities. There is a political dimension to the shift in Jacks Hill, as well, but this is something to which I return in the next section.

It bears mentioning here that this genealogy of gang formation and the escalation of violence in Jacks Hill was the dominant one offered up by community members who were still reeling, still in the middle of things, so to speak. By July 2005, after a combined raid by the Jamaica Defense Force (JDF) and the Jamaica Constabulary Force (JCF) that resulted in the arrest and removal from the community of approximately twenty known gunmen (though not the two gang leaders), villagers whispered less and began offering up genealogies that moved beyond the community. In other words, they began to frame their discussions about the violence that emerged at the local level in a way that examined not only the links that community members built on family connections to other communities near or far, but also those generated through the establishment of more illicit connections rooted in political and economic networks that stretched beyond the family. For them, as for many Jamaicans, this meant thinking through the connections among violence, political parties, weapons distribution, and the drug trade to redraw the usual maps of globality. Expanding the scale of analysis in this way provides another kind of answer to the question "Why now?"

GENEALOGIES II: NATIONAL AND TRANSNATIONAL
CIRCUITS OF VIOLENCE

I mentioned earlier that the newspaper reports of Jason's disinterment noted the presence of "outsiders." Karyl Walker (2004b), a reporter for the *Jamaica Observer*, wrote: "Residents claimed that the clashes were being perpetuated with the assistance of badmen from the nearby Grant's Pen community and as far away as Tivoli Gardens in West Kingston. 'The boy dem have dem friction but since dem start knock head wid man from Grants Pen and Tivoli the gun thing get plenty,' said a resident who didn't want to be identified. The police, while confirming that men from other areas had infiltrated Jacks Hill Village, could not say if they had come from Grants Pen or Tivoli Gardens." By December, after the major gun battles, reporting on the involvement of "outsiders" was much more concrete: " 'Men are brought in from Tivoli, Bread Lane and Grants Pen,' said Detective Inspector Donovan 'Hucks' O'Connor of the Half-Way-Tree Criminal Investigation Bureau. 'With the assistance of men in the area they are the ones causing most of the problems' " (Walker 2004a).

Similarly, although community members mentioned connections that individuals in Jacks Hill had with people from other areas in Kingston when they talked with me in December 2004, it was not until July 2005—when things were, as many people put it, "back to normal"—that they elaborated on these outside connections without lowering their voices or looking over their shoulders. By that time, it was also known to community members that Selwyn's gun had been found in Tivoli Gardens and that it was part of a generalized circulation of weapons between West Kingston, August Town, and Jacks Hill.

Grants Pen, Tivoli Gardens, August Town—these are the so-called inner-city communities in and around Kingston whose names evoke the landscape of political and drug-related violence that is ordinarily a defining feature of gang warfare in Jamaica. Historically, these communities have been referred to as "garrisons," a term originally used by the demographer Carl Stone (1986) to denote political strongholds led by "top rankings" in which any significant social, economic, or cultural development occurred only under the auspices of the dominant party leadership, and where residents seeking to oppose or organize against the dominant political party risked suffering personal and property damage.[4]

Most analysts trace the development of garrison communities to post–Second World War urbanization and the disruption of traditional social orders and networks (Sives 2003). With the urban economy unable to absorb the rapidly expanding labor market, unemployment rose dramatically, and growing discontent among new migrants was fueled by what Stone (1988) argued was an expectations gap. The new population of "sufferers" became vulnerable to politicians who discovered that they could be enticed to become party loyalists with promises of political spoils. As the opposing parties built their cadres of supporters willing to win elections by any means necessary, political gangs developed with the intention of intimidating voters and cementing political garrisons. Leaders of these gangs maintained close links with politicians, creating a situation of democratic clientelism, which later became known as political tribalism (Headley 2002; Stone 1983). In other words, due to the legacies of British colonial rule in which the majority of the population had never been involved in formal politics, a system of paternalism characterized the emergence of democratic nationalism in Jamaica, one in which loyalty to a personality became a key aspect of partisan politics. Over time, the foundations of partisan identity shifted, but the dominant experience of political participation became one of violence (Sives 2010).

During the late 1950s and 1960s, existing gangs became tied to political leaders, and political partisanship became more directly linked to the distribution of state resources, with housing foremost among these. By the mid-1970s, the "sufferers'" physical neighborhoods were polarized as units in newly constructed large-scale housing developments downtown were given only to supporters of one or the other political candidate; thus, Tivoli Gardens developed as a JLP enclave, and Arnett Gardens, for example, developed as a PNP enclave. Within these communities, party activists pushed out minority party supporters, in many cases forcing them to set up squatter communities elsewhere.[5] At the same time, the strengthening of black power and internationalist movements meant that rival political neighborhoods—now spatially segregated—also became increasingly ideologically polarized (Sives 2010). Since residents of garrison communities operate with a profound distrust of the police, the "dons," or area leaders, become the political authorities in the area. These dons not only mediate the links between formal and informal economic and political enterprise, but they also perform state-like functions, such as security, mediation of domestic and other disputes and determination of guilt and punishment, help with access to health care and education, and sponsorship of community events such as beauty pageants and children's Christmas "treats" (Charles 2002; Harrison 1982).[6] This kind of assistance is crucial in spaces where the neoliberal state has abandoned people to what one resident in a study on violence in inner-city communities funded by the World Bank termed "bare survival" (Levy 1995: 43) and works to reconfigure previously taken-for-granted relationships among citizenship, governance, and legitimacy, particularly in urban areas (Jaffe 2009).[7] Several academic and editorial commentators have gone as far as to argue that garrison communities are states within a state, that "the Jamaican state has no authority or power [within them] except in as far as its forces are able to invade in the form of police and military raids."[8] However, Amanda Sives (2010: 139) has pointed out that "while the dons may operate independently from the state in certain respects and fulfill important functions as a result of the failure of the state . . . they remain connected to the political directorate and engaged in the formal networks operating within the state."

Though the locations of the original so-called garrison communities have remained constant through the years, the social organization of crime began changing in the mid-1970s. At that point, the more intense export trade in ganja coincided with the oil crisis and the foreign exchange and balance of payments crises (Stone 1988), and the concomitant implementation of structural adjustment policies worsened patterns of inequality and increased poverty (Harriott 1996). During the late 1970s and moving into the 1980s, growing unemployment and an increased cost of living prompted a move from political partisan violence to turf violence (Harriott 1996, 2004; Levy 1995). In other words, dons became less beholden to politicians, although they were still loyal to their party (Charles 2002; Sives 2010). In part, this was because after the 1980 elections, which were particularly bloody (more than 800 of the almost 1,000 murders that year were attributed to political campaigning), several area dons were sent abroad while others began pursuing full-time criminal activity in Jamaica (Headley 2002). The clamping down on the ganja trade and the newly transnational organization of political gangs led many to go into cocaine and crack distribution, both in the United States (principally New York and Miami) and in Jamaica (Sives 2002, 2010). The hard-drug business also generated a trade in illegal high-powered weapons, which has ensured easier access to guns for the general population.[9] This new organization of violence has had a major effect on the residential patterns of the urban poor, many of whom are forced to flee deteriorating war zones as their homes and places of employment were destroyed (Eyre 1984, 1986). Because rival politically affiliated gangs continue to challenge the state's claims to legitimacy and authority (which is already challenged, of course, by various leaders' own involvement in the industries of violence in Jamaica and by internationally documented instances of criminality and corruption among the local security forces), several crime-reduction plans have been initiated in the past decade, and task forces have been commissioned to write reports and give suggestions for reducing political and gang violence. Despite these efforts, however, there were more than 1,600 murders in Jamaica in 2006, 2007, 2008, and 2009, though all major crime categories decreased in 2010, with the number of murders totaling 1,428 (Matthews 2011). Part of this increase in murders and other violent crimes prior to 2010 might be attributed to political campaigning, as general elections were held in September 2007. Yet the intensified wave of crime and violence might also be attributable to what Anthony Bogues has identified as a decline not only in the hegemony of the creole nation-state but also in the influence of radical modes of self-making that were rooted in Rastafari and black nationalism. For Bogues, this situation has facilitated the dominance of the "shotta," who is quickly replacing the area leader within communities. The "shotta" is a figure who is focused on amassing enough capital to influence the two-party system, who sees no need to root his initiatives within the rhetoric of black suffering and redemption, and whose rule is established through the power of death (Bogues 2005).

When Jason brought heavily armed associates (some of whom were members of his extended family) from Grants Pen and Tivoli Gardens to Jacks Hill, therefore, he was also engaging in what the anthropologist Faye Harrison (1988) has termed "the politics of social outlawry" by redrawing the space of existing turf wars to encompass a rural hillside community. But Jason was not the only one with "outside" connections. Macka also mobilized contacts he had with both JLP-dominated areas in August Town and the People's National Party stronghold of Maxfield Park to bring both weapons and associates to Jacks Hill. This war, a classic feud in some senses (Evans-Pritchard 1940), was therefore not drawn strictly along the lines of political affiliation, although politics did end up mapping onto broader disputes related to power, status, and influence in the community. Once in Jacks Hill, both sets of "outsiders" realized that here was a community where there was little police presence and fairly dense bush, as well as youth who had few prospects for their own futures, several of whom were only too happy finally to be participating in something they felt had been unavailable to them. That is to say, because this was a community where the most thrilling social events might be a fish fry at the Adventist Church or the occasional pay dance party hosted by one of the younger middle-class community members, several youth felt it was "boring." Many were excited, therefore, about the chance to be involved with the sorts of community intrigue they knew happened elsewhere.

In fact, during the run-up to the 2002 elections, politics became a unifying force between the two gangs. For several terms, Jacks Hill had a JLP councilor (this is the local representative for the community to the MP) but an MP from the PNP. Most of the older families in the area had a history of voting for the PNP, but by 2001 even some of the more progressive middle-class community members were becoming frustrated with their MP, in part because he rarely gave significant attention to the community since the local representative was from the opposition party. The councilor, who was from a neighboring hillside community and had known the youth in Jacks Hill since they were children, began mobilizing people to consider voting for the JLP MP in the next election. Jason, it was said, was very active in this regard—registering people to vote, organizing a busload of Jacks Hill community members to attend the JLP conference as delegates, and paying youth 4,000 Jamaican dollars (just under US$100 in 2001) to vote JLP. The mobilizing worked, and there is now a JLP MP for East Rural St. Andrew, the community's electoral district. Yet the fragile unity generated by a common political struggle was ephemeral, fizzling shortly after the elections, because Macka's crew allegedly refused to pay Jason's group the correct amount for some public work that was done in the district. The gang war thus escalated.

While ties to politically factionalized communities in Kingston seemed to exacerbate this escalation, these same ties may ultimately have brought about the end of the war. Initially, when middle-class homes were being broken into, the police did not seem to pay much attention, in large part because no one was hurt and firearms were not regularly used. But after one middle-class woman was brutally raped, and after gunmen began openly sitting on the road with their AK-47 machine guns leaning against trees, the police increased their presence in the community and Jacks Hill became one of the priorities of Operation Kingfish, the counter-narcotics and anti-crime task force initiated by the government in October 2004. As police became a more regular presence in the community—both on the road and in the air in helicopters—community members also became less reluctant to provide information to authorities.

Nevertheless, because the increased police presence did not seem to calm things down immediately in the community, one middle-class community member took it upon himself to work through his own political connections to, as he put it, "find out what was happening in Tivoli Gardens to create this situation in Jacks Hill." His connections did not admit outright that JLP activists from Tivoli Gardens were involved in Jacks Hill's war, but they did suggest that the army be included in any discussions about problem solving. Representatives from the JDF therefore met with a Jacks Hill spokesperson, promising to put its military intelligence unit into play in the community. Community members were surprised at how much the JDF already knew. It had photographs of the main players; it also knew that guns were moving from Tivoli Gardens to Jacks Hill and that specific individuals were circulating between the two communities. When JDF helicopters began flying over the community to map the footpaths that lead from the area into the Blue Mountains, the leadership within Tivoli Gardens is rumored to have pulled their people out of Jacks Hill, leaving Ryan's crew without a significant source of external support or supplies. Then, one Sunday in May, the JDF raided Jacks Hill. Although one of the two gang leaders had yet to be captured in early 2009, by July 2005 community members for the most part had moved back into their homes; it was possible again to walk on the road without fear; the shop and the bar at the top of the hill had reopened; and only the absence of some dozen people and the presence of charred buildings marked violence on the landscape. "Back to normal," indeed.

GLOBALIZATION AND NEW FRONTIERS

I want to suggest that it is productive to think through the emergent violence in Jacks Hill in relation to the concept of the frontier. In her book *Friction*, Tsing (2005: 12) uses the concept of the frontier to imagine, as she puts it, "the links between heterogeneous projects of space and scale making, as these both enable capitalist proliferation and embroil it in moments of chaos." In her work in Indonesia, she uses the idea of capitalist frontiers to talk about how opportunistic logging companies "discovered" the Kalimantan region, "opening" it to foreign speculators and then leaving it when it was no longer easily profitable, in the meantime generating activism locally that drew from the language of the global environmental movement to bring attention to nature and "nature loving." For Tsing (2005: 28), a frontier is "an edge of space and time: a zone of not yet—not yet mapped, not yet regulated." Frontiers are spaces of desire. They have, she writes, "their own technologies of space and time: Their emptiness is expansive, spreading across the land; they draw the quick, erratic temporality of rumor, speculation, and cycles of boom and bust, encouraging ever-intensifying forms of resourcefulness" (Tsing 2005: 32). Yet frontiers are not actually empty; nor are they infinite or infinitely productive. Instead, they are vulnerable to quick reversals of fortune when the violence and destruction that characterize processes of frontier making are no longer merely distractions and confusions but become full-blown crises. Eventually, somebody blinks, and what looked like "development" or "opportunity" just the other day suddenly seems less valuable than fool's gold. The frontier is abandoned.

In the story I have related in these pages, Jacks Hill became a frontier of sorts, a spatial and temporal edge in Tsing's terms, but, like the logging industry in Kalimantan, not one that is easily reconciled with the notions of the frontier that were developed in the late nineteenth century (about which I say more later). By this, I mean that Jacks Hill, within the memories of its inhabitants or the archives of English plantation owners, has never existed as a space of abandon. To the extent that it was "wilderness," it was wilderness cultivated by slaves and, later, small-scale landholders who had created community in waves since at least the early 1800s. Not much later, the village was populated (and administered) by at least one significant representative of the state and its formal institutions—first, the rector of the Anglican church in the 1890s, and later, in the 1940s and 1950s, middle-class nationalists, many of whom were themselves leading figures within organizations such as the Jamaica Agricultural Society, the Jamaican Water Commission, the *Jamaica Gleaner*, the People's National Party. To theorize the proliferation of violence in Jacks Hill in relation to a frontier concept therefore requires that we consider that frontiers may be created through the dissolution of hegemony, not only by its originary absence (Meeks 1996; Roitman 1998).

Moreover, while Jacks Hill became a violent frontier zone, this was not directly the result of capitalist opportunism. In Jacks Hill, there are no material resources to exploit—certainly not the ones that are usually attractive. There is no industry to speak of; there are no significant contracts to monopolize for the employment of one's followers; and although there have been a few people who have grown marijuana in the district, these typically have been not large-scale transnational operations but small fields supplying an internal trade. Instead, Jacks Hill became a frontier through the redirection of an already existing circulation of power, influence, and illegality that proliferates in Jamaica through the development and splintering of formerly politically affiliated, and now turf-related, gangs. What made Jacks Hill an attractive frontier for "outsiders" was its absences and weaknesses—not what it held but what it lacked. There was (and still is) no police post in the district; there was no conspicuous or regular surveillance; the ties between poor and middle-class community members had weakened; and the Community Council had all but stopped meeting. And critically, there were few economic opportunities locally, creating conditions that might make gang recruitment or coercion easier.

On one hand, then, it seems plausible to argue that Jacks Hill became a frontier as a result of the state's neglect, of its marshaling of resources to other, more politically connected communities. This is what has resulted in the immiseration of those who have been unable to mobilize work-related networks within Kingston or abroad, given the declining opportunities locally. For these community members, the promises of citizenship have long been bankrupt, and their own ability to participate (in markets, in political life) has long been circumscribed. In this context, other forms of authority emerged to take the place of the state—in this case, neither NGOs and other multilateral institutions nor privately owned companies (Trouillot 2001) but gang leaders and drug dons. On the other hand, the state had not completely disappeared. Members of the opposition party and the army *knew* what was going on in Jacks Hill; they *knew* who the main players were. They simply did not *act* until the situation reached crisis proportions.

Indeed, once the cycles of violence dislocated the majority of poorer community members—effectively making them temporary refugees—and once the threat to middle-class lives became too much to bear, the state's authority was reasserted and the "crisis" was redirected. Through the military and the police force, the Jamaican state effectively contained the local geographical spread of political violence and violence related to drugs and gangs, which is already transnational in its scope, to limit its movement into new frontiers. That it was able to accomplish this in Jacks Hill but not—until May 2010—in Tivoli Gardens (despite four previous attempts over the course of twelve years) is precisely because Jacks Hill *was* still that "zone of not yet," not fully incorporated into the broader circuits of violence and power that have characterized communities such as Tivoli Gardens for the past four decades.[10] This should highlight the temporal dimension of frontier-ness and suggests that frontiers do not "open" and "close" but, instead, act like tides, waxing and waning according to the pull of complex negotiations among governments, capital, and populations.

Janet Roitman makes this argument in her study of the "garrison-entrepôt," a kind of frontier zone that competes with the state as a site of wealth creation, accumulation, and redistribution achieved through violence, new patterns of sociability, and new forms of political and economic subjectivity. Her work in the Chad Basin reminds us that, "despite the proliferation of financial, commercial, and even military relationships that seem to evade certain forms of state power, the consolidation of the latter is equally palpable" (Roitman 1998: 297, 2005). If we view the events in Jacks Hill from this perspective, we might interpret current intensifications of violence as marking not only a colonization of, or assertion of sovereignty over, new frontiers, but also the parallel desire to reinscribe the borders of governmentality, borders that are, as Veena Das (2007: 167) writes, "instituted through sporadic, intermittent contact rather than an effective panoptic system of surveillance." One of the greatest challenges facing contemporary states—in the Caribbean and beyond—has to do, therefore, with the processes by which frontiers (of space and of time) should be managed. I am thinking here not about the management of territorial boundaries that became critical to state formation within some Caribbean locations in the mid-twentieth century—for example, Trujillo's drive to centralize the Dominican state by purging the Republic of its Haitian and Haitian–Dominican citizens in 1937. Instead, I am thinking about those boundaries that mark the limits of sociocultural citizenship that have been rooted in dominant nationalist notions related to families, economics, and politics. I have attempted to show that in Jamaica, these processes of frontier management have created a sense of unpredictability and arbitrariness, and it is this unpredictability that sets populations adrift, creating new frontier moments.

A temporally driven understanding of frontiers, then, prevents us from imagining them primarily as liberated zones, liminal spaces where rules fall away and innovation reigns.[11] Indeed, focusing on temporality in relation to the frontier might compel us to a reconsideration of the relationship between frontiers and camps. These two sorts of time-spaces are often positioned as diametrically opposed—one, open chaos and lawlessness; the other, hyper-disciplined, the state of exception that not only proves the rule (Agamben 1998) but that is the rule (Gilroy 2000; Mbembe 2001), just as for Aimé Césaire (2000 [1950]), fascism was not external to European liberal democracies but foundational to them.[12] Like other theorists examining similar questions, Agamben's quintessential example here is the Nazi concentration camp, though other observers have taken the concept of the "camp" to spaces beyond Europe such as post–Patriot Act Guantánamo Bay (Butler 2004), slave plantations (Gilroy 2000), apartheid South Africa and Palestine (Mbembe 2003), contemporary socialist China (Farquhar and Zhang 2005), favelas in Rio de Janeiro (da Silva 2009), and NGOs such as Médecins sans Frontières (Redfield 2005).

I would like to think about whether it would be productive to imagine the frontier and the camp not as opposites but as negative images, especially under current conditions. That is, I ask whether we might conceive of states of "bare life" as the result not only of processes of total control but of its lack (Piot 2010). Can we think about neoliberalism as creating a similar effect through active neglect and calculated absence, the "zones of social abandonment" that João Biehl (2005) writes about? In other words, might we position something like Orlando Patterson's (1982) discussion of slavery as a form of "social death" that results from the nature of the plantation as a total institution as the reverse image of, for example, James Ferguson's (2006) figuring of contemporary sub-Saharan Africa as a "shadow," a snapshot of abjection and inertia, the result of a total absence of institution?[13] Because neoliberalism *creates* the new frontier space for opportunistic circuits through a remapping of the administrative purview of the state, particular populations (sometimes entire regions) fall through the cracks, as it were, comprising, in Ong's words, those "staggering numbers of the globally excluded" (Ong 2006: 23) who become stateless and illegitimate, stripped of all claims to political or social citizenship, not unlike those slaves on New World plantations.

Yet we know that even on slave plantations, African and creolized men and women developed forms of individuality, subjectivity, and community—dare I say it, forms of agency. And we also know that, despite current processes of privatization, corporatization, and deregulation, excluded populations continue to complexly negotiate both state and parastatal organizations to assert claims—politically, economically, and socially (Ong 2006; Slocum 2006).[14] Even Catarina, the subject of Biehl's study of the socially abandoned in Brazil—those "ex-humans" who exist in a purgatorial space "between encompassment and abandonment, memory and non-memory, life and death" (Biehl 2005: 4)—finds creative ways to reassert her humanity, largely through talking and writing.

Frontiers are thus also, as Tsing (2005: 32) asserts, "imaginative projects." However, as we have seen, the creativity they might engender is only materialized through profound violence. In many ways, this is a metaphor for the Caribbean region itself—a "frontier" not only for anthropological theory, as Michel Rolph Trouillot so insightfully put it in a now classic essay in the *Annual Review* in 1992, but also for the creation of new worlds, new forms of economic production, and new conceptualizations of political citizenship.[15] That these were innovations forged through violence—both spectacular and mundane—is the legacy of expansionism that remains with us today. I end this chapter by reflecting on these more broadly drawn innovations to think through how the category of frontier might be a useful framework through which we might view some of the challenges for state formation within the Caribbean region, and particularly within Jamaica.

HISTORY, FRONTIERS, AND STATE FORMATION

When Frederick Jackson Turner first laid out his Frontier Thesis at the American Historical Association meetings in Chicago in 1893, he was concerned with the announcement by the bulletin of the Superintendent of the Census for 1890 that the U.S. frontier was officially closed. For Turner (1963: 3), the environment created by the Western frontier—"the meeting point between savagery and civilization"—was what gave Americans a unique temperament and what distinguished them from Europeans. Because of the constantly moving outer edge of settlement, he argued, the frontier engendered the rugged individualism of American nationalist ideology. It both generated and reproduced "that coarseness and strength combined with acuteness and inquisitiveness; that practical, inventive turn of mind, quick to find expedients; that masterful grasp of material things, lacking in the artistic but powerful to effect great ends; that restless, nervous energy; that dominant individualism, working for good and for evil, and withal that buoyancy and exuberance which comes with freedom" (Turner 1963:37). But for Turner, it was not merely that the frontier catalyzed a particular personality type. The individualism encouraged by frontier living also promoted democracy and equality. In other words, the cultural ecology of the United States promoted the most perfect rendering of liberal democratic social and political institutions. As a result, the so-called closing of the frontier, for him, created an uncertain future. Of course, like the climate theories of development and other forms of environmental determinism and Social Darwinism that proliferated in the late nineteenth century, Turner's thesis has been roundly critiqued—for its easy association between character and institutions, personhood and polity; for its lack of specificity (and inaccuracy) in relation to particular details; and for its erasure of the Mexicans and Indians, among others, who were pushed out of the way in the name of Manifest Destiny.[16]

Nevertheless, as the American studies scholar Richard Slotkin points out, the myth of the frontier is the longest-standing nationalist origin story in the United States. This is so, he argues, because "its ideological underpinnings are those same 'laws' of capitalist competition, of supply and demand, of Social Darwinian 'survival of the fittest' as a rationale for social order, and of 'Manifest Destiny' that have been the building blocks of our dominant historiographical tradition and political ideology" (Slotkin 1994: 15). As ideology, the frontier myth supports an association of democracy and progress with social mobility, expansion, and exploitation, at the same time masking the conflicts and forms of oppression involved in these processes (Slotkin 1973, 1994). This is true not only for the early colonial period in the United States, but also for the period between the mid-eighteenth century and the abolition of the slave trade in British Jamaica in 1807.[17]

In his recent book about what he calls "mortuary politics"—the social and political meanings ascribed to beliefs and practices associated with death—Vincent Brown (2008: 57) reminds us that "Jamaica's dynamic and profitable economy consumed its inhabitants." By this, he means that in the middle of the eighteenth century, when Jamaica was Britain's most significant colony in the New World in terms of both profits and population—Jamaica received more enslaved Africans than any other single British colony and about 25 percent of the total African immigrants to the Americas during the last half of the 1700s—the death rate for both Englishmen and Africans was exceedingly high. Yet the potential to generate fantastic wealth continued to pull British adventurers to the island. After all, as Brown (2008: 16) points out, "The average property holder on the island held more than thirty-six times the assets possessed by his counterpart in the thirteen North American colonies."

These adventurers and these Africans were meeting at a time when the first phase of Western imperial expansion was at its height—the period just before the Haitian Revolution would reorient colonial practices and visions. And they were meeting in a space that was seen as atavistically Other, a colonial no-man's land, a liminal space where, as classical anthropological accounts of ritual would have it, "normal" rules were suspended (Gennep 1960; Turner 1969, 1974). While he does not use the language of the "frontier," Brown (2008: 16) tells us that we might characterize Jamaica during this period as an "enterprise zone, a territory organized by the government on behalf of business interests." In this zone, he continues, "Profit taking prevailed over civic investment. . . . Jamaicans built few schools and no universities. Public works projects were conducted only for the benefit of commerce. Instead, people went to Jamaica hoping to win their fortunes as quickly as possible, living fast, and, if need be, dying young" (Brown 2008: 16).

The historian Trevor Burnard (2004: 19) is even more scathing in his representation of white Jamaicans' ambition for wealth:

Jamaicans were addicted to ostentatious display and devoted to luxury. They spent their money on lavish feasting, copious drinking, and all manner of sexual and sensuous delights. Jamaica was a gambler's paradise rather than a philosopher's retreat. "Careless of futurity," white Jamaicans showed little commitment to their native or adopted land, educating their children, if they had any, in England and caring little about developing and maintaining institutional structures. Everything was sacrificed on the altar of getting rich quickly. Jamaica was not a land of long-term planning. Its white citizens loved risk and hazard, their schemes were always vast but seldom well planned, and they "put no medium in being great and being undone." They were inordinate risk takers, but their passionate natures and fiery, restless tempers did not encourage a persevering spirit. One of the great themes of Jamaican history was the speed with which plans were made and begun, then laid aside in favor of fresh novelties. Excess and speculation rather than restraint and planning were their watchwords.

In other words, early colonial Jamaica was organized—economically, politically, socially—to support mercantile capitalist development on the frontiers of the New World, frontiers that were nevertheless fully integrated within a broader system of Atlantic exploration and exploitation (Hornsby 2005) and that, of course, were also profoundly racialized.

For anthropologists of an earlier era, these frontier spaces would have been known as the culture spheres of "Plantation America," that region from the eastern coastline of Brazil through the Guyanas and the Caribbean and into the southern United States, a region characterized by the plantation-based production of monocrops for export alongside small-scale peasant production of staples; rigid class lines within a context of multi-raciality; and "weak" community structures and "matrifocal" family organization (Wagley 1957). For liberal anthropologists of the mid-twentieth century, and especially for those influenced by the "culture at a distance" and "culture and personality" studies that for a time dominated post–First World War research in the United States, understanding the historical development of this culture sphere would "serve as a frame of reference for our studies of the contemporary societies and cultures of the Americas" (Wagley 1957: 3), just as for later economists — and especially those within the region — understanding the working of plantation economies would explain industrialization and underdevelopment in the twentieth century (Beckford 1972; Best and Levitt 1969).

I am also interested in the legacies of these early patterns, but not to argue for direct continuities between then and now. Instead, I want to think about how we might position these historical patterns in relation to post-colonial state formation. If we understand Jamaica as initially having been explored, expanded, and exploited by the British as a frontier, and if by this we mean that the logics of social, economic, and political organization privileged the boom-and-bust cycles of capitalism rather than other, more person-centered forms of social engineering, then we must think about the legacies of this history for colonial state formation both before and after 1865, as well as for postcolonial state formation. I want to argue that we must acknowledge that these histories and these experiences generate the terrains of what is possible, examples for roads that might be taken, and norms through which people develop expectations about hierarchy, leadership, and patronage. With this in mind, I briefly probe two different, though related, phenomena: the customary practice of granting slaves provision grounds and the centrality of practices related to death and dying.

The enormous literature on the resistance practices of slaves on plantations, and of emancipated slaves after abolition, has often positioned slaves' provision grounds as critical spaces not only for the development of internal markets and the accumulation of fairly significant amounts of currency by people who were themselves considered property, but also for the elaboration of worldviews and lifeways that were, to a degree, separate from the institution of the plantation.[18] Yet there were, as Burnard (2004: 153–54) points out, also two principal contradictory effects of the sorts of autonomy made possible by slave grounds. The first has to do with the structural vulnerability faced by slaves. This vulnerability was rooted in the fact that provision grounds, while giving slaves a degree of economic independence, also tied them to land—indeed, to specific plantations—instilling in them a sense of commitment and loyalty to "their particular patch of ground and their particular plantation," as well as a "wary conservatism typical of peasants and petty commodity producers." As the result of connections Afro-Jamaicans made between genealogy and locality through the belief, for example, in the inalienability of family land, and because slaves' attachment to property was a customary right but not one that was legally protected or recognized, white plantation owners were able to secure their hegemony. Being tied to provision grounds, therefore, created a structural ambiguity for slaves who were still dependent on the continued benevolence and patronage of particular plantation owners or estate managers. This ambiguity, Burnard (2004: 155) argues, "made them conservative and encouraged, on most occasions, a temporary truce between slaves and whites because whites were not only the principal predators on plantations but also sometimes the only protectors slaves had."

The second contradictory effect of slave provision grounds, Burnard argues, was the intensification of disputes among slaves over property. As Burnard (2004: 164) points out, "Slaves stole . . . from each other constantly," and oftentimes the only protection they had from thieves—especially when the thief was from a different plantation from the victim—was the intervention of their masters. As a result, criminality was enhanced by the policy of providing slaves with provision grounds, and even more so when slaves were given access to markets. Burnard (2004: 169) maintains that giving slaves property rights within the context of plantation America thus weakened solidarity among slaves and solidified the racial and economic hegemony of planters: "On the one hand, the tendency of slaves to engage in capitalist market-oriented activity worked, in the long run, against the logic of plantation slavery because it reduced slaves' dependence on the bounty of the master and thus reduced his control over them. On the other hand, private property and market exchange fractured slave communities."

I discuss what I feel is one potentially critical effect of this phenomenon momentarily, but for now, I turn—even more briefly—to the centrality of practices related to death and dying to the formation of Jamaican social worlds. Vincent Brown argues against a sense that the demographic turmoil of late-eighteenth-century Jamaica precluded social and cultural development, stressing instead that the turmoil *produced* norms, expectations, and institutional structures appropriate to the system of plantation exploitation. "It is thus less revealing to see the extravagant death rate in Jamaican society as an impediment to the formation of culture than it is to view it as the landscape of culture itself," and he writes, "the ground that produced Atlantic slavery's most meaningful idioms" (Brown 2008: 59). What Brown is suggesting here is that we understand the ways creole populations (slaves and masters, overseers and traders, maroons and indentured laborers) as having created selves *through and in relation to* conditions of death and disease, not *in spite of* them.

For both of these historians, particular forms of structural organization created a set of relations — social, economic, and political — and these relations gave rise to a set of customs. In other words, there is a historical social ecology to cultural production, and therefore the processes of cultural production and institution building must be seen as grounded within a political economy of available possibilities. In other words, based on Burnard's analysis of slave provision grounds, we might come to the conclusion that notions about the relationships among space, protection, and patronage far predated the post–Second World War period of nation building. Patterns for conceptualizing and organizing influence, authority, loyalty, and land use in relation to the social and economic hierarchies of class and culture were, in fact, established during the period of slavery and solidified in the post-emancipation period during which the majority of former slaves remained tied to the estates, at least until the collapse of the sugar industry in 1846. And extrapolating from Brown's assertion that death was the "principal arena of social life" (Brown 2008: 59) during the height of the plantation system might lead us to argue that violence and the specter of violent death was in fact foundational to state formation in Jamaica, during the colonial period and beyond, and that it therefore stands to reason that the development of political institutions in the post–Second World War period might occur through an armed process of carving up space and garnering allegiance through the distribution of scarce resources such as job and housing contracts, among other things.

Now, let me make an analytic leap. The forms of partisan and gang-related violence that permeate social life in Jamaica are thus not problems of culture, as is so often posed. I will continually come back to this issue in the chapters that follow, but I raise it here to make a point about how nationalist slogans and myths generate popular sensibilities about the culture of particular groups. Slotkin (1994: 43) proposes an alternative thesis that rethinks the relationship between landscape and ethos, arguing that "the particular forms taken by the developing political economy of the Metropolis—its modes of production, its system for valuing social and economic goods, its peculiar culture and history of social relations, its characteristic political institutions—inform the decision to seek Frontier wealth, and determine the kind of people that will go (or be sent) to the colonies, the kinds of resources they will be interested in, the ways in which they will organize their exploitation and governance of the territory."

Here, Slotkin grounds the frontier myth of rugged American individualism in terms of a set of structural relations of power that change over time rather than as the result of cultural complexes that extend across time. "The disadvantage of acknowledging this process in a theory of American development—and perhaps in bourgeois development as a whole," he continues, "is that it brings to the fore those patterns of class conflict and oppression that Western democracy is supposed to have abolished" (Slotkin 1994: 43). The ideologies that supported the particular form that exploration and exploitation took in the Americas during the early colonial period, in other words, were meant to obscure the actual class relations and conflicts that developed over time. Moreover, they created the conditions for apprehending progress and development in terms of adherence to a particular set of cultural values rather than through the lens of a historical political economy. This has been one of the most profound legacies of British colonialism in Jamaica and continues to have some of the most devastating effects in relation to notions of citizenship and belonging.

Three weeks passed between the time Selwyn was killed and when his autopsy was conducted. Winsome was grateful to get the autopsy date as soon as she did, since, as she mentioned to me, several people had been killed in early March but still had not been scheduled by the beginning of April because there was such a backlog of bodies. Three days after she arrived in Kingston, she was finally called in to identify him. As she waited in the morgue, the police brought in another victim. This one had been shot and then nailed to a makeshift cross, a crucifixion-cum-cautionary tale, she supposed. After the autopsy was finally conducted, I drove Winsome to the funeral home downtown to drop off the clothes she wanted Selwyn to wear in his casket (which was to be open at the funeral) and to inspect the undertaker's work. As we reached the front door, I hesitated, unsure about whether she wanted privacy or company.

"You scared to see him, Deborah?" Winsome challenged.

"Do you want me to see him?" I asked, by way of reply.

"Yes, man, you must come."

Behind the curtain separating us from other families inspecting the bodies of their loved ones, we slowly pulled back the sheet that covered Selwyn's naked and embalmed body. Winsome lovingly pointed out every single shot to me — touching his right eye, his left shoulder, his side. Her fingers lingered longest on the big hole in his chest, the shot from his own gun. "Him look good," she said, "them do a good job with him." As we readied ourselves to leave, Winsome stopped briefly at the curtain. She turned her head back to Selwyn and said, very casually and with the slightest of waves, "bye baby." In that instant, I was immediately catapulted eight years back in time to a beautiful summer afternoon. I was driving back up the hill after a very long day at the library, grateful for the cooler air that began to surround me as I rose above Kingston. Hearing an insistent oncoming horn as I approached one of the narrow switchbacks in the road, I paused to allow the other motorist the right of way. When the car emerged from the blind corner, I realized it was Selwyn and Winsome in their red two-seat MG, careening around the bend. They noticed me but did not stop. I caught a quick glimpse of Winsome laughing, and then, as they zinged down the mountainside together, she flung her arm up in a wave.

Deviant Bodies, 2005/1945

On 5 October 2005, several armed men firebombed a dwelling in southwest St. Andrew near downtown Kingston, possibly in reprisal for an earlier incident that had occurred as part of a feud between men from two areas in the district. Four people were killed in the blaze; they were unable to escape the burning house because a padlock secured the veranda's iron grille. One of them was ten-year-old Sasha-Kay Brown, who spent her last moments pleading for help from her neighbors. "'The little girl climbed up on the grille and called out the names of almost everybody who lived on Barnes Avenue, begging them to come and help her,' one neighbor recalled. 'But when we ran out of our houses and tried to assist her, the gunmen fired at us. The last thing we heard the little girl said [*sic*] was that the fire was burning her, then her voice just faded'" (Sinclair 2005b). The gunmen also shot and killed the family's dog, whose body was later found in the burned-out yard.

On Friday, 5 October 2007, gunmen entered a home in the East Kingston community of Rockfort and sprayed forty-eight-year-old Violet Williams and her eighteen-year-old daughter Christina Bryan with bullets. This double murder was understood to be a reprisal for a triple murder that had occurred an hour or so earlier in which the victims were a four-month-old baby and her parents, twenty-seven-year-old Marlon Hurd and eighteen-year-old Shaineta Smith. According to the report in the *Daily Gleaner*, those responsible for the latter incident went on to kill seventy-year-old Joan Richardson and her nine-year-old grandson: "Residents said Miss Richardson was at home bathing her grandson when the gunmen entered her home and shot her in the head. They then chased her grandson and shot him several times. His nude body was dragged from under a cellar" (Sinclair and Rose 2007). It is speculated that Richardson's son had been involved in a feud among rival groups within the community. A few days later, gunmen used gas and fire-bombs to ignite a house located close to that of Violet Williams and her daughter. Six children were inside at the time, and the heavily armed men "hid in the dark backyard and called out the names of the children one by one, hoping they would step outside, so they could kill them" (Sinclair 2007). They were anxious to kill another child as revenge for the two children who had been murdered the previous Friday.

For Kingstonians inured to the day-to-day violence that surrounds them, these murders were nonetheless stunning. For many newspaper and radio-show commentators, they marked a new level of brutality and cruelty— "cold and ruthless death squads" (Blaine 2005) using children in the settling of scores between grown men. The economist Cedric Wilson, guest columnist for the *Gleaner*, argued in the aftermath of the Barnes Avenue killings that they signaled a new phase of war. "The ruthlessness of the crimes being committed are the acts of twisted supermen," he stated. "This is [a] new breed of criminals without soul or conscience, evil men for whom the conception of good and evil is irrelevant" (Wilson 2005). These comments imply that while there had been a spatial and systemic logic to the patterns of crime and violence, the murders on Barnes Avenue and in Rockfort could not be assimilated within that logic and thus were apprehended as exceptional, evidence that Jamaica has developed a "culture of violence." This phrase itself is so taken for granted that it is commonly used as if its meaning is universally understood and agreed on. In the executive summary of the National Security Strategy green paper of 2005, for example, it appears this way: "The continuous growth in the number of violent incidents causes many Jamaicans at home to live in fear, and influence [*sic*] those in the diaspora to abandon their dream of resettling on the 'rock.' It is now conceded that Jamaica has spawned a culture of violence in its most negative form, which is abhorrent to its values and stands in the way of every kind of social progress" ("A National Security Strategy for Jamaica" 2006). For many commentators, Jamaica is seen as a "killing society" (Hermione McKenzie, president of the Association of Women's Organizations in Jamaica, quoted in Sinclair 2005a), and crime is understood as a "way of life" in which the gun is a symbol of manhood (Chevannes 2001). By corollary, sexual violence, according to Women's Media Watch, is normalized as a part of an overall "inner-city" culture of violence characterized by political violence, drugs, and gangs ("Why Jamaican Men Rape" 2006), a culture that is seen to be glorified through media and thereby reproduced.

Viewing violence as a primordial aspect of Jamaican culture mobilizes a certain kind of essentialism, one in which it is "not merely that the violence has an internal semiotic (and therefore to understand the violence one has to understand the culture)," as David Scott (1997: 146) has written, "but that the semiotic of the culture is—at least in part—violence, and *therefore* in order to understand the culture one has to understand the violence." In other words, the notion of a "culture of violence" presupposes a kind of savagery, harking back to earlier forms of scientific racism that defined black populations as natural, wild, and uncontrollable. This is a vision held not only by Jamaicans in Jamaica but also by those living abroad, a point made poignantly clear by the fact that crime was one of the biggest agenda issues during the Jamaica Diaspora Foundation conference in Kingston in June 2006, at which overseas Jamaicans identified violence as the number one factor inhibiting their own return and their ability to conduct business in Jamaica, and by the decision in late 2005 to stop reporting weekly crime statistics in the newspaper and to remove crime reportage from the front page of the *Gleaner*. This last action was taken in part because Jamaicans living abroad complained that constant front-page coverage of murders not only made foreigners wary about visiting Jamaica; it also made U.S. citizens discriminate against resident Jamaicans on the basis of hailing from such a violent nation. Their concerns highlight how, for many U.S. nationals, the association of violent crime with particular immigrant groups intensifies the periodic eruption of nativist and anti-immigrant sentiment that has played so large a role in class and racial formation in the United States (Brodkin 2000).

In this chapter, I think through the proliferation of discourse about the "culture of violence" seen to characterize Jamaican society and to accom-

pany migrants from Jamaica into metropolitan diasporic locales.[1] I will argue that the culture of violence discourse has its roots in the earlier mobilization of the "culture of poverty" trope, itself the result of a culturalist
approach to understanding inequality that became solidified in the aftermath of the Second World War (Yelvington 2006a). This is an approach in
which difference is mapped in terms of "culture," and "culture" itself becomes a force that is seen to determine the behavior, outlook, and potential of entire groups. Within U.S. anthropology, this culturalist approach
emerged as a result of an attraction among scholars to psychoanalysts and
Gestalt psychologists in the early twentieth century. In the years leading
up to the Second World War, however, a commitment developed to a more
interventionist social policy grounded in social science research. In all of
the big "race relations" studies of the early twentieth century—Gunnar
Myrdal's *An American Dilemma*, the report of the Moyne Commission on
labor riots throughout the West Indies in the late 1930s, and, less explicitly,
the reports following the riots in Chicago of 1919 and the riots in Harlem
of 1935—researchers probed the various social institutions that shaped the
lives of New World black folk in order to determine the extent to which
these institutions fostered a cultural complex that encouraged positive attitudes toward dominant development paradigms. To the extent that they
did not, the communities in question were deemed deviant, even pathological. In what should be a familiar story to any student of social science
research of the early twentieth century among African descendants in the
Americas, paramount among the institutional forms that were seen to both
generate and reproduce this deviance was the family. I will focus on this
preoccupation in these pages to attempt to clarify how gender and sexual
norms have been mobilized by states in ways that reproduce racial and
class hierarchies through the idea of "culture." In other words, my analysis
in these pages is intended to provide one window through which we might
explore how the biopolitical management of race has also "regulated our
desires, shaped what we understand to be both legitimate and prescribed,
taboo and prohibited, expressions of black sexuality and gender identity,
across the diaspora" (Stephens 2009: 33).

Moreover, I will demonstrate that characterizing and managing diverse
class cultures within African American populations by way of the discourse
of dysfunction that arose in relation to the formation of black families was,
in fact, a transnational project that has had particular but related effects

among different diasporic (in the sense of a worldwide black community) populations and one that also has moved with people as they create diasporas (in the sense of transnational migrant communities). The historian Karin Rosemblatt (2009: 607) has argued that the transnationalism of this project was facilitated not only by the networks among scholars that stretched across national boundaries, but also by a notion of inheritance— "with its cultural, biological/genetic, and economic registers; its conflation of biology and environment; and its insistence on the centrality of family to cultural and economic processes"—that provided the conceptual glue connecting race, class, and culture for scholars in a variety of locations. Probing this project, therefore, can tell us something about how links were posited—and institutionalized through policy—between the economy, family, and political participation for communities of African descent in a range of locations at a particular moment. Moreover, this kind of investigation can help reveal how the institutionalization of these links has produced a kind of epistemological violence that continues to pervade contemporary popular analyses of actually existing violence among black populations "at home" and "abroad," even though the political and economic basis for these links has shifted fairly radically. Most broadly, therefore, this chapter is concerned with black people's relationships to states across imperial and generational moments, specifically in terms of how the movement from a mid-twentieth-century emphasis on state-centered industrial modernization to the global neoliberalism of the late twentieth century and early twenty-first century affected how black masculinity and black family formation have been positioned in relation to development paradigms. I suggest, finally, that since in the contemporary period family is not tethered to economic participation and production in the same way that it was during the modernization moment of the mid-twentieth century, there is no longer any ideological basis for rooting economic underdevelopment in faulty family formation.

DISCOURSES OF DEPRAVITY: THE CULTURALIZATION OF POVERTY AND VIOLENCE

Throughout the period of Atlantic slavery, marriage was a contested issue. Within the West Indies, it is generally accepted that patterns of marriage and family life among slaves developed in opposition to slavery and were based, as the historian Mary Chamberlain (2006: 6) has argued, on "a communitarian philosophy of society, in which lineage and kinship are foregrounded as structuring practices, through and in which the individual and his/her sense of self is inextricably bound" (see also Higman 1976, 1984; Sutton 1984). This would contrast with the sexual violence and promiscuity that characterized slave societies, especially in the early period of New World imperialism, and that resulted in the characterization of black Africans and West Indians—but not white men—as aggressively and abnormally hypersexual.[2] While marriages among slaves were not encouraged or recognized until the late eighteenth century, slaves did form families and generated a complex marriage system encompassing patterns that included ego-focused bilateral kinship networks, ancestor-oriented descent lines, and visiting relationships. These patterns were expressed differently depending on factors that had to do with the size of plantations, the nature of work, and the color and provenance of slaves. Once marriage was promoted by both civil and religious authorities, it was understood by slaves "not as the prerequisite to family formation," Chamberlain (2006: 23) argues, "but its opposite: as confirmation and celebration of a couple's loyalty and fertility." In the post-emancipation period, when planters and missionaries alike attempted to socialize within the newly freed people the values of working for wages and paying for medical care and education, former slaves reconstituted families in their own interests. In other words, they created families not merely to accept the European family models championed by missionaries,[3] but in ways "that controlled the reproduction of the single commodity the planters needed most of all, and that they universally bemoaned was in short supply—the labor force" (Chamberlain 2006: 27; see also Putnam 2002; Roberts 1998).

While colonial administrators worried about the high rates of illegitimacy revealed by the censuses of 1843 and 1890 and argued that illegitimacy created a situation in which "the foundational elements of good citizenship are thus lacking and the progress of the State is hindered" (Registrar General of Jamaica, quoted in Chamberlain 2006: 29), the colonial state did not explicitly involve itself in Afro-Jamaican family formation until the early twentieth century. Prior to that time, Afro-Jamaican promiscuity and the high rates of children born to unmarried women (approximately two-thirds from the period of emancipation through the present) were understood by observers either as signs of their irredeemable savagery and immorality, or as the results of victimization and disadvantage. By the 1920s and

1930s, some uplift-oriented middle-class Afro-Caribbean men and women began to pay more attention to family formation and parenting practices, writing about their concerns in the West Indian publications that were emerging within Afro-Caribbean migrant destinations throughout Central America (Putnam 2007, 2008). This is significant because migration, in this case, seems to have prompted concern among black middle-class activists with family patterns among poorer West Indians, just as it did in the United States in the wake of the Great Migration north (Frazier 1966 [1939]; Gaines 1996; Higginbotham 1993). Nevertheless, these concerns did not immediately translate into policy recommendations. According to the historian Lara Putnam (2007: 1), despite interest in the sexual mores of Afro-Caribbean populations among observers, missionaries, and bureaucrats in the Colonial Office, "There was little emphasis placed on the social, cultural, or psychological consequences of Afro-Caribbean domestic forms."

In the immediate aftermath of the Civil War in the United States, on the other hand, the Freedmen's Bureau, a federal agency established in 1865 to protect and aid emancipated slaves in the South, began to concern itself with black family structure. Newly emancipated slaves were not only encouraged to marry but faced imprisonment and, in some cases, denied pension payments if they decided not to (Ferguson 2004). In this way, Roderick Ferguson (2004: 85) reminds us, the bureau played an active role in the attempt to "rationalize African American sexuality by imposing heterosexual marriage upon the freedman through the rule of law and as a condition for citizenship." The burden of responsibility for former slaves thus was shifted from the government and former slaveholders to the patriarchal husband, now seen as legally responsible for the well-being of the household. This federal attempt was short-lived, as the bureau was discontinued in 1869. Nevertheless, the groundwork was set for linking patterns of family formation to legitimate economic and political participation in a newly united nation-state.[4]

In fact, in his classic essay "Governmentality," Michel Foucault (1991: 92) traced these connections back further, to the introduction of economy in the sixteenth century — "the correct manner of managing individuals, goods and wealth within the family (which a good father is expected to do in relation to his wife, children and servants) and of making the family fortunes prosper" — into the realm of political practice. For Foucault (1991: 92), during the early colonial period, "economy" referred to "the wise government of the family for the common welfare of all," and governance was therefore to exercise over all of the inhabitants of a state "a form of surveillance and control as attentive as that of the head of a family over his household and his goods." By the late nineteenth century, then, it was already commonplace to understand both economic and political activity in relation to the governance of family structure. Thus, in both the United States and Jamaica, family structure became a way to measure progress and assimilation into the post-emancipation state (see also Lowe 2006). White heteropatriarchal middle-class families thus became the standard against which African American and Afro-Jamaican families were judged, and racialized heteronormativity "became a regulatory regime" (Ferguson 2004: 85).

By the aftermath of the worldwide economic Depression, region-wide labor riots, and the beginning of the Second World War, West Indian family formation became newly situated as a policy concern within the British Colonial Office, and a link was created between poverty and what looked to the middle-class government officials and social welfare workers like parental irresponsibility. This was also the case in the United States. In part, this shift in policy-oriented attention to lower-class black families in the United States and the West Indies was the result of a movement away from the biologically driven understandings of race that undergirded the various strands of scientific racism throughout the mid-nineteenth century to the early twentieth century and toward anthropologically and psychologically oriented analyses of human difference.[5] By the mid-1920s, many prominent U.S. anthropologists were elaborating a Durkheimian notion that positioned culture as a set of shared mental patterns that led to particular behaviors. Margaret Mead, Ruth Benedict, and Edward Sapir, influenced by Freud and other psychologically oriented theories of human development and interaction, pushed the idealist theory that "culture was the product of both psychic and historical factors, that it was functionally integrated to some extent, that it was patterned, and that cultural configurations were historically emergent" (Patterson 2001: 80).

The early culture and personality studies — such as Benedict's *Patterns of Culture* (1934) and Mead's *Sex and Temperament in Three Primitive Societies* (1935) — generated an interest in the discovery of core value orientations among cultural groups and directed attention away from the more radical theories of social organization and change that had emerged during the

Depression years. Concurrently, institutions that supported social-science research during this period—the Rockefeller philanthropies, especially the Social Science Research Council, established in 1923; the National Research Council; and the American Council of Learned Societies—became particularly concerned with the psychology of acculturation. As Thomas Patterson (2001: 87) has argued, these foundations supported research geared toward the war effort—in other words, toward helping to determine "the covert value orientations of the recipient cultures as well as the psychological characteristics of individuals from those cultures who might accept or reject elements from the donor culture under the particular circumstances of contact." However, the concerns regarding value orientations and acculturation were reflected not only in the culture-at-a-distance studies of national societies within the U.S. sphere of influence but also in the race relations literature that had been emerging in the United States during the interwar years. And just as in the studies of Third World development and revolution that emerged in the aftermath of the Second World War, research on U.S. race relations relied on psychological understandings of personality development, identity formation, and the influence of frustration and aggression on behavior (Herman 1995).

For example, Gunnar Myrdal's study *An American Dilemma*, commissioned by the Carnegie Corporation and ultimately published in 1944, was geared toward examining the causes of the continued inequalities between blacks and whites in the United States to create policy that would transform race relations (though not necessarily the structural arrangements on which they were grounded).[6] Myrdal focused on a number of the institutional dimensions of social, economic, and political life, but undergirding his analysis was a concern with the so-called disorganization of African American family structure, a disorganization that "constructed African Americans as figures of nonheteronormativity who could potentially throw the American social order into chaos" (Ferguson 2004: 88). Myrdal drew from E. Franklin Frazier's arguments that slavery, mass migration, and urbanization had deleterious effects on black family structure but arrived at different resolutions for change. Frazier rooted the solution to the black familial pathology of so-called matriarchal gender relations in an acceptance of what Ellen Herman (1995: 189) has called "capitalist patriarchy"—a condition whereby "black men would be as free as white men to accumulate property, sell labor power, and otherwise function within the marketplace."

In other words, he felt that the only way to transform the broader structural inequalities facing black Americans in the post-Depression era was to integrate them fully into the economic life of the United States, including them, for example, in the industrial workforce. These arguments about the employment of black men as the corrective to matriarchal deviance had become common sense by the 1960s, and propping up this vision of black masculinity became "a preferred method of tackling poverty, illegitimacy, inadequate housing, poor academic achievement, and a host of other community problems, including rioting" (Herman 1995: 190).[7] Myrdal, however, understood these issues as being rooted in a fundamentally moral and psychological dilemma. For him, race relations were "an index of struggle within the U.S. psyche," a problem, as he wrote, "in the heart of the American" (Herman 1995: 179). Racism thus became framed as a psychological rather than an institutional issue, and deviant family structure was seen not only to index psychological harm vis-à-vis proper gender identity, but also to perpetuate it and even to exacerbate it by generating the frustration that could ultimately lead to uncontrollable rioting.[8]

The West India Royal Commission sent to the British Caribbean after the labor riots that swept through the region in the late 1930s produced a report (known as the Moyne report, after the head of the commission) similarly stating that one of the causes of the labor problems in the region was a dysfunctional family structure among poor and working-class black West Indians. This structure was characterized by high rates of illegitimate births, "loose" family organization, and "careless" upbringing of children. For the authors of the report, dysfunctional families were not necessarily framed in terms of psychological deviance, but were seen to have generated a lack of economic productivity and motivation and, therefore, a lack of ability to participate politically in an engaged and thoughtful way. The report ultimately recommended a movement toward independence for the West Indian colonies, as well as the establishment of an Office of Colonial Development and Welfare that not only would see to improvements in housing, education, public health, and land resettlement, but would also foster more responsible parenting and sexual restraint.[9]

Sir Frank Stockdale, the first comptroller of social welfare and development for the Colonial Office, agreed with Lord Moyne that the family—or the lack thereof—was the root of most of West Indians' social problems (Chamberlain 2006). In 1941, Stockdale appointed Thomas Simey social welfare adviser for Jamaica. Simey was the Charles Booth Professor of Social Science at the University of Liverpool and was a key proponent of modern social engineering and social policy. By the time of his appointment, Frazier's *The Negro Family in the United States* (1966 [1939]) and Melville Herskovits's *The Myth of the Negro Past* (1941) were the two dominant explanations of black family pathology. Simey, who took a Frazierian approach, shared Stockdale's belief that the "material and moral impoverishment of the family led to impoverishment of social life, and of the community as a whole" (Chamberlain 2006: 33), and his understanding of the relationships among citizenship, poverty, and family form reflected dominant thinking in this regard within England. He believed that sociological studies could contribute to a broader understanding of the problematic familial institutions that were prevalent among the majority of the population and, therefore, to the development of solutions to the problems to facilitate a transfer from Crown Colony government to self-rule. His own survey of social conditions in Jamaica—*Welfare and Planning in the West Indies* (1946)—set the pattern for future family studies by delineating types of mating practices and by arguing that there seemed to be a close correlation between color, occupation or economic level, and family type (Simey 1946). These findings were echoed, though modified in various ways, by scholars whom Simey invited to study social conditions in the region, including Edith Clarke (1966 [1957]) and Madeline Kerr, whose study *Personality and Conflict in Jamaica* (1952) was also influenced by the functionalist psychologically oriented studies of family life in the United States.[10] The context within which these studies were conducted was one in which people were captivated by both the possibilities and challenges offered up by impending political independence and the need to socialize within Jamaicans a sense of belonging and civic responsibility that would orient them toward a sense of common nationhood.

The growing commitment to social engineering in relation to New World black populations was accompanied by a newly hegemonic industrial development ideology that positioned the patriarchal family at the heart of economic productivity, the reproduction of labor, and educated consumption (Reddock 1994; Smith 1966). Within this context, which stretched across the Atlantic, the roles were clear: men labored, and women reproduced their labor by seeing to the health and welfare of the household. Deviating from this norm was seen as a cultural rather than a structural problem, not only in the West Indies but also in the United States. This ideological norm would also be supported institutionally within the early independence constitutions throughout the British West Indies, as Tracy Robinson has pointed out, within which women (and children) gained rights of citizenship through their relationship to men. Although this legally sanctioned gender stratification was corrected with gender neutral language after the 1970s, Robinson (2003: 250) argues that, because the dominant ideology of men as heads of households persists, "Women's visibility as citizens . . . is never far from the reproach of transgressive citizenship," especially if they are unmarried mothers. Ferguson (2004: 85) explains the ideological link that was made between households headed by women and poverty, then, as follows: "Within a national context that has historically constructed the heteropatriarchal household as a site that can absorb and withstand material catastrophes, African American poverty was often explained by reverting back to the question of African American intimate relations and denying the irresolvability and historicity of state and capital's own exploitative practices." The family studies that were commissioned during this period reproduced this view, and implicit within them were concerns regarding the political futures of postwar African Americans and black Caribbeans.

Of course, later studies modified the value bias and Eurocentric stress on male dominance and the nuclear family by suggesting that lower-class family forms were creatively adaptive—solutions to problems faced in other spheres of their lives—and that while lower-class people shared the general values of the society, they also were able to "stretch" these values to make them fit their own circumstances (Dirks and Kerns 1976; Gonzalez 1970; Greenfield 1966; Rodman 1959, 1971; Rubenstein 1980, 1983; Stack 1974).[11] What is key for my purposes here, however, is, first, that family formation was seen to reproduce racialized difference in the Caribbean, as Alissa Trotz (2003: 11) has argued, and therefore "hegemonic representations of families (as different, respectable, normal) are central to stratification processes and have contributed to the disempowerment of the vast majority of Caribbean peoples."[12] And second, because black peoples' sexual practices and family organization were seen to be related to the viability of economic development and statehood, they became problems to be addressed at the highest levels of government, as they also were in the United States during the same period.

In fact, in addition to the emphasis on scholarship, one of the first activities of the Office of Colonial Development and Welfare staff in the West Indies was to visit the mini–New Deal programs of the Roosevelt administration in Puerto Rico and the U.S. Virgin Islands, visits that were organized by the Rockefeller Foundation. Unlike Britain, the United States did not initially adopt a welfare approach to issues of social development. Instead, U.S. officials took a scientific approach, establishing a policy of population control and institutionalizing home economics education. The home economics movement emerged in the United States at the turn of the twentieth century and was designed, as Rhoda Reddock (1994: 225) has argued, to draw households "into relations with the market as a consumption unit and to bring housework in line with capitalist modernization, stressing rationality, professionalism, and scientific principles." By the mid-1950s, based on research conducted in Puerto Rico and Jamaica funded by the U.S. Conservation Foundation (see Blake 1961; Stycos and Back 1964), the general agreement was that overpopulation (the result of promiscuity and high illegitimacy rates) was the main reason for the region's economic problems and the Puerto Rico model (sterilization among lower class women) was put forward as a solution (Briggs 2002; Reddock 1994). Laura Briggs (2002) has argued that these kinds of collaborative investigations should direct our attention to the syncretisms between overseas development and domestic welfare or poverty policies. In other words, as I have been attempting to show here, at a time when British dominance in the Anglophone Caribbean world was waning and the United States was therefore showing more interest in the region, both the U.S. and West Indian sociological literature posited a link between "the poor" (or, in the case of the West Indies, the "lower classes") and "sex patterns," patterns that ultimately became proxies for race (Briggs 2002: 178). These patterns, in turn, constituted poor black people as unassimilable to the national mainstream and therefore excluded them from the normative categories of citizenship (Ferguson 2004).

By the time Oscar Lewis (1965, 1975 [1959]) coined the term "culture of poverty," therefore, the sexual and kinship patterns that constituted poor black people as deviating from the idealized cultural norms of the United States and Jamaica were already elaborated through research and policy.[13] However, the traits Lewis listed as characteristic of a culture of poverty—

simple language; a great need for sex and excitement; a propensity to rage, aggression, and violence; an inability to be alone and a constant need for sociability; a high incidence of early sexual unions outside the context of marriage and thus of illegitimate children; an emphasis on appearances; a lack of participation in the major institutions of the larger society (with the exception of jail, the army, or the public welfare system); an orientation to the local and an inability to see beyond immediate problems; and a value on "acting out more than thinking out, self-expression more than self-constraint, pleasure more than productivity, spending more than saving, personal loyalty more than impersonal justice" (Lewis 1965: xxvi) — served to further entrench the culturalist view of social inequality, partly because his books were published by popular presses, and partly because his ideas were reproduced in the U.S. policy arena by people such as Daniel Moynihan (U.S. Department of Labor 1965).[14]

In other words, because "stable" families with male breadwinners were seen as the motors of modern, industrial economic growth in both the United States and the West Indies during the mid-twentieth century, regulating the sexuality of lower-class blacks — especially urbanized, industrialized, lower-class blacks — became a key aspect of the state's relationship to black populations. Thus, African Americans and Afro-West Indians whose families deviated from the normative model of heteropatriarchy were seen as "reproductive rather than *productive*, heterosexual but never *heteronormative*" (Ferguson 2004: 85) and were therefore subjected to discursive regulation that ultimately, according to the logic of culturalist development paradigms, blamed them for their own poverty and, after the dismantling of the welfare state in the United States and the implementation of structural adjustment programs in Jamaica in the late twentieth century, abandoned them to the whims of the market. As Diane Austin-Broos (2005: 184) has elaborated in her discussion of the politics of moral order — those "forms of thinking and practice that naturalize a people and their social circumstance as the product of a moral deficit, deviance, or degeneracy" — institutions of the state in fact activate and reproduce this kind of culturalism, with the consequence that "the disordering capacities of the state and market society are projected onto those against whom that power is used" (Austin-Broos 2005: 184).

This sort of culturalist hegemony was not unique to scholarship concerning the black family and the reproduction of poverty. It also suffused scholarship on the African diaspora, shifting focus in this area away from the more internationalist scholarly and political movements that had developed among black communities worldwide during the early decades of the twentieth century.[15] This is an important parallel story because it reflects the extent to which shifts in scholarly vision also frame the range of political projects that can be imagined at any particular moment.

Brent Edwards (2001: 49) has argued that the term "diaspora" entered scholarly literature in the United States during the 1950s as African American scholars became interested in the transnational black influences on anticolonial movements in Africa. Diaspora, on one hand, became a way for U.S. scholars to think through differences of opinion regarding "the political scope of *Pan-Africanism* in the independence moment" (Edwards 2001: 55), as well as a way to explore the question of origins. It was thus a concept that, in his words, was "resistant or exorbitant to the frames of nations and continents" (Edwards 2001: 52) in relation to both cultural politics and realpolitik. However, as the Cold War wore on, and as African nations gained independence, diaspora became reduced to its cultural aspects "rather than precisely a means to theorize both culture and politics at the transnational level" (Edwards 2001:55; see also Frederickson 1999; Von Eschen 1997).[16] The question of origins became a question of culture, and here again we are confronted with the anthropological enterprise.

While St. Clair Drake (1975: 11) advocated a comparative analysis of diaspora populations oriented toward coordinating action to, in his words, "complete the worldwide task of Black Liberation," earlier comparative scholarship on blacks in the New World was shaped by a Boasian focus on acculturation and the diffusion of particular cultural traits across what were then known as "culture areas." Herskovits, Boas's student, was particularly interested in the different degrees to which New World black populations retained, adapted, and reinterpreted cultural practices understood as African in derivation. Friends with many of the Harlem Renaissance bigwigs (Zora Neale Hurston was one of his research assistants), Herskovits felt that clarifying the African derivation of African American cultural practices in particular would counter claims of those like Frazier, who asserted that black Americans had no significant cultural legacy and therefore contributed nothing culturally or politically to the United States. Herskovits's idea was that providing evidence of this cultural legacy through "scientific" study would not only bolster self-esteem among African Americans but also lessen racial prejudice (Yelvington 2006b). Critics and sympathizers alike understood the model Herskovits developed—his "scale of African-isms" (Herskovits 1941)—as more of a classificatory scheme than a theory. Yet it nevertheless has also provided one blueprint for imagining that New World black populations might share a history and, by implication, might be able to construct a common future based in part on countering the denigration of "things African."[17]

At the same time, the kind of culturalist analysis that Herskovits mobilized also heralded, as Penny Von Eschen (1997: 162) has argued, a shift from the vocabulary of political economy to the language of moralism," a move that, she argues, was the result of post–Second World War race liberalism spurred by the emergent Civil Rights Movement, as well as by the anticommunist fervor of the early Cold War period. This move had two conservative effects. First, as I have noted, sociological analyses of race and class began to privilege a focus on culture over a focus on socioeconomic inequality. Within the academy, this had the effect of supporting a liberal view of development that naturalized capitalist competition and of portraying racism as "an anachronistic prejudice and a personal and psychological problem, rather than as a systemic problem rooted in specific social practices and pervading relations of political economy and culture" (Von Eschen 1997: 157). Practically, the cultural model put forward by intellectuals such as Oscar Lewis; Michael Harrington, whose book *The Other America* (1981 [1962]) was said to provide the impetus for President Lyndon Johnson's War on Poverty; or Nathan Glazer and Daniel Moynihan, whose *Beyond the Melting Pot* (1963) was also taken up in policy circles. This cultural model directed attention away from the overall political economy of American capitalism and how it "uses, abuses, and divides its poorly organized working class" (Marcus 2005: 47) and toward psychologically oriented assimilationist strategies for eliminating poverty. These strategies emphasized self-help, but not the kind of self-help that looks like grassroots political organization among a class *for itself*.

The second conservative effect of McCarthyism was that activism toward black liberation began to privilege a focus on nationalism over a focus on internationalism.[18] In Von Eschen's (1997) analysis of how the Truman Doctrine and Cold War politics led black Americans to become increasingly exceptionalist to secure demands for rights at home, she argues that liberal African Americans eschewed a previous emphasis on the oppression of black peoples worldwide to secure particular kinds of rights "at home." Of course, as she shows, this was not necessarily a freely made choice within black activist circles: anticolonial activists experienced significant repression at the hands of the government during the early Cold War period. Yet to legitimate the emergent sense that the United States should lead the "Free World" and to shape international perceptions of American race relations, the Truman administration and the State Department offered a compromise that narrowed the scope of what constituted a black community.[19]

Herein lies the root of the epistemological violence generated by the turn to culturalist analysis, both in relation to social and economic inequalities and in terms of diasporic community formation. The question of where black populations stood in relation to states (an important question for black Americans after the failure of Reconstruction and for colonial blacks especially after the Second World War) became secondary to the question of how blacks in the West were connected to roots, to Africa, on one hand, and to the individual states in which they sought to become full citizens on the other. Although the language of cultural politics has enabled a critique that can be construed as anti-nationalist,[20] it abandons the impetus within *inter*nationalism toward imagining alternative ways to constitute political community. That is, culturalism not only obscures our understanding of the ways imperial and nationalist projects have been developed transnationally, producing similar challenging effects for black populations in diaspora, but it also makes difficult the elaboration of alternative frameworks for the analysis of social issues. It derails, for example, a global political economic analysis that would frame violence in Jamaica within a more historical and relational context while providing a way to slot new forms of so-called social deviance into existing paradigms in ways that make them seem interchangeable. Thus, the "culture of poverty" easily morphs into the "culture of violence," a paradigm that is so evidently taken for granted within responses to the high levels of violent and spectacular crime in Jamaica, such as those with which I began this chapter and to which I now return.

The sense that Jamaica is a hotbed of out-of-control violent crime is not confined to the territorial space of Jamaica itself. It also travels along the same circuits as Jamaican migrants, largely because of some Jamaicans' involvement in the crack trade that began to develop in the early 1980s in the United States as a result of the relocation of political-party "activists" from Jamaica to the United States by party leaders after the bloody elections in 1980.[21] American newspapers chronicled the involvement of these drug gangs (largely without being aware of their transnational political networks), and early reports exuded a sense of bewilderment at what was apprehended as a shockingly ruthless new presence on the scene. Jamaican posses, the "newest and most violent organized crime groups," inspired awe among law enforcement agents attempting to devise ways to stem their tide. "I've never seen a group splatter themselves like the Jamaicans do," said Senior Special Agent William D. West of the U.S. Immigration and Naturalization Service (INS) to a reporter from the *Washington Post*. "They actually try to take people out in public places. They don't care if innocent people get hit in the cross fire." U.S. Attorney Joseph E. diGenova confirmed this assessment. "What you have here is a real violence-prone, extortion-oriented, organized crime group that can move into a neighborhood or an area," he said, "take it over [and] terrorize the inhabitants" (quoted in Churchville 1988). Similarly, in a special report in *Newsweek*, an agent with the U.S. Bureau of Alcohol, Tobacco, and Firearms (BATF) argued, "Today's ghetto gangs, especially the Jamaican posses, are far more violent than the Mafia. . . . If they don't kill you, they'll kill your mother. . . . The Cubans and Colombians don't want to deal with them because they're so dangerous" (quoted in Morganthau et al. 1988: 22). In the same report, a police investigator in Dallas stated, "Torture and maimings are posse trademarks as well. . . . A lot of groups have a potential for violence, but [the Jamaicans] demonstrate it daily." Finally, in an article in the *Miami Herald*, Joseph Vince, assistant special agent with the Miami Bureau of Alcohol, Tobacco, and Firearms, described Jamaican posses as the "most vicious and violent gangs" in the United States, possessing a style that is "bold and bloody." "They have shootouts in the street," he continued. "They have indiscriminately sprayed bullets into crowds, mowing down people at dance halls, taverns, soccer fields and picnics. . . . They have even held guns to the heads of their drug customers." And Tom Truman of the Kansas City district office of the BATF declared that the Jamaicans were fascinated by firearms: "They like to have their photos taken with guns in their belts, very much like the posses in the old western pictures" (quoted in Cohen 1988).

By 1988, most reports estimated that posses comprised approximately 10,000 members across the United States and were responsible for at least 1,400 drug-related murders (see, for example, Treaster 1988), and journalists were attempting to make sense of the connections between drugs and arms; between gangs in Florida, Philadelphia, New York, and elsewhere in the United States and those in Kingston; and between Jamaican gangs in the United States and political machinations in Jamaica. Readers learned when posse members began to migrate—in many cases, illegally—to the United States and how they organized their operations and networks, not only in cities such as Miami, Philadelphia, and New York, but also in the Midwestern and Appalachian outposts that they had "invaded" (Morganthau et al. 1988: 24). Yet what one most strikingly takes away from these accounts is, first, a sense of the seeming ineffectiveness of the various coordinated police actions designed in collaboration with the U.S. Park Police, the Drug Enforcement Administration (DEA), the BATF, and the INS to control the influence of the Jamaican posses—actions with quaint names, such as Operation Caribbean Cruise and Operation Rum Punch, that reveal how most Americans see the region. Second, one cannot help but feel the urgency of an impending encroachment of unpredictable and spectacularly ruthless criminality, the result of Jamaican posses being "clannish, cunning, and extraordinarily violent" (Morganthau et al. 1988: 20).

This urgency was replicated in reporting in Canadian and British newspapers, which tracked the new presence of posses (called "Yardies" in the United Kingdom) through America and for whose readers the United States serves as a cautionary tale, both with respect to the burgeoning crack business and in terms of the violence associated with the drug and arms trade. For example, an early article in the *Globe and Mail* of Canada explained, following the shooting of two young women by a man who was believed to be a member of a Jamaican posse based in Brooklyn, "Posse gangs are violent Jamaican gangs that have established networks throughout the United States and are starting to make inroads in the Toronto area. The gangs are known to operate crack houses and tend to infiltrate a city's poorer areas" (MacLeod 1989). A year later, the *Toronto Star* reported that Jamaican gangs were responsible for four shooting deaths and an "exceptional surge in gun-related crime." While Metro Police Chief Bill McCormack argued that the police department would "not let it get out of hand as it has in New York and other parts of the United States," the article continued by listing a variety of "horror stories," incidents in which Jamaican posse members had proved themselves to be "hard, Uzi-toting thugs . . . whose only aim is to control as much territory as possible, within which they have the unrestricted 'right' to sell crack," a proclivity developed and "nurtured on the free-enterprise drug market in the United States" (Mascoll 1990). In Canada, too, the gangs were seen as moving from urban centers of Jamaican migration, such as Toronto and Montreal, to smaller cities such as Ottawa.

What was different about the reportage in Canadian newspapers, however, was the emphasis on how the broader Jamaican community was being stigmatized as a result of the posses' activities. In other words, the majority of law-abiding Jamaican migrants to Canada worried that "the violence and crime now publicly associated with blacks, especially with recent shootings in Toronto, have 'held the Jamaican community hostage to the actions of a few'" (Abraham and Hum 1994). The rise in "black crime" created a dilemma for Canadian law enforcement agencies, as well, because they did not, at the time, officially collect statistics on the ethnicity of criminals, fearing that this would fuel bigotry (Davis and Grieg 1987). Detective Dave McLeod, an intelligence officer who specialized in organized black crime, explained: "The Jamaican faction is largely disproportionate to its representation in the population at large. But there's a timidity based on the politics that we have as Canadians, as opposed to the Americans, that virtually binds us to not recognizing black crime because it's black. And that's because of other social-conscience issues that have nothing to do with the recognition of a criminal pattern" (quoted in Appleby 1992a). Nevertheless, while Jamaicans represented half of the black community in Toronto, it was informally estimated that they were responsible "for far more than 50 per cent of the black-crime mosaic" (Appleby 1992a). Journalists acknowledged that this situation caused various rifts within the black community in Canada. While other West Indians felt compelled to constantly make clear that they were not Jamaican, Jamaicans themselves needed to consistently reiterate that the perpetrators of violent crime were only a small minority of Jamaican migrants to Canada. Within a special series published by the *Globe and Mail* in 1992, what seemed most alarming for those concerned with stopping the crime wave was the fact that the bulk of those being arrested for these crimes were born not in Jamaica but in Canada. This led many reporters to take a more structurally oriented approach in their analysis of violence, and their focus emphasized the effects of the economic recession, unemployment, and discrimination in Canadian schools, among other factors (Appleby 1992b; see also Armstrong 1994). At the same time, seemingly excessive violence was always noted as the distinguishing factor of Jamaican posse activity, and this was seen to require explanation as an element of both Jamaican history and culture.

Within the United Kingdom, early newspaper reports also focused on the sensationalism of Yardie violence.[22] As "the most terrifying crime syndicate to emerge since the Mafia," Yardies were portrayed as "Jamaican-born gunmen who kill with ruthless pleasure" and as "notorious Caribbean gangs of crack-cocaine dealers whose taste for extreme violence knows no bounds" (Gardner 1988; Hennessey et al. 1993). They also document the connections between the emergent crack market in the United Kingdom, which is far more lucrative than in the United States, and the American drug scene. In fact, Scotland Yard had closely followed events in the United States during the mid-1980s and had developed detailed intelligence on the links between Jamaican crime gangs in the United States and Britain by 1987 (Davis and Grieg 1987). Yet the special units developed to deal with the so-called Yardies—a crack unit at Scotland Yard and Operation Dalehouse—had been shut down by the early 1990s, leaving law enforcement officers unclear as to how they would fight the intensified presence of crack and violence on the streets of London, as well as the emergent market in heroin. After a botched attempt to use an informant to infiltrate Jamaican gangs, Scotland Yard developed Operation Trident in 1998 to address what it termed black-on-black gun crime and to track the movements of gang members, many of whom were thought to have entered Britain after having been deported to Jamaica from the United States or after having fled trouble in Kingston.[23] By 2001, Scotland Yard officers believed, "Murders now being committed in London are a direct result of feuds involving gangsters in the fiercely political enclaves of downtown Kingston or Spanish Town. . . . Hardened Jamaican criminals regularly fly in from Kingston—bringing with them their culture of violence" (Davenport 2001).

As must be evident, within all this reporting the emergence of Jamaican gangs is explicitly theorized as a transnational phenomenon. Awareness of Jamaican drug gangs in the United States is sparked by a request by Interpol to the BATF in 1984 to track weapons that had been shipped to the Kingston wharves from Florida. Individual gang members move between Jamaica, the United States, Britain, and sometimes Canada, and gangs themselves have branches in cities throughout their international network. Drugs are moved across borders in an effort to develop the greatest profits, and so on. The violence associated with these gangs is also transnational; it is one commodity among many that circulate between Jamaica and its various diasporas.[24] Like that of other commodities, the consumption of violence generates an experience that then marks an entire potential market. We might therefore think about the consistent representation of Jamaican gangs as excessively, spectacularly ruthless as a kind of "branding" process in which Jamaicans successfully mobilize one of their so-called natural resources (a cultural proclivity for violence) to generate an important niche for themselves within emergent global capitalist markets. "Brand Jamaica" thus not only includes such commodities as reggae and Rastafari, sun and sand, but also a terrible tendency toward uncontrollable, culturally reproduced violent behavior.

Critics of media portrayals that present Jamaicans as culturally violent generally have emphasized the broader effects of this culturalist perspective on the violence of Jamaican drug gangs, effects I mentioned earlier in relation to Canadian reportage. In the context of the United Kingdom, for example, all blacks—indeed, all black and Asian immigrants to Britain— are seen as potential Yardies and are therefore framed as invading aliens who constitute "a racial 'stain' on a hitherto uncontaminated and unspoiled landscape" (Murji 1999: 187; see also Small 1998). Even when television documentaries about Yardies root the gangs in Britain within political conflict and deteriorating social and economic conditions within Jamaica, they do so, as the sociologist Karim Murji (1999: 191) has argued, to explain "a 'drugs and guns' culture in Jamaica in a way that many liberals might find appealing." In other words, attempts to explain a culture of violence nevertheless reproduce the notion that violence is, in fact, a cultural trait, "something for which we might expect someone to discover a gene sooner or later" (Murji 1999: 191). The effect of this perspective on the black British community as a whole can be devastating, as Tracey Skelton (1998: 27–28) has argued, as it may cause "damage through lost potential and opportunity, and may even establish the context for actual physical harm in the most extreme cases." In other words, media portrayals that present Jamaican violence as a natural characteristic of black men in particular perpetuate prejudices and undergird the forms of nationalist racism that became especially foundational to British national identity after the arrival, en masse, of West Indian immigrants after the Second World War (Gilroy 1987). In these portrayals, the consistent representation of black men as savage, ruthless, uncontrollable, and highly dangerous easily supports popular sentiments that they "do not belong, they are not like 'us,' they are not British, they should not be here" (Skelton 1998: 37), sentiments that enjoy their most virulent and public expression after events that are understood as racial disturbances: the Notting Hill Carnival riots of 1976, for example, or the Brixton riots of 1981.

Significantly, the report by Lord Scarman after the Brixton riots also recycled the discourses of family dysfunction that had become hegemonic during the mid-twentieth century, further solidifying the popular perception of a link between culture and violence. As Paul Gilroy (1987: 104–5) has explained,

> Scarman's discussion of the black community in the Brixton area begins with a section on the family which reproduces the stereotyped image of black households beset by generational conflict and torn asunder by antagonism between authoritarian parents, who are inclined towards Victorian-style discipline and their British-born children who operate with a more permissive set of mores. The pathological character of these households is established in the text by a discussion of the effects of male absence and of male presence which is "supportive but seldom dominant." According to Scarman, the resulting "matriarchy" undergoes "destructive changes" under the impact of British social conditions and the disintegration of this basic structure of life is part of the chain reaction which ended in the Brixton riot.

For Gilroy, the explanatory logic of the Scarman report is as follows: cultural conflict leads to generational conflict, which leads to family breakdown, which leads to an identity crisis, which leads boys to the public sphere of the street, where they engage in crime, and girls to the private sphere of the home, where they breed, only to perpetuate the pattern of dysfunction into another generation. In other words, while poverty and racism create the conditions for the potential eruption of forms of disorganized public protest and "mugging,"[25] it is a faulty family structure that enables cycles of dysfunction to reproduce themselves, thereby maintaining black Brits outside the legitimate boundaries of citizenship in the United Kingdom.

Once established as hegemonic, this kind of culturalist analysis of inequality and its effects is constantly available and can be mobilized in relation to any episode of violence. For example, in April 2007, Prime Minister Tony Blair publicly stated that "the spate of knife and gun murders in London was not being caused by poverty, but [by] a distinctive black culture" (Wintour and Dodd 2007), one characterized, in part, by bringing up youth "in a setting that has no rules, no discipline, no proper framework" (Wintour and Dodd 2007), and no father. This comment ran counter to analyses given by others in his administration, who stressed that black youth were disproportionately impoverished and therefore disproportionately represented within the criminal justice system in England. Blair based his statement on the comments of a black pastor who later argued that his remark to Blair—"When are we going to start saying this is a problem amongst a section of the black community and not, for reasons of political correctness, pretend that this is nothing to do with it?"—was taken out of context. Blair also advocated an "'intense police focus' on the minority of young black Britons behind the gun and knife attacks" (Wintour and Dodd 2007), leading many community leaders to fear heightened police profiling and discrimination. Finally, he argued, "We need to stop thinking of this as a society that has gone wrong—it has not—but of specific groups that for specific reasons have gone outside of the proper lines of respect and good conduct towards others and need by specific measures to be brought back into the fold" (quoted in Wintour and Dodd 2007).[26]

In the case of Toronto, an exploration of blogs and newspaper editorials that address the 9 percent increase in Toronto's homicide rate in 2005 reveals a similar anti-immigrant stance, rooted again in faulty family structure. For many commentators, although Jamaicans constituted only 7 percent of the city's population of 2.5 million, they were seen to be responsible for 80 percent or more of the city's gun crime and certainly for the bulk of the city's murders. Jamaica, in these accounts, is seen as the "birth place for the gang culture now taking hold of the city," and Jamaicans are thus positioned as "utterly ruthless and remorseless psychopaths" (Chuckman 2006) who come from "fatherless homes" (John Macfarlane, editor, *Toronto Life*, quoted in Goldstein 2006; see also Rivers 2005). These Jamaicans bring to Toronto a " 'born fi dead' culture" (Garvey 2005) that is proliferating because of "poorly screened immigration and multiculturalism policies that encourage immigrants to hang onto their culture no matter how dysfunctional or destructive" (Chuckman 2006). In this view, Jamaicans are born into a pathological culture of violence that they carry with them as they migrate to Toronto, infecting an otherwise peaceful, tolerant, and, by some accounts, overly generous Canadian ethos.

There are, of course, other ways to understand the relationships among family structure, economic stability, migration, and violence. The 1992 series in the *Globe and Mail*, for example, examined the roots of Jamaican posses within Jamaica and explored how poverty and hopelessness contributed to the development of violence. In the articles, the attention to family structure was framed differently from the sorts of analyses I have so far provided. One author quoted Flo O'Connor, coordinator of the Jamaican Council on Human Rights in Kingston, at length. "The problems you have been having in Canada and elsewhere are indicative of the wider breakdown of the family structure in our country," she argued. Though it seems she is about to reproduce the discourse of dysfunction here, she quickly takes another tack. "We were never one for a nuclear family—90 per cent of the people in Jamaica came from what is euphemistically called single parents, and there was nothing wrong with that." She continued, "We had a very clear focal point of authority, which is the mother. When mother had to go to work, we had a very highly developed extended-family structure, a very strong support group—every adult was responsible for every child." O'Connor contended that two developments had undermined that structure: "One was the wave of migration in the fifties, the seventies and the eighties. The second, far more far-reaching, is the development of political partisan tribalism." She maintained that these processes were linked because Canadian employment preferences for domestics, nurses, and teachers encouraged migration led by women, and because other adults had also migrated, moved to rural areas to escape inner-city violence, or been killed, youth were growing up with different role models—corrupt policemen, dons, and enforcers. In this kind of context, she asked, "Where is the guidance going to come from?" (quoted in Appleby 1992a).[27]

While many Jamaicans of all classes also reproduce (and sometimes celebrate) the notion that Jamaicans are particularly violent, and that this violence is part of what defines a Jamaican sensibility, others offer more nuanced understandings of how family structure, economic stability, migration, and violence are linked. In her seminal essay on popular notions of heritability, Austin-Broos challenges the scholarly perpetuation of racial hierarchy as the invariably dominant organizing principle of Jamaican society. She argues instead that if we read discourse on race in relation to articulations of class, color, and gender, then the notion of "inheritance" emerges as both a biological and cultural marker of the perpetuation of hierarchy. In other words, Austin-Broos's research subjects articulated a concept of inherited identity that was both historically and environmentally rooted. "People are as they are today due to the colonial past," she argues, following one group of her informants. But "the notions of heritable identity that contest this view emphasize a different inheritance. . . . They focus on a 'history of freedom' that followed abolition. The creation of family, class, and nation is intimately associated with this history and seen as the creation, over time, of newly secured identities especially for people identified as 'black.' Both these positions operate from ideas of environing condition; one which reproduces hierarchy and the other which comprises the practice of freedom to realize and equality of condition" (Austin-Broos 1994: 222).

Many of the middle-class individuals she interviewed said that lower-class Jamaicans demonstrate an aggressiveness that keeps them outside "respectable society"; this is so because, as one middle-class woman told her, "the slavery thing is still in them" (Austin-Broos 1994: 223). In part, we might see this as one effect of the discourse of absolute difference that emerged after the Morant Bay Rebellion in 1865, an event that marked a switch from the language of universalism that dominated abolitionist discourse to one that foregrounded an absolute and irreconcilable racial and cultural difference (Hall 1995). The lower- and working-class Jamaican women with whom Austin-Broos worked, however, articulated a different notion of heritability because they positioned the present in relation not only to the colonial past, but also to an international system in which racial and class hierarchies have intensified. For one woman, the inheritance of this situation produced the violence of the "ghetto." As Austin-Broos (1994: 226–27) argues, "In her view, 'youth' not sustaining a 'cultural standard' and becoming 'barbarous' is an issue of heritable identity, not the product of 'breeding' or even an undisciplined environment, but rather of discrimination no longer counterbalanced by a sustaining black community."

This is the type of nuanced approach that is not typically rendered within media, especially not during moments that are understood as crises. Instead, as I have shown here, the argument that black youth are violent because they have been raised within households that deviate from the normative pattern of sexual relations and family formation provides both a racialized and a sexualized justification for exclusion from the legitimate community of the nation-state. Even more critical, because violence is positioned as external to the formation of states such as the United States, the United Kingdom, and Canada, rather than as constitutive of them, there is in fact no way to explain violence in these states without attaching it to "deviant" immigrant groups. Although anthropologists, historians, and other social theorists have convincingly demonstrated that violence is and has been part and parcel of nationalism—in both the initial struggle for statehood and the ongoing efforts to construct a notion of citizenship[28]— bloggers, editorialists, and policymakers, by positioning violence as external to the process of state formation, all reproduce the notion that violence is a cultural rather than a structural phenomenon (even though they may identify factors such as poverty as producing violence in particular contexts). They also perpetuate analytic discourses that position New World blacks as culturally deviant and therefore ultimately unassimilable to the nationalist ideals that characterize the states in which they find themselves. In other words, actually existing violence both generates and reproduces a particular epistemological violence that has become the dominant framework through which many understand the place of black people in relation to states.

VIRGINITY TESTING AND STERILIZATION

So far, I have analyzed how cultural deviance has been framed in terms of a faulty masculinity that results in an aberrant matriarchy that, in turn, prevents black populations from fully participating in society according to the terms of modern citizenship. I end this chapter by considering how ideas regarding gender, family, and citizenship may have shifted from the mid-twentieth century to today and what this might mean for the ways scholars analyze the mapping of citizenship onto black bodies.

On Tuesday, 29 July 2003, in response to the release of a report outlining the pervasiveness of sexual and other abuse in children's homes in Jamaica, the opposition parliamentarian Ernie Smith proposed virginity testing of girls younger than sixteen. "I am proposing mandatory medical examinations of all schoolgirls returning to school to determine if their virginity is still intact," he stated (quoted in "MP Suggests Virginity Tests" 2003). Smith was supporting MP Sharon Hay-Webster of South Central St. Catherine, who had suggested that young unmarried women undergo compulsory sterilization if they had more than two children. Hay-Webster argued that with the intensification of poverty and unemployment and no drop in the number of unplanned pregnancies, policy measures needed to be taken to prevent people from increasing the burden on an already overburdened state. "We possibly need to look at state control of parenting," she said, "and maybe we need to look at tubal ligation of mothers who come in with a second or third child and can't take care of them" (quoted in "Tubal Ligation Proposal Causes a Stir in House" 2003).

Hay-Webster's and Smith's proposals for the compulsory sterilization of women and virginity testing reproduce the hegemony of the mid-twentieth-century view that women are responsible for deviant masculinity and that lower-class black people's excessive sexuality places them outside the boundaries of responsible citizenship. In the early twenty-first century, however, these ideas could not stand, and the proposals were met with a great deal of public censure. The human rights groups Jamaicans for Justice, Women's Inc., and Women's Media Watch issued sharp critiques of the proposals, arguing that they not only violated people's privacy (as well as the principles of equality, freedom, and democracy) but also showed a bias consistent with broader gender ideologies in Jamaica that needed to be tackled head-on. These and other organizations advocated for public education programs to be made available to schoolgirls to provide better information regarding reproduction and contraception and for the prosecution of the typically older men who take advantage of young girls under existing laws. Joyce Hewitt, coordinator of public education and legal reform at Women's Inc., went a step further: since the responsibility for unplanned or unwanted pregnancies does not lie exclusively with young women, she suggested, "If they are considering surgical procedures for the ladies then they should consider vasectomy and lobotomy for the men" (quoted in "The Eye of the Beholder" 2003).

This, indeed, was the tenor of several letters to the editor published in the *Jamaica Gleaner* and the *Jamaica Observer*, many of which were posted by Jamaicans living overseas. "Castrate the men," one letter writer from Canada argued. "Now, there is a solution to poverty, and whatever else ails the Jamaican society" (Rankine 2003). Another letter writer lamented, "Again it is the poor girls, who are already abused, who are targeted for further humiliation and abuse. . . . When will we begin to make a public example of men who have had sexual relations with girls under the age of consent and got them pregnant?" (Falloon 2003). Letter writers typically insisted that education—not sterilization—was the most effective way to combat teen pregnancy. "When is the last time you saw a female graduate [of the University of the West Indies] with three to four children hanging around her skirt tail?" asked the pseudonymous Blue Falcon (2002) in a letter to the editor of the *Jamaica Gleaner*. "Maybe we need to start the education process in the House of Parliament!" Sylbourne Sydial (2003), leader of Facilitators for a Better Jamaica in London, extended this argument to indict Jamaican leaders for their bankruptcy of vision. "Instead of dealing with the core sickness," she offered, "they are going for the symptoms. . . . What should be tackled is the core sickness in our society of joblessness, lack of hope in certain sectors, developing our nation to be self-sufficient."

These letter writers were pushing government representatives to see teenage pregnancies that resulted from sexual abuse and the high percentage of Jamaican children born into poverty not as problems in a vacuum, but as symptoms of broader structural and educational inequalities. Yet as I have outlined, this was not the first time that the Jamaican state tried to intervene in these broader problems by policing the sexuality of working-class black women, thereby attempting to control how families are formed among poor Jamaicans and to inculcate a commitment to the culture of respectability. Whereas the Moyne report envisioned Jamaican nationhood as being forged in part through the privatization of women's labor and the development of nuclear working-class families headed by male industrial workers, the context today is much changed.

While the industrialization-by-invitation policies pursued in the immediate post-independence period spurred a degree of economic growth, the social structures of the colonial period nevertheless remained basically intact until Michael Manley mobilized the symbols and rhetoric of black power and Rastafarian redemption during the electoral campaign of 1972 and in his declaration of democratic socialism in 1974. During the 1980s, many of Manley's attempts at economic redistribution were rolled back, yet his policies that addressed family structure and women's rights — and here I am thinking, for example, of the repeal of the so-called Bastard Laws, the establishment of a Women's Bureau, and the implementation of a minimum wage for household helpers — have had lasting impact within a new context in which national development strategies targeted women's labor on an unprecedented scale. Women ultimately displaced the traditional male working class as priority plans for economic development turned to the expansion of free-trade zones, offshore data processing, and tourism (Ford-Smith 1997). Moreover, women have come to represent the bulk of Jamaica's internationally mobile labor force. Since 1965, when immigration restrictions in the United States became less stringent, migration from Jamaica (as from the West Indies more generally) increasingly has been driven by women. Like earlier Jamaicans who settled in the urban United States, these women have tended to concentrate within the industries of personal and professional services and government employment. More recently, they have been recruited as teachers and health-care workers.

Because women now make up the bulk of students at the University of the West Indies; because women's migratory labor is now fueling Jamaica's remittance economy; because successful "higglers" are garnering significant market shares and therefore defining consumer trends among lower-class Jamaicans;[29] and because dancehall has created new spaces in which black women's bodies are displayed and celebrated (Cooper 1993, 2004; Niaah 2004; Ulysse 1999), it is no longer possible or feasible to privatize women's labor and public personas. Within the context of contemporary neoliberalism, then, calls for virginity testing and forced sterilization — the latest attempts to dis-alienate the social body through gendered reconstructions — were immediately denounced, almost ridiculed. They were pounced on as misguided, last-ditch efforts by ineffective politicians to implement short-sighted solutions to longstanding problems that had at their root the long-term effects of economic and social inequality within and beyond Jamaica.

What I want to argue here is that *neoliberalism means that the family is no longer viewed as either the primary unit of economic participation or the principal engine of economic growth*. Instead, the current emphasis on entrepreneurialism — with the entrepreneur as a figure that, to a degree, can be extricated from the context of family—releases the natal family unit from the burden of being apprehended as the most critical factor in relation to economic production, as it was during the mid-twentieth century. Across the world, new kin relations are being defined and mobilized to advance new economic arrangements, and this has worked, in some contexts, also to transform principles of descent and land use (see, for example, Ellison 2009). Within the Caribbean context, the neoliberal logics of flexibility have converged, as the anthropologist Carla Freeman (2007: 252) has argued, with the kinds of "reputational flexibility" associated with the "oppositional politics of the Caribbean subaltern." In other words, the sorts of practices that have been seen to define working-class egalitarianism, such as entrepreneurialism and individualism (Wilson 1973), are now also seen to facilitate participation in the global capitalism of the twenty-first century, despite the fact that these two forms of flexibility are, as Freeman (2007: 255) puts it, "grounded in oppositional logics." This means that the flexible dynamics of West Indian family formation, within the current context, could be construed as an asset and, if mobilized as such, could stand as a quintessential example of creating what Cathy Cohen (2004: 30) has called "a new radical politics of deviance."

Of course, these changes do not mean that family formation—especially black family formation and its attendant emphasis on cultivating a proper masculinity—has somehow suddenly become a political non-issue, both in relation to contests for the state in the United States and Jamaica and in terms of the various kinds of black nationalist "common sense" (Lubiano 1998) that have emerged in both locations. Instead, as we have seen, the culture of poverty discourse (in which black men are irresponsible, selfishly status seeking, and incorrigibly undomesticated) has given way to the culture of violence discourse (in which black men—because they have been undomesticated—are susceptible to the pull of gangs and the street, through which they become pathologically incapable of demonstrating empathy or human compassion). Black men have become problematic in new ways, their marginality defined in relation to new institutional configurations. In the first instance, poor black men are "problems" because they are not household heads, stable breadwinners, and actively present (patriarchal) fathers to their children. In the second, poor black men are "problems" because they cannot gain a significant foothold in legitimate entrepreneurial activities (because they were fatherless) and are therefore responsible for the violence that perpetuates poverty and insecurity. In the first case, their pathology is diagnosed in relation to their roles in the family; and in the second, it is diagnosed in relation to their roles in the economy. Either way, faulty black masculinity is to blame for economic underdevelopment and persistent poverty. This is the rationale that undergirded segregation in the late nineteenth century, that ushered in the welfare reforms of the 1980s and 1990s,[30] and that supports the systematic denial of the basic goods that were previously understood as the rights of citizenship in the current neoliberal era.

This looks like a gloomy situation, indeed, but there is nevertheless a real opportunity. If, due to the nature of broader economic shifts globally, the family is no longer the primary unit of economic productivity and political engagement, and a late-nineteenth-century sexual division of labor is not idealized in the same way that it was during the mid-twentieth century, then we are presented with new ways to invigorate the analysis of social inequality and to interrupt the perpetuation of discursive violence against black people worldwide. First, we must abandon the idea that the nuclear family is the primary unit through which populations can engage the state (see Fineman 1995). Second, we must attempt to chip away at the hegemony of culturalist discourse regarding family formation and faulty black masculinity, even as the Christian right attacks, among other things, the *Roe v. Wade* decision in the United States, and despite the emergence of the male-marginalization discourse in the West Indies. And third, we must explore new ways to organize our political and economic loyalties and to formulate our notions of how transnational and diasporic alliances and commitments should be forged, broken, and remade.

It is not incidental, I think, that Brent Edwards's *The Practice of Diaspora* (2003) and Michelle Stephens's *Black Empire* (2005) — two of the "big books" on diaspora in recent years — address the burgeoning forms of black internationalism and pan-African anticolonialism during the interwar years. This was the period, after all, when middle-class intellectuals, as well as migrant manual laborers, were encountering each other in metropolitan centers and backwoods barrooms, thinking through what it might mean to be a worldwide community of politically agential black folk (see Putnam forthcoming). What might it mean that, on the heels of historiography that emphasized black working-class politics and as part of the current scholarly focus on constructing relational histories and anthropologies, we are revisiting an earlier moment when people struggled with questions about the relationships between nationalism and internationalism, racial solidarities and class solidarities? Does this reflect a broader move to make an analysis of class relations and the state more paramount within scholarship of diasporic "communities"; to think beyond the moment of culturalist identity politics by locating other moments during which people imagined being in and belonging to a global community? For me, the significance of these two books lies in their implicit urge to envision alternative models of community formation. This is, of course, a particularly pressing issue in the current global context, in which it is not only the sovereignty of formerly colonial states that is coming into question but also the ideology of neoliberal capitalist development itself. Perhaps in analyses of these pre–Cold War moments—in conjunction with another look at the various radical feminisms that developed throughout the twentieth century—we might find useful tidbits that can help us to challenge and transform the new imperialisms that confront us today.

Spectacular Bodies, 1816/2007

> Early colonial Jamaica was much more than a failed settler society; it was
> an abundant garden of power and terror. Demographic turmoil, rather
> than terminating social development and stifling cultural practice, was a
> seedbed for particular forms of being, belonging, and striving appropriate
> to this world of relentless exploitation. It is thus less revealing to see the
> extravagant death rate in Jamaican society as an impediment to the for-
> mation of culture than it is to view it as the landscape of culture itself, the
> ground that produced Atlantic slavery's most meaningful idioms. Death
> served as the principal arena of social life and gave rise to its customs.
> VINCENT BROWN, *THE REAPER'S GARDEN*

If it is true that dead bodies have political lives, as Katherine Verdery (1999) has so forcefully argued, and that these lives — or after-
lives, as in the cases she discusses — have something to do with how
people come to imagine political transformation, then something
must be said about the spectacularity of the murders I have so far
been describing. Body parts chopped up and tossed into gullies;
dead "dons" buried and exhumed; children burning to death in
broad daylight: these are macabre scenes staged for public appreciation. What sorts of politics might these scenes embody? What
kinds of social worlds do they index? Verdery's context, of course,
is Eastern Europe, and the bodies are largely those of historical per-

sonages, characters within nationalist mythologies. Elsewhere, however, we confront similar dynamics involving ordinary people — the ritual murders, witch hunts, and occult economies that John Comaroff and Jean Comaroff (2000) describe in South Africa, the vigilante squads Daniel Goldstein (2004) analyzes in Bolivia, the lynching parties Jacqueline Goldsby (2006) parses. All of these scenes evoke a particular sense of temporality; they mark the moments of post-socialism, post-apartheid, post-industrialization, or post-Reconstruction. In this chapter, I think through the spectacularity of violence in Jamaica, but I want to resist the temptation to read it as something that characterizes the postcolonial. Instead, I want to approach spectacular violence as foundational to Jamaican experiences, especially after the British takeover from Spain in 1655, and to read twentieth-century explanations of violence in Jamaica in relation to what they tell us about how we have experienced the postcolonial moment.

Most Jamaicans, including the editorial staffs of both major daily newspapers, are now willing to publicly link the current crisis of gun violence to the development of political parties in the mid-twentieth century. They have also become willing to point out the hypocritical "empty moralising" of politicians who, on one hand, denounce murder, yet on the other hand, mobilize their own constituencies militarily during election periods (see, for example, "Henry Bats for Reparation" 2007). In other words, there is currently some public clarity in acknowledging the historical legacies of democratic state formation and the development of armed communities. What is less clear is how to think through the relationships between these local experiences — and by local, I mean the ways community-level and national-level struggles have been articulated over time — and global forces, such as the international trade in drugs and arms, neoliberal capitalist consolidation, and global media. This murkiness means that the more distant histories of imperialism and slavery that continue to inform the spectacularly performative aspects of local struggles often take a back seat within contemporary explanatory paradigms to a more immediately resented dimension of social reality — the metaphorical American foot that is seen to be bearing down on Caribbean necks.

Here I explore this kind of causal displacement as a problem. It is a problem because attributing the spectacularly performative nature of murder in Jamaica primarily to U.S. influence erases particular kinds of continuities between the "old" and "new" empires, and in doing so it creates the conditions for world leaders such as former Prime Minister Tony Blair to fail to seize the possibilities of the two-hundredth anniversary of the abolition of the slave trade, expressing "deep sorrow" for Britain's role in the slave trade but refusing to apologize outright ("Tony Blair's 'Sorrow' over Slave Trade" 2006). While many scholars have dealt with the socioeconomic legacies of slavery, taking different positions on how conditions during slavery have shaped contemporary patterns of socio-racial stratification, family formation, and economic dependence,[1] few have chosen to think through how slavery—and more specifically, the practices of discipline and punishment during slavery—might provide insight into contemporary patterns and forms of violence.

In chapters 1 and 2, we saw people responding to what the anthropologist Michael Taussig (1992a: 24) has called "the creation of terror through uncertain violence" by internalizing it, attaching themselves to an existing discourse to suit the condition of ever intensifying dimensions of dread. Here, instead, I focus on the process of projection, how certain realities are displaced on others, intentionally or not, or what Joseph Roach (1996) characterizes as "surrogation." By mobilizing this term, Roach seeks to illuminate a social process of remembering and forgetting in which substitutes for great loss—in the Caribbean, histories of genocide and slavery—never fit neatly into the spaces they are designed to fill. Surrogation therefore is a process not only of replacement but also of erasure, of "forgotten substitutes" (Roach 1996: 5) as much as of creative reinventions. Roach therefore wants us to think through performance genealogies, the sorts of kinesthetic and symbolic reserves and archives that are mobilized by generation after generation to attune ourselves to how the past lives in the present.[2]

Let me be emphatically clear that I am not suggesting there is a straight line to be drawn between the forms of violence practiced by plantation owners and overseers vis-à-vis the men and women they considered property and the sorts of murders I have been discussing in these pages. Instead, I want to think through repertoires of spectacular violence as just that: techniques of performance that have developed over time and that are made available through a variety of public forums for improvisatory citation or reprisal, what the performance studies scholar Diana Taylor (2003: 21) has called "a constant state of againness."[3] By this, Taylor means to draw attention to how a concept of repertoire differs from that of archive, with repertoire constituting those embodied forms of verbal and nonverbal ex-

pression that transmit knowledge, not strictly as a sort of deterministic historical memory, but as an ongoing process of building from the past to the
present (Taylor 2003: 19–24). This notion of repertoire provides a way for
us to imagine continuity in more complex terms, a complexity that in this
case must be contextualized in relation to the thorny dynamics of empire
and, more specifically, of the transfer from British to American imperialism.

Jacqui Alexander (2005) has argued something similar in relation to how
the "psychic economies" of earlier colonial moments continue to operate in
today's neoliberal era. Alexander is interested in how heteronormativity becomes pivotal to state formation, a hegemonic requirement for citizenship,
during three seemingly disparate moments: the initial Spanish colonization
of the New World when, in 1513, Balboa massacred Indian "cross-dressers";
the neocolonial criminalization of gay and lesbian sex in the Caribbean; and
the neo-imperialist militarization in the United States. She argues that the
practices that structure and mediate heterosexuality within these three moments actually traffic across them: "The practices—the very mechanisms
through which state and nation are mediated—would have different effects
that bear on the contextual arrangements in which they find themselves,
which in turn shape their capacity to travel, to overlap, and circulate within
and among these formations" (Alexander 2005: 192). Yet, travel they do,
across space and time. Alexander (2005: 194) calls the result of this travel,
of ideological continuities and reworkings, "palimpsestic time." This is a
framing of time that positions it as layered rather than linear and that therefore deconstructs evolutionary narratives of progress, development, and
enlightenment.

For the context that structures my interests, I argue that an intellectual and popular focus on Americanization not only obscures how earlier
imperial histories of spectacular violence continue to inform contemporary enactments, but it also blinds us to how violence itself is organized
transnationally. That is, it privileges a model that sees the national space
as threatened by what is ostensibly "outside" rather than appreciates the
multifaceted and intricate ways "outside" and "inside" have always been co-
constitutive.[4] To make this argument, I first probe Jamaica's revised national
cultural policy for the insights it can offer about how this kind of nationalist
boundary making, within the realm of policy creation, strengthen culturalist—rather than historical—notions of cause and effect. I then turn to an
analysis of historiography that addresses slave punishment and death, ma-

terial artifacts on display in a Great House outside Montego Bay, popular music, and myths to think through how memories of forms of bodily torture during the period of slavery circulate, thus becoming available for mobilization in the present. If, as Vincent Brown (2008: 59) argues, death was the "principal arena of social life" in early colonial Jamaica," and if, as we know, spectacular death was a central custom of the social world of slavery, then we must be as imaginative about these legacies as we are about the varied and complex ways we engage "America" in the contemporary world.

SPECTACULAR ALIENATION AND AMERICANIZATION

In his classic *The Society of the Spectacle* (1967), Guy Debord analyzes the forms of capitalist alienation and oppression that developed in the second half of the twentieth century. He argues that the rise of the consumer society and the proliferation of the media created a society of the spectacle, in which "all of life presents itself as an immense accumulation of spectacles" and "everything that was directly lived has moved away into a representation" (Debord 1967: no. 1). Debord uses the terms "spectacle" and "spectacular society" to refer not only to the media, but also to all of the institutions of democratic society: production, education, and politics, in addition to consumption and leisure. In this way, he asserts that the spectacle society is a total system, but one whose organization does not depend on the concentrated coercive power of a totalitarian fascist regime. Instead, the power of spectacularity relies on a kind of hegemony that is infinitely more diffuse. The spectacle society reflects the domination of the visual image in all transactions (including human relationships), the supremacy of the commodity, and the victory of alienation. Indeed, for Debord, the spectacle society is one in which social relations are mediated by images:

> The spectacle is the moment when the commodity has attained the total occupation of social life. Not only is the relation to the commodity visible but it is all one sees: the world one sees is its world. . . . Alienated consumption becomes for the masses a duty supplementary to alienated production. It is all the sold labor of a society which globally becomes the total commodity for which the cycle must be continued. For this to be done, the total commodity has to return as a fragment to the fragmented individual, absolutely separated from the productive forces operating as a whole. (Debord 1967: no. 42)

For Debord (1967: no. 44), the spectacle is "a permanent opium war," exciting only passivity and de-politicization through its distraction from the creativity promised through revolutionary action. He writes: "When the real world changes into simple images, simple images become real beings and effective motivations of a hypnotic behavior. The spectacle as a tendency to make one see the world by means of various specialized mediations (it can no longer be grasped directly), naturally finds vision to be the privileged human sense . . . the most mystifiable sense [that] corresponds to the generalized abstraction of present day society" (Debord 1967: no. 18). This, of course, is what Slavoj Žižek (2002), echoing Jean Baudrillard's notion of hyperreality, picks up on in his analysis of the terrorist attacks on the World Trade Center of 2001. For Žižek, our life as spectacle has led to a passion for the real, which ironically can be experienced only as spectacle:

> This means that the dialectic of semblance and Real cannot be reduced to the rather elementary fact that the virtualization of our daily lives, the experience that we are living more and more in an artificially constructed universe, gives rise to an irresistible urge to "return to the Real," to regain firm ground in some "real reality." The Real which returns has the status of a(nother) semblance: *precisely because it is real, that is, on account of its traumatic/excessive character, we are unable to integrate it into (what we experience as) our reality, and are therefore compelled to experience it as a nightmarish apparition.* (Žižek 2002: 19)

In his later *Comments on the Society of the Spectacle* (2007 [1987]: 8), Debord is explicit about the notion that this diffuse spectacular power represents "the Americanisation of the world," to which there is no outside, but in the earlier essay he does not give an explicit chronology of the development of the spectacle society beyond offering it up as the logical result of postwar capitalist developments. Other scholars, however, have attempted to pinpoint its origin more explicitly. Walter Benjamin (1999), for example, has argued that the alienation and commodity fetishism of the spectacle began in the Paris Arcades of the nineteenth century and was further institutionalized with the emergence of department stores in and beyond Paris. And several scholars have made the argument that the World's Fairs offered up a particular kind of spectacular alienation, a commodified consumption of the real "Other" that tricked spectators into a sense of separateness and distance through the occlusion of the imperial projects that generated such forms of exhibition (see, for example, Breckenridge 1989; Mitchell 1991; Rydell 1987). Yet for me, the kind of capitalist spectacularity Debord explores has its origins not in post-industrial Europe or postwar America but in the slave markets throughout the New World, the "scenes of subjection" that Saidiya Hartman (1997) so brilliantly analyzes.[5] Caribbeanists much more accomplished than I have demonstrated that New World plantations must be seen as early instantiations of capitalist production and slaves as proto-proletariats, which suggests that we might think about the global circulation of American consumerist patterns as continuous with spectacular slave discipline (Mintz 1989; Mintz and Price 1992; Trouillot 2002).

I point this out to make an argument about how the idiosyncrasies of Eurocentric theory production and the post–Second World War focus on Americanization and the globalization of consumerist fantasies collude in the silencing of these earlier imperial histories of slavery.[6] In other words, Debord did not theorize how colonial formations have been central to the configuration of Western society and therefore, like many other scholars, ignored the constitutive role of slavery and racial terror in the development of Western modernity.[7] As a result, the focus on commodification and consumption unfortunately provides little insight into how spectacle is continually breached by the fallout from colonial formation. If, following Taussig (1986), we understand terror as the mediator of colonial hegemony and torture as that which links the body to the state, then we must acknowledge that the spectacular violence on which colonial slave societies were founded produced, both in the past and in the present, a constant disruption of the kind of alienation Debord proposes.[8] In other words, "forgetting" particular genealogies of terror not only erases the relationships between slavery and colonial state formation, but it also actively obscures how the past lives in the present. As Barnor Hesse (1999: 130) has argued, Debord "inserts a soft-focused lens on the history of the West's exploitation and dehumanization of 'non-Europe' and consequently blurs the relation between contemporary manifestations of racism and the constitutive contamination of liberal-democratic values." The silencing of these relations is not a problem that is unique to European theorists, and it more generally leads to a particular kind of myopia when analyzing contemporary phenomena such as the spectacles of violence I have been discussing—a myopia to which few are immune.

For example, the Jamaican literary critic Carolyn Cooper argues that the performative posturing and spectacular violence associated with particular young people in Jamaica is the result of the "complicated socialization processes of Jamaican youths who learn to imitate and adapt the sartorial and ideological 'style' of the heroes and villains of imported movies" (Cooper 2004: 147). She goes on to argue that, because it is relatively inexpensive for urban Jamaicans to go to the cinema to see the latest imports from the United States, and because so many Jamaicans have access to American television through legitimately or illegitimately procured cable connections, the influence of U.S. versions of heroic masculinity and gun violence are inescapable, even for Jamaican filmmakers. These filmmakers, in turn, cannot help but reproduce "these distorted images," which "are greedily imbibed by gullible Jamaican youths searching for role models" (Cooper 2004: 147). Cooper supports this point by giving the example of the dancehall star Ninjaman, who stated in an interview that after he saw the Jamaican cult movie *The Harder They Come* (1972), he wanted to become a cowboy. The movie, in Cooper's words, "created a taste for the feel of the gun" (Cooper 2004: 147). Cooper issues a caveat here, arguing that there is also an "indigenous tradition of heroic 'badness' that has its origins in the rebellious energy of enslaved African people who refused to submit to the whip of bondage" (Cooper 2004: 147). As a result, she argues, there is a certain degree of ambivalence about "badmanism" among Jamaicans; yet it is clear that, for her, what we might call the "positive badness" of antislavery and antiestablishment freedom fighters cannot stand up, in the contemporary era, to what she understands as the "negative badness" of American popular culture.

The political scientist Obika Gray is somewhat more nuanced in his explorations of what he calls "badness-honour" in Jamaica. In *Demeaned but Empowered: The Social Power of the Urban Poor in Jamaica* (2004), Gray extends his earlier *Radicalism and Social Change in Jamaica, 1960–1972* (1991), on subaltern subjectivities and social movements in Jamaica. By way of a historical exegesis of gang violence in Kingston, he seeks to clarify the contours of the Jamaican state during the period that led up to independence and throughout the postcolonial era. Gray is particularly interested in how the state has negotiated, drawn legitimacy from, co-opted, and capitulated to what he calls "power from below" (Gray 2004), and he thus foregrounds how the cultural practices and sensibilities of the urban lumpen proletariat have had a critical hand in forging the taken-for-granted shape of politics in Jamaica. Gray's book, however, is an attempt not only to characterize the Jamaican state, but also (and perhaps more importantly) to understand the social dynamics of subject formation among urban lower-class Jamaicans and how they have changed since the 1940s. This is where he expands on his earlier arguments regarding the role of American popular culture in the development of Jamaican "badmanism" (Gray 1991).

Like Cooper, Gray (2004: 99) focuses on how American cinema, particularly the Hollywood westerns that were shown at theaters in many working-class neighborhoods in Kingston, projected "images of savage violence, animated gunplay and romantic melodrama [that] proved compelling for the cinema-going poor." For Gray (2004: 99), the westerns' moral codes, in which "good" (white cowboys) always triumphed over "evil" (Indians, often) were not only popular entertainment but also a form of ideological socialization that, coupled with the newsreels that also were shown in the theaters, "affirmed the virtues of American society and the moral struggle of the United States against communism and other evils." Through cinema, therefore, as well as through popular music, radio broadcasts of American evangelists, magazines such as *Time* and *Photoplay*, Disney comics, and American visitors themselves, the Jamaican poor could not escape the bombardment of American culture and its assertions of universality (Gray 2004: 100).

Gray (2004: 101) argues that "the simulacrum of American experience" was not the only influence on Jamaican lumpen throughout the second half of the twentieth century. He also cites particular strains of Africanity (Rastafarianism, among others), a waning British influence, and the emergent political institutions. But the American experience seems to have emerged as the dominant one, especially by the 1960s. That, he argues, is when Rastafarian cultural nationalism mixed with Hollywood gangsterism, a mixture that wedded race pride and criminality to produce "hybrid social types—neither wholly Jamaican or fully North American in sensibility" (Gray 2004: 102). For Gray, this is the origin of "badness-honour," a repertoire of power that rests on the "affirmation of a violent, stylized outlawry *in the name of rescuing a racially impugned self*" (Gray 2004: 131). Yet the purported "hybridity" of this figure seems to present a problem in that it implies an aborted process of indigenization. He argues that while some inner-city dwellers were able to creatively adopt and adapt American popular forms within a Jamaican idiom, for the majority this was not possible:

Indeed, locals with limited or no direct contact with American society and culture experienced nostalgia for the culture and ambience of that nearby industrial society as if it were their own. One consequence of this de-territorializing effect of America's cultural reach was that many among the urban poor experienced a palpable cultural disruption. For many Jamaicans, there was a disjuncture between the misery and hardships of their lived experience on the island and the imagined experience of participating in the material well-being, consumer tastes and popular culture imported from a highly industrialized society. This contact with distant American others through travel, film, music, radio broadcasts and pulp fiction therefore transported Jamaicans — including large contingents of the urban poor — into an American-dominated and worldwide political, economic and cultural space. (Gray 2004: 100)

While it is true that the United States became the dominant cultural, political, and economic force in the Caribbean region in the mid-twentieth century, this paragraph raises many questions. What does Gray mean by "cultural disruption"? What does it look like? What are its effects? Is the kind of "cultural disruption" brought about by American media qualitatively different from that brought about by British colonialism? If so, how? Is "nostalgia" for American ways of life distinct from the nostalgia for empire that is sometimes expressed by those at all levels of Jamaican society? Beyond a short description of some musical performers, influenced by the figure of the black American hipster who wore dark sunglasses and otherwise appropriated "a medley of expressive styles and affective-libidinal norms" (Gray 2004: 108), we do not get any concrete examples of how Gray links the influence of American *popular culture* to the development of political gangsterism in Jamaica.

In a way, this precisely reflects the problem of America in the postcolonial Caribbean of the twentieth century. While some inroads have been made in thinking through the role of Americans — as consumers and distributors — in the drug and weapons trade throughout the Western Hemisphere (see, for example, Nordstrom 2004, 2007), and in exploring the effects of the political "influence" wielded by nearly constant U.S. intervention (military and otherwise) throughout Latin America and the Caribbean particularly since 1898 (see, for example, Gregory 2006; Maingot and Lozano 2005; Neptune 2007; Renda 2000; Roorda 1998), it is much more difficult to quantify the effects of cultural influence. Moreover, because of the power dynamics that shape the processes of cultural change, creolization, amalgamation, and innovation, influence itself is always and already problematic, always and already available for blame in relation to local social issues. Meanwhile, the forms of corporal violence elaborated during slavery—forms of violence that resonate with contemporary bodily mutilations—remain untheorized in relation to contemporary realities. This can pose particular kinds of problems when trucked into the arena of policymaking.

TOWARD JAMAICA, THE CULTURAL SUPERSTATE

As has been amply shown, one of the ways that states become social actors in everyday life is through the establishment of national cultural narratives. That states "have actively engaged in the production of national fantasies of communitas" (Aretzaga 2003: 396) is demonstrated by the plethora of anthropological and historical studies of cultural policies and the concomitant literature on cultural politics and cultural struggles.[9] As an aspect of governance, the formulation of cultural policy embodies a form of social engineering because it creates blueprints for the generation of ideal citizens, legitimating social hierarchies through metaphors of "distinction" or "taste" (Bourdieu 1984).

However, within postcolonial contexts a sense has existed that the making of cultural policy is a form of counter-hegemonic practice geared toward reorienting national sensibilities away from European colonial aesthetic hierarchies and toward a valuation of that which is seen to be indigenously generated. This especially has been the case for states that have maintained complex political ties to empire during the postcolonial period (for example, Puerto Rico; see Davila 1997; Ramos-Zayas 2003), but it is also a more general phenomenon in which newly independent states face the prospect of defining cultural difference while maintaining significant political and economic connections to the former imperial power. From the point of view of state officials, the emphasis is on modernization with a difference. In Jamaica, the policy that was adopted at independence in 1962 and subsequently revised during the mid-1970s as a result of the more general sponsorship of cultural policymaking in newly independent states by the United Nations Educational, Scientific, and Cultural Organization (UNESCO) reflects exactly this emphasis.[10] The new cultural policy, adopted in 2003 and titled *Towards Jamaica, the Cultural Superstate* maintains this focus, but it reflects a less hopeful context in which a greater urgency exists regarding the realization of *actual* independence (Ministry of Education, Youth, and Culture [MEYC] 2003).

Indeed, the policy begins by outlining contemporary realities, listing increased crime and violence, drug trafficking, and Americanization as some of the urgent challenges facing Jamaicans: "Jamaica must contend with the paradoxical opportunities and threats of globalization, the penetrating cultural presence of the United States with its influence on the cultural integrity and identity of our population, and the leadership role Jamaica must play in Caribbean cultural activities" (MEYC 2003: 9). The sense that Jamaica has a leadership role to play within the Caribbean is underlain by a more general and profound disillusionment with a creole nationalist project that has collapsed (Bogues 2002; Carnegie 2002; Meeks 1994; Scott 1999; D. Thomas 2004). Within this context, the domain of "culture" is held up as a way to get back on track, to rebuild a national community in the face of both internal and external threats. And the invocation of the term "cultural superstate," although nowhere defined in the policy, could perhaps be seen as a call to action in this regard. The stated goals of the cultural policy are to affirm national identity and a sense of pride that is "founded in the historic courage and resilience of our people," to "foster the participation of all in national life and promote investment in national cultural development" (MEYC 2003: 5), to "discover the things that make for peace and build up the modern life" (MEYC 2003: 8); and to "reflect in its expression the notion of cultural excellence and international achievement that our people have established over the years" (MEYC 2003: 8).

I have discussed the new policy at length elsewhere (Thomas 2005). Here I echo the discussion of culturalism in chapter 2 by taking up just two of the dominant tensions within the policy: first, the notion that culture is dynamic versus the insistence that culture has boundaries; and second, the attempt to promote cultural diversity versus the need to protect cultural integrity. I do this to show how a presentist perspective can generate a notion of "culture" that is corporate (in the various senses of the word) and therefore an entity through which action can be taken. The first tension underlies the assertions that there are "unique cultural manifestations and distinctive style that can be considered to be quintessentially Jamaican" (MEYC 2003: 5) or that there is a Jamaican "cultural integrity" (MEYC 2003: 9) that can be penetrated—and subsequently diluted and made inauthentic—by other ("foreign") cultures. From this vantage point, "culture" needs to be protected by the government, which, it is argued, must "recognize, protect and promote all cultural expressions and products developed by the Jamaican people in the course of our history, including all forms of African retentions, European based traditions, intellectual expressions and products, nation language, Rastafarianism, folklore, jerk concept, *et al*, including any form or expression notable or recognizable as Jamaican and which would be a source of national pride and identity" (MEYC 2003: 17).

The sense here is that Jamaican culture is quantifiable and recognizable, although the terms of this recognition are unclear. On one hand, what is recognized is a sense of heritage—"our connection to our past" (MEYC 2003: 29)—which, as the "reservoir of creativity in Jamaican society" (MEYC 2003: 30), is to provide inspiration for action in the present. But the framing of culture as heritage always puts us in the bind of viewing change as loss. That is, if "heritage" implies that a cauldron exists filled with cultural practices developed in the past on which we can now draw to confront contemporary situations, then change must mean cultural loss. This equation evokes a kind of Herskovitsian model of culture as a quantifiable series of traits that might be retained, reinterpreted, or abandoned rather than a more processual view of cultural transformation that instead privileges people's own creativity and responsiveness to a broader context (LeRoi Jones's "changing same," 1963, or Mintz's and Price's "underlying grammatical principles," 1992).

But "heritage" is important in the cultural policy not only because of the kinds of insights past practices may bring to bear on the present, but also because it is a potential source of income. In assessing the extent to which public and private agencies have mobilized to showcase Jamaica's heritage to a global audience (by gaining recognition, for example, as a UNESCO World Heritage Site), the policy concludes that "there have been serious inadequacies as over the last few years we have failed to capitalize on our heritage product for economic advantage" (MEYC 2003: 30). With this statement, heritage becomes "product," a commodity for sale in a competitive global marketplace (an issue to which I return in chapter 5), and as with all products, we must then be concerned with uniqueness and quality control. This raises the issue of "authenticity," a concept that comes up in several places throughout the policy. For example, it is argued that we must "assure authenticity" in relation to "traditional knowledge bearers" (MEYC 2003: 30), that within the tourism industry we must promote a "more authentic cultural expression of the Jamaican people" (MEYC 2003: 38), and that when training tourist workers, we must ensure "the authenticity of our product and information" (MEYC 2003: 39). Whereas in an earlier moment, claims to "cultural authenticity" were "a crucial element in resistance to colonialism" (Khan 2004: 11), providing the tools to dismantle colonial assertions that black and brown West Indians were either culture-less or culturally inferior, these claims are now mobilized mainly within the frame of commodification. Yet defining the "authenticity" of a particular product or practice is never a neutral proposition. Rather, it involves a process of external evaluation that, as many scholars have pointed out, is always interested and always reflects a political agenda (Jackson 2005).

The tension between viewing culture as either dynamic or bounded also emerges in relation to the policy's approach to social engineering. It is argued that the cultural policy must "be concerned about the type of person we seek to shape through our culture, education and social systems" (MEYC 2003: 10). The view of culture as dynamic is reflected in the statement, "We create the culture that simultaneously creates us" (MEYC 2003: 10); yet a more and more bounded vision emerges as the policy outlines the need to "seek consensus on the Jamaican person that we need to create" (MEYC 2003: 10). According to the policy, this person is ideally committed to national and regional development, should understand Jamaica and the region, should "assume his/her role in the unending process that is called human development" (MEYC 2003: 11), should know the history of Jamaica and the Caribbean and should see himself or herself both in national and regional terms, should be multilingual so he or she can be "competitive in a global economy" (MEYC 2003: 11), should recognize "his/her place within the cultural diversity of Jamaica and thereby promote tolerance, respect for others, and peace in communities," and should be "open to experiencing other cultures" (MEYC 2003: 11).

The focus on developing particular kinds of citizens is where the policy is most explicit about its disciplinary objective. Here, the aim is to generate the sense that the state is not outside its citizens but is imminent within each of us (Althusser 2001). This becomes more transparent if we raise the questions that haunt each of the earlier statements: How would a commitment to national and regional development be learned and subsequently manifested? What are the aspects of Jamaica and the region that must be understood? What is our role in the process of human development? What aspects of Jamaican and Caribbean history should be foregrounded? How do we come to find our "place" in relation to other sub-national communities, and does this necessarily breed peaceful respect? And, finally, how "open" should Jamaicans be to "other cultures"? Which ones, and in what ways? None of the answers to these questions are givens, yet calling attention to the processes of naturalizing ideological positions into "common sense" also allows us to make visible how broader power dynamics shape the notions of appropriateness, "authenticity," and value that are institutionalized through the educational system and other spheres of civil society.

This point brings me to the second tension: that between the "promotion of cultural diversity as an important element of national identity" (MEYC 2003: 9) and the sense that Jamaicans must be protected vis-à-vis those "foreign" cultural influences assumed to be deleterious to the cultivation of the ideal citizen. This tension is most evident in discussions about the arts and the idea of cultural loss or endangerment: "On one hand, communities benefit from contact with other cultures, receiving a kind of cultural stimulation and fertilization from this exposure and openness. On the other hand, however, cultures in communities require special considerations and programmes for their development and may be endangered by the imposition or dominance of other cultures, especially those of more technologically advanced societies" (MEYC 2003: 10). The policy thus suggests that an important equilibrium must be maintained between embracing cosmopolitanism and valuing that which is considered to be distinctly Jamaican, that there must be a way to be global on Jamaicans' terms.

With the following statement, the policy also implicitly alludes to the global dimensions of racial prejudice and discrimination by defining those elements of the Jamaican experience that should be privileged: "While not restricting our global capacity, there is a need to foster and promote as a means of priority our Caribbean and African international identity, while mindful of the importance of all other aspects of our diverse reality" (MEYC 2003: 14). A delicate balance is being performed here, a two-step that seeks to privilege the histories, cultural practices, and experiences of black Jamaicans without undoing the creole model of national cultural identity. This issue arises again in the discussion of "excellence" (the assertion that

Jamaica is *likkle but tallawah*, a phrase that means that the physical, spiritual, and metaphysical strength of Jamaica far outweighs the island's small size). Excellence, the policy states, is the "reflection of the undying, unrelenting spirit of a people determined to rise from the ashes of enslavement to the prowess that was the history of their earlier civilization. It is the embodiment of that vigour and energy that fashioned the tales of protest and rebellion so notable in the pages of our history" (MEYC 2003: 18). Here, "prowess" is attributed to Jamaicans' African heritage, which, while unstated, is positioned as the fount not only of a history of protest and rebellion but also of current achievements worldwide. As blackness is carefully privileged in these two examples, diversity emerges within the policy as a problem in two registers: internally and internationally.

Internally, diversity is a problem of national inclusion or exclusion. The policy recognizes over and over that Jamaica is "composed of several and varied communities, each with its own cultural characteristics" (MEYC 2003: 9) and that therefore a national cultural identity must "include aspects of each community as they interact to create a common system of being, thinking and doing, and the individual's cultural identity will be based on his/her familiarity with the cultural characteristics of the community of which s/he is a part as well as in relation to the surrounding community/communities" (MEYC 2003: 9). The national motto is invoked to talk about the "historical reality" of Jamaicans who were "forced to discover ways and means to live together in relative racial and cultural harmony" (MEYC 2003: 16). However, the problem that is identified within the cultural policy is that the diversity of Jamaica "can only be successfully expressed if each community is afforded opportunities to promote [its] specific and unique identity and expression" (MEYC 2003: 16), but that "over the years our formal processes have emphasized our European past far more than our African, Indian, Chinese and other heritage" (MEYC 2003: 29). Appeals to creolization, therefore, have not been seen to remove the conditions that have made possible a continued marginalization of (especially) cultural practices that are seen as "African" in derivation.

This is so because, as most recent work on creolization has maintained, cultural mixing does not occur in a vacuum but is shaped by broader power dynamics (Khan 2001; Puri 2004; Sheller 2003). By emphasizing processes of rupture and creativity, and by stressing the development of a shared cultural and social repertoire that can provide the basis for a national identity, much of the early work on creolization tended to obscure the actual conflicts that occurred and power relations that shaped these developments.[11] In fact, the process of creolization has taken place *within* historical and contemporary relations of domination and subordination at local, regional, national, and global levels (Mintz 1996; Mintz and Price 1992). These dynamic relations of power have constrained the extent to which the various visions, practices, and aesthetic norms of particular groups (in the case at hand, lower-class black Jamaicans) have been represented within the creole formation at any given moment. This policy refers implicitly to this when it calls for the government to "foster and promote opportunities for full expression of Jamaica's vibrant grassroots culture, recognizing the contribution of this sector to the dynamic Jamaican product that we now boast" (MEYC 2003: 17). Here we see a recognition that ideologies of creoleness have tended to obscure existing (racial, class, and ethnic) inequalities.

Because there is often an unwillingness to talk about these structures in explicit terms, the power dynamic shaping both cultural expression and the formulation of cultural policy is often displaced to dynamics that occur outside the purported cultural boundaries of the nation-state. In other words, if diversity is something that must be carefully managed internally, it is all the more critical to intervene to protect Jamaican cultural integrity from what is often portrayed as a foreign (U.S.) cultural "invasion," while simultaneously acknowledging how important particular cultural "interactions" have been. "Our cultural diversity has been enriched not only by the strong spiritual forces that have co-habited within our borders . . . but also by the constant interaction with foreign cultures over the years" (MEYC 2003: 16). By privileging "interaction," the policy advocates a kind of cultural transformation in which the partners in the process of cultural exchange are more or less equally positioned. From this point of view, it becomes important to call for the government "to provide and promote opportunities for Jamaicans to engage or interact with foreign cultures" (MEYC 2003: 17) and to "provide for our people opportunities to experience the excellence of foreign cultural expressions through exchanges and co-production agreements both within our shores and in other parts of the world" (MEYC 2003: 19).

However, this sense of interaction also feeds into a notion that cultures are bounded (that "foreign" cultures are not always already present within Jamaica) and that therefore there are instances in which cultural interaction will be perceived as a threat. This is what leads the policy to emphasize, in the section on "Culture and Education," the development of stronger links between the educational system and cultural institutions. It posits that if there were a greater "cultural component in the school's curricula" (MEYC 2003: 26), and if youth learned more about Jamaican history, then Jamaicans would be empowered "to participate fully in national development" (MEYC 2003: 27). Again, this places the burden of social and economic development on "culture" rather than on, say, a good land-reform or job-creation policy.

What is even more critical, though, is the assumption that what underlies the "upsurge in violence and anti-social behaviour" (MEYC 2003: 26) about which people are justifiably concerned is a cultural *absence* that is "aggravated by the extensive diet of foreign influences provided to [youth] by an expanding cable market" (MEYC 2003: 27). That youth are singled out as especially vulnerable is made clear in the following passage: "This [media expansion] has serious implications for a Jamaica whose population is essentially a young one, with more than 60% of the Jamaican population comprised of persons in the 0–30 age cohort. This group represents active participation in the cultural process. They watch more television, use the [I]nternet and consume certain cultural products like popular music, and are usually confronted with a wider range of social and cultural problems" (MEYC 2003: 27). These issues resurface in the "Culture, Technology, and Media" section of the policy, which states: "One of the fundamental challenges of culture from age to age is the tension between traditional knowledge as promoted and upheld by societies and transmitted, largely through orature to the next generation as somewhat sacrosanct, and the quasi-sacrilegious embracing of new technologies by the now generation" (MEYC 2003: 41). The idea presented here is that "local cultures, especially in developing societies like Jamaica, are at risk of disappearing as the young embrace the new values and realities brought to their living rooms by way of these new technologies. Because of these technologies, our societies, and especially our young, are constantly bombarded by foreign influences and values" (MEYC 2003: 41).

In these two areas, the policy links current "anti-social" trends in the behavioral patterns of children and youth in Jamaica directly to "worrying deficits in their social skills, personal integrity, self and national awareness." It also relates these "deficits" to "declining parental care and supervision, the absence of positive role models and deficiencies in the formal and informal educational and cultural systems" (MEYC 2003: 27). The argument here is that there is a direct correlation between "alternative communications media, drug abuse, teenage pregnancy, and, increasingly, to crime and violence" (MEYC 2003: 27).

That all of Jamaica's most pressing social problems are attributed to U.S. media is striking in the degree to which it rehearses Debord's critiques of the centrality of mass culture and mediation to the social reproduction of domination.[12] Moreover, the vision that youth are somehow endangered and uncritical consumers reflects an inability to think through how local hierarchies of power both shape the assessment that "foreign cultural influences" are solely negative and ignore how youth produce visions of transnational cultural practice that resonate for them. The fact that youth often symbolically occupy the contested terrain of nationalists' deferred (or even derailed) development dreams does not preclude them from elaborating their own.

Nevertheless, the antidotes to Jamaica's various social ills that are presented in the cultural policy are to "encourage the development of programmes that reinforce the attitudes and values relevant and necessary for social cohesion and peaceful co-existence, devising as well policies and programmes to arrest the negative and dysfunctional cultural values and practices to which children and young people are increasingly and uniquely susceptible" (MEYC 2003: 28); to "give direction and support to programmes that encourage children and youth to think creatively and to learn about diverse cultures in order to encourage national pride and openness to other cultures, nurture a sense of national identity and awareness and foster tolerance and respect and faith in one's own culture" (MEYC 2003: 28); and to "strengthen and consolidate domestic experiences of local expression in order to reduce the impact of these foreign cultural products" (MEYC 2003: 41). While it is true that one of the hallmarks of the current period is a greater centrality of media in relation to the formation of social worlds and imaginative possibilities (Appadurai 1990), the formulations in the cultural policy reproduce the idea that youth are especially endangered (and male youth in particular), reflecting a more general problem: an inability to see their aspirations (expressed through their cultural productions and practices) as valid expressions of their understanding of their own social positions.[13] But this is something I discuss in more detail in the next chapter. Now, instead, I address the preoccupation with U.S. media by turning to that which is elided in these kinds of discussions: the continued legacy of British imperial violence. Tracking a range of ways this past still circulates in the present can help recover genealogies that have been displaced by the contemporary discourses of American consumerism and domination.[14]

IMPERIAL VIOLENCE AND THE EXEMPLARY SPECTACLE

The historian Eliga Gould (2003: 497, 474) has written that the early eighteenth century Atlantic world constituted a zone of "chronic war and violence," a "zone of conflicting laws where Britons were free to engage in forms of violence that were unacceptable (whether in Britain proper or in Europe's law-bound state system)." This peculiar freedom and its necessary counterpart — slavery — generated a system whereby power was maintained through performative demonstrations that drew from existing repertoires of punishment developed within Britain that were then adapted to New World contexts, in part as a result of what slaveholders learned about the cosmological systems of those over whom they ruled (Brown 2006, 2008). For example, European slave traders and plantation owners learned that Africans believed that when they died or if they were killed, they would return to their homelands and be reunited with lost kin and friends in the spiritual world. As a result, the practice of mutilating the bodies of rebellious slaves was commonly used as early as the seventeenth century to deter revolts and to demonstrate that planters had power even over the spiritual worlds of enslaved people (Brown 2006; Egerton 2003). Brown (2006: 182) tells us that by the eighteenth century, planters hung the bodies of rebels in public places to demonstrate "that the dead remained in Jamaica" and, with similar intent, threatened to deny the final rite of passage to those slaves who committed suicide.

While eighteenth-century English punishment practices were not uniform among the colonies, all allowed a range of torture that included "branding, burning, hamstringing runaways, amputating limbs, castrating accused rapists, and conducting private executions" (Egerton 2003: 150). These were techniques that the historian Douglas Egerton describes as common throughout the U.S. South, where white judges also often sentenced rebellious slaves to death by execution and then turned their corpses over to local surgeons for mutilation. "In extreme cases," he writes, "white authorities resorted to torture and dismemberment while the accused remained alive" (Egerton 2003: 149). In most cases, as well, slaveholders required that slaves witness the executions of their fellow bondsmen to demonstrate the risks involved in challenging the status quo.[15] Also common in Jamaica were the decapitation of slave rebels' corpses and the display of their heads atop poles in public areas—the fate of the leader of Tacky's Rebellion in 1760 (Egerton 2003), as well as of countless runaways (Brown 2006); the burning of bodies; and the chopping of ears, noses, and feet. And, of course, one need only read the Jamaican planter Thomas Thistlewood's dry recounting of when, how, and with whom he had intercourse to realize the extent to which sexual violence was expected and worked into the fabric of ordinary occurrences (Hall 1989).

Of course, these eighteenth-century practices within the British Caribbean were profoundly influenced by the Haitian Revolution and the fear of revolt it inspired among planters throughout the Atlantic world. In many ways, this is ironic, given that it was well known at the time that the brutal treatment of the slaves in Saint-Domingue was part of the impetus for rebellion. One need only read the first ten pages of C. L. R. James's classic *The Black Jacobins* to feel the intensity of depravity that slaves confronted in that French colony in the late eighteenth century:

> The slaves received the whip with more certainty and regularity than they received their food. . . . Whipping was interrupted in order to pass a piece of hot wood on the buttocks of the victim; salt, pepper, citron, cinders, aloes, and hot ashes were poured on the bleeding wounds. Mutilations were common, limbs, ears, and sometimes the private parts, to deprive them of the pleasures which they could indulge in without expense. Their master poured burning wax on their arms and hands and shoulders, emptied the boiling cane sugar over their heads, burned them alive, roasted them on slow fired, filled them with gunpowder and blew them up with a match; buried them up to the neck and smeared their heads with sugar that the flies might devour them; fastened them near to nests of ants or wasps; made them eat their excrement, drink their urine, and lick the saliva of other slaves. One colonist was known in moments of anger to throw himself on his slaves and stick his teeth into their flesh. (James 1989: 12–13)

Although James was writing in the late 1930s, George Lamming repeats this passage, among many others, in his treatment of history in *Pleasures of Exile*

(1992), an example of the ways knowledge about slavery circulates in (and beyond) print, a point to which I return later.

Spectacular punishments were also gendered, as Doris Garraway notes. She argues that slave masters in Saint-Domingue blamed women—rather than malnourishment, exhaustion, and the violence of slavery—for infertility and brutally penalized those whose pregnancies did not result in healthy offspring: "Abortions were brutally punished by fitting an enormous spiked iron collar around a woman's neck to be worn day and night until she bore a child for the master. Both mothers and midwives were severely whipped when infants were either stillborn or afflicted with common tetanus, known as lockjaw, which colonists attributed to the slaves' practice of witchcraft" (Garraway 2006: 222).

Lest we imagine that these modes of terror were the result of the whims of one or another planter, Diana Paton's discussion of punishment and state formation in Jamaica shows us that they were actually legislated. Paton (2004) reveals that slave courts were specific about how and when particular body parts should be removed from individual "criminals" and often also ordered specific severed pieces to be nailed to significant landmarks.[16] While these sorts of public performances of power were common throughout Europe in the early modern period, they continued in Jamaica long after their abolition in England (Brown 2006). Moreover, the new forms of punishment that were implemented in Jamaica after the abolition of slavery under the guise of introducing modern techniques of discipline—forms such as the treadmill—did not eradicate the practice of older corporal violence and, in fact, were themselves ultimately seen as continuous with plantation owners' largely unfettered power over the bodies of workers during the slavery period (Paton 2004). In other words, abolition reflected a less clear transition from slavery to freedom than is often popularly perceived (Hartman 1997; Paton 2004). If we recall that public flogging was maintained as a form of criminal punishment in Jamaica for most of the twentieth century, and that even today intermittent arguments are made in the editorial pages of Jamaican newspapers for the reintroduction of public hanging, we might make the same argument for the achievement of political independence.

The spectacular here becomes part of the fabric of everyday life; it becomes an expected dimension of visual performativity that nevertheless disrupts the alienation of commodity fetishism through its hyper-racialized embodiment. It is this everydayness that many current scholars of violence highlight. I mean to evoke here not the many excellent analyses of the kinds of structural violence that infuse everyday life among communities throughout the globe (for example, Farmer 2003) but, instead, the work of those anthropologists who deal specifically with how spectacular violence itself is incorporated within and reproduced through the processes of everyday life.

For example, Maria Victoria Uribe (2004) draws from Arjun Appadurai's work on the various kinds of everyday resistance to processes of globalization in India (Appadurai 1998, 2002) to explore contemporary violence in Colombia and its relationship to the mass killings of the 1950s referred to as "La Violencia." She argues against scholars who have linked mass violence to linguistic, religious, or ethnic differences among populations and instead foregrounds how the massacres during La Violencia relied on—and reinscribed—the production of minor differences among otherwise similarly positioned individuals (Appadurai 2006). In other words, those who were killed were not "Others." Nevertheless, the manipulation of their dead corpses produced alterities because, once they were killed, bodies were reconfigured by using an inventory of butchery practices drawn from everyday life that also evoked common conceptions of the body among the population. In this way, chopping up an already dead body with a machete and rearranging limbs and organs served the agenda of disorganizing the body, "depriving it of its human nature and turning it into a macabre allegory" (Uribe 2004: 88), allowing it to be consumed as a warning.

Similarly, Daniel Goldstein analyzes how urban slum-dwelling Bolivians take the law into their own hands to make demands on a state that is unwilling or unable to provide security. For him, the lynching of thieves by other members of the community is a "form of spectacular cultural performance, a means for people ordinarily excluded from the political, economic, and social mainstreams of Bolivian society to force themselves violently into the public eye" (Goldstein 2004: 3). Spectacle, for Goldstein, is a form of political action (rather than political passivity), a performance of visibility. In this case, while the spectacles of vigilante violence call attention to the structural violence faced by those on the margins of the state, they also provide insights into how gender norms are expressed and materialized. In his account, women who participated in the lynchings explained that they were "sacrificing to provide for their children and defending their homes and property with their lives" (Goldstein 2004: 203). They saw this as part of their roles as women and mothers, and participation in the violent actions that had come to shape their everyday lives therefore became one way to enact these gendered expectations.

Finally, Veena Das's recent attempt to understand how the riots against the Sikhs in Delhi in 1984 were worked through within the realm of the everyday demonstrates how survivors incorporate their experience of violent events — events that threw everything they previously considered solid into question — into their ongoing relationships. Das (2007: 7) argues that after events that forever change what we know to be true, recovery occurs not through "grand gestures in the realm of the transcendent but through a descent into the ordinary." In other words, mourning, adaptation, and forgiveness can occur only by reinhabiting the world, a process that is necessarily ongoing.

Yet in thinking about the examples of spectacular violence that I have discussed so far in this text, there was no single riot, no massacre, no extremely violent event that appeared as an aberration from everyday life, no one occurrence that resulted in a new reckoning of time — dividing that which happened before the event from that which happened after. What we have instead is a series of events that provoke ever increasing levels of shock and disbelief but that nevertheless are quickly enfolded into the realm of imaginable possibilities. In a way, this mirrors how people must have come to terms with the various techniques of discipline during slavery, the ever more macabre stagings of warning and rebuke. These performances of spectacular violence cannot just disappear from the repertoires of rule; instead, the various techniques of embodied violence developed by the British during and after the period of slavery still exist as potential resources for those Jamaicans who attempt to publicly display their own power. In other words, there are historical precedents for the mutilation of corpses and the burning alive of black bodies, just as there are for the motivation to use dismembered and disfigured bodies as exemplary spectacles. Yet as is evident from this discussion, it is not usually this history that is engaged when interested parties grapple with the causes of contemporary violence in Jamaica.

In her attempt to think through the relationship between the so-called modern phenomena of racial and religious "Othering" and earlier moments of differentiation, the literary critic Ania Loomba (2007: 604) argues that "the central tenets of early modern European slavery were formulated by both repeating and reformulating medieval as well as non-European ideologies of difference."[17] Through an analysis of medieval conversion romances and their portrayal of European and Christian mastery over the Eastern world (and Islam) through the religious conversion of an elite, but fair-skinned, foreign woman, she demonstrates that elements of what we now consider modern discourses of racial and religious difference not only have earlier provenances but were also shared by Western and non-Western populations. Loomba links the development of these discourses to the global geopolitics of the medieval period, to the historical forms of material and ideological exchange among the populations in question. She does so to challenge how we periodize the development not only of racial ideologies but also of global relations of exchange and contact. Importantly, she suggests that "what appears as avant-garde in early modern literature about the East is a reworking of a legacy, a memory formed by hostility and exchange, love and fear, over several centuries, shaped most persistently by literature and repeatedly evoked to manage new anxieties" (Loomba 2007: 609–10). With this, Loomba is pushing us to understand that a repertoire of racial discourses developed in relation to a global political economy of material and ideological exchange as early as the medieval period and that these discourses then became available for mobilization, though not necessarily in the exact same forms, during later periods—most notably, during the period of the transatlantic slave trade and the colonization of the Americas. It is precisely this concept of continuity that I emphasize in imagining how particular forms of violence established during the slavery period form a repertoire on which people might draw in their contemporary lives. This link is never simple, of course. "What we have to understand," Taussig (1997: 26) reminds us, is that "it is not merely some horrific process in which imagery and myth work out from a political unconscious to be actualized, but rather a socio-historical situation in which the image, of crime, for instance, is no less real than the reality it magnifies and distorts." It is this situation, this *process*, that I grapple with here.

For many Jamaicans, neither the history of slavery—and, in particular, the experiences of embodied terror—nor the history of resistance to slavery is part of everyday acts of memory and identity formation. There is a historical dimension to this silencing (Trouillot 1995), one that has to do with a de-valorization of "things African" during the British colonial period and a postcolonial emphasis on modern development within the context of the "Out of Many, One People" motto that was adopted at Jamaica's independence in 1962. This is, of course, is an issue that has been discussed widely, but permit me one example here. Upon the granting of independence, which occurred on 6 August, the Emancipation Day commemorations that had been held annually throughout the island on 1 August since the abolition of slavery in 1838, and that had enjoyed various periods of revival throughout the early twentieth century, were abandoned for the celebration of the end of colonial rule. Emancipation Day ceased to be a public holiday, it is said, because commemorating the abolition of slavery would have been divisive, constantly reminding the descendants of slaves and slave owners of their antagonistic history (Williams 1997). While not all Jamaicans ceased to celebrate Emancipation Day, the keepers of that history became marginalized in relation to dominant mid-twentieth-century discourses that positioned explicit gestures of racial pride as anathema to creole multiracial nationalism.

For the literary critic Joan Dayan (1998: xvii), these histories of slavery and the resistance to it are canonized in Haiti within the space of vodou practices, which she views "as ritual reenactments of Haiti's colonial past, even more than as retentions from Africa." She argues that the "dispossession accomplished by slavery became the model for possession in vodou" (Dayan 1998: 36), and that the history of slavery is given substance through time, and in the space of everyday practice, by the *lwa*, the hundreds of spirits that make up the Haitian pantheon of gods. In Jamaica, no such contemporary island-wide ritual practice exists through which the histories of slavery and resistance to slavery are made manifest in ordinary everyday settings. By this, I do not mean to argue that there are no African-derived cultural practices that were creatively developed to deal with New World contexts, but rather that these cultural practices were very spatially specific, with none enjoying national hegemony.[18] There are, however, other communicative forms within Jamaica's public sphere through which these memories are made available.

I am thinking, for example, of the myths that form part of a national popular literary tradition, such as the White Witch of Rose Hall. This is the story of Annie Palmer, a white Jamaican woman and the widow of John Palmer, who had inherited the Rose Hall and Palmyra estates, about ten miles outside Montego Bay, from his granduncle in the early nineteenth century. Annie Palmer was the only child of an estate-owning family in Hanover who had also spent time in Haiti, where, it is rumored, she learned witchcraft. She was said to be "restless, ambitious, dark-tempered and strong-willed" (Black 1966: 17), a woman who poisoned her husband and killed him after he went into a rage when he found out she was having an affair with a young slave. After his death, and after the flogging to death of her slave lover (who was blamed for her husband's death), Annie Palmer began to manage the estates and was said to be a particularly cruel overseer, making frequent use of the "spikes and iron collars, the stocks and flogging posts" (Black 1966: 20) that peppered the lives of slaves on the Rose Hall estate. After one of her slaves attempted to poison her and was condemned to death, Annie Palmer asked that the head be delivered to her after the execution, stuck onto the end of a bamboo pole, and "placed above the corn house, a short distance from the great house itself, where in the fierce heat it festered and decayed, as did all hope in the hearts of those who saw it" (Black 1966: 22). Even the village *obeahman*,[19] it is argued, feared Annie Palmer, for he believed her black magic was stronger than his own. She was said to ride her horse at night, taking lovers (slave and white) and then killing them by mysterious fever. After setting her sights on a cooper who rejected her advances, the story goes, Annie Palmer fell off her horse and was strangled to death.[20]

The Rose Hall Great House fell into disrepair from that time and has only been restored in the past forty years. In my recounting of the tale here, I have drawn quotations from the story of the White Witch of Rose Hall from the published version by the historian Clinton Black.[21] But this is a story that would be familiar to any Jamaican, because it is one of the legends one learns as a school-age child, the details of which—and especially those details related to how she mistreated her slaves—are indelibly imprinted in one's consciousness. Like the circum-Atlantic performances Joseph Roach analyzes, the myth of the White Witch renders legible and repeats many of the tropes I have been discussing: the corruption of plantation societies; the complex but fundamentally unequal relationships that develop within them; the violence that structures these relationships; the obscuring of violent structural inequalities by such means as (black) magic and fetishization; and the ultimate vindication and redemption of those "at the bottom." In other words, this cultural myth-cum-performance event reminds us not only of what we already know but also of what we are constantly in danger of forgetting, and this reminder is perhaps all the more powerful because of the gendered "twist" in the story.

Great houses themselves can serve as repositories of particular kinds of memories regarding slavery, although these are usually sanitized memories that present the luxury and grandeur of the life of plantation owners but neither the excruciatingly hard labor nor the forms of terror and torture that were the daily lot of slaves. Yet after discussing this part of my research with friends, I was directed to visit the Greenwood Great House, just a few miles outside Montego Bay.[22] Greenwood Great House is situated on land originally granted to Hersey Barrett for his role in the British takeover of Jamaica from Spain in 1655. By the late eighteenth century, the Barrett family had amassed more than 85,000 acres of land in Jamaica and 2,000 slaves and in 1790 built the great house as a guesthouse. At one time, the house was the residence of Richard Barrett, speaker of the Assembly and custos of the parish of St. James (he was also a cousin of the poet Elizabeth Barrett-Browning). Now owned by Bob and Ann Betton, Greenwood Great House has won a Musgrave medal for excellence in heritage preservation and is one of twenty-nine great houses that have been declared national monuments by the Jamaica National Heritage Trust.

The Bettons bought Greenwood Great House in 1976, about a year after they had decided to relocate from England to Jamaica (a homecoming for Bob Betton). They have maintained the home in a condition as close to original as possible, displaying an unparalleled collection of antique furniture, fixtures, and china and offering daily tours that are advertised by vacation companies and cruise ships, as well as in the *Rough Guide to Jamaica* and *Lonely Planet*, guidebooks that are geared not only toward the all-inclusive mass tourism market but also to more rugged travelers who seek "authentic" experiences. On their biggest day, the Bettons hosted more than six hundred people from all over the world, but the number of visitors ebbs and flows with the ups and downs of the tourism industry more generally. While many of the visitors are tourists—principally Americans and

Canadians—the Bettons also receive a steady stream of Jamaicans, many of whom tour Greenwood Great House as part of a high school, university, or church field trip.

At the end of the tour, visitors are confronted with a series of slave irons that the Bettons found on the property, as well as what they call a "man trap"—a disciplinary device for runaway slaves—that they obtained from an antique dealer in Kingston. The tour guide pauses at these displays, discussing the contexts of use for both the irons and the trap. I asked the Bettons about how visitors respond to this part of the display, and they said it varies. African Americans, they noted, tend to become either angry or pensive, in some cases even breaking down in tears or treating Ann Betton with contempt, assuming that she is a descendant of the Barrett family. Some Jamaicans also react in this way, but on the whole, the Bettons said, Jamaicans were typically more taken with the "duppy" (ghost) stories that are associated with the house than with the visual reminders of slavery. The Bettons argued that this is a reflection of a more general discomfort among black Jamaicans with discussing slavery, something that has only recently begun to change. Yet many Jamaican visitors—principally those Bob Betton calls the typical "roots" Jamaicans—react with comments such as, "Dem white people wicked, eh?," which indicate an understanding of the racialized economy of social hierarchy during slavery and, to a degree, identification with the plight of those at the bottom of that hierarchy. Bob Betton has gotten the sense that educated Jamaicans, by contrast, and Jamaicans who have been able to make the transition from the lower classes to the middle classes tend to be "more sensitive" or "uptight," expressing embarrassment and disbelief or indicating that they prefer to forget that aspect of their past. Displaying the artifacts of terror therefore places Greenwood Great House within a more general dialogue about a history of violence in Jamaica and the impact of that history on the present.

Perhaps the most pervasive communicative form that transmits information regarding the repertoires of violence during slavery, however, is popular music—in particular, the forms of roots reggae that emerged in the 1970s. I am thinking here of certain classics: Bob Marley and the Wailers' "Slave Driver," for instance, originally released on the album *Catch a Fire* (1973). Marley sings:

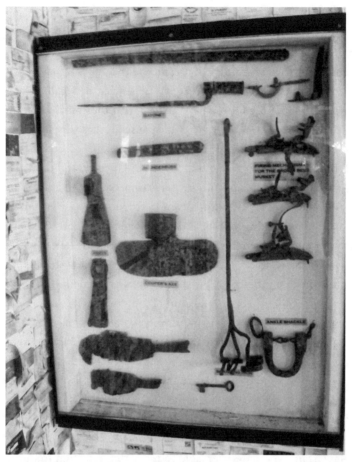

Display at Greenwood Great House. PHOTOGRAPH BY DEBORAH THOMAS.

Man trap at Greenwood Great House. PHOTOGRAPH BY DEBORAH THOMAS.

Iron implements at Greenwood Great House. PHOTOGRAPH BY DEBORAH THOMAS.

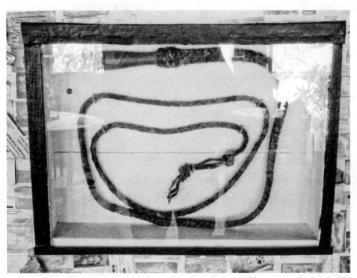

Whip display at Greenwood Great House. PHOTOGRAPH BY DEBORAH THOMAS.

Every time I hear a crack of the whip
My blood runs cold
I remember on the slave ship
How they brutalized their very souls . . .

And, of course, Burning Spear's "Slavery Days," originally released on *Marcus Garvey* (1975):

Do you remember the days of slavery?
Do you remember the days of slavery?
And how they beat us
And how they worked us so hard . . .
With shackles around our necks . . .
Oh slavery days! Oh slavery days!

In most reggae songs that evoke slavery, the impetus for "remembering slavery days" is not to chronicle the abuses endured by slaves, which might account for some of the lack of specificity in this regard when compared, for example, to imperial penal codes. Instead, these memories are vocalized partly to instill pride in the "children of Israel" who "run away from plantations"—in other words, to celebrate the resistance of the ancestors. Here, I am referring to "Sons of Slaves" (1974), in which Junior Delgado asks his compatriots, "Are we not the children of slaves? / Are we not the children that run away from plantations? / Are we not the children of Israel?," then follows by asking, "How long will it take you to give us just a little justice?" In some cases, that last question becomes a warning. The chorus of Bob Marley and the Wailers' "Slave Driver" gives notice that "the table is turned." And in "Slave Master" (1982), Gregory Isaacs cautions:

Slave master comes around and spank I with his whip, the whip
But if I don't get my desire
Then I'll set the plantations in fire
My temperature is getting much higher
Got to get what I require.

At a moment, then, when most Jamaicans remained wary of any articulation of black power, despite the degree of opening enjoyed by more radical social and political ideologies brought about by Michael Manley's turn to democratic socialism in 1974, Rastafarians and reggae musicians were pushing the population to reevaluate the role of slavery in the nation's political, social, cultural, and economic development.

In this way, the "memories" of slavery evoked by Burning Spear and other artists served also to emphasize a sense of continuity between slavery and the modern economic development projects that they saw as maintaining black Jamaicans—indeed, black people worldwide—in a position of perpetual structural marginality and disenfranchisement. There are several obvious examples here. Joe Higgs's "More Slavery" (1975) argues:

> Still down here in slavery
> Still down here in slavery . . .
> They remove the chains but they use us with brains (still down here in
>   slavery) . . .
> It's more than four hundred years (we were brought here in heavy
>   chains) . . .

And Don Carlos's "Plantation" (1984), originally on the album of the same name, states:

> Look into my history
> I can recall the days of slavery
> How they treat our ancestors
> They treat them so bad
> They let them work the plantation
> Even plough the earth
> They work them and work them
> They work them to death
> Now they wanna come play the same tricks on us, no-oh
> You ain't gonna play the same tricks on us, no-oh
> A mister wicked, back 'way
> You are vampire, back 'way
> Slave driver, back 'way
> You are vampire, back 'way

Even more explicit is "Modern Slavery," recorded in 1983, in which the Wailing Souls decry "modern, modern slavery" in both Jamaica and southern Africa. Linking the past and present in this way opens the door for calls for justice and, in some cases, reparations. "When will this payday be . . . for these retired slaves?" asks Culture in the "Payday" (2000).

The songs I have listed were all enormously popular in their time and remain so today. They have been integral to the development of a popular consciousness regarding the centrality of slavery to contemporary inequality and the importance of developing a sense of black pride and achievement, despite Jamaica's colonial history. As such, they stand as public iterations of ideas, memories, and institutional forms that provide alternatives to hegemonic nationalist ideologies. These songs—alongside the spaces of myth and the physical symbols of the plantation era that dot the landscape of Jamaica—articulate part of what Paul Gilroy (1993: 36) famously called a "counterculture of modernity." Within these spaces, the spectacular violence of slavery is given a read that is simultaneously terrifying and vindicating. It is acknowledged as constitutive of—rather than external to—the development of Jamaican social relations even as it is understood to have been part of a more generally global system of racial domination.

That the violence of slavery is, finally, part of a repertoire through which we apprehend current patterns of violence in Jamaica might be made apparent by looking briefly at a couple of more contemporary (though now classic) offerings. The first, "Murderer" from Buju Banton's seminal 'Til Shiloh (1995), links the tit-for-tat taking of life within ghetto communities both to the political machinations discussed in chapter 1—"Stop committing dirty acts for the high officials"—and to rampant structural inequality. Notably, the perpetration of violence is endemic to all classes within Jamaican society—"It's like an epidemic and you won't find a cure; / Upper class you could be rich, middle class, whether you are poor, / Only the righteous won't feel insecure." Given that the song is framed within the language of prophetic biblical vindication, as well as psalmist meditation, it is not surprising that Banton's solution lies in Jah's redemptive powers:

> Don't let the curse be upon your children's children
> Abednigo, Shadreck, Meshek, Daniel in the den
> Jonah in the whale's belly, but he was never condemned
> Job with the leprosy, and he still reached heaven
> He will do for you everything He has done for them.

Here, those who stand by their beliefs and refuse to "bow"—to pressure meted out either by civilians or by governments—are redeemed. (We will see echoes of this concept, as well, in the two chapters that follow.) Violence in this rendering has its roots in the persecution of Jah's chosen people by corrupt states bent on crushing the righteousness of those former captives wandering through the wilderness of Babylon.

The second song, Bounty Killer's "Look" (which was deemed unfit for radio play at the end of 1999 when it was released in Jamaica), is generally less biblical in its language and more explicit about the structural violence of poverty and the hypocrisy of elected officials:

> Look into my eyes, tell me what you see;
> Can you feel my pain? Am I your enemy?
> Give us a better way, things are really bad,
> The only friend I know is this gun I have.
> Listen to my voice, this is not a threat;
> Now you see the nine, are you worried yet?
> You've been talking 'bout you want the war to cease
> But when you show us hope, we will show you peace . . .
>
> Look down on my shoes, can you see my toes?
> The struggle that we live nobody really knows;
> Stop and ask yourself, would you live like that?
> And if you had to then, wouldn't you bus gun shot?
> Look into the schools, tell me how you feel;
> You want the kids to learn without a proper meal;
> Den what you have in place to keep them out of wrong?
> If they drop out of school dem a go bus dem gun.

For Bounty Killer, the violence that plagues Jamaica is merely the result of ghetto people's attempts to survive within conditions that are not even suited to animals: "For you to stay alive, you've got to rob and kill . . . / 'cause man a live like dog." The only thing that will quell the power of the gun, in this case, is real social transformation. Although he does refer explicitly to the history of slavery, he lays out its legacy. Taken together, therefore, these songs allow us to make a connection between the vivid spectacularization of violence during slavery and contemporary forms of discipline (and sovereignty) that are enacted by both shottas and the state.

SPECTACLE, THE POPULAR ARTS, AND VIOLENCE

By the time C. L. R. James arrived in the United States in 1938 for what would become a fifteen-year stay, he had just published *The Black Jaco-*

bins, his seminal account of the Haitian Revolution, and had already become a leading figure not only within the Trotskyist movement but also within the global struggle for black liberation. In fact, he had been invited to America by the Trotskyist Socialist Workers Party to embark on a vast speaking tour that was designed to work through the party's relationship with black Americans. While in the United States, however, James became a quintessential ethnographer, a student of American economic and political processes, popular and elite cultural production, manners and mores. His overarching preoccupations had to do with issues of race in the United States and the potential for revolution in America, and in thinking through these issues he was drawn to analyze the popular films, novels, and comic strips that, in his view, had become increasingly violent after the Great Depression began in 1929. He was especially interested in the emergence of gangster-detective fiction and films and sought to understand "the conditions in which these new arts, the film, and with it the comic strip, the radio and jazz have arisen in order to see exactly why they become an expression of mass response to society, crises, and *the nature and limitations of that response*" (James 1993: 122).

In *American Civilization* (1993), the collection of essays that emerged from this U.S. sojourn, James argues for a complex relationship between fiction and reality. He contends that we must approach the gangster film or novel not as a literal representation of desire, but as embodying a more general ethos related to the economic crisis of the Depression. For James, the gangster and the detective are not opposites; instead, they are complementary sides of one character complex, and this character complex represents the frustration of an American population in the throes not only of economic disintegration but also of a collapse of expectations. The gangster-detective, he writes, is "the persistent symbol of the national past which now has no meaning—the past in which energy, determination, bravery were certain to get a man somewhere in the line of opportunity. Now the man on the assembly line, the farmer, know that they are there for life; and the gangster who displays all the old heroic qualities in the only way he can display them, is the derisive symbol of the contrast between ideals and reality" (James 1993: 127). In other words, the emergence of the gangster in popular fiction and film, as well as the violence that propels gangster stories, reflects an intense sense of bitterness and rage, now externalized by a population reeling from a crisis of confidence in relation to achieving the "American dream." Without safety nets or other institutional spaces of either production or authority on which to rely, James (1993: 127) argued, Americans began to idealize those individuals "who go out in the world and settle their problems by free activity and individualistic methods." However short-lived their success, gangsters take matters into their own hands; they make a difference; they effect change. Post–Depression era Americans thus lived vicariously through this persona.

James did not see this idealization of the gangster character as a form of alienation. Neither did he understand the consumption of popular film and fiction to be a form of commodity-induced passivity. Instead, he conceptualized the intensified representation of violence within popular art forms, on one hand, as reflecting a lack of faith, an abandonment of the social contract that had previously been hegemonic. On the other hand, the public expressions of this abandonment also stood as a process of politicization, as the release of a fearful and enraging insecurity that had long been simmering under the surface. This release was made possible by the Depression, "which made Americans begin to realize that the ground under their feet was unsure" (James 1993: 159). In other words, where Debord saw alienation and de-politicization, James saw a potentially productive crisis of legitimacy. The effect of this politicization, however, was also potentially disastrous, for James perceived the deep dislocations brought about by the economic crisis of 1929 as harbingers "on a vast social scale of the most striking social and political actuality of our time—the emergence of the totalitarian state" (James 1993: 148). He continued: "The possibility of totalitarian power arises only when the suppressed hatreds, antagonisms, frustrations, burst irrepressibly into the open. At this period, it is clear that the social, political ideas of the old regime are exhausted and recognized as such by the vast majority. The function of the totalitarian state is to substitute a new state organization and a new ideology for the old" (James 1993: 148). While both Debord and James ultimately are attempting to account for forms of total political repression, I believe what James gives us that Debord does not is a sense that there is a historical genealogy that is global in scope that continually disrupts the alienation of the spectacle. This genealogy can be made visible through the apprehension that repertoires of spectacular violence are engaged in response to specific provocations, material or otherwise, over time. James's analysis, then, must prompt us to think through the spectacularity of contemporary violence in Jamaica vis-à-vis specific geopolitical crises that have to do with economic marginalization, debt, and political corruption, to name just a few examples — crises that, in other words, have longer histories than that of the media infiltration of the United States throughout the twentieth century.

I end this chapter by claiming the following: arguing that the U.S. media have created a taste for violence among Jamaicans relies on two presuppositions. The first has to do with the notion of boundedness that pervades these discussions. This is a boundedness that always predates a sort of contagion by what is outside (where Britain already exists on the inside). Yet there really has been no point since 1776 at which we cannot speak of American cultural, economic, and political influence in the Caribbean, despite the fact that this only became dominant in the second half of the twentieth century. And second, there is the sense that there is some kind of baseline where British influence is merely civil and institutional. This is a presupposition that leaves no room to explore the real institutional and ideological legacies of colonial violence.

We should instead think about contemporary violence in Jamaica as having emerged from layered histories and therefore as having layered, and sometimes unexpected, effects. On one hand, the legacy of British imperial slavery provides a template of spectacular techniques through which conquest over the bodies of others is either literal, as in both the expected and arbitrary forms of punishment meted out to slaves, or symbolic, as in the practices of displaying tortured and dismembered bodies to discourage breaches of the hegemonic order. This legacy does not disappear with decolonization; rather, it is compounded and augmented by the new techniques of power associated with intensified U.S. political, economic, and cultural influence since the Second World War. During this period, salient techniques of spectacularity include the opportunities for the cultivation of illicit wealth through association with the drug and arms trade, the cultivation of consumerist desires, and the promise of migration. Power over the body in this context is exemplified in similar techniques, but it is also managed through regulations guiding who may or may not travel and, relatedly, who may or may not develop the power to consume (not only products but also ideas and styles). The spectacularly violent incidents that I discuss in these pages, then, might be best understood as an ongoing performance of how the everyday is shot through with a dangerous history, a history that has rendered certain black bodies ever public and vulnerable.

4

Public Bodies, 2003

Chapter 3 outlined some of the parameters for a discussion of the relationships between culture and history, culture and policy, and culture and memory. In this chapter, I turn more explicitly to the realm of representation. Rather than focusing on representations of slavery, however, I will be preoccupied with how representations of Jamaicanness—and the discourses that circulate around these representations—are produced and consumed in relation to the categories of citizenship that emerged initially in the postcolonial period and that subsequently have been transformed in the neoliberal moment. This necessarily means that I want to think overtly through the analytic frames of gender and sexuality, since it is through these frames that the ideas of appropriateness and respectability that have undergirded black people's relationship to the colonial and postcolonial states have been imagined. As I will show, it is also through these frames that contemporary anxieties about the transnational are expressed.

I begin the chapter with a discussion of the controversy that erupted in print and over the airwaves concerning a statue titled "Redemption Song" that was erected during the summer of 2003. The statue, designed to commemorate the abolition of slavery, ended up generating heated debates that brought to light how differences along the lines of gender, generation, color, class, and religious and educational background influence people's consumption and appreciation of public representations of Jamaican culture and history. In thinking through how these black bodies became flashpoints, I show that the arguments that raged in the newspapers and on the airwaves rehearsed ongoing struggles over the terms of cultural citizenship — struggles whose racial, gendered, and sexual dynamics are constituted transnationally. Jamaicans *in diaspora* wrote themselves into the national space throughout the extended period of debates, not just to stay connected, but also to play an active role in the co-construction of the nation. In doing so, they reproduced and sometimes sharpened the borders of the nation even as their own spatial dispersion held the potential to deconstruct those very borders.[1]

I move from the discussion about the parameters of citizenship that were inspired by the "Redemption Song" statue to one about those that suffuse the production of popular culture, particularly the gangster genre of popular fiction and film. I am especially interested in how the space of the nation is imagined primarily within the *Yardie* trilogy, written by Victor Headley, and in *Bun' Him!!!* by Macka Diamond (billed as Jamaica's first "official" dancehall novel), and secondarily in the films *Belly* (directed by the African American Hype Williams) and *Shottas* (directed by the Jamaican-born Cess Silvera). I do this to demonstrate that where elite nationalist representations (such as the formulation of cultural policy) are defined by boundary making, even though the discussions surrounding particular representations are transnational in scope, popular culture is always already imagined and produced through transnational channels (and is recognized to be so by its participants). Because of this, it is forced to engage intra-diasporic hierarchies and stereotypes and to be explicit about the sorts of masculinity and femininity that can move across borders. I suggest that "transnational Jamaica" is engaged differently in these two forms of cultural production as the result of two related phenomena, one having to do with the contexts within which the art forms are produced, and the other with the sorts of critical mediation that has characterized the two forms. I am intentionally invoking Inderpal Grewal's provocative *Transnational America* (2005) here to suggest that Jamaica, like America, is a globally circulating entity that holds within it particular expectations and sensibilities that can be consumed without having to set foot in its actual territorial space. This is the case, on one hand, because the transnational sphere of Jamaica (its migrant communities) spans the globe, and on the other, because people's mediated experiences of Jamaica—reggae music, athletes—have been so profound.

Despite the divergence related to notions of what constitutes the appropriate spatial frame for imagining citizenship, these two forms of representation do share ground on one issue: the policing of sexuality. The various responses to the "Redemption Song" statue should recall for us the discussion in chapter 2 about a particularly situated notion of how class position and social mobility are related within the national space and how this relation is lived and embodied through family formation. For a middle-class or a striving middle-class consuming public, then, class articulates in complicated ways with education, religion, generation, and notions of vulgarity to create boundaries on appropriate expressions of sexuality. Popular films and novels, on the other hand, work to police sexuality through the idealization of a caricature of masculinity that transcends not only class but also national boundaries.[2] Within these popular cultural offerings, homosexuality, especially—as well as other sexual practices that are considered "deviant" even when performed by heterosexual couples (such as oral sex)—is represented as a foreign pathogen encroaching on the social body of Jamaica by threatening this caricature of masculinity. The scaffolding of national boundaries therefore is strengthened by protecting this masculinity, often through explicit sexual violence. In both cases, therefore, notions of the appropriate expression of sexuality and intimacy define the edges of authentic citizenship in transnational Jamaica. In both cases, as well, a notion of "respect"—one that always evokes the presence of an externally observing public—is mobilized to legitimize this authenticity, even as it takes different forms as it moves across class, cultural, and territorial terrain.

I argue that these convergences are the result of apprehensions regarding the experience of transnationalism in the neoliberal context. While it is true that transnationalism has been a frame through which Jamaicans have defined their relationships both to a wider world and to the nation-state since the late nineteenth century, the intensification of migration after independence has generated somewhat contradictory effects. On one hand, as I have attempted to show throughout these chapters, working-class and poorer Jamaicans are experiencing greater autonomy, and their cultural forms of expression have become more prominent within a general public sphere. On the other hand, as neoliberalism erodes the promises of sovereignty on various levels and as Jamaicans living within North America and the United Kingdom come to experience "global citizenship" as ever more profoundly racialized (Clarke and Thomas 2006), new sorts of anxieties have emerged about the future. In other words, it is not just those who are developing cultural policy for the state but also citizens at home and abroad who are apprehensive about the effects of diaspora and transnationalism, and these apprehensions are related to the new vulnerabilities and uncertainties that have eroded regulatory norms of the mid-twentieth century related to gender, sexuality, and the family and their relationship to citizenship, even as these norms were vehemently contested. These apprehensions are expressed within both popular forms of cultural production and responses to elite representations. Underlying them are questions regarding what new norms governing gender, sexuality, and the family might characterize the contemporary transnational sphere.

"REDEMPTION SONG"

Although it is one of the larger islands in the Caribbean, Jamaica is nevertheless a small place. It is, however, a small place that boasts two major daily newspapers — one of which is the oldest consistently published newspaper in the Western Hemisphere, and both of which are published online — as well as a number of smaller daily and weekly publications targeted to various sectors of the population. Several radio discussion and call-in shows also are aired throughout the day. Unlike television or the Internet, radio in Jamaica is a global medium that privileges the local (in this case, the national space) *even when* people call in from overseas. Similarly, when Jamaicans in diaspora write e-mail letters to the editor to both daily newspapers, they are usually addressing issues that have emerged in Jamaica, not those they face where they are living. As a result, the level of participation in locally developed public debates is very high, both directly, as Jamaicans across the country (and throughout the diaspora) write letters to the editor or call in to the radio shows, and indirectly, as they use the radio shows and newspapers as stepping stones for their own kitchen table, veranda, and rum shop deliberations. What I am trying to get at here is that Jamaicans, wherever they are, are always ready to add their two cents to a local controversy.

During the summer of 2003, the debates about "Redemption Song" became just such a controversy, and one that happened to emerge during a moment when there was a heightened level of "crisis talk" in Jamaica. By this, I mean that discourse regarding the extraordinary level of crime and violence, the various failures of politicians, and the lack of economic opportunities had become ubiquitous in the public sphere and in private discussions, leading many to insist that "Jamaica mash up completely." Teresa Caldeira (2000: 19) has called this kind of discourse the "talk of crime," the "everyday conversations, commentaries, discussions, narratives, and jokes that have crime and fear as their subject." This is a kind of talk, she argues, that is contagious and that is not only expressive but also productive—of opinions and perspectives as well as landscapes, public space, and social interactions. As I have noted, crisis talk has a long history in Jamaica, and it has typically bubbled over when there have been significant transformations in the political economy of labor within and beyond "the rock." Because these are transformations that generate doubts and uncertainties regarding the future, crisis talk typically has produced intensified attention, on the part of government and civic leaders, to two dimensions of social life in Jamaica. One has to do with the issue raised in chapter 2—the gendered dynamics of the social body (especially the strength and nature of working-class families)—and the other with the public representations of Jamaican-ness that circulate both locally and in the international sphere. That these dimensions are related is an argument I hardly need to rehearse here. The statue, therefore, served as an embodiment of more general concerns about the future and its relationship to the past.

"Redemption Song," created by Laura Facey Cooper and unveiled by Prime Minister P. J. Patterson on 31 July to commemorate Emancipation Day in 2003, stands at one of the busiest intersections in New Kingston, the heart of Kingston's commercial district. It marks the entrance to Emancipation Park, a six-acre tract of land that the National Housing Trust spent 100 million Jamaican dollars (U.S. $1.6 million) renovating in 2002 as part of the then prime minister's ongoing attempts to commemorate those who endured slavery. Prior to its revitalization, the land went largely unused except as an occasional entertainment venue. Now, with creative landscaping that includes three fountains, a stage, and a fitness trail, and with an ice-cream truck and kiddie rides nearby, Emancipation Park has become a well-used public space, home to concerts as well as political protests, fitness enthusiasts as well as tourists.

The statue itself features bronzed figures of a nude man and woman resting on a concrete basin as if emerging from a pool of water. The figures stand more than 3.5 meters tall on a base into which were initially etched

"Redemption Song," by Laura Facey Cooper. IMAGE COURTESY OF THE
JAMAICA GLEANER COMPANY, LTD. COPYRIGHT THE GLEANER COMPANY
LIMITED, 2003.

the words first uttered by Marcus Garvey and then immortalized by Bob
Marley: "None but ourselves can free our mind."[3] Facey Cooper's design —
which cost about $75,000 to build — won first place in an open competi-
tion judged by a committee of leading figures in Jamaica's arts scene that
included David Boxer, curator of the National Gallery, and Rex Nettleford,
then the vice-chancellor of the University of the West Indies, the founding
director of the National Dance Theatre Company of Jamaica, and a cultural
consultant on countless national committees and international boards.

Letters to the editor and commentaries by columnists on the statue appeared almost daily in the newspapers throughout the month of August and into September, and debates raged on the radio call-in shows. At the end of October, sentiments on the statue still ran high enough for the Reggae Studies Unit of the University of the West Indies to host a forum discussion among reggae artistes, intellectuals, and other interested individuals at which the predominating sentiment toward the statue was hostility. Although some saw hope in the statue and felt that it embodied strength, vigor, and pride, there had been enough calls for the statue's removal by the end of August that an opinion poll was conducted in early September. Despite the ongoing vociferous opposition to the statue, the poll ultimately revealed that the majority of Jamaicans of voting age actually felt the statue should stay at the entrance to Emancipation Park (Observer Reporter 2003).[4] As a light-complexioned Jamaican, Facey Cooper herself came under fire, with several people suggesting that since her "whiteness" would prevent her from having a visceral identification with slavery and emancipation, her monument would naturally lack a powerful resonance among those who *would* purportedly identify with people who had been enslaved: "Being white, instead of placing the theme of Emancipation in the very specific context of the enslavement of African peoples now living in Jamaica, she has universalized it, making it a generic emancipation in which she can also participate. . . . *Redemption Song* does not speak to most Jamaicans. . . . It does not express the Jamaican experience using symbols that Jamaicans find understandable, approachable, *ours*" (Graham 2004: 175, 178). Ultimately, the statue was compared — unfavorably — to well-received liberation-struggle monuments in Barbados, Guyana, and Haiti. What was all the fuss about?

REPRESENTATIONAL VIOLENCE

One of the processes I have kept coming back to throughout these chapters is how anticolonial political and intellectual elites of the mid-twentieth century promoted new ideas about cultural citizenship as part of their push toward political independence. I have already explored how gender relations and family formation were systems through which they attempted to engineer cultural practices in the service of economic development and political stability. Yet many also worked within the sphere of symbolic representation, cultivating the notion that previously denigrated Afro-Jamaican beliefs and practices should be valued and institutionalized as the foundations of Jamaica's national cultural identity. They thus established various community-based arts organizations and festivals, part and parcel of the social-welfare work and democratic political nationalism, current at the time, that promoted particular notions of progress and development (D. Thomas 2004).

For many among the political and cultural elite who gained power during the transfer from British rule, however, these notions of progress and development were not consonant with the cultural forms and institutions that Jamaicans evolved during the period of slavery. The irony, then, is that while nationalist intellectuals and activists, who were overwhelmingly middle class, sought to confer recognition on working-class Afro-Jamaican forms and institutions by using them as the foundation of a national cultural identity, they also saw them as hindrances to political and economic development. In other words, by carving out a distinctive place for the elaboration of a cultural heritage, creole multiracial nationalists attempted to inculcate both a cultural identity and the acceptance of hegemonic structures of postcolonial political authority. Percy Hintzen has identified these simultaneous endeavors as the two key dimensions of nationalist projects in the Caribbean. He argues that "national elites became the agents of modernity and the instruments of equality" (Hintzen 1997: 63) through a developmental discourse that masked postcolonial relations of power and undermined "the symbolic power of ethnic nationalism," which, in his view, is essentially a discourse of race (Hintzen 1997: 66).

Indeed, in Jamaica the tensions between various strands of black nationalism and creole multiracialism have informed cultural politics from the establishment of Crown Colony rule to the present. On one hand, the early movement to promote a new (anticolonial) vision of cultural citizenship remained wedded to British institutions and to the idea that these institutions would socialize the population within values that by then had been constructed as uniquely belonging to the respectable middle classes, such as discipline, temperance, collective work, thrift, industry, Christian living, community uplift, and respect for formal education. On the other hand, it gave symbolic primacy to historical events and select cultural practices deemed relevant to the majority of the population. As I have already noted, at independence in 1962, this two-step emphasized social modernization with a difference: the cultivation of "middle-class values," "respect-able" family structures, community mobilization, and political participation would facilitate Jamaica's economic growth alongside a public re-valuing of those aesthetic practices that had been denigrated by colonial authorities.

Elsewhere, I outline the connections between broader political and economic initiatives and the tensions between creole multiracial nationalism and diverse black nationalisms over time (D. Thomas 2004). Here, I will just reiterate that, while the government's legitimation of aspects of Jamaica's African cultural heritage broadened the public space in which notions of national identity could be debated, the actual process of privileging particular elements of Jamaica's African cultural heritage also marginalized alternative visions. The attempt to consolidate a nationalist state, to inculcate soon-to-be-ex-subjects with a sense of national belonging and loyalty that would naturalize new relations of authority, validated a particular kind of citizen and a specific vision of cultural "progress" and "development" that prioritized creole multiracial integration around the model of nationalist "respectability." But this was not the only vision of progress available to Jamaicans at the time of independence or afterward. Competing understandings of Jamaican identity and political struggle have been rooted in a sense of racialized (and, relatedly, transnational) citizenship. These competing understandings in large part are what shaped the diverse reactions to "Redemption Song."

Jamaicans who did not appreciate the statue tended to root their opposition in the nudity of the figures. Taking offense to nudity operated here on several levels. Many Jamaicans were offended because they understood their foreparents as having been humiliated in their nakedness. They thus felt the statue was disrespectful. As John Campbell (2003) wrote from Miami, "Did our ancestors stand naked for slave masters and fellow slaves to view them in their nakedness in public? For God's sake, couldn't they at least cover their private parts? Shame, shame, shame on all of you who allowed this to happen." Others agreed. Antonnette Thomas (2003) wrote, "When I think of emancipation from slavery, I think of being able to wear clothing, finally!" And Stephanie Bygrave, a thirty-seven-year-old self-employed woman in Kingston, offered her opinion to the columnist Claude Mills (2003): "Dem shoulda cover them up with a loin cloth or something. What the artist is saying about black people? And why dem coulden free up them mind inna dem clothes?" Several letter writers, therefore, advocated that the statue's figures be clothed or that foliage be placed strategically nearby.[5]

Others were worried about how "outsiders" would respond to the figures' nudity. A Jamaican woman living overseas argued that the statue "merely reinforces the stereotypes of black people as sexualized beings" and asked, "What does it say to people who link sex and tourism in the Caribbean?" (Mills 2003). Celia Jackson of Kingston felt that the figures were inappropriate for children's viewing, stating that it was "poor taste to have a sculpture with male and female genitals exposed and so exaggerated erected in a public place" (Jackson 2003). The statue also prompted an extended debate on the size of the penis and the extent to which it was representative of the average Jamaican man. Some suggested that the size of the flaccid penis might make some men feel intimidated and insecure about their own endowment, while others expressed concern that "the emphasis on the genitals of the man could have the effect of reinforcing stud like mentality in the psyche of our males" (Richards 2003).

Some letter writers linked the nudity of the statue to a decline in local (Jamaican) values and a tendency to follow foreign fashion. "We are also losing our values, respect, culture, discipline, way of life, and want to follow the rest of the world, going down the negative road," one wrote. "This is not our culture, style, or taste. I expect to see these kinds of things when I travel to Italy and other European countries" (Campbell 2003). Echoing many other concerned citizens, Ricardo Smalling of Kingston wondered why "we look at a magnificent work of art and all we see is sex. . . . Our ability to reason seems to be tied to sex and sexuality and everything has to be lowered to that level" (Smalling 2003). C. Kelly of Portmore agreed, arguing that the statue only adds to the "growing lack of respect shown to each other," which is embodied through the omnipresence of sex and sexuality (Kelly 2003).

Several saw the objection to nudity in the statue as hypocritical for this very reason. "Listen to the language of our entertainers. Look at the dresses worn by some of our young and not so young girls. Nothing is left to the imagination," Marilyn Delavante (2003) wrote to the *Gleaner*. "Consider the behavior of so many who exhibit vulgar and explicit behavior," she continued, "add to this the immoral sexuality of men who abuse under-age girls and women." Delavante's sentiments were echoed by Christopher Burns, who asked, "Why is it that we embrace readily the slackness of the dance-hall and the vulgarity of the dirty dancing, yet react with shock at another form of (lifeless) art?" (Burns 2003).

This invocation of dancehall reflects the widespread popular debate that surrounds the music and associated culture of contemporary youth. Because dancehall lyrics in large measure have diverged from "conscious" reggae's emphasis on social critique and redemption, instead reflecting a ghetto glorification of sex, guns, and the drug trade, many middle-class observers have referred to dancehall derisively as "slackness" music. In particular, they have seen dancehall fashions and women's highly sexualized dance moves as vulgarly degrading to Jamaica's moral fiber. Their everyday judgments of working-class Jamaican women who spend enormous amounts of money and time getting ready for dancehall sessions rather than, purportedly, investing in their own or their children's educational and occupational advancement, again reflects an impetus to reassert the culture of respectability by circumscribing the mobility of black women's bodies. These judgments also reflect an ongoing concern, a fear even, among certain middle-class and upper-class Jamaicans regarding the power of lower-class production of popular cultural to shape both behavior and public perceptions of Jamaica and Jamaicans. Carolyn Cooper has used the dancehall trope of the "border clash" to identify these kinds of discursive scenarios. She argues that border clashes exemplify the "ideological conflicts between competing value systems in Jamaica" (Cooper 2004: 35) — conflicts that are rooted in class and color hierarchies — and, moreover, that they continue to emerge in the public sphere mainly because elite Jamaicans fail to take popular culture seriously as a means of expressing and enacting an alternative worldview among poorer Jamaicans.

That many of the responses to the nudity seemed also to break down along class lines became clearest in the deliberations about whether Jamaicans could accept nudity as "art." On 6 August, the *Gleaner* published an editorial in defense of the statue, in which the editors asked whether "prurience, like beauty, is in the eye of the beholder" ("The Eye of the Beholder" 2003). They went on to suggest that the strong negative responses to the statue disguised "a deep, unconscious guilt in the psyche of those who express shock at the sensuality of the figures rather than delight in the symbolism the artist envisioned." Furthermore, like several letter writers, the *Gleaner* editorial pointed out that "representation of the naked human figure has been an art form since the beginning of time," citing Michelangelo's "David" in particular. The editorial concluded by arguing that there should be "restraint and more mature reflection on the artistic merits of the work" ("The Eye of the Beholder" 2003b).

Many others echoed these sentiments, concluding that opposition to the statue revealed a sense of continued mental and social enslavement and that black men and women in Jamaica were "still unable to accept themselves as beautiful" (Gallimore 2003). Marva Chambers of Kingston called for more open-mindedness. "Why is it that we as a people can only tear down and never see or appreciate the positive side of anything that has happened in this country?" she asked. "Is it that we are so afraid of our own nakedness, or is it that after 41 years we have not been truly emancipated?" (Chambers 2003). Kevin Young (2003), writing from Florida, refuted the idea that latent Eurocentrism was behind opposition to the statue, arguing instead that "misguided conceptions of morality" and a "lack of appreciation for artistic expression" — in short, ignorance — were to blame. George Witter (2003), writing from England, concurred. "If this 'masterpiece' was created by an American, European, or anyone else except a Jamaican," he wrote, "it would be treated as brilliant modern art." The multimedia producer Tommy Ricketts took this notion one step further to argue that "there are many persons who are not ready to deal with emancipation and this is a Talibanish trait in highly religious countries, like Jamaica. Anywhere else in the world intelligent people would appreciate this" (quoted in Harold 2003). The cultural critic Narda Graham, in response to these kinds of comments, explained why many Jamaicans would have seen the statue's nudity not as "art" but as an offense to public decency: "Some commentators have suggested that since Jamaica has a highly sexualized culture, it is surprising that Jamaicans should be disturbed by nudity in public art. In fact, the opposite is true. It is exactly because we are a highly sexualized culture that nudity in art is shocking to many, since for a large number, nudity equals sex — not purity, rebirth, freedom, or nobility. . . . Therefore, most Jamaicans do not expect or wish to see anatomically precise nudity on a public piece of art" (Graham 2004: 175).

Others explained the opposition to "Redemption Song" by seeing it as just one more example in a long history of "middle class misrepresentation[s] of struggle" (Harold 2003) and by taking issue with the tone of intellectuals and artists who ridiculed those Jamaicans who did not appreciate the artistic merits of the statue. Dwight Smikle (2003) described this patronizing tone in the following manner: "'We are in the great house and we know what is best for you. You after all are just ordinary Jamaicans and we are the refined ones who can appreciate the fine work of art that we have given to you.'" Similarly, the *Observer* columnist Lloyd Smith (2003) argued that the statue was "thrust on the nation by the Patterson administration with a certain degree of contempt for the Jamaican people who are still being seen by many of our politicians, the intelligentsia, the upper middle class, and the last vestiges of the plantocracy as illiterate ignoramuses who do not know what is good for them." And Cooper, who dedicated a series of newspaper columns to criticizing various aspects of the statue, condemned the paternalism that infused the dismissiveness of the middle class and the elite of those Jamaicans who did not appreciate the statue:

> In its consolidation of the myth of mindless African physicality the monument is, at core, a reification of enslavement, and an excellent example of what the Jamaican artist, Omari Ra, wittily describes as an "apesthetic." The selection of this monument, which so thoroughly offends the sensibilities of a substantial number of the African Jamaican population, by a small panel of experts out of touch with popular opinion is a validation of the right to rule of the "out of many, one" elite. Indeed, this contemptuous image of "emancipation" may be read as a re-enactment of the politics of the Abolitionist Act which paid compensation to slave masters for the loss of services to which they were presumed to be entitled. (Cooper and Donnell 2004: 7–8)

Here, Cooper invokes an elite-controlled public sphere and how it continually recalibrates the axes of social differentiation to its own advantage. Annie Paul, a cultural critic and Caribbean art historian, elaborates on the aesthetic implications of these recalibrations: "This public space is configured as a supposedly neutral, colourless, raceless, secular sphere which while claiming to erase all difference actually privileges a Euro-American worldview in which despite the racial background of the majority of Jamaicans it is most unnatural to talk of an African or black aesthetic and most natural to look to European and American heritage for fitting antecedents" (Paul 2004: 130).

These critics were responding to what they saw as a lack of respect given by cultural elites to the cosmologies of poorer, black Jamaicans and, in particular, to their ideologies regarding publicly displayed nudity in a commemorative statue that, in their view, was supposed to have emphasized the role of black Jamaicans in the abolition of slavery. Further, at issue here was a clash of class-related understandings not just of aesthetics (Bourdieu 1984), but also of historical causality. Complaints about the seeming "passivity" of the figures reflected an underlying concern with agency. The prayer-like posture seemed to many to invoke the idea that British policymakers, influenced by the moral arguments of abolitionists, bestowed emancipation on passive Jamaicans. It did not, in other words, symbolically represent slaves' taking their own freedom by burning fields or running away. As prayerful supplicants, the statue's figures instead portrayed the newly liberated slaves as innocent children entering a new life as freed people with unencumbered hearts and bodies, a portrayal that also invoked the class paternalism commentators decried. Moreover, underlying people's discomfort with the figures' nudity was their own critique of primitivism: not only were they certain that, as rebels torching sugar estates or runaways forming maroon communities, slaves were unlikely to have been naked, but they were also convinced that had the figures been representing middle-class "brown" Jamaicans, they would have been clothed.

Thus far, I have been positioning the various responses to "Redemption Song" in relation to a color–class binary, with working-class black Jamaicans as the purveyors of an authentic nationalist vision (as well as the victims of a racial slight) and middle-class commentators as appearing "uncritical about their class origins, blasé about nudity in public monuments, strongly influenced by a Eurocentric cultural aesthetic, disrespectful of non-elite opinions, and deeply invested in the status quo" (Smith 2006: 38). Faith Smith has rightly pointed out that this sort of positioning is reductive and misses important nuances within some of the letters to the editor that came out both in defense of and in opposition to the statue. Indeed, one might, as she suggests, usefully read an appreciation of the figures' nudity as beautiful, not as a capitulation to Eurocentric conceptions about taste, but as evidence of the appreciation of a symbolic (non-sexual) oneness with God the Creator. Moreover, we could (and should) parse what it means that middle-class intellectuals who have tended to support the often in-your-face sexuality of dancehall—what many in both the middle class and the respectable lower classes refer to as "slackness"—as a form of cultural resistance, understood these representations instead as vulgar.[6]

In other words, ideas about status, foreign-mindedness, respectability, and aesthetics do not, of course, map quite so neatly into class "camps," and we should not speak of middle classness as if it is unified, static, and merely conservative or of working classness as if it is uniquely committed to rejecting colonial strictures. Working-class communities also police the boundaries of respectability, and both lower-class and respectable middle-class Jamaicans have a long history of denouncing elites for their decadence and immorality. That history has been documented as far back as nineteenth-century planters' diaries and travel narratives (I am thinking especially of Lady Nugent's excoriation of the Jamaican planter class as decadent) and as recently as the various responses to the inauguration of Carnival in Jamaica in the early 1990s (Edmondson 1999b). What this should reveal, again, is that questions about representation, about belonging, and about the future are expressed through questions about gender, sexuality, and appropriate forms of intimacy—and these questions cut across class and status differences.

Nevertheless, those middle-class Jamaicans who have truly thrown their lot in with working-class folk, for political or personal reasons, largely have been seen as class traitors, and as Annie Paul (2004) has argued, there is still a tendency for those who see themselves as elite arbiters of cultural taste within the Jamaican public sphere to see lower-class and working-class aesthetic sensibilities and production as uneducated and unenlightened, in need of molding and refining. There is also a clear difference, it seems to me, between certain middle-class critics' defense of dancehall and those same critics' very vocal disappointment with other Jamaicans who dismissed popular objections to the statue's vulgarity out of hand. This difference is rooted, I believe, in the contexts of production and consumption of the arts in question. In other words, dancehall—like other popular arts in Jamaica—is a collective and performative cultural practice that is routinely revised and refined by participants within the cultural milieu in which it arose. "Redemption Song," on the other hand, as a piece of public statuary commissioned by the government and designed by one (middle-class) artist to represent "the masses," is far from being self-representative and dialogic.

It is worth noting here that the bulk of the discussions about nudity focused on the male figure. This is so partly because the black female body is always a public body, always visible, always metaphorically naked. Indeed, as the literary theorist Daphne Brooks (2006: 7) has argued, "The iconography of the black female body remains the central ur-text of alienation in transatlantic culture."[7] And as the feminist legal scholar Martha Fineman (1995: 189) has argued, discourses conjoining poverty and single motherhood conspire to constitute these mothers as culturally deviant and, therefore, perpetually public and unprotected by privacy laws: "Poor single mothers not only fail to conform to the nuclear-family model but also do not live up to the norms of 'independence' and economic 'self-reliance' that underlie our normative images of American families. Occupying either the category of poverty or that of single motherhood places women (along with their children) into the realm of 'public' families." Typically, within the context of policy intervention, black women are "public" while the black men who are also integral to sex and reproduction are hardly mentioned or sanctioned, and this silence, in effect, covers up the male body. But with "Redemption Song," the male body was in full view, laid bare to speculation and controversy, and its presence in the public sphere raised a storm. Thus, the statue, which both emerged from and generated "crisis" discourse that had to do with notions of cultural citizenship, publicly exposed the double standard regarding gendered bodies by making the black male body the center of debate. Yet the crisis discourse that centers the black female body when the objective is control and nation building is undergirded by the same logic as the crisis discourse that centers the black male body when the objective is representation. By this, I mean that, in a way, the uncovered male body in "Redemption Song," fashioned by a whitish middle-class woman and appearing passive and therefore insufficiently masculine, is apprehended as a reflection of more general contemporary concerns about the so-called marginalized black man, a man who—because he is surrounded and primarily influenced by women in the household, in the school setting, and in the workplace—cannot help but fail in today's world.[8] In both cases—cases that provide a kind of negative image for each other—the real questions have to do with how citizenship is imagined and how that imagination is gendered.

In addition, the debates about the statue revealed something about what is important to Jamaicans transnationally. Because the Caribbean was initially developed in relation to global circulations that began to emerge in the late fifteenth century, and because migration has long been undertaken as a strategy for individual, familial, and national development, Jamaican-ness far exceeds the *place* of Jamaica, and alternative visions of citizenship have challenged nationalist commonplaces regarding territorial rootedness and local authority. Indeed, Charles Carnegie (2002: 80) has argued that "particular historical and structural conditions have produced cultural pre-dispositions toward imagining community in global terms and enabled a matching cultural circuitry for building translocal images." Concerns about the figures' nudity and purported passivity resonated in a global sphere partly because of the daily humiliations faced by many Jamaicans in dias-pora as a result of racial discrimination and xenophobia. Thus, Jamaicans in diaspora were moved to contribute to debates that solidified the place of Jamaica, even as that place exceeds its boundaries.

This is not new. Since the late nineteenth century, migratory Jamaicans have been central to the consolidation of diasporic nationalisms. Initially, Jamaican men traveled beyond the country's shores to build the Panama Canal, to construct railroads or work in the emerging banana industry in Costa Rica, to develop Cuba's sugar industry after the First World War, and, after 1943, to perform various kinds of agricultural labor in the United States. As a result of these intra-regional and international circulations, at any given moment during the end of the nineteenth century and begin-ning of the twentieth century, an average of one-quarter of the working-age male population was "in foreign." While migrated men often faced racial and class subordination abroad, the experience of migration and participat-ing in a regional labor force also gave them access to a wider range of ideas and experiences than those locally rooted in Jamaica.[9] Panama, Costa Rica, and Cuba were fields that bred many new leaders within Jamaican popu-lar movements, such as Marcus Garvey, Alexander Bedward, and the three founders of the Rastafari movement. It was not only popular leaders, how-ever, who were politicized by their migratory experiences, but also middle-class Jamaicans, especially those who landed in the Jim Crow United States (James 1998; Watkins-Owens 1996). For many of these Jamaicans, it was their first experience of an arbitrary racial discrimination that was un-mitigated by their educational and social status (as it would have been at home). Italy's invasion of Ethiopia in 1935 also catalyzed an increased sense of ethnic, racial, and pan-Caribbean identification among West Indians in the United States. In fact, the first Jamaican nationalist organization was founded in 1936 not in Jamaica but in New York City, the main port of entry for the first wave of West Indian migrants who were not agricultural laborers.

While women did not figure as migrants as extensively as men until the late twentieth century, their working lives were also changing during this period as the fragmentation of rural holdings during the last two decades of the nineteenth century led many women to leave agricultural work (where they predominated until the 1880s) to seek other employment avenues. Meanwhile, the development of the banana industry in the late nineteenth century catalyzed the growth of a middle class, which itself created a demand for new services, including domestic work. When domestic service work was at its peak in 1943, many rural women migrated to urban areas to seek jobs within that industry. As maids in middle-class households, these newly urban women were confronted with considerably diminished autonomy and were subjected more directly to class and racial discrimination (Austin-Broos 1997). This restructuring disadvantageously incorporated lower-class black women more squarely within colonial hierarchies of color, class, gender, and culture in terms that devalued their customary political, economic, and sociocultural roles.

While the emergent nationalist movement in Jamaica attempted to forge a local sense of Jamaicanness that, despite struggling against these hierarchies, nevertheless reproduced aspects of colonial racial and gender ideologies (partly through its emphasis on the domestication of women's work and its consolidation of middle-class authority and leadership), many working-class and middle-class Jamaicans were increasingly developing a diasporic consciousness that not only provided the potential for organized *political* movements from multiple loyalties and locations, but also generated a notion of Jamaican culture and economy that spanned territorial borders. These two different visions of community would struggle for supremacy throughout the second half of the twentieth century, and this struggle also shaped public discourse around the controversy I outline here.

Ironically, while several commentators ended up noting with great disappointment that a statue meant to unite the population had actually divided it, in a way the statue *did* unite Jamaicans—but not in the way many anticipated. Instead, Jamaicans were united in a common conversation about the sorts of images that should appropriately reflect Jamaicanness. The controversy provided a venue through which people re-created the space of the nation and insisted on the legitimacy of the nation-state in the face of a global situation they felt increasingly powerless to transform. That this was a unity that was not harmonious is clear. The divisions of color, class, religion, and education (among others) that haunt Jamaican society—not only "on the rock" and in the diaspora, but also between those "on the rock" and those in diaspora—always lurk not too far beneath the surface. As a result, they are ready to erupt publicly in response to provocations big and small during periods when significant transformations in labor practices force a renegotiation of the relationships between nationalist consolidation and global political and economic trends. The public debates that raged about nudity, racial agency, gender relations, and sex that were embodied by the "Redemption Song" monument reconstituted and concretized Jamaican specificity even as they seemed to reflect its dissolution, addressing the most pressing issues Jamaicans face today. They were about the place of racial respect in relation to nationhood.

RESPECTABILITY MEETS RESPECT

I use the term "racial respect" as a kind of counterpart to respectability, intentionally invoking the anthropological work on cultural duality that emerged in the 1970s, just as the hopefulness generated by the political independence of many Caribbean territories began to wane. Cultural duality has been one of the dominant tropes through which researchers have identified central tensions within Afro-Caribbean societies. Because Peter Wilson's ethnography of Providencia (Wilson 1973) positioned values at the heart of the analytic model, and cultural duality as the definitive core of the social system, his account in many ways is both the most seminal early ethnography of West Indian cultural duality and the most contested. His argument was that Caribbean societies should be approached and analyzed according to two opposed themes, beliefs, or value systems: reputation and respectability. He contended that these two systems lived in the structure of these societies and within the minds of individuals and that they provided the basis on which social roles were evaluated.

Respectability, as Wilson defined it and as I have been using it, is rooted in the system of stratification imposed by the old colonial social order. It was reproduced through the teachings of the colonial church and was associated with "whiteness," British culture, and formal authority. Reputation, on the other hand, was defined as the response to colonially induced dependence. It was egalitarian, "black," and based on individual achievement measured by and against the performance of one's peers. As such, reputation was seen as a leveling device within systems where socioeconomic mobility for more than the very few was, in fact, unattainable. However, Wilson argued, because reputation was a solution to the scarcity of respectability, its realization sometimes involved acts that, in the view of the respectable, were antisocial or characteristic of illiterate poor people. He maintained that the conflict between respectability and reputation was a dialectical struggle that took place between whole groups and in the minds of single individuals and that it was resolved differently at different moments in the lifecycle. Moreover, he argued that lower-class recognition of middle-class respectable values was as much a part of the tension between the two systems as was their far more frequent rejection of those values in practice (Sutton 1974).

Wilson (1973: 148) also claimed that women were more concerned with respectability and men with reputation, and that, therefore, men and women participated in different, though overlapping, value systems. In fact, he alleged that because women enjoyed preferred status during slavery, they were more committed to an "alien value system." The evidence he provided for these claims revolved around the different ways men and women socialized publicly. In his ethnography, women's social lives centered on the church and kinship networks, while men's were based in friendship crews. Finally, Wilson argued that the system of reputation, because it championed equality and therefore embodied the "true" nature of Caribbean societies, could (and should) become the dominant system through, for example, women's eschewal of colonial values and educational-curriculum reform.

Critiques of Wilson's formulation have been copious. Several scholars have argued that, by misreading the sexual division of labor that arose on the plantations and focusing only on men's response to colonial domination and locating the production of countercultural values in men's activities, Wilson was unable to see that women also engaged in activities and held values that were independent of, and often opposed to, those represented by the dominant colonial system (Besson 1993; Sutton 1974).[10] Moreover, because Wilson's study did not address how relationships between ideology and social structure changed over time, it missed the role of power and economic dependence in shaping the overall social system and therefore developed a limited (and reactionary) perspective on the role of the church, education, and marriage in people's lives (Sutton 1974). As a result, Wilson wrote about the two value systems as if they were freely selected by social actors instead of examining how the two systems were integrated into a single cultural order, as well as how power relations between men and women were tied to structures of both meaning and hierarchy (Douglass 1992; Yelvington 1995).

Notwithstanding Wilson's significant misreading of both the history of West Indian gender relations and how the material and ideological dimensions of peoples' lives are constituted by — and constitutive of — these relations, his attempt to demonstrate how duality operated at both the individual level and the societal level remains a key to understanding the political implications of black lower-class cultural practices and aesthetics. A more rigorous examination of how gender, race, and class articulate to form a single social field in Jamaica, however, would require that we situate his concern with nation building within a global frame of reference, both historically and in the present. As I demonstrated in chapter 2, within the context of mid-twentieth-century nationalism, privatizing women and cultivating respectability within the domestic sphere was part of a more general concern with state formation and development. During the post–Second World War period, when the nation was extolled as the most modern form of social organization, this concern with state formation was, by extension, a push toward cultivating respect within an international public sphere.

Jamaican nationalisms at the beginning of the twenty-first century, however, are no longer primarily rooted in this kind of vindicationist respectability, partly because the influence of the sector of the professional middle classes who gained state power at independence as cultural and political brokers in the lives of poorer Jamaicans began to decline after the 1960s. By the mid-1990s, the intensification of transnational migration and the increased political, economic, and social influence of the United States had created a situation in which many black Jamaicans were able to bypass middle-class leadership, reaching their goals instead by capitalizing on newly developed niche industries and on their own networks of family and friends in Jamaica and beyond. These shifts have bolstered the autonomy of working-class Jamaicans, giving them relatively greater ability to eschew conventional middle-class modes of respectability and to define progress and citizenship through their own cultural idioms and innovations (Robotham 2000; D. Thomas 2004). Of course, these idioms center on popular music and the other aspects of popular cultural production that emerge from it. At the same time, the contemporary geopolitical context has resulted in a situation in which discrepancies in income and wealth have increased, unemployment has risen, and education has become an increasingly gender-stratified pursuit, and in which it is not only progressively more difficult to achieve local goals without "foreign" intervention (whether at the level of government or family), but also that survival is often impossible without the "remittance culture" that has come to characterize Caribbean societies more generally (Page 2006). These are the contradictory realities that also must be seen as informing both the reception and the production of cultural expressions.

In chapter 3, I argued that, because the development of national cultural policy is geared to defining and promoting that which is seen as indigenously Jamaican, boundaries are erected to bracket out that which is perceived to be foreign. I mentioned that youth were seen as being particularly susceptible to foreign media and therefore were not typically positioned as discerning cultural producers in their own right. Here I revisit this argument through an analysis of forms of cultural production that have been created by and for Jamaican youth. Victor Headley's *Yardie* trilogy and Macka Diamond's *Bun' Him!!!* — as well as the films *Belly* and *Shottas* — open windows onto imagined transnational communities of Jamaicanness, communities that are defined by the contours of violence and sexuality. I mine these popular novels, and more briefly the films, to think through the limits of citizenship, which are being envisioned and reproduced for a "mass" audience not only within Jamaica but also throughout its diasporas.

SEX, LIES, AND TRANSNATIONAL TRAFFICKING

That Jamaican cultural production has hit mainstream America is demonstrated by the fact that even the *New York Times* has jumped on the dancehall bandwagon. A fashion spread written by Steve Garbarino in the newspaper's *Sunday Magazine* of 30 May 2004 presented dancehall and reggae artists wearing Gucci and Versace at Coronation Market and other locations in Kingston's tough downtown neighborhoods. The emphasis throughout the piece was on "keeping it street," on the chaos, authenticity, and rootsy sexuality embodied through a politics of cool that was generated, ironically, by wearing high-price designers' clothes in low-income areas. The "realness" of the street, here, was rooted in violence — or, rather, in the ever existing possibility of violence at street dances in West Kingston. Indeed, violence is central to many popular representations of Jamaica within contemporary film and fiction, not only in those stereotypical representations produced by so-called outsiders. Indeed, locally grown filmmakers and writers have been behind the proliferation of a transnational black gangster genre whose screen life begins with *The Harder They Come* and moves through such offerings as *Rockers, Children of Babylon, Dancehall Queen, Third World Cop, Belly,* and *Shottas* (about which I say more later), as well as those that have been released straight to DVD, such as *Rude Boy* and *Rollin' with the Nines.*[11] It is the centrality of violence within these films that many Jamaicans decry, especially those migrant Jamaicans who daily combat stereotypical assessments of their communities that are based on the participation of a non-representative few in the real-world circuits of the drugs and weapons trade.

Yet these are the circuits that animate the *Yardie* trilogy, a series of popular gangster novels written by Victor Headley, a Jamaican who migrated to England at age twelve. The trilogy, set in the late 1980s and early 1990s, narrates the saga of "D.," a Kingston gang member who was sent to London to solidify the U.K. branch of the gang's distribution chain but who instead eludes his contacts and sets up his own empire, quickly becoming the top man in London. The three novels — *Yardie, Excess,* and *Yush!* — chronicle the ups and downs of D.'s life as a don, as well as the ins and outs of the various interlocked sectors of black London. In *Yardie,* we meet D. as he arrives at Heathrow Airport. He realizes quickly that "he was in no hurry to get back to Jamaica and the hardship of day-to-day living in the ghetto" (Headley 1993: 6) and that, "for anyone coming from a poor background in Kingston's tenements, England, no matter how tight things were getting, was still a more comfortable environment to live in" (Headley 1993: 27). This is why he decides to do whatever it takes to stay in London rather than completing his mission and returning to Kingston. He visits Donna, his first love who migrated some years before, and through her brother Leroy (who runs a record store) makes the necessary contacts to establish himself in the "business." Soon he is driving a fancy car and wearing fancy clothes and enjoying the privileges of donmanship: money, women, and respect. All the while, however, D. is developing a crack habit that makes him unpredictable and hotheaded, traits that can prove deadly on the street. Moreover, aspects of his past haunt him, particularly the death of his older brother Jerry, who as a youth in Kingston was on his way to becoming a top don himself but did an about-face, becoming a respected Rastafarian who was murdered after attempting to prevent the infiltration of the drug trade into his community. In *Yardie*, D. finally finds out who was behind the murder — as it happens, a member of a rival drug gang in London named Blue — and exacts his revenge.

Although D. is not convicted for killing Blue — at the last minute, the prosecution's star witness "decides" not to testify against him (the witness is Blue's girlfriend, whom D. has raped) — he is deported and jailed in Jamaica. Thus, in the beginning of the trilogy's second installment, *Excess*, D. is in Jamaica, where, having been sprung from the much harsher conditions of jail there by his former don in Kingston, he is getting much needed rest and relaxation among family members deep in the country. Now cured of his crack habit by one of the community elders, a roots man, D. returns to London, where his crew has had to reorganize to avoid the increased police scrutiny brought about by his arrest. According to Charlie and Sticks, his partner and right-hand man, the scene has changed while D. was gone — the crew has had to work hard to sustain a peace treaty with its main rivals and to contain the turf wars that have developed as several locally led gangs have emerged. This news is sobering for D., and he spends much of the novel contemplating his decisions in life, thinking through what it would mean to be a real "family man" to either of his children's mothers in London (he already has three children in Jamaica), strategizing about how he might get out of the drug trade and become a legitimate businessman, and even imagining returning to Jamaica and opening a business. *Excess* thus reveals much more about the general rhythms of life in black London and provides far more context regarding the racism and police brutality that are a part of daily life for West Indian migrants. In fact, the second novel begins at a funeral for a sixteen-year-old boy who died while in police custody, a boy who had been mistakenly identified as a purse snatcher for whom the cops were looking. Thus, throughout *Excess*, we follow the storylines of this boy's younger brother Harry, who eventually leaves school and becomes a dancehall DJ, and his uncle Chris, who teaches black history and counsels youth at a local community center. We also come to know something about interethnic relations, since Harry and two of his friends become involved in an incident with a South Asian shopkeeper who refuses to sell them alcohol because they are underage. Harry's friend Donovan shoots the shopkeeper, and the three boys go on the run. These stories provide a backdrop for D.'s entry into the music-promotion business and Charlie's foray into artist management, but the main drama is still propelled by the rivalries between the drug gangs. Because one of the local crews, headed by a Black Brit named Simon, has encroached on D.'s turf, Sticks (D.'s right-hand man) takes it upon himself to pay Simon a warning visit. As a result, Simon organizes a hit on Sticks, who is killed coming out of a dance with D. at the end of the book.

In *Yush!*, Simon's crew goes after Linton, another of D.'s close associates; thus, the third novel in the trilogy centers on the process of avenging deaths and reconsolidating turf, a process made more difficult by the arrival, in the first pages of the book, of Lancey, a hard-line cop from Jamaica who has been brought to England by Scotland Yard to help neutralize the Jamaican drug gangs. D. has a history with Lancey, who, it turns out, arrives in the United Kingdom with his own agenda: before he became a cop, Lancey had worked with Skeets, D.'s don in Kingston, whom he continued to protect while working for the Jamaican police. His involvement with the trade grew, and when Blue was arrested for the murder of D.'s brother, Lancey arranged for his release, destroyed the records of the arrest, and sent him out of Jamaica, all because Blue was moving drugs for him. In England, Lancey is therefore intent on extorting a cut of the profits from the various crews while appearing to shut them down. Simon agrees to cooperate, but D. refuses, at which point Lancey organizes a raid on the house of the mother of one of D.'s children, Jenny (whom he marries at the beginning of *Yush!*, even as he continues his relationship with Donna, who spends most of the third novel in Jamaica arranging the purchase of land and the construction of a home for their eventual return). D. must mastermind a plan that simultaneously deals with Lancey *and* Simon, thus handling both his personal and his professional business. He carries out his plan the day before Donna and their baby daughter are due back from Jamaica, and while he successfully kills both Simon and Lancey, D. is shot and is rushed to the hospital. *Yush!* ends, as *Yardie* began, at Heathrow. Charlie is there to meet Donna's flight, but we, like her, come to the end of the trilogy without knowing whether D. has survived. Equal parts fantasy, action thriller, and morality tale, the three books provide windows onto — and are themselves part of — debates regarding the transnational circuits of crime and violence.

The *Yardie* trilogy was originally published by X Press, which Headley founded in 1992 with two former journalists to provide a venue to support and distribute black pop literature and to make available "the type of literature that the black person in the street (people outside of academia) would want to read — literature that addressed black issues, was contemporary in its appeal, and accessible to and in touch with the lives of black people at the grassroots in Britain" (Forbes 2006: para. 10). By the mid-1990s, X Press novels had become so popular that mainstream presses such as Pan Macmillan picked up several of the X Press books for second printings, and other presses sought to take advantage of the identification of new reading publics by entering the market for black popular literature.[12] *Yardie* thus inspired a proliferation of novels about Jamaican drug and crime organizations, and this proliferation was paralleled in nonfiction throughout the 1990s with the publication of memoirs and journalistic accounts of the transnational circuits of Jamaican drug posses such as Pauline Edwards's *Trench Town, Concrete Jungle* (2001), Father Richard Ho Lung's *Diary of a Ghetto Priest* (1998), Laurie Gunst's *Born fi' Dead* (1995), Geoff Small's *Ruthless* (1994), and, more recently *Shower Posse* (2003), written by Duane Blake, son of the legendary Vivian Blake, leader of the Shower Posse gang throughout the 1980s.[13] In general, these books seek to provide some context for the development of drug posses, to give greater depth to the problem than is usually offered by sensationalist media reports on violence within black communities in Britain and the United States.[14] They tend, therefore, to highlight the poverty, underdevelopment, and political corruption that characterize particular communities in Kingston, linking these to circuits of poverty, underdevelopment, and political corruption that are global in scope. In other words, they position gun violence and crime among Jamaicans and others within more general patterns of supply and demand in a global underground economy.

This broader context, however, was not immediately evident in *Yardie*, the trilogy's first installment, and thus Headley (as both author and co-founder of the press) was criticized for reproducing stereotypes and glorifying the violence of the gangster lifestyle. Headley himself refers to this criticism obliquely in the prefaces to the second and third books. In *Excess*, he reveals that, after *Yardie* was published, "The press had gone over the top and got me into an awkward position, between a rock and a hard place, as they say" (Headley 1994: vii), and that as a result he began to decline requests for interviews. He argues that the real morality tale of *Yardie* was that "because of deprivation, lack of opportunity and general sense of frustration, a great proportion of Black youth is resorting to 'any means necessary' to stay alive, to be able to afford the material trappings they see all around" (Headley 1994: viii). We should hear echoes of Bounty Killer here. And in *Yush!*, Headley writes (somewhat less obliquely):

> At first, I got really phased [*sic*] by the way the media jumped up and labeled me without a hearing. I guess the system has us trapped in some kind of stereotype mentality, but then when some black people attacked me for "glorifying drugs and violence," it got me thinking. . . .
>
> On the other end, the youths on the streets really made me feel good, like I was doing something positive by writing my stories. As that is what they are; stories that express the black experience in the West in the 90s. And they do not glorify anything, I call them "intelligent gangsta stories." (Headley 1995)

Criticism from the community is also likely to have shaped the way Headley crafted the second two installments of the trilogy, even if only unconsciously. I have already mentioned his emphasis on context in *Excess*, and this is an emphasis that continues in *Yush!*. For example, in one scene we come upon the characters watching a television documentary about violence and the drug connection in Jamaica, a documentary that, the narrator tells us, "kicked up a storm in the black community" (Headley 1995: 35). The characters decry the bias evident in the film, one of many that "seemed to be part of an overall strategy to label black people and perhaps try to justify some immigration practices" (Headley 1995: 35), and they worry about the effect of these sorts of media offerings both on the Jamaican community in London and vis-à-vis the tourist economy back home. Moreover, we are told again and again in both *Excess* and *Yush!* that the only way for poor black youth in England to make something of themselves is to amass capital through the drug trade and then eventually invest it solely in legitimate businesses. Charlie explains this to a young DJ as follows: "You don't want to spend your whole life dodging bullets on the street, right? . . . If you start out poor, and the system only leaves drugs for you to make money, the difficult step out of that is to get legit, earn a living up front'" (Headley 1994: 263). This is not only D.'s dream but also Simon's, who is portrayed several times throughout *Yush!* as struggling to keep the business together only until he has finished constructing his gym, a project he anticipates will free him from the drug trade within six months.

Literary critics, for their part, have tended to vindicate the *Yardie* novels, using them, on one hand, as fodder for their own critiques of how literary canons consistently ignore "pop lit," thereby reproducing the sorts of racism and classism that devalue popular cultural production (Farred 2001; Forbes 2006). On the other hand, they have demonstrated that the representations of black immigrant life in the *Yardie* trilogy reveal "the ideological and fiscal bankruptcy of the third World nation-state" (Farred 2001: 291), as well as "the final demise of traditional British society," a society that continues to "'bar the door' to its black citizenry" (Collins 2001: 77, 95). In other words, the *Yardie* novels not only make patently clear that the days of acculturation and colonial respectability are over but also signal a new understanding of national space. This is a space Grant Farred (2001: 294) characterizes as a "Malthusian postcolonial black Atlantic, where the cargo is distinctly different but the cost in human life is not so dissimilar from that of the middle passage." This is an extreme characterization, perhaps, but it nevertheless succeeds in linking an earlier moment of global capitalism, one that depended on the slave trade to generate wealth, to the current one in which the drugs and arms trades are the highest grossing "industries" in the world (Nordstrom 2004).

In this space, as Curdella Forbes (2006: para. 31) has argued, "Home has nothing to do with physical geographies," and D.'s survival depends on his ability to mobilize the transnational networks that link Kingston to London, New York, Miami, and Toronto in a never-ending series of migrations and deportations, shipments and investments. These networks crystallize what Johanna Roering (2007: 223) has termed an "alternative city," in which migrants are neither integrated nor acculturated but that acts as a way station of sorts within a more general tendency toward nomadism. D. himself recognizes London as a node within a broader constellation of similar spaces. We see this in *Yush!*, where Headley has him reflecting back to his first days in London. "Though he didn't really know the English scene in the beginning," he writes, "when he checked it out it was the same all over anyhow. The hustlings, the danger, the enemies, the very same scene everywhere" (Headley 1995: 85). Farred analyzes this sensibility in terms of D.'s experience of the postmodern: "[D.] is deliberately rootless, in touch with a transnational world through the cell phone, making deals; he and Charlie invest in property for economic, never psychic, reasons. . . . Headley's men have links to many parts of the globe; *their business ensures them a temporary residency, never citizenship, a relationship to the nation they rejected even before they left the Caribbean*" (Farred 2001: 301; emphasis added). In a way, this sort of nomadism—a nomadism that entails a *general* rejection of the category "citizenship"—complicates the notion of diasporic longing because it cuts across the home–abroad dichotomy. That is, if Kingston is no different from London is no different from Toronto, then living through the networks of these "global cities" (Sassen 1991) requires men like D. to locate "home" in some other kind of space. Music—in particular, dancehall music, itself an integral part of transnational circuits of production and consumption—can serve as such a space, as it not only provides news and information about what is going on in Jamaica, but it also offers a temporary solid ground for Jamaicans living abroad. Indeed, Farred suggests that D. and his crew live their lives through popular culture, the only medium of exchange they truly trust—in the only arena where they sometimes even feel, if only momentarily, at "home" (Farred 2001: 301).

It is not incidental, then, that it is through music that D. initially begins his foray into legitimate business, or that legitimacy is linked to marriage and life as a "family man." Charlie makes the latter point most explicitly at D.'s wedding when he admonishes him, "'Now that you're gonna get legal, you'll have to keep clean'" (Headley 1995: 3). Yet it is also true that after D. returns to London in *Excess*, he takes time before getting back into the swing of things on the street, content to let his associates handle his business while he allows himself to enjoy domestic life, first with Donna and then with Jenny. For D., this is an ongoing struggle, however, as the settling of old wrongs on the street exerts a constant pull and because he has a deep and abiding sense that women—despite their integral involvement in the various revenge plots that are orchestrated throughout the three books— are ultimately not worth losing your head over. In the end, we cannot be certain about whether he will be the one gangster who lives to prove that it is, in fact, possible to make a successful transition from the informal to the formal economy, from ladies' man to family man.

This issue is also raised in *Bun' Him!!!*, the debut novel by the dancehall

DJ Macka Diamond that has been billed as "Jamaica's FIRST official dance-hall novel," a billing made all the more official by the parental advisory logo on the cover warning about explicit content, a logo one might usually see on a compact disc. "Bun' Him," in fact, was a hit recording for Macka Diamond (with DJ Black-er). It was originally released as a single in 2005 and was included on VP Records' *Wild 2 Nite* rhythm compilation compact disc in 2006. While the book was originally distributed by Sangster's Book Stores and its subsidiaries, VP Records also decided in 2008 to place the anniversary edition prominently throughout its network of record shops, thereby ensuring its availability for a downtown dancehall audience. In *Bun' Him!!!*, unlike the *Yardie* trilogy, the gangster plot is not the main narrative thread, but it does provide the underlying context that moves the action forward.

The novel introduces us to Sandra, a woman from a Kingston ghetto who has managed to snag a wealthy husband, Larry. Larry is a good provider (labels and brand names dot the landscape of *Bun' Him!!!* like sand on the beach) but cannot satisfy Sandra in bed. She keeps this bit of dissatisfaction to herself while faking orgasms with Larry and maintaining the illusion of happy matrimony in front of her friends—even her best friend, Tiffany, with whom she grew up—because she figures it is a sacrifice she can make for the security Larry provides. Tiffany, who has no idea that Sandra is only pretending that all is well in her life, resents Sandra's smugness and is envious, constantly weighing what she has against Sandra. As a case in point, Tiffany's relationship with Ricky, a taxi driver, seems to pale in comparison with Sandra's marriage, because Ricky cannot provide Tiffany with the material things she needs to feel secure.

One night, after she is again unfulfilled by a late night romp with her inebriated husband, Sandra decides to go with Tiffany and her older sister Mitsie to a dancehall session being held as a memorial for the legendary dancer Gerald "Bogle" Levy. She returns home after 7 A.M. to find an irate Larry, who attempts to strangle her and then wrestles her to the floor, all the while yelling at her and punching her in the face. When it seems she is trapped, Sandra grabs Larry's gun from under the bed and points it at him, at which point Larry backtracks and begs Sandra for mercy. After what seems like an eternity, Sandra orders Larry out of the house. The following day, the enormity of the evening's events sinks in for both Sandra and Larry; Sandra worries that Larry will not come back and wonders what she will do if he does not, and Larry worries that Sandra will not take him back and hopes for reconciliation. They do, of course, reconcile, but Sandra is still committed to keeping her marital difficulties from Tiffany, pretending that her disappearance for days was due to some innocent romantic time in the country with Larry and not to her attempts to hide her bruises and his attempts to woo her back. This only makes Tiffany more envious of Sandra and more impatient with her own relationship, an impatience she makes patently clear to Ricky, who subsequently beats her publicly with no intervention from bystanders, who know that "only a fool would get involved inna man an woman affair," and then rapes her at knifepoint. Ricky's assault is so severe that even Tiffany's mother wants her to call the police, but Tiffany declines to do so, musing that Ricky "had enough friends in the area that wouldn't take too kindly to such a move" (Diamond 2007: 83). Like Sandra, Tiffany keeps the incident to herself, but her tension is evident.

Meanwhile, Sandra, whose night at the dance has her longing to go out again, despite the repercussions, begins to scheme to go to Asylum, a popular nightclub in Kingston. She cons Larry into thinking that the school event she must attend will last longer than it will, skips out as soon as she can, and meets Mitsie at the club. Larry is willing to be conned, however, because he has plans of his own. He calls Tiffany (she had given him her number some time earlier) and asks her for some "private" time. Feeling this is her chance, even though Larry is her best friend's husband, Tiffany jumps into the affair, enjoying its material rewards, including a new car and clothes. Meanwhile, Sandra is enjoying temporary freedom at Asylum when she runs into Calvin, her first love, who had migrated to the United States and become involved in the drug business and who recently had been deported back to Jamaica. The sparks fly, and Calvin presses Sandra for her phone number, which she does not give and instead takes his. Sandra, of course, cannot stop thinking about Calvin and eventually gives in to the affair.

We should not, however, imagine this as a romantic return to a first love, because we soon find out that the couple's high school romance actually began as a dare, with Calvin and his friends meaning to "break [Sandra and Tiffany] in one at a time and then form the line" (Diamond 2007: 118) — in other words, to run a train on them. Yet Calvin fell for Sandra, so only Tiffany was the victim of their battery, something about which Sandra never knew. Here we are confronted with how thin the line is between love and assault, and it forces us to notice something about how insecurities are played out through the disciplining of sexuality. Although the novel positions Tiffany and Sandra as opposites in many regards, this positioning in fact only obscures the principal thing they share: a generalized experience of sexual violence. For me, this is not just about chauvinism and masculine bravado. It reflects an insecurity within the novel itself, an inability to tell the "good" woman from the "bad" in the absence of more traditional regulatory forms of discipline, a confusion about the expression of interpersonal intimacy within a neoliberal context in which masculinity and femininity have been brought into question (and under scrutiny). Again, what we are seeing is anxiety about the transnational refracted through sexual politics.

Throughout the rest of the novel, we follow Sandra and Tiffany as they manage their respective affairs, both becoming pregnant for their lovers. Sandra's pregnancy inspires Calvin to leave the drug business and go legit, but only after one more run. It also prods Larry into wanting to focus on satisfying Sandra rather than running around with Tiffany, so each character must decide his or her fate. Calvin, distracted by his desire to become a family man, tells Sandra about his planned drug run. His sexual rejection of one of his drug mules after she has provided him with oral sex, however, has her threatening to abort the mission. This prompts him to give her the beating of her life, one that is capped with (supposedly consensual) sex and that results in her acquiescence to the mission, much to Calvin's relief. Sandra, although she is in love with Calvin, decides that he cannot offer her the stability that Larry can. "Walking away from Larry would actually be easy," she muses. "It wasn't like she loved him. She didn't, the only thing she loved about him was his money" (Diamond 2007: 227). We see her continuing to weigh her options: "And that was what made the situation tricky. Money! . . . . . . Security! . . . . . . That was what it was all about, nothing more, nothing less. And if she did leave Larry for Calvin, what did the future hold? . . . . . . With him there was no guarantee, and with no guarantee, where would that leave her and her baby, especially if something was to happen to him?" (Diamond 2007: 227–28). Sandra decides to call Operation Kingfish and inform the authorities of Calvin's plan. The police swarm Calvin at the airport as he is waiting for the plane to take off for Miami, and he and his various associates are arrested and either killed or thrown in jail. Larry meanwhile decides to end his relationship with Tiffany. He takes her to dinner and tells her about Sandra's pregnancy. Tiffany, reeling from the news, does not even get a chance to tell him she is pregnant before she is shot several times by the enraged Ricky. She dies on the spot but not before she is able to plant doubts in Larry's mind about the paternity of Sandra's unborn child.

As the months go by, Sandra and Larry both mourn Tiffany's death; Ricky is hunted by the police; and Sandra begins to visit Calvin in prison (sometimes bringing their newborn daughter), but never tells him that she is the one who landed him there in the first place. One day on the way home from a visit, she is so distracted that her car is hit by a truck at an intersection, and both she and the baby are hospitalized in critical condition. Because their injuries are so severe, Larry is asked to donate blood, and this is how he finds out he is not the father of Sandra's child. He waits to confront Sandra about this until she is out of her coma and on her way home, then greets her at the door with her bags already packed, ordering her out of his life. Sandra, in tears, can think of no one to call except Maxine, a childhood friend turned Christian, and the book ends with Sandra arriving at her old friend's home. It is clear throughout the last chapter that Macka Diamond's sympathies do not lie with Sandra. Her narrative voice even tells us at one point that Sandra is a "Cold, Selfish, Self-Centered BITCH!!!" (Diamond 2007: 268), and on the last page of the novel, we are explicitly confronted with the moral of the story: "The grass is not always greener on the other side, sometimes the grass only looks greener because it's painted, so sometimes it's best to stick to the evil that you know, and never forget. . . . [U]nfair game play twice!" (Diamond 2007: 279).

As in the *Yardie* trilogy, dancehall music animates the pages of *Bun' Him!!!*, with snippets of lyrics from popular songs ending most of the chapters. Also as in *Yardie*, the social worlds of the characters in *Bun' Him!!!* are territorially bounded only insofar as "the law" occasionally catches up with one or another of them and—temporarily—puts them out of commission by locking them in jail or deporting or extraditing them. Even these moments only represent a blip within an easily reconstituted transnational Jamaica, in which the United States in particular is a taken-for-granted presence, whether because of the circuits of migration or the drug trade or the ubiquity of the "brand names" and media stars that are popular with Jamaican youth. Despite the best intentions of nationalists concerned with cultural patrimony, therefore, this transnational sphere is the hegemonic spatial frame of reference for youth, contextualizing their interest in "things foreign," their attempts to forge relationships, and their efforts to move forward in life. The transnational sphere is also the dominant spatial referent within the social worlds that populate *Shottas* and *Belly*. This is a sphere, moreover, that links dancehall and hip-hop cultures through the processes of both production and consumption, as well as through the transnational reach of popular music publications (as well as their extended institutional spaces) — publications such as *The Source, XXL, F.E.D.S.*, and, in Jamaica, the afternoon *Star*, as well as other, occasional newsweeklies — that provide the main source of critical mediation for these forms.

Shottas was shot and edited by the Jamaican-born director Cess Silvera in 2001. Although the film premiered at the Toronto Film Festival in 2002, it did not secure a distributor (Sony Pictures) until four years later, because a rough cut was taken from Silvera's studio in 2002, and millions of bootleg copies hit the streets throughout the United States and in Jamaica. Even though Sony did not release *Shottas* until November 2006, it won the best picture award at the *Source Magazine* show in 2002 because the bootleg copy had so thoroughly saturated the market.[15] For the authors of urban fiction like *Yardies*, the legitimacy of their representations rests in part on their own street credentials. Films like *Shottas* and *Belly* instead tend to root their authenticity in the use of dancehall and hip-hop artists in leading roles. Silvera, however, is also tantalizingly cagey about his own background in interviews, contributing to the aura of mystery and danger. While early reports claimed he was raised in Miami and then earned a bachelor of fine arts degree at New York University's film school, later press coverage refers to him as a "reformed bad-ass" who made *Shottas* because, in his words, "I was close to either prison or death, and didn't like none of those two options." Later in the same interview, Silvera explains that he and his brother wrote the script in two days and began shooting two weeks later, but adds, "You don't want to know how I financed it." And when talking about a sequel to *Shottas*, he warns, "I'm going to make sure I keep my gun on the table while I am editing it."[16] It is statements such as these that position *Shottas* as an authentic gangster film written and directed by an authentic gangster.

The film's story centers on Biggs and Wayne (played, respectively, by the musician Kymani Marley and the dancehall DJ Spragga Benz), childhood friends who grew up in the volatile Waterhouse area of Kingston during the 1970s. As children, they rob a truck driver at gunpoint to secure visas to go to Miami, where Biggs's mother already lives.[17] Fast-forward twenty years and we are back in Jamaica meeting a now grown-up Biggs who has been deported for his involvement in the drug trade in the United States. Wayne is at the airport to greet him, having been deported several years earlier. Wayne shows Biggs what he has been able to accomplish since his return to Jamaica—a mini-empire complete with a mansion in Jacks Hill, legions of people from whom he regularly extorts "taxes" in exchange for the protection he and his compatriots provide, and connections to influential politicians. Biggs is impressed but lets Wayne know that, in Miami prior to his arrest, he lived the best life there was to live, "and likkle Jamaica cyan do dat fi me."

After Wayne's little brother is killed by the police, and after his political connection orchestrates a bungled attempt on his life, the two friends obtain visas to return to the United States, along with their friend and partner in crime Mad Max (played by Paul Campbell), to reestablish themselves on the streets in Miami. There they live the high life, taking over the business from Biggs's former rival, Teddy Bruk Shot (played by DJ Louie Rankin). When Teddy attempts to arrange a side business directly with people in Jamaica, Wayne and Biggs find out and shut him down. In retaliation, Teddy sends a crew to kill Biggs and his team, and just as we hear Biggs talk about "kicking back" a little bit, taking a break from the business to travel with his girlfriend, Teddy's men storm into the house. A *Scarface*-style shootout ensues from which no one but Biggs and a presumably fatally injured Mad Max emerge. After mourning Wayne, dropping Max at the emergency room, and taking his own revenge on Teddy, Biggs stares out over the water on Biscayne Bay.

Belly, released in 1998 by Lionsgate / Fox Studios and directed by Hype Williams, who is best known for his string of popular hip-hop videos in the mid-1990s, also engages these transnational circuits. However, *Belly* draws our attention to how people within these transnational social worlds develop hierarchies of "badmanism" among the black folk that populate them. In other words, what *Belly* adds to the story I am telling here is an engagement of intra-diasporic complexity. The film itself chronicles a moment in the lives of the best friends Tommy and Sincere (played by the rappers DMX and Nas, respectively), who grew up together on the streets of Queens, New York, and who support themselves by robbing local businesses and dealing dope. Their story is ultimately a morality tale that indexes the power dynamics among blacknesses through space and language.

One night after robbing a strip joint, Tommy hears a news report on MTV about a new form of heroin that is so potent it has only to be applied externally to be effective. According to the newscaster, the new drug is on its way to the United States via "conduits in Jamaica and throughout the West Indies." Tommy decides this can be a lucrative new business for him and enlists the support of Sincere, who, despite his own growing desires to become legitimate, ultimately capitulates to Tommy's wishes. Tommy then drives to the estate of the Jamaican drug don Lennox (played by the dancehall DJ Louie Rankin) on Long Island to ask for financial backing and Jamaican suppliers. Because Lennox initially resists the partnership, Tommy asks him if he is too scared to try a new business. Lennox responds by turning his attention completely to Tommy for the first time during the visit, saying, "Don't you ever bring that scared business to me. You're looking at the toughest rass claat Jamaican in the United States of America. I run shit. I kill for nuttin." With that, Lennox promises to think about it, but not without indicating that Tommy will owe him a big favor for his consideration. Lennox's language here is an important, yet subtle, tool through which Williams indexes the realism of *Belly*'s underworld. Unlike many films in which African American actors portray Jamaican characters, Williams actually hired Jamaican artists for *Belly*. This is significant because in this film, as opposed to movies such as *How Stella Got Her Groove Back*, the accent and the proficiency with Jamaican patois are critical registers of the kind of "authentic" badman-ism Williams needs to portray in this narrative.

With Lennox fronting the money for the new business, Tommy organizes a crew to travel to Omaha to set up the distribution system. The money starts to roll in for the New Yorkers, at the expense of the local crew led by Rico, who sports giant spectacles and styles his pressed long hair in a flip. Resenting the competition, Rico places an anonymous call to the Federal Bureau of Investigation (FBI) to rat out Tommy's crew. The Feds descend on the headquarters of Tommy's business in Omaha, and the crew falls, landing the point man, Knowledge, in jail.

Meanwhile, Lennox calls in his favor from Tommy, and they travel together to Jamaica. As they are driven through the streets of Kingston with Tommy coughing from the strength of the Jamaican spliff they are smoking, Lennox shows Tommy the "pure sufferation" of Kingston's ghettos and takes him to a dancehall session at the Jamaica Gates club (where Sean Paul is giving a live performance). There he points out Kingston's top don, Sosa, who is so well protected that "no one can touch him," Lennox says, "not even me. It will have to be a man from out of the country." That man, of course, is Tommy, and he is happy to oblige. By the time Tommy returns to New York, the FBI has seized his home (and imprisoned his girlfriend Kisha), so he goes on the run.

With Tommy in Atlanta dealing dope and Sincere slowly getting out of the business and onto a new, more spiritual path, Knowledge sends Shameek (played by the rapper Method Man) to Omaha to retaliate against Rico, which he does handily. Back in Jamaica, the news comes in that Lennox was behind the hit on Sosa, and Sosa's crew—led by Chiquita, a dancehall queen-cum-assassin—mobilizes to avenge their leader's death. They travel to New York and ambush Lennox at home. In the gun battle that ensues, Lennox manages to kill all of Sosa's men with high-powered guns, but Chiquita surprises him by jumping him from behind and slitting his throat from ear to ear. Here is where we see most clearly how Williams maps a hierarchy of badness onto regionalized and nationalized modalities of blackness. At one end of the spectrum is the Omaha-based Rico, who is portrayed as "soft" because of his "country" hairdo and style of dress and because he rats out the big-city boys who are dipping into his business. Within the context of urban America, Tommy is the one who inspires fear, but he seems anxious in the Long Island home of "the original don dada" Lennox and awkwardly out of place on the streets of Kingston. But in the end, the baddest of them all is a Jamaican woman who kills Lennox not with the impersonal technology of guns but by getting close enough to slit his throat. Again, we see gender operating as a site of unpredictability within the transnational network of violence in which Jamaican blackness is the most powerfully violent of the three representations, but it is the one that also perishes in the end.[18]

This has the effect of redirecting *Belly's* narrative away from an exploration of the points of convergence and divergence among diasporic blacknesses and toward an exegesis of African American spiritual redemption, a move that takes our attention away from the anxieties about transnationalism and the sorts of masculinity and femininity that are possible within this sphere. Instead, the film ends on New Year's Eve in 1999, and the new millennium is ushered in with Tommy turning over a new leaf and with Sincere and Tionne, the mother of his baby (played by "T-Box" Watkins of the group TLC), in Africa, where, according to the concluding voiceover, Sincere is experiencing life "like a whole new beginning."

Shottas and *Belly* should be seen as complementary expressions—two sides of the transnational coin, as it were, outlining a common framework from different perspectives. With the novels, they play an important role in the ongoing debates about how to get ahead and how to make a future. Some of this debate transpires on websites: *Shottas* has a page on MySpace, for example, and bloggers often refer to *Belly*, and sometimes even to D., when discussing models for "gangsta" lifestyles. But this sort of debate is also generated within the print form. It is not insignificant, for example, that *Bun' Him!!!* ends with a page of "discussion points" that include "Do you think there is any valid reason to cheat on your partner?"; "What if you are not satisfied in your relationship, how would you address such a situation?"; and "What is your take on the whole Bun-fi-Bun issue?" That page also contains a series of questions that ask the reader what he or she would have done in any of the main characters' shoes. By ending in this way, the novel is clearly positioning itself as a tool for sparking discussion, not just as a cultural product that people are expected to uncritically consume and mimic.

Similarly, while Headley's male characters are often apprehended as irredeemably misogynistic, it is also the case that the book creates spaces for debate about appropriate gender relations. This is done not only through D.'s internal struggle but also through the various female characters who animate the novels. Sweetie, for example, having had a similar migratory trajectory to Charlie's and D.'s, represents a sort of Jamaican authenticity vis-à-vis gender relations that characters such as Jenny and Charmaine (D.'s and Charlie's wives) cannot because they were born and raised in England. This becomes evident when the three women begin to discuss one of the popular soap operas they are watching on television. In the show, the female character is unhappy in her marriage and has an affair, something Sweetie denounces as "foolishness." "A woman mustn't gwan dem way deh," she argues, to which Charmaine responds, "You're right . . . but that happens a lot over here. And these soap operas influence people to an extent" (Headley 1993: 98). Jenny defends the character, asking why, when a man does the same thing, nobody thinks anything of it, and argues, "If a man messes about you can't stay with him." Sweetie responds by insisting, "A woman must know how to cope with dese problems," because "dat is how Black man stay" (Headley 1993: 99). Throughout the conversation, Sweetie and Charmaine place more emphasis on whether the man takes care of his responsibilities than on his fidelity, and the three women discuss the differences in women's roles in Jamaica and Britain, with Sweetie noting that in the United Kingdom, "From a woman have a child the State looks after her, gives her a flat and money weekly. In Jamaica, if you don't have a man to help you, t'ings rough" (Headley 1993: 100). The issue is no more resolved in this conversation than it is in D.'s life, for although he marries Jenny, it is clear that the Jamaican-born Donna has his deepest love.

It is also not incidental that in both the films and the novels, a point comes at which the gangster wants to settle down and become a family man. We could read this simply as an attempt to reinscribe a normative worldview regarding family and sexuality. However, what makes this trope striking is that the desire for stability is expressed through a longing for more traditionally rendered modes of intimacy. That this is framed within the language of heteropatriarchy only reflects that this is the language that is available to these characters, but if we take a broader view of what is really going on, we see again that they are experiencing life as nomads within a transnational context in which gender relations (and intimate relations more generally) are shaken up. The desire, therefore, is actually to re-create an observable space called "home" amid circulation and to solidify gender roles that have been called into question.

Moreover, while women are often portrayed as commodities, pretty things you might pick up and hold for a short time but that you eventually will put back because you cannot really afford them over the long haul, they are also indispensable to the action. They are informers, protectors, double-crossers, and, most of all, when included in the inner circles, loyal co-conspirators. The sexism of these novels thus is one about which there is a constant internal discussion that is necessarily transnational.

Let me be clear that I am not making these points to apologize for either the gender norms that permeate these characters' worlds or the sexual violence that often disrupts them. Indeed, sexual violence is ubiquitous throughout the *Yardie* trilogy and *Bun' Him!!!* and the films and thus exerts one of the limits to the kind of transnational citizenship that is otherwise imagined in these popular culture offerings. While sexual violence explicitly drives the action in *Bun' Him!!!*, in *Yardie* we are confronted with numerous instances of sexual violence that render this sort of abuse pedestrian. For example, at D.'s club one evening, we see Sticks beating his girlfriend for talking to another man. He is eventually stopped by his friends, but one gets the sense that they intervene more because they do not want him to draw too much attention to the crew than because they feel the abuse is wrong. In another case, D. stops a man from stabbing and killing his girlfriend because she wants to leave him for another man, arguing that it is not worth it to do time for a woman: "'Nough more ah dem out deh star. Make she gwan, don't waste your life over dem t'ings deh, man" (Headley 1993: 85). And D. himself roughs up the pregnant Jenny after she complains that he is on the road rather than with her preparing for the baby's arrival. Finally, of course, there is D.'s rape of Blue's girlfriend, the incident that leads to his arrest. It is this last incident that elucidates D.'s misreading of the complex cultural landscape in which he finds himself, his "misunderstanding that England is not merely an extension of Jamaica," as Kezia Page (2007: 8) has put it. It is Charlie who has to explain that this kind of "rash action could bring some heat on his friend. It wasn't like dealing with Yard women who would never go to the police" (Headley 1993: 127–28). In other words, there is a limit to the transnational imagination of citizenship, one that has to do with how sexuality is wielded, managed, and—sometimes violently—policed.

Nowhere is this clearer than in the case of homosexuality, and it is transgressive sexuality more generally that consistently draws the borders of Jamaicanness by delineating that which is foreign and dangerous. As Faith Smith (2011: 10) argues, the recent increase in public preoccupation with the question of non-normative sexualities must be seen in relation to the contemporary context of neoliberalism, a context within which postcolonial liberation and autonomy become the freedom to assert control over one's sexual autonomy, defined as wholesome, normative, straight. While sexuality is not a theme that is explicitly explored in either *Belly* or *Shottas*, both the *Yardie* trilogy and *Bun' Him!!!* take pains to address it. In *Excess*, we are confronted with a side story designed to explain one of the ways that West Indian youth in England lose interest in school and become vulnerable to the life of the street. Harry, the fourteen-year-old brother of the youth who is killed by police at the beginning of *Excess*, is reprimanded in school, and his mother, Lorna, and uncle Chris, a community worker, must meet with the principal to find out what happened. The teacher explains, "Well sir, as part of the new curriculum we teach pupils to respect other people's cultures and lifestyles. . . . The incident happened during a class discussion on sexuality. Apparently . . . Harry disrupted the class and used abusive language towards the teacher who happened to be of a minority group" (Headley 1994: 57). Chris responds:

> I know that we can't change the curriculum in your school. . . . I also know all about this idea of a multi-cultural society and the so-called "equal opportunity" policies you're talking about, believe me. But I want you to understand something. The majority of black parents don't really want their children to learn about practices they don't agree with. Because of these . . . topics you teach here, my nephew is refusing to come back to school. As a result, you have another fourteen-year-old black pupil who is likely to lose interest in education and find himself running the streets. Don't you think it's disturbing? (Headley 1994: 58)

Cynicism about the lack of rewards for playing by the rules haunts both school-age youth and the community workers who counsel them. (Harry mentions to Chris that his older brother had been the best student in the class, and that obviously did not get him anywhere.). It may be a compelling explanation for the halfhearted coast from school to the informal economy, but here it is sexuality—and more specifically, homosexuality—that prompts an immediate break. There is no compromise, no slow drift away from the formal institutions of the state, only a cultural impasse that is resolved by finding another school for Harry to attend. In *Bun' Him!!!*, too, homosexuality is positioned as a foreign practice. When Calvin first sees Sandra at the club, he is confused when she does not immediately give him her phone number and wonders whether she is a lesbian. "He hoped it wasn't so," Macka Diamond (2007: 101) writes, "but with the way Jamaica was moving, if what he suspected was so, disappointed as he would have been, it wouldn't surprise him too much, seeing that everything wha gwaan a foreign was now common practice a yard." Calvin's wariness about the possibility that Sandra might be a lesbian seems almost like a gratuitous, perfunctory attempt to get the obligatory chastisement of homosexuality out of the way, but in *Excess*, Harry's assault of the teacher actually pushes an element of the plot forward. In both cases, sexuality marks the limit point of Jamaicanness—and thus of the transnational space of Jamaica—as there is no space for sexual alterity within a Jamaican experience, migrant or not.

That homosexuality marks the boundaries of citizenship in the Caribbean is not news. Jacqui Alexander (1994, 1997, 2005) has spent a career demonstrating the various ways Caribbean states, in their criminalization of non-procreative sex, reproduce a nationalism rooted in heteropatriarchy while obscuring their own complicity in the processes that undermine the sovereignty that ostensibly was granted at independence. The nationalist state, she writes, paradoxically protects women by prosecuting certain forms of domestic violence while also criminalizing lesbians; it polices the meanings of masculinity and femininity while also facilitating a global political economy of desire through its tourism industry; it "mediates the massive entry of transnational capital within national borders, but blames sexual decadence (lesbian and gay sex and prostitution) for the dissolution of the nation" (Alexander 1994: 6).[19] For Alexander (2005), these contradictory processes have their roots in the initial colonization of the region, a period when the violence of heterosexualization was made manifest through the murder by Balboa of Indian "cross-dressers" in the early sixteenth century.

Makeda Silvera makes a similar argument when she tracks normative conceptualizations of heterosexual patriarchy to the linking of production and reproduction during the period of slavery:

> Reproduction served not only to increase the labor force of slave owners, but also, by "domesticating" the enslaved, facilitated the process of social control. Simultaneously, the enslaved responded to dehumanizing conditions by focusing on those aspects of life in which they could express their own desires. . . . . Because [sex] was tied to attempts "to define oneself as human," gender roles, as well as the act of sex, became badges of status. To be male was to be the stud, the procreator; to be female was to be fecund, and one's femininity was measured by the ability to attract and hold a man and to bear children. In this way, slavery and the postemancipated colonial order defined the structures of patriarchy and heterosexuality as necessary for social mobility and acceptance. (Silvera 1992: 529–30)

In part, this understanding of social mobility was also a response to colonial constructions of black sexuality as natural and wild, evidence of an incapacity for self-control and, therefore, for self-rule (Rosenberg 2004).

Within Jamaica, as elsewhere, gendered dynamics during slavery produced notions of sexuality and masculinity that would come to define the parameters of anticolonial struggle. Anthony Lewis and Robert Carr have traced the gendered dimensions of relationships between Europeans and Africans on the plantations, identifying pivotal events—such as Tacky's Rebellion in 1760—that brought about significant shifts in policy and practice. These shifts would transform local constructions of masculinity and its relationship not only to creole indigeneity and status hierarchies among slaves but also to political struggle and open rebellion (Lewis and Carr 2009). Lewis and Carr demonstrate that the privileging of locally born black men in the late eighteenth century gave them more options and greater economic flexibility within the slavery system and thus served to consolidate their interest within the ideological framework of white patriarchy. During the post-emancipation period, free colored men came to replace Europeans within the Jamaican power structure and began to construct a notion of Jamaicanness that was rooted in the process of creolization. Afro-Jamaican men, Lewis and Carr argue, thus needed to define their legitimacy as representatives of an emergent nation by their resistance to the hegemony of European systems of value in relation to masculinity, and they did this partly through religiosity (Christianity), which they reframed (through the transnational missionary activity of African American preachers and through movements such as Garvey's Universal Negro Improvement Association) as serving a pan-Africanist agenda. The emergence of black "proto-nationalism" at the turn of the twentieth century, then, involved "the creation of a body politic that [was] gendered male in its battle with the 'white' (colonial) master" (Lewis and Carr 2009: 9), and the policing of masculinity thus became a *nationalist* project. For Lewis and Carr, this moment provided the foundation for a contemporary context in which "overdetermined notions of race and religious values compete against individual rights to act and to be in the construction of national identity" (Lewis and Carr 2009: 1).

Yet it is not merely the patterns developed during the period of colonial slavery that support the policing of heterosexual patriarchy. Elizabeth Povinelli (2006: 16) has argued that it is liberalism itself—its derivation from European empire and its concomitant conceptualizations of citizenship—that creates the ground to which normative notions of sexuality and belonging cohere. In her ethnography of ideas about subject formation and modes of sexual relation in liberal settler colonies—among radical faeries in the United States and aboriginal communities in Australia—she argues that "the intimate couple is a key transfer point between, on the one hand, liberal imaginaries of contractual economics, politics, and sociality and, on the other, liberal forms of power in the contemporary world." Love, therefore, is seen to secure "the self-evident good of social institutions, social distributions of life and death, and social responsibilities for these institutions and distributions" (Povinelli 2006: 16). Thus, it is empire in its broadest sense that requires the violent policing of gender and sexual norms, past and present.

Jamaica often has been positioned as exceptional in relation to the level of violence that is deployed to police these norms, even within the context of the Caribbean.[20] However, Cecil Gutzmore (2004: 124) has made the point that, because patriarchy and homophobia are structuring principles of both Caribbean societies and the seemingly more liberal societies to which Caribbean people migrate, what sets Jamaica apart is not its apparent brutality but "the overt virulence of the homophobia at the expressive level within both secular and religious popular culture." Gutzmore identifies several belief systems that undergird virulent anti-homosexual action, among them selective religious fundamentalism, the conflation of homosexuality with pedophilia, and the primordialist assertion that before European conquest, Africa was a homosexual-free zone. These belief systems are largely shared among Jamaicans (and others) both on and beyond "the rock," but the stakes one might have in these systems differ based on one's vantage point vis-à-vis the nation.[21] In other words, the threat to the body politic, to the community, is imagined and experienced differently whether one is inside Jamaica battling structural adjustment or a sex tourism industry or inside the United States battling racial discrimination, xenophobia, or exoticism. These differences are reflected in the novels themselves and, perhaps, in the audiences who read them.[22]

We might productively ask, therefore, whether the deconstruction of territorial borders that is written into popular cultural production is ultimately trumped by the reproduction, sharpening, and violent policing of these borders vis-à-vis notions of appropriate sexuality. The homophobic sentiments that undergird the transnationally driven imaginations of Jamaicans at home and abroad—not just among the usual suspects whose lyrics demean men who "bow" (Saunders 2003), but also among those offerings from female DJs such as Tanya Stephens, who argues that men who want oral sex must have picked up the habit abroad, because "wi nuh support dem tings deh dung a yard"[23]—are also reproduced by those who consider themselves middle class and striving middle class. Here, as we have seen, certain kinds of exposure that purportedly are generated through movement (though not necessarily mobility) are seen as decadent, and "America" is felt to be the origin of particular forms of "slackness."

Transgressive sexuality, however, is not the only purported immorality seen as emanating from the United States. As we have already seen, many Jamaicans also identify media saturation and neocolonial dependent development as unconscionable. This is the dancehall artist Lady Saw's point in the song "What Is Slackness?"[24] If we take seriously Saw's questions about why sexually explicit movement is seen as slack but policies ensuring that poor Jamaicans will never have access to the same level education, health care, or housing as rich Jamaicans are not, then we must also recognize that she is identifying the central tension that has animated this chapter. That is, anxieties regarding Jamaicans' position within a neoliberal global economy (whether they reside "on the rock" or "in foreign") are expressed and debated through the language of sexuality. As I have attempted to demonstrate, the critique of the centrality of respectability to mid-twentieth-century development ideology had to do, in large part, with the status of racialized identities within the (trans)national public sphere. Today, the righting of old racial wrongs is still a critical project, and apprehensions about this project are still broached within the framework of sexuality through the language of *respect*, itself a term of address among working-class Jamaicans that asserts a shared (and equal) humanity.

I have been mobilizing the term "respect" in a variety of ways throughout this chapter. It has been used to invoke the presence of an external observer; a sense of self-respect that is rooted in a nationalist pride that differentiates Jamaicans from North Americans and Europeans; a sense of respect toward others that is seen as increasingly absent, given the levels of interpersonal violence; an appreciation for cultural frameworks alternative to one's own (most pointedly with reference to middle-class respect for the cultural practices and beliefs of working-class and lower-class Jamaicans); an acknowledgment of the difficulties of being a black transnational migrant in the United States or the United Kingdom; a counterpart to the discourse of respectability; the deference that is given to a leader who is revered and not merely feared; and, finally, a validation of the cultural innovation and consciousness of youth. What these various usages share is the quest for recognition that processes of racialization have been integral to the elaboration of ideologies concerning gender and humanity (or the lack thereof), that imperialism and racial ordering have shaped global movements past and present, and that conceptualizations of citizenship have been both imagined and institutionalized in racial terms, terms that themselves emerge from and create configurations of class, gender, and sexuality. In other words, *real* respect would entail a validation of racial subjects who are still confronted with the legacies of slavery and colonialism and the recognition of the integrity and legitimacy of a class-coded set of cultural practices and values that diverge from those "respectable" practices that have been (and, in many cases, still are) promulgated by political and cultural elites, middle-class professionals, and most religious communities as the proper foundation for citizenship.[25] As the plethora of letters from Jamaicans in diaspora complaining about "Redemption Song" suggests, this respect is urgently necessary in the contemporary moment in which "Jamaica" evokes stereotypically gendered and racialized expectations related to service, tourism, and the drug trade.

On one hand, therefore, neoliberalism has generated increased power in the public sphere for lower-class black Jamaicans to define cultural citizenship on their own terms. The decline in the strength of the creole nationalist state has diminished the power of its disciplinary domesticating arm. Popular-culture norms, values, and practices therefore have taken greater space in many national imaginaries, marking a refusal of class paternalism and a decline in the hegemony of respectability paradigms as the arbiters of modern progress. In Jamaica, this has dislodged the centrality of particular configurations of social value that had maintained relatively rigid links between color, class, and cultural capital. Yet the contemporary global situation also exerts a different kind of *discipline*—with effects that create new anxieties that are expressed in terms of "crisis." The Jamaican state's decreased ability to meet the social, educational, and occupational needs of its citizens has articulated with the reassertion of racial hierarchies internally and national hierarchies globally, hierarchies that are still acutely experienced as part of an old global imperial order that, rather than waning, has actually intensified (Sassen 2000; Trouillot 2001). Because racial hierarchies have not disappeared, and because racial discrimination is still acutely felt not only at individual but also at structural levels, racial vindication is still a critical project. That this is a project that is often expressed through the elaboration of notions of appropriate masculinity and femininity, and that it is implemented in complex and diverse ways — ways that often confound analysts and activists — reflects not only the persistence of racial distrust but also a changed generational vision in which "uplift" is often felt to be as constraining as "downpression" (Ulysse 1999). We should not think that respectability is dead, however, or that Jamaicans of diverse class backgrounds no longer have any investment in its realization. This is not a zero-sum game, as should be clear by my attempts to show that one of the axes around which both respectability and "racial respect" seem to cohere is that of sexuality.[26] The call for racial respect, however, *must also be* a call for a new orientation in which the success or failure of various development schemes is *not* contingent on the policing of black working-class women's bodies and in which the elaboration of notions of citizenship are not tethered to heteronormative conceptions of the social body.

Resurrected Bodies, 1963/2007

"Rastas on Rampage in MoBay—Eight Persons Killed." So screamed the headline of Jamaica's daily afternoon paper, the *Star*, on 11 April 1963. Two days, later the *Daily Gleaner* led its news coverage with four articles under the heading "8 Killed after Attack on Gas Station. Two policemen, Three Ras Tafarians among the Dead." And by 10 A.M. on that fateful Holy Thursday morning, RJR (then Radio Jamaica and the Re-Diffusion Network; now Radio Jamaica) reported: "Three people are now known to have died in this morning's uprising by Rastafarians in Montego Bay."[1] For those who today understand Rastafarians as primarily advocating a philosophy of universalism (the "One Love" Bob Marley sang about), and even for those who prefer to foreground Rastafari's ideological roots in black supremacy and pan-Africanism and its more general black nationalist stance,[2] news of a "rampage" or an "uprising" by Rastafarians would seem anomalous. But during that immediate post-independence period in Jamaica, fear and disdain were the attitudes most commonly directed toward Rastafarians, not only by those in the middle and upper classes, but also by many working-class Jamaicans. This means that events that were primarily local in scope generated national attention and concern.

In this case, the high level of concern was marked by the fact that the prime minister at the time—Sir Alexander Bustamante—flew to Montego Bay, Jamaica's second city, accompanied by the commissioner of police, the top command of the Jamaica Defense Force, the security chief, two ministers of government, and several police from the head-quarters in Kingston. Once in Montego Bay, Bustamante mobilized police forces from St. James, the parish of which Montego Bay is the capital city, as well as from the neighboring parishes of Hanover, Trelawny, and West-moreland, to join with civilians in the roundup of Rastafarians.[3] Ultimately, because of the actions of five "bearded" individuals who were motivated by a land dispute, more than 150 Rastafarians were arrested, jailed, beaten, and tortured. In addition to three of the five who were involved in the attacks on the gas station, a nearby motel, and an estate manager's home, an unknown number of Rastafarians died as a result of the torture, and many more were permanently scarred. Since the 1990s, a group of Rastafarians in western Jamaica has kept a public vigil commemorating "Bad Friday," and in 2007 the vigil was folded into the yearlong schedule of events designed to com-memorate the bicentenary of the abolition of the slave trade. At these com-memorations, elder Rastafarians offer testimony about their experiences, asking that the government make a formal apology to the Rastafarian com-munity and that it consider reparations of some sort.

Because instances of state violence against members of a population di-rect our attention to how citizenship is defined at any given moment of time, in this chapter I use the example of this event—now known euphe-mistically as the Coral Gardens "incident"—to think in a somewhat dif-ferent way through the questions that animate each chapter of this book: Who has been included in the national body of Jamaica, and how has that changed from the mid-twentieth century to the early twenty-first century? How have threats to the body politic been imagined and eradicated? And how do those who have suffered as a result of their exclusion envision re-dress? Asking these kinds of questions can help us to revisit how citizenship is imagined for today's world. Moreover, it compels us to think about both the limits and the possibilities of reparations as a framework through which we might seek greater recognition of the historical rootedness of contem-porary inequalities, not only in Jamaica, but throughout the black world.

I argue that the call for an official apology for and investigation of the events at Coral Gardens is crucial because it directs attention to two im-portant processes that I have been addressing in various ways throughout these pages. First, it acknowledges that citizenship is not a static, universal-

The stage at the annual commemoration of the Coral Gardens incident, Montego Bay, Jamaica. IMAGE COURTESY OF JUNIOR "GABU" WEDDERBURN.

ist notion but is characterized by and rooted within processes of racialization, which are themselves developed transnationally and can change over time (Gilroy 2006; Thomas and Clarke 2006). Second, the call for reparations directs greater attention to the political economy of class formation (Biondi 2003) and its relationship to nationalism and development (Brodkin 2000), thereby destabilizing culturalist notions of violence. In other words, taking reparations seriously—despite the various important critiques that have been leveled at reparations movements, public apologies, and Truth and Reconciliation Commissions—could mean thinking anew about how to explain the violence that plagues our societies today.

This chapter also has a side story—one that has to do with how we think about archives and how various sorts of archives might be mobilized to support contemporary goals. If we agree that certain forms of violence are written out of nationalist narratives even as they define the terms of belonging, then we must understand the testimonies given at events such as the Coral Gardens commemoration as counter-nationalist narratives. These sorts of counter-narratives cannot be framed merely as a way to fill in the blanks of an unfinished history, what Joseph Roach (1996: 26) would see as "the disparities between history as it is discursively transmitted and memory as it is publicly enacted by the bodies that bear its consequences." Of course, they do also serve this purpose, in this case standing as rhetorical strategies through which a general fear of black radicalism is named and linked to past processes of class formation and nation building. More importantly, however, the counter-narratives offered up by Rastafari elders are also performative building blocks through which community solidarity, authority, and futures are envisioned. These visions incorporate not only the immediate desire some have for compensation for wrongs done to particular individuals and families in 1963, but also the long-term project of reorganizing our notions of both political and cultural citizenship. One example of how this is being done today is Rastafarians' mobilization around issues of cultural ownership and the legal protection of cultural heritage and practices. For those involved in the effort, this has necessitated a greater engagement with the Jamaican government, something that, in an earlier political moment within Rasta, would have been considered completely anathema. A delicate tightrope act thus is being performed here that must navigate between the movement toward community empowerment within the context of the Jamaican state's attempt to develop a unique "brand Jamaica" within a global marketplace, a neoliberal consumerist ethos whereby culture itself becomes a commodity to incorporate and consume, and the institutional sites of transnational governmentality that have created the channels through which this navigation might occur.

EVENTS AND AFTERMATH

Inspired by Maurice Halbwachs's (1992) pioneering work on social memory, historians have long been interested in how national narratives stand as acts of collective cultural memory and in how these memories and myths then take embodied forms as memorials and monuments (see, e.g., Connerton 1989; Gillis [ed.] 1994; Lorey and Beezley 2002; Olick 2003; Sturken 1997). Because these scholars have seen memory as contextually contingent, and therefore as a dynamic force in the creation and undoing of narratives of collective belonging, the elaboration of cultural memories has become a way to critique nationalist historiography.[4] Here, the insistence has been that "'memory work' is, like any other kind of physical or mental labor, embedded in complex class, gender, and power relations that determine what is remembered (or forgotten), by whom, and for what end" (Gillis 1994: 3). That this kind of work is also gendered has been an assertion of feminist researchers concerned with these issues (Hirsch and Smith 2002), with the implication that "monumentalizing, memorializing, and testifying can be viewed as a form of mapping and charting of social and physical relationships" (Mains 2004: 197). This body of scholarship has focused on reading monuments, memorials, and other commemorative practices as situated versions of history to reveal the various dimensions and dynamics of power that shape truth claims.

Anthropologists have drawn from the insights of these scholars in their efforts to ethnographically understand how remembering and forgetting are also located within the practices of everyday life, and not just concretized within monuments and other kinds of memorials. Veena Das's work is perhaps the best known example of this perspective (Das 2007), but I am also thinking, for example, about Irina Carlota Silber's analysis of how Salvadorans countered national policies of postwar reconstruction by mapping the connections between private memories of loss and collective memories of civil war on their everyday (unmarked) landscape. Silber (2004) shows that this is one way in which public memory and history remains in the hands of those who continue to be marginalized by a state that claims to be acting in the interests of reconciliation. Liisa Malkki's work on memory and national cosmologies among Hutu refugees also has demonstrated that these processes are neither static nor predictable but contingent on people's differing, and changing, circumstances — in the case she discusses, the extent to which they were incorporated into their adopted "homes" (Malkki 1995). Memory, in these studies, is never unitary, and histories are always relational. The politics of memory — like those of identity — must always therefore be understood through reference to the particular historical, geopolitical, and ideological contexts in which memories are made and recalled (Trouillot 1995). In other words, as David Scott (2008: vi) has put it, "Memory is always memory-in-the-present: the exercise of recovery of the past is always at once an exercise in its re-description, an exercise in arguing with the past, negotiating it, a persistent exercise in the questioning and repositioning of the assumptions that are taken to constitute that common life."

Black memory, it is claimed — and, more specifically, New World Black memory — constitutes something of a special case in this regard, as it is produced and reproduced within a context often characterized by "an absence of ruins." This title of Orlando Patterson's second novel is meant to foreground experiences of rupture, pastlessness, and fragmentation that are often seen as constituting the historical and discursive context for the majority of New World African populations. Indeed, three generations of writers and literary critics have attempted, in different ways, to reconstruct the lives of those who were or would become slaves, to glean insight into their aspirations, their imaginations, and their day-to-day movements, by putting together a mention in a diary here, a list in a log there (for example, Baucom 2005; Hartman 1997, 2008; James 1989; Patterson 1967). These acts of reconstruction, just as much as those of memorialization, are oriented toward the creation of a historical consciousness that other scholars have argued is to be found within the oral traditions—spiritual and secular— that have been elaborated and transmitted within marginalized communities throughout the diaspora. In both cases, we are presented with a sense of the archive, the spaces that must be mined to serve the goal of understanding how we come to be who we are (Bogues 2003; Farred 2003; Price 1985, 1998, 2007; Trotz 2004).

These spaces of black memory, of course, often stand in opposition to forms of state memory and therefore constitute a kind of minority report, what Anthony Bogues calls "dread history." This is a history of radical utopian desire that "attempts to excavate from the practices and ideas of the subaltern resistance movements in the Caribbean a worldview in which hope is rooted in a conception of the bourgeois colonial world turned upside down" (Bogues 2003: 179).[5] Michael Hanchard has argued that, while states are often also interested in incorporating aspects of this worldview, they are not necessarily committed to transforming the discursive conditions that generated it. He writes, "A state that honors a once-marginalized and feared subject or citizen is simultaneously acknowledging that, in hindsight, a prior regime or series of regimes might have erred in the fundamental exclusion and marginalization of a particular figure or event in the national past. In rehabilitating marginalized and excluded figures and events, states are not rehabilitating the past but, instead, the past's representation in national-state narrative" (Hanchard 2008: 53). However, Hanchard continues, there is an ulterior motive to black memory that remains at odds with this rather sanitizing move on the part of states, because it is geared to making contemporary claims "about the *relationship* between present inequalities and past injustices" (Hanchard 2008: 48; emphasis added). In other words, the alternative archives of black memory ultimately can be mobilized to serve the cause of reparations.

But I am getting ahead of myself. If, as Scott (1999: 82) has argued, an "archive is not merely a collection; rather, it is a *generative* system . . . that governs the production and appearance of statements," then we must see the testimonies of Rasta elders at events such as the commemoration of the Coral Gardens "crucifixion"—which is how several elder Rastas refer to the incident—as creating an archive through which memory not only forges and instantiates the community's histories and social relations but also charts the range of possible directions for the future at any given moment. The anthropologist Carole Yawney argued as much when she discussed the two forms of discourse she saw as characterizing Rasta ideology and sociality: iterative discourse, which she understood as primarily codified and formulaic, and generative discourse, which she saw as producing creative, unique, and far-ranging frameworks for understanding and acting (Yawney 1985, cited in Homiak 1999; see also Yawney 1978).[6] For Yawney, generative discourse was produced by charismatic elders who shared a special talent for "teaching," those elders who were truly visionary and could inspire vision in others. To be sure, she was discussing these discursive forms in relation to the private reasoning sessions that initially constituted the primary mode of coming to Rasta and engaging the way of life. But these private sessions have their public and semi-public corollaries in events such as the Coral Gardens commemoration, nyabinghis,[7] and international "trods," performative pedagogical occasions that serve simultaneously to produce and celebrate the community's archives, to inspire young Rastas, to solidify the bonds of sociality within and between Rasta communities, to strengthen elders' positions as revered "ancients," and to generate debate about future paths based on the aspects of the archives that are emphasized at any given moment (Homiak 1985, 1990, 1999).[8] These sorts of events are especially critical in a context where there is very little public knowledge about what happened that Easter weekend in 1963, even, in many cases, among Rastafarians themselves.

In fact, very little scholarly attention has been paid to the Coral Gardens affair. It is mentioned briefly in Terry Lacey's *Violence and Politics in Jamaica, 1960–1970* (1977), which is where I first encountered it as a graduate student. There, however, it is discussed as one among several incidents that provoked a "nervous national bourgeoisie" (Lacey 1977: 85) to believe that

Rastafarians, as a whole, were ready to revolt violently against the Jamaican state, thereby justifying a security policy that, Lacey argues, was rooted in "conspiracy theories." Similarly, James Mau (1968), an American sociologist who conducted research in Jamaica in the 1960s, discussed the Coral Gardens incident briefly to demonstrate that middle-class and upper-class Jamaicans have consistently viewed the Jamaican "masses" as hostile, menacing, and ready to revolt at any moment. Rex Nettleford treated the Coral Gardens incident somewhat more substantially in his classic *Mirror, Mirror: Identity, Race, and Protest in Jamaica* (1970) to show how Rasta became associated in the minds of the Jamaican middle-class public with crime and violence. He, like Lacey and Mau, argued that the government's response to the events at the gas station and beyond amounted to an "overkill" resulting from "a pathological fear of violence" from particular sectors of the population (Nettleford 1970: 83).[9] However, like that of the Green Bay Massacre of 1978, the official archive of what happened at Coral Gardens is slim.[10] The actual events of that Holy Thursday are usually related merely as a way to introduce the main story of Coral Gardens, which is not the event but the aftermath — the government roundup and criminalization of Rastafari. Yet it seems worthwhile to revisit the day itself, as well as the events leading up to it, not only to understand how in extraordinary circumstances some ordinary people become "criminals" while others become "vigilantes," but also to apprehend how the recounting of events can take on mythical dimensions, with dissonant versions refracting the particular end games of different narrators, like a "tell" in poker. To do this, we must begin the story long before that Easter weekend. I will start with the version of events that appeared in the *Jamaica Gleaner* as that newspaper reported both on the "incident" itself and on the ensuing trial.

In February 1962, Hubert Stewart, overseer at Tryall Farm (a section of the Rose Hall estate), confronted Rudolph Franklin, who had been cultivating land on the property, allegedly without formal tenure. Franklin was the leader of the group of five or six "bearded" men who began the day of 11 April 1963 by setting fire to the Shell gas station in the Coral Gardens section of Montego Bay. It was reported that someone who worked at the gas station had told Stewart that Franklin had captured land on the estate and was using it to burn coal, so he went to remove him accompanied by a police corporal from the Rose Hall station. During the argument that ensued, the corporal fired five shots, one of which punctured Franklin's intestines and another of which nicked his shoulder. Franklin was admitted to the Montego Bay Hospital and was subsequently charged with possession of ganja. On his release from the hospital, he was sentenced to six months' imprisonment. After he finished serving his prison sentence, he returned to the community, telling people he would get revenge for what had happened to him.[11]

Rastas do not typically dispute this official version of why Franklin and his peers planned the events that later transpired in Coral Gardens, although the exact dates might differ slightly. Prince Williams, for example, discusses the motivation behind Franklin's revenge this way:

> These Rastaman. Some are Rasta, some nah Rasta. Them live up in the hills of Coral Garden on a plantation owned by the same Rose Hall owner/farmer. Now it's owned by a white man. These bredrin live in the hills, they do their farming. Lots of cultivation, plant food and plant ganja too. These bredrin share with the people around them. They share with the estate owner.
>
> This man that they do these things toward, this Rudolf Franklin, he wasn't no Rastaman. He just similar now like how wear dem beard and go round said way. The man a no Rasta. But they want to rob this brother of the wealth that his father die and leave, a piece of land. . . . And they did take it. And they said they allowed some money, but Rudolf say him nah want nah money fi him land. They give him some land that he can farm. They did so on the Coral Garden property. But is like, every year, when reaping time comes, the said man come and reap, and Rudolf don't reap nothing. Maybe he's thinking what's going down. And when they look, dem come and hold him up further, seh you're too near down yah so, so they hold him up further in the hills. The next year when the harvest come to perfection to reap, same thing happen. So Rudolf haffi take it to mind and know seh something gwan now. The third year when they move him up further, further, further inna de hills, and he create him food and the same thing happen, that's the time that they shoot him, that's the time they give him the seven shot. And then he go to prison with the seven shot inna him. . . .
>
> This was the revenge he carry back from prison. Ca the doctor tell him seh seven months the period of time him have to live from the bullet he pick up. Him seh, No mahn, anytime the seven month come mi

haffi carry somebody with me. Exactly the seven months, he comes out of prison. He and a few guys that around him start a revolution in their own category by making spear and covering themself with cow skin and making some science weapon, bow and arrow . . . And they attack these guys that run the estate — the head man, the butcher and the bookkeeper. The man-dem start until the police informed and the police come in and him kill the inspector and a couple of de estate owners. (Williams 2005: 115–17)

This version of events is corroborated by many of the elders who were rounded up after the Coral Gardens incident, including Ras Noel Bennett from Trelawny. After Bennett was released from prison, he went to the community from which Franklin had come to glean the whole story from community members. As he recounted it, he asserted that Franklin's father had owned land on the Rose Hall estate that he had passed on to Rudolph, and the government of Jamaica wanted to buy it from him to build a gas station. Franklin told them he did not want to sell, but the government officials told him they would put money in an account for him at the bank for the land. Months passed, and the officials noticed that none of the money had been drawn from the account. They visited Franklin again to ask why he was not drawing the money. Franklin told them he did not want the money, he wanted land, and the government gave him a parcel near where he had already been farming vegetables, including herb.[12] Ras Bennett, like Prince Williams, told me that Franklin's crops were destroyed three times just as they were ready to reap and that after the third time, he was ready to take revenge. Zoith Jarrett, also known as "Nose," offered similar testimony at the Coral Gardens commemoration in 2008:

Now brethren, hear me. . . . Rudolph was like my brother. When Rudolph get shot, 1961 October, it was a Thursday evening. When them shot Rudolph, them put Rudolph into a jeep to lie down pon him belly and take him to the hospital. . . . That was 1961, October. Rudolph go to hospital and him spend three week in the hospital. When him come out of hospital, him go to prison for six months. When Rudolph come back from prison . . . a Saturday, 1962, June, when him come I was the first person that Rudolph buck [up]. . . . Him seh to me seh, "Nose, where you going." Me seh, "Me going downtown to pick up two pants." Him seh, "All right . . . when you come back me waan see you." . . .

Accidentally me nuh see him the Saturday night. The Sunday morning bout 8 o'clock we buck up, and when we buck up, [there were] three of us. King Alphonso father was the elder one to us at that morning. Him seh to King Alphonso . . . we call him Uncle Charlie, him seh, "Uncle Charlie, I gwine do something, and me know unoo [nah] gwine like it, but when I go perform my works I don't want to see none of unoo around." . . . And him seh to we the Sunday morning, "Uncle Charlie, me go a prison go spend six months. Me spend three week a hospital and the doctor tell me seh, when me go dead me a go start smell meself before me dead because me a go decay." . . . And him call three name, him seh anytime him gwine dead, him de carry the three man with him. Well accidentally him only get one . . . Mr. Fowler . . .

And him haffi do it. Because if you living at a place disturbing no one, having the community people around you doing nothing that is wrong, why you think I should come and interrupt you. All Rastaman answer that question. Why should I come and interrupt you. If I interrupt you . . . what you going to do? Destroy me. So me have to take what me get . . . That's the way it goes mi bredda. (Public testimony given at the 2008 Coral Gardens commemoration)

These accounts corroborate the motive theory that was developed by the police soon after the events of Holy Thursday transpired. Indeed, Selbourne Reid, a retired police officer who was stationed in Montego Bay at the time of the Coral Gardens incident, writes that police were often called in to remove Rastafarians who were trespassing on the Rose Hall estate and that they were usually accompanied by the estate's tractors and bulldozers to destroy both their crops and their dwelling places (Reid 2009: 87–88).[13] Familiar with both Franklin and the more general issue of squatting, the local police therefore understood the murders as a local problem, not the result of a wide-ranging conspiracy to overthrow the Jamaican government. Nevertheless, the reaction of both the government and local civilians suggested fear of the latter. But again, I am getting ahead of myself.

Another Ras who grew up in the area where Rudolph was farming but who now lives abroad — and who asked not to be identified — tells a somewhat different story. He reminds us that at that time, Rose Hall estate was the only employer in the area, and owned all the surrounding lands that made up the communities of Salt Spring, Flower Hill, and others. Across the road from the estate along the beach, an area that is now populated by hotels, was an old slave village called Little River. Life centered around the Rose Hall factory, and the residents of all these communities worked on the estate in one capacity or another, and in some cases were given customary use of land within their communities to cultivate gardens. No one, he says, held formal tenure to either their property or their houses, and the post office, the police post, and the factory were all connected to the estate. Moreover, cultivating anything other than a small garden — in other words, clearing lands by bushing and burning — would bring trouble from the ranger for the estate, Pa Galley. This Ras contends that Franklin and at least two of his co-conspirators — Lloyd Waldron and Clifton Larman — attended Cornwall College in Montego Bay, the most prestigious high school in western Jamaica. These men were therefore not ordinary cane cutters but had positions such as timekeepers, and Franklin himself worked in the Chemistry department of the estate, supervising the mixing of chemicals that would be used to spray for mosquitoes, among other things. These men were also at the center of a burgeoning black power sensibility, talking with other workers about the realities of the slave trade, about the Maroons and Marcus Garvey, and about the need to change their situation. To some villagers, Franklin and his brethren were considered militants, despite the fact that they were well loved within the community.

In the early 1960s, as this Ras tells it, Mr. Owen Hale was brought as the manager to Rose Hall from another plantation. Hale was seen among workers as someone who was more explicitly racist than the previous manager, and he was concerned with the emergent sensibility of racial pride among the workers. Hale demoted Franklin from his job and sent him back into the fields, and pressured the other brethren to also leave the estate; Waldron, for example, ended up taking a job with the Public Works Department. Rather than work in the fields spraying fertilizer, Franklin opted to quit his job, at which point he began clearing land for cultivation down in a valley behind the community of Flower Hill rather than in the area of Lennon, where community members were given rights to cultivate. For a time, Ranger Galley looked the other way because he was married to a woman whose brother was also cultivating there. However, four or five years later, when Franklin began building a house, Mr. Hale found out and sent orders for Franklin to move off the land. The first delegation to visit Franklin chopped down his crops, as did the second, but Franklin persisted.

The third delegation, however, included Hale, Ranger Galley, the book-keeper at Tryall, two policemen from Rose Hall, the head ranger for the estate, and a district constable. As they came upon Franklin and another farmer, the Ras argues, Mr. Hale said, "You don't hear yu mus' go?" The Ras claims that members of the delegation said Franklin picked up his machete and began threatening them, and that they shot him in self-defense; however, he says he was told by the son of the other farmer that Franklin displayed no hostility, and that it was Hale who eventually shot him, not the policeman as was the official report. For the Ras, this was significant because it is part of a longer history of those with state authority taking responsibility for crimes committed by private persons. He contends that the delegation put Franklin's body in their jeep and dumped it in the nearby churchyard where a group of schoolchildren eventually found it, covered with dried blood and grass. At this point, Franklin was taken to the hospital, and then to jail. The Ras remembers that when Franklin returned to the community after serving his sentence, he was a changed man.

The *Gleaner* reported that by Palm Sunday, 7 April, Rudolph Franklin was seen meeting on the Rose Hall property with four other Rastafarians, and for the next several days, according to court testimony by local community members familiar with those who were ultimately charged with murder, these men were heard making comments such as, "Brother it is our time now."[14] This version of the story is corroborated by the Ras, who said that on that Sunday morning, Franklin appeared at his home with four brethren he did not know. Because Franklin was close with his mother, the Ras was not surprised to see him, but he did notice that they seemed "serious." The five men ate what his mother gave them, and when they were leaving, Franklin called to the Ras, who was a young boy at the time, telling him to take care of himself because he did not know when he would see him again. By the following Tuesday, he says, people in the area were saying they saw Franklin and some Rastamen going into the valley with whips and strange armor. "Everybody sensed something was going on," he recalls, "but no one thought what happened Thursday was in the making."

Let me return to the *Gleaner*'s account. At 4:25 A.M. on Holy Thursday, Franklin and four other men[15] — Lloyd (Felix) Waldron, Noel Bowen, Carlton Bowen, and Clifton Larman — arrived at Ken Douglas's Shell station at Coral Gardens and confronted the lone attendant, George Plummer. Plummer testified that all five men had weapons, including hatchets, machetes, spears, guns, and a whip, and stated that he feigned adherence to the principles of the Rastafarian faith to escape. The five men then sprayed the station with gasoline and set the building on fire. Two cars parked behind the station were also splashed with gasoline and set ablaze.[16] From the gas station, the men proceeded to a nearby motel, the Edgewater Inn, where they attacked a guest, Ken Marsh, a salesman from the parish of St. Andrew. Marsh had emerged from his room when he heard the watchman and the owners of the motel shouting. He ran to the dining shed, and the five men cornered him and hacked him to death with a machete. The men continued up through the hills behind the motel toward the home of the overseer of the Tryall Farm, Hubert Stewart. On the way, they met the estate's headman, Edward Fowler, whom they chopped to death.

Stewart told the court that at 6 A.M. on 11 April, he heard stumbling and chopping in his dining room, so he got out of bed, grabbed his gun, and opened the door to the dining room. There he saw four men, including Franklin, demolishing his home. Stewart said that when he pointed and fired his revolver, a fifth man—whom he identified as Clifton Larman—chopped him on the hand with a spear. He escaped through a back door with his family and ran through the cane fields. Noel Grossett, the bookkeeper at Tryall Farm, also heard the commotion at Stewart's house and ran when he saw Franklin coming toward him with a whip, but Franklin spared him. After smashing more furniture in the house and threatening to burn the house down, the five men left and started moving toward Rose Hall Farms by way of White Gut Marl. Grossett testified that on the way he heard Franklin say "Time is against us" and "We want Hayles and Williams." Hayles would be Mr. Hale, the manager of Rose Hall Farms, and Williams was the corporal at the police post at Rose Hall.[17]

By this time, the police had been alerted to the various events taking place, and a squad under the command of Inspector John Fisher rushed initially to the gas station, carrying only batons and guns that, for the most part, were unloaded. Once there, the police realized the incident was not isolated, and several more cars were dispatched to the area. Three police cars were joined by one belonging to a civilian, Albert Causwell, an assistant manager at Marzouca's Capitol in Montego Bay, who was on his way to Kingston but stopped to assist the police. Altogether, there were fourteen uniformed and plainclothes policemen in the party of four vehicles. They ascended into the hills around Rose Hall to White Gut Marl, and when they saw five Rastafarians walking toward them, they stopped their vehicles and got out of the cars armed with rifles, revolvers, and batons.

The police shouted to the Rastafarians to halt and drew their weapons, pointing them at Franklin and his crew. Corporal Clifford Melbourne fired three shots, and one of the Rastafarians fell. Another constable with a gun also pulled his trigger, but since he was not one of the few policemen whose guns were loaded,[18] Franklin's crew realized they had the advantage and began to attack the police with their weapons. The police ran, some attempting to pick up stones and throw them at Franklin's crew, without success, and headed toward a nearby golf course.[19] As the police were running, the supervising inspector fell, and Noel Bowen, one of Franklin's men, began to slash him with a machete. One of the police turned back to help the inspector and ended up shooting and killing Bowen. Felix Waldron was also shot and killed by a policeman. While trying to get away, Causwell, who was also armed, attempted to crouch through a wire fence. Two of Franklin's crew were nearby and began hacking him. Melbourne fired a shot toward them, at which point one of the Rastafarians threw a spear that struck Melbourne. Franklin and one of his men then ran to Melbourne and began chopping him in the head with a machete and hatchet. Both Causwell and Melbourne were dead, and Franklin was badly injured.[20] By this time, another police squadron arrived led by Assistant Superintendent Bertie Scott, who was shot and killed before he got out of the car. Then Franklin—coming around a corner with a police service revolver—was fatally shot by police. By 9 A.M., three of the five "bearded" men (Franklin, Noel Bowen, and Felix Waldron) and two policemen (Melbourne and Scott) had been killed.

For those in the community, the Ras states, that Thursday morning was "pure chaos." They stood on the ridge overlooking Rose Hall and noticed several cane fields on fire and several streams of people running up into the hills. They were wondering what was going on, and by the time the crowds arrived to their area, they were told that "Rasta kill a whole heap of people from Tryall and Spring Bush, and Brother Ruddy [Franklin] was involved." What follows is the account of the events of that Holy Thursday day that he came to piece together from friends of his who saw portions of what transpired. Franklin and his men, he says, went to the gas station because they knew the watchman had a gun and they wanted to take it with them on their mission. At that very moment, a white man and his wife drove up to purchase gas. The watchman wouldn't open the door and the white man "got antsy," so they ended up killing him and lighting up the gas station. They then proceeded to Fowler's house. Fowler had testified in circuit court in Montego Bay that he was one of the delegation that went to move Franklin off his land, and that Franklin had drawn his machete prompting them to shoot him in self-defense. However, according to the Ras, Fowler was not in fact one of the delegation, but that another man who had been there refused to testify to this version of events, so Fowler took responsibility for it, allegedly falsely. When Franklin and his men found him, Franklin cut his throat with a hatchet. There was a witness to this killing, but Franklin told him to run free since they were not after him. The men continued to Stewart's house, where the maid was in the kitchen scalding milk. Franklin told her to "carry out the busha," but Stewart's wife saw them and warned her husband, who then ran for his gun. Stewart shot at Franklin—the bullet grazed him above his eyes—and then ran through the back door with his wife into the cane fields. This is when Franklin and his men started chopping the house, and setting the fields on fire.

They continued on through the mountain to an opening that led through the community of Mount Zion to the factory at Rose Hall in order to kill Mr. Hale in his office. However, at White Gut, they met the police, who were also coming through the valley toward Rose Hall. They heard the policemen ask the inspector to distribute the bullets, and when they determined the police were unarmed, they began striking them with the whips, machetes, and hatchets they were carrying. "I don't know how many of them got killed in there," the Ras says, "eventually they shot Ruddy in his eyes . . . and he fell." He continues, "Clifton and the other brother somehow managed to escape. It must have been close to two weeks that they were on the loose, and it was bedlam in Flower Hill, people didn't sleep." What this Ras wanted to emphasize, however, was that Franklin and his men had a very specific agenda that was related to their own mistreatment at the estate. In other words, this was not a diffuse "Rastafarian uprising," as it had been reported in the news, but a specific revenge for what they felt to be racist and unjust treatment. "This was not just a random mad something," the Ras argues, "every step along the way there were people who were not killed." Nevertheless, the hysteria that was generated by these events mobilized security forces and civilians alike to hunt down Rastafarians, not only in the area where these events took place, but across the island.

Two days later, according to the *Gleaner*, Holness Rhoden, a truck driver from Salt Spring, arrived at the Montego Bay police station with Carlton Bowen and Clifton Larman, the men who were now being charged with murder and conspiracy to commit murder. He testified in court that he had heard about the search for Bowen and Larman on the radio and that at about 10 A.M. on 13 April, he had set out with a party of villagers from his district for the Rosehall Mountains. The villagers came upon Bowen and Larman, who were armed with machetes. Rhoden shouted to the two men, accusing them of being the men for whom the police were searching, and Bowen and Larman began advancing on the party. Rhoden fired his gun, shooting Larman in the foot. Bowen pleaded for him not to shoot again, arguing that they had just been following the orders of their leader (Franklin), and Rhoden led the two men out of the bush and into the back of his truck. The Ras tells us that this particular roundup was not spontaneous, but that Rhoden, in fact, was the unofficial leader of a more generalized vigilante group that had been terrorizing Rastas in the area long before the "incident" itself. Moreover, he insists, Rhoden was supported in this effort by local ruling JLP party members who supplied him with guns. Incidentally, again according to the *Gleaner's* trial reportage, Rhoden admitted that several days later he shot another Rastafarian in the same area where they had found Larman and Bowen, spurred by the police campaign of "mopping up" Rastafarians and believing him also to be one of the five men involved in the Holy Thursday killings (he was not).[21] The police charged Bowen and Larman; several days later, they also charged Leabert Jarrett.

Under questionable circumstances, the three accused men gave statements incriminating themselves in the events of that morning.[22] Their trial, which began on 16 July, lasted twenty-nine days, with an additional four days of summation, making it the longest murder trial to have been conducted in the parish of St. James at the time. The defense—a team of lawyers who would each subsequently become quite well known in Jamaica, and one of whom eventually became the Jamaican High Commissioner in London—argued both insanity and "diminished responsibility."[23] In the end, however, all three men were sentenced to death by hanging. In May, Jarrett was released on appeal, and on 2 December 1964, Bowen and Larman were hanged and buried in the prison compound.[24]

As in any representation of events, we are confronted here with a set of gaps that are generated by differences in social position, in political affiliation, and in personal relationships. Tina Campt (2004: 14) has argued that these gaps are fruitful spaces that "exceed and at the same time contest the claim of any representation to render its referent comprehensively or with complete accuracy or veracity." They illuminate, in her view, the social technologies of memory, those material and meaning-making processes through which understandings of events "are transported, absorbed, and preserved by and among individuals in society" (Campt 2004: 13). In doing so, gaps reveal the dynamics of dominant social relations but also potentially provide openings for alternative assertions of purpose. With this in mind, there are two important points to underline, I believe, when thinking about the discrepancies between the versions of events presented at the Coral Gardens commemoration and within the Ras's testimony.

The first has to do with the Ras's positioning vis-à-vis Franklin. Because he was close to him—Franklin "would go to the market in Montego Bay and would come back with a big bag of patties just for the children. . . . To have an adult from the community come up like that, he was so gentle . . . and we loved him"—the relationship gives him a privileged vantage point from which to see the events of that Easter week in 1963 because he was actually nearby. Most accounts of the events that brought on the government roundup are offered by Rastafarians who lived outside the immediate areas of Salt Spring and Flower Hill, and these men relate Franklin's story somewhat offhandedly, as a necessary but ultimately inconsequential backdrop to more important proceedings. This is because most of them also say they never knew him and, in fact, never even knew where Coral Gardens was, in many cases becoming aware of the context for their mistreatment only after having arrived in jail and consulted with other Rastas there. For them, the events of the day were important only insofar as they precipitated the aftermath, the mass "crucifixion" of Rastafari. Franklin's story thus achieves a sort of mythical status in relation to what began on 11 April 1963, because clarifying the specifics, the ins and outs of what happened and how, is not really the point of any Rastafarian testimony about Coral Gardens.

Second, and relatedly, the Ras argues that Franklin was a Rasta, while many other Rastafarians who offer testimony at the commemoration argue that he was not. The Ras emphasizes Franklin's *livity*—his gentleness with children and older community members, his willingness to share, his commitment to the well-being of black people—pointing out how people were drawn to him as a teacher and a faithful friend. This is a point that was corroborated by the former police officer Selbourne Reid when I spoke with him in Fort Lauderdale, where he is now living. Reid argued, in fact, that Franklin was a real leader among youth in the area because he "always shared" with the people. In contrast, other Rastafarians contend that Franklin gave "true" Rastafarians a bad name because he carried out a personal vendetta in a way that undoubtedly would have consequences for the larger community. Whether this is the case or not, it again reflects a particular positioning in which it is not the events that matter but the aftermath. Privileging the aftermath in this way serves specific goals that are not related to the past and the popularizing of a more inclusive, truer history, but are oriented toward the future and the development of community-wide agendas.

Gaps also exist, of course, between the Ras's version of events and the "official" story that appeared in the newspaper and during the trial. These gaps raise other sorts of issues that call into question the ways social hierarchies operate in Jamaica, the histories of these hierarchies in relation to colonialism and slavery, and the effects of these histories in terms of the extent to which the state and its security forces are perceived as legitimate. But I will say more about these issues below.

Discrepancies notwithstanding, it is nonetheless a fact that the events of Holy Thursday morning put into motion a series of processes because Franklin was *perceived* to be a Rastafarian, and his actions were *perceived* to be part of a more general revolt. This is what provoked the mass hysteria among neighbors and government officials, and this is what caused Prime Minister Bustamante to initiate a roundup campaign through which more than 150 Rastafarians from four parishes were arrested on charges that ranged from vagrancy and unlawful possession to being a suspected person, being in possession of dangerous drugs, and being in possession of dangerous weapons. Because of the limited accommodations of the Montego Bay police lockup, Rastafarians were taken to jails in towns as far away as Lucea (in the parish of Hanover), Savannah-la-Mar (in the parish of Westmoreland), and Falmouth (in the parish of Trelawny).[25] At a JLP meeting later that April, the prime minister justified these actions, arguing that it was his prerogative to call on the army when necessary: "'When I was officially told that the life of two policemen were snuffed out . . . I ordered the army down there, that's my right. I will order them again as often as it is necessary.'"[26] The week after the events at Coral Gardens, the government also began a campaign to eradicate the cultivation of ganja in Jamaica and conducted raids against those suspected of growing and distributing ganja.[27] The government also initiated a policy of eighteen-month minimum mandatory sentencing for anyone using or possessing ganja. For Hugh Small, Esq., son of the judge who presided over the case, these campaigns and policies have had long-term injurious effects on the population in general, in part because they were introduced just as Jamaica became an independent democratic country. Introducing mandatory minimum sentencing laws for ganja offences "along with other developments," he argues, "placed a tool in the hand of the Police to oppress persons who used ganja, even in the privacy of their homes, and to frame many persons." He continues, "It severely eroded confidence in the justice system from which it has not recovered" (e-mail communication, 11 January 2011). Rex Nettleford further argues that the war on ganja effectively became a war on Rastafari (Nettleford 1970). Because this is the period when Jamaica was also pioneering the mass tourism industry, we must understand these sorts of punitive actions not only in relation to the domestication of a local population, but also in terms of the pacification of an international audience.[28]

While there was overwhelming public sympathy for the actions of the police and the prime minister in the aftermath of Coral Gardens, there was also a degree of criticism. Not surprisingly, the most consistent organ of critique was *Public Opinion*, the weekly newspaper published between 1937 and 1974 by the PNP, then in opposition. It ran several editorials accusing the government of panicking and creating a situation in which "clean-living middleclass young men in St. Andrew Parish form themselves into a midnight militia, rounding up any stray gardener they find, beating the daylight out of him and sending him home or turning him over to the police who arrest him as a vagrant" (Maxwell 1963a). It also published a series of letters by Mortimo Planno, a Rastafarian elder, seeking to explain the vision of Rastafari (Planno 1963a, 1963b); excerpted a flyer that had been distributed by the "Militant Rastafarian Brethren Repatriation Front" that focused on the specific cause of Franklin's actions that Holy Thursday morning, bringing to light the instances of police harassment and torture of Rastafari (Maxwell 1963c); and reported that the Bar Association had initiated plans to investigate what had really happened at Coral Gardens ("Dennis Marshall's Seven Days" 1963).[29] However, while members of the PNP critiqued the government for the wholesale scapegoating and criminalization of Rastafari, they typically did so within the language of universal human rights and in that way reproduced the view that was put forward in the pioneering study sponsored by the University of the West Indies in 1960 that Rastafarians could—indeed, should—be assimilated into Jamaican society (rather than repatriated to Africa).[30] In other words, the dominant oppositional perspective was that Rastafarians "have rights just as the Christian Scientists, Roman Catholics and Jehovah Witnesses have rights" (Maxwell 1963c); that they were a "symptom" of more general problems within Jamaican society; and that while we should not attempt to stamp out Rastafari, we must "remove the conditions which create them . . . the poverty, filth, frustration and death that they are faced with" (Maxwell 1963a; see also Maxwell 1963d). These instances of public opposition seem to have fizzled fairly quickly. As a result, the only ongoing archive of the aftermath is that of the Rastas who experienced it.

LIVING OUTSIDE THE BODY POLITIC

Throughout 2007, I had casually been following the various events and debates that were related to the commemoration of the bicentenary of the British abolition of the slave trade in 1807. On 3 April, an article in the *Jamaica Gleaner* announced that on that very Friday—Good Friday, as it happened—survivors of the Coral Gardens incident would hold an anniversary commemorative "groundation" as part of the bicentenary calendar of events. I immediately called my friend Junior Wedderburn to see if he could travel with me on such short notice. Junior, a Rastafarian from Portland, Jamaica, has lived in the United States for twenty-five years. He was the musician for the dance company with which I had performed and now plays in the Broadway musical *The Lion King*, as well as with his own group, Ancient Vibrations, a dance and drumming company that showcases Afro-Jamaican drumming forms such as Kumina and Burru, some of the roots of reggae music. He rearranged his schedule and became my research partner.

During the plane ride, Junior confessed that, although he and the older Rastafarians who mentored him were no strangers to harassment at the hands of the police and other agents of the state, he had never heard about Coral Gardens or about the suffering of the elders there in 1963. In part, he felt that this was the result of the particularly uneasy structural position of families like his when he was growing up. Working-class black people throughout Jamaica who were reading or hearing about what happened at

Coral Gardens were likely to have felt sympathy for the Rases, he argued, because of a sense that the government's actions were motivated, at least in part, by a desire to undermine the development of black pride. However, because Rasta and black pride were so intertwined at the time, and because people like his parents saw Rasta as a fearful thing—even though they had been influenced in the development of their own black pride by movements such as Marcus Garvey's—they would not have wanted to discuss the incident for fear of driving their children toward Rasta. Moreover, as Junior saw it, Rastas, unlike Christians or Jews, never needed to mobilize the specter of suffering to attract new followers, so while stories of persecution were well known among the community, they were not positioned as foundational to the faith. At any rate, Junior was as eager as I to hear the stories, to try to find out "what really happened" on that fateful "Bad Friday," and to learn what kind of reparations were being envisioned.

We arrived in Montego Bay and made our way to Dump-Up Beach, where the commemoration was being held. At the gates of the venue were several food and clothing vendors, as well as a group of people playing kumina drums and singing. We stood outside for a while, checking out the scene and scanning the crowd for anyone who seemed to be involved with the day's events, someone we could talk with about what had happened during the days that followed Holy Thursday 1963. We were led to Empress Enid, who subsequently took us to Icient Iyah, and the three of us went to a nearby restaurant to talk.

They both shared their stories, which, like all narratives of extreme suffering, were harrowing. Ras Iyah, born on Emancipation Day (1 August) in 1936, told of being betrayed by people in his own community who felt emboldened by the prime minister's alleged order to bring in all Rastafarians "dead or alive." He remembered being tied to two other men and led down the road to police who were waiting there, beaten the whole way. The three men were tossed in the back of a truck and taken to a jail in another town because the one in his district was already full. Once there, police grabbed the men, tossing them into cells by their arms and legs. Cells that were made to hold three people held twenty-five and thirty men, who struggled to breathe fresh air while covered in their own blood and filth. For eighteen days they were only nominally fed, and for eighteen days they were tortured, beaten with the butts of guns, among other things. "What can I say about it?," Iyah asked Junior and me rhetorically. "Every cruelty that is done to any human being, police did to Rasta in that crucifixion." Finally, they were called before the court: "They said, 'now Rasta, you are brought up here for obstructing the police and their duty. So I and I said, 'Your honor, how could I and I obstruct police and their duty when there were no policemen present? It was the people that take the command . . . that take the law in their hands, and rope I and I, and beat I and I. . . . I and I don't have any charges; them that beat I and I have charge.'" After investigating Iyah's case more fully, and those of the two men who were tied to him, a judge set them free, finding no charges against them. Iyah was finally released from prison, but the effects of those beatings are still visible in the scars on his body and the uncertainty of his gait.

Empress Enid, who was born in Montego Bay in 1932, was in her last trimester of a pregnancy in April 1963. She remembered that, on that Thursday morning, she woke up and heard people saying, "Rasta kill police"; that war was breaking out between Rasta and police. She did not believe this right away, but by that evening, the rumors had spread enough for her to become worried, and at 4 A.M. the next day, she heard a police van roll up close to her gate and stop. At that time, she said, she was still "combsome," but her child's father was dreadlocked, so they jumped out of bed. Unsure of what to do, and unable to run or hide because it was so late in her pregnancy, she decided to hide her husband inside the house. She took the mattress off the bed, leaned it up in the corner of their room, and tied him inside it. She then went outside. "I up and down," she remembered, "and up and down. I rub the belly and I ball, I rub the belly and I ball." The police came to the gate, but they did not enter. "King Selassie keep dem weh," she said.

Later that day, she rested near the standpipe in her community and watched the police shoot a Rastaman as he was going up the steps nearby. They shot him three times, then continued to beat him, she said, "until him discharge." Only then did they take him to jail. Later, she went to the jail and saw all of the Rastafarians out in the hot sun of the yard being beaten. When they asked for water, they were sprayed with hoses. She could not stand to watch and went home to give her husband, still inside the mattress, water and food. That night, she went into labor prematurely. "I bleed like a cow," she said. "When I start bleed, I bleed so 'til I white like a piece of white marl. . . . I bleed, me mean seh me bleed out heavy blood. . . . And the Saturday nine o'clock the baby come, but I never have any strength because all the blood gone. I was weak, so weak I couldn't stand up. That baby lived seven days and take three spoon of tea for the seven days, and him die." The next Monday, things had died down, and the child's father was on his bicycle returning to work. The police removed him from his bicycle and arrested him. On Wednesday, they took him to court and fined him $500 for disorderly conduct.

Other accounts of these events are available but difficult to find.[31] In June 1963, John Maxwell, then the editor of *Public Opinion*, published the testimony of William Cole of Trelawny, a Rastafarian artist:

> At about 3 o'clock on Good Friday "a body of people come down on me with gun and stick and started to break the house door with a force, and demands me out of the house. My wife get frighten and run with the baby. They come into the house and find me under the bed because I heard them crying for me to come out so they could beat me. . . . [A] man lift up the sheet of the bed and point his gun at me and I came out. They start with their stick dem and they gun to murder me in the worst condition. Then they take me away to the Deeside lockup."
>
> "They say 'we locking up all you people who carry beard.'"
>
> From Deeside he was taken to Wakefield where he was manacled to another Rastafarian, Vincent Ellis, who had been trying to buy a ticket to see a film at the Wakefield movie-house when he was "captured." On the way to Falmouth, Mr. Cole said, "the same continually murderation was going on in the police transport. They mashed out my toenail with their police boots, spit in my face and juk me with they batons. But the worst position was in Falmouth.
>
> "At Falmouth they asked me my name and I told them and they began again to murder me and Ellis all the while telling us 'go back where you come from.' It was about 15 to 16 of them was in the station beating us. One of them was a police in uniform.
>
> "Some of them had batons and some had all kind of big stick and it was in the station there that they try to kill us. They beat us until Ellis' foot swell big so, and they beat me until my hand burs' and they break my knee-cap besides which they hit me in my back so bad that my semen run out of my line for three days straight."

He lost consciousness in the police wagon on the way to Montego Bay but they continued to beat him according to his fellow prisoner Ellis who was still shackled to him.

About three days after he was jailed at Montego Bay he lost consciousness in the cell. "The prisoners shouted out that I was dead and the police got a doctor to see me. He said I should get three days hospital treatment but the police only close the door and left me there.

"In the cell there were about 18 of us and three bunks. Some of us slept on the bunks, taking turns according to who was most badly hurt, most of us slept on the concrete, resting our heads on each other for pillow. Some had to stand up because we couldn't all sleep at the same time. We had to sleep in shifts. Those that were standing up sang and talked to keep themselves awake."

William Cole was brought before the court about a week after he was jailed. He was charged with an unspecified breach of the Road Traffic Law . . . He was granted £25 bail and was bailed by a relative of his wife's.

He went to a doctor and was treated for his injured hand which was so mangled that the bone was affected. The doctor treated him for his other injuries.

He then employed a lawyer and when he went to court the second time he found that the charge had been altered and was now "Contemplating of creating war," in his words. His lawyer, Hewart Henriques, successfully argued that no evidence had been presented, no accusers had appeared and Mr. Cole was freed . . .

It was not until he had been in jail for some days that William Cole was able to get any clear idea of what had caused him to be taken there along with all the other Rases. "We got to understand what happen at Rose Hall and we got to understand that Bustamante said to bring in all Rastas dead or alive." (Maxwell 1963b)

Michael Kuelker, a professor of English at St. Charles Community College in St. Peters, Missouri, published an account by Prince Elijah Williams, part of a more general oral history of Rastafari:

At the time of the Coral Gardens insolence, I-man was 20 years old. I never know where they call Coral Garden.

Thursday evening, April 1963, some of the people around seh, "Prince, why you nah go trim? You know, police pon Rasta in a conflict inna Montego Bay." I say, "Fi wha?" These were people who live in the Wakesfield community and work in Montego Bay. They see I pass when I leave form mi yard, go a shop or go a market. Gas station burn in Coral Garden, policeman get shot. They say, "Wha'appen, Prince? You nah go trim? You nah go shave?" I have my precept, my dreadlocks. I reply to dem seh, "If dem in conflict with police inna Montego Bay, a dem nah Rasta. Look over and we inna Trelawny." How could I be guilty of wheh dem do in Montego Bay? I say, "No mahn, I nah go trim." Why should I trim?

That was Holy Thursday. On Friday morning, the sound come through the bed I lay pon. I look through the window and see gun and bayonet. When they come out of the main, the road going to Falmouth, that's where the police get out of their unit and take it on their foot. A whole heap of police, some from Montego Bay.

Skenchie, my son, was about six-week-old. Ruth were there bathing him, and I lie down pon the bed. The place was silent. And then you can hear the sound from the horses' feet running on the ground. I hear the sound of these big bulls of Bashan, men of war. When I hold up my head and look through the window, it was an army going to war. . . .

I watch the bayonet glitter against the sun ball. The bayonet and the gun, the crash helmet they have on, likewise glittering in the sun. Going to war, *Roman soldiers going to war* against people who have *no* ammunition, no weapon, not even stone.

I run from deh, go through the cow pasture, so as to go tell the rest of bredren-dem. . . . We see them gather and they were down on us like dead meat. The community—puppa, momma, breddah, sista, auntie, cousin, in-law, everyone—the people the police get load up truck, drive in a car, ride bicycle, ride motorbike and pon foot. Our own brothers and sisters hungry fi destroy I-n-I structure. When I hear the beating and the dragging foot pon the earth, I know they come fi Rasta.

It became late, about 4:30 or 5 o'clock. Mi listen to the people when they talk while me sit down in the cane fields. The cane field, that's where I give up I-self. I catch the voice of one of the district constables, one who is not that wicked. I call him by name, William Talk, from Friendship, and he said to I seh, "A who dat? Prince?" "Yes, mahn." By the time I reach him, I am taken by the civilians, and nuff lick and nuff kicks and nuff box. When I reach the barbed wire, they nah bother to lift me up, just draw I between the barbed wire. Bust mi two foot, nuff cut, pure blood. A nuff blood they take from I structure. The same people I grow amongst, eat with, talk with, drink with everyday.

I come like a dead stranger to what they told me later.

That morning, mi family were brutally hangled. Ruth were made to stand in the sun. If she were to falter and sit, they were ready to strike her. She and mi son, Skenchie, at that time six weeks old, burned up in the sun the whole day. The police-dem and civilian woman comb out Ruth's locks. I see fi I-self. She had nuff locks. Combed out one by one. In 1963 we were well covered with locks.

These are the torture that Babylon bring upon Rasta. Blameless Rasta. I never think seh the people-deh would handle dem so. (Williams 2005: 7–10)

The elders I have had the opportunity to track down and interview with Junior Wedderburn and Ras Junior Manning, who until his death in March 2010 was the principal organizer of the Coral Gardens commemoration, offer variations on these themes: beatings with batons so hard and so extensive that the police themselves came away with marks on their own arms from the ricochet; stoning and the mashing of toes with gun butts; and trimming, or the removal of beards and hair with any instrument available, from broken bottles to knives and machetes. Their testimonies share a framing of the aftermath of the Coral Gardens events as an epic war between the forces of good and evil. Here, it is not only the police but also those civilians mobilized by the police who become "Roman soldiers"— those representatives of a pagan society, also indexed by Rastas as "Babylon,"[32] who bullied Christians and were thus destined to fall. Like Christ, Rastafarians are persecuted and betrayed by those they know, subjected to extraordinary physical harm both directly and indirectly. The injustices done are rendered bureaucratic through the most inconsequential pedestrian resolutions—a fine levied here, a petty charge there. Nevertheless, at the annual commemoration of the suffering of those elder Rastafarians who were affected by the aftermath of the Coral Gardens affair, there are no victims, only resurrected soldiers. There, the elders' stories become performances: familiar phrasings are repeated; the rhythmic crafting of particular cadences are punctuated by rhetorical flourishes. "Rasta suffer bad, bad," they shout, and the public memorializing becomes a generative force, a form of reparation and redemption through which the bonds of community are energized. Rasta, they assert with pride, once persecuted and maligned, is now the symbol through which Jamaica is most recognized across the world. Job persevered, and his fortunes were restored.

It is worth pointing out that the brutal terror these elders describe refers, of course, to only the most visible and coordinated harassment of Rastafarians. Those who came to Rasta in the 1940s and 1950s, and straight up through the 1970s, experienced random acts of terrorism by the Jamaican state, acts that in part served to solidify a sense of collective identity (Price 2009).[33] Many elders speak of emerging from nyabinghi rituals only to encounter the police, who would then arrest them and shave off their locks. Others recall being seized and beaten for no reason; evicted from their homes; fired from their jobs; and chased down, stoned, and tortured by both civilians and police, the latter of whom also had individual Rastafarians under surveillance and sometimes broke up meetings and marches (Chevannes 1994). Indeed, Reid (2009: 89) remembers that when he joined the police force a few years before Jamaica's independence, images of bearded Rasta men were used during target practice to stand in for the face of a criminal. And as recently as the 1980s and 1990s, examples abound of elders being denied entrance to public businesses or Rastafarian children being removed from prestigious schools because they refused to trim their hair. Although to a millennial international public Rasta has come to symbolize peace, love, and unity, to a mid-twentieth-century Jamaican public, Rastafarians' radicalism evoked fear—indeed, dread—because from their emergence in the 1930s through the first decade of independence, Rastafarians were seen as a threat to the consolidation of the Jamaican state, particularly after the outbreak of the Second World War, when marches and meetings led by Rastafarians were suppressed because they were thought to heighten racial tensions (Jan van Dyck 1995). As a result, they marked the boundaries of citizenship during both the colonial and immediate postcolonial periods.

This perceived threat was largely based on the Rastafarians' early rejection of the authority of the British monarchy (and, later, of the Jamaican nationalist state) and their allegiance to His Imperial Majesty Haile Selassie, who was crowned emperor of Ethiopia in 1930. Like many diasporic blacks in the early decades of the twentieth century who embraced various forms of Ethiopianism, pan-Africanism, and internationalism, Rastafarians espoused an ethic of black self-determination that inverted the colonial order, advocating for a type of black supremacy (Hill 1983; Maragh 2007 [1935]; Pettersburgh 2003 [1926]). As Rupert Lewis (1998: 154) has pointed out, they did so within a social milieu in which "the racist attitudes of the white landowning and merchant class, the colorist behavior of the brown people, and the hankering of black Jamaicans after lighter skin color formed a dominant ethos." Even among black peasants, Lewis notes, admiration of and loyalty to plantation owners and the British Crown was strong. Within this context, it was not only the government but also ordinary Jamaicans who came to view Rastafarians as hoodlums. For example, Frank Jan van Dyck (1995: 71) reminds us that in 1951, after a "bearded man" murdered Sidney Garrell and attacked his girlfriend, Bernadette Hugh, as they were enjoying the beach off Palisadoes Road in Kingston, extensive public resentment and hostility was expressed toward Rastafarians, not only by elites, but also by dockworkers on Kingston's waterfront who went on strike, he writes, "because they refused to work with bearded men from squatter areas any longer." Indeed, Jan van Dyck (1995: 71) quotes workers from newspaper reports at the time saying the Rastas should "go away, shave their beards and mend their ways."

This view of Rastafarians as hoodlums was only reinforced by events such as Prince Emmanuel's all-island convention in 1958, a nyabinghi that was to have culminated in a return to Africa, for which brethren had prepared by selling all their belongings; the Coronation Market riots of 1959; Reverend Claudius Henry's repatriation attempt in 1959, for which he sold as many as 15,000 tickets at a shilling each without ships' materializing on the appointed day; and Henry's subsequent plan to train an army that would deliver the Jamaican state to Fidel Castro before repatriating to Africa in 1960.[34] Moreover, some held a view that Rastafarians were also involved with radical political youth movements. Reid (2009: 91–93) explains that Franklin and his men worked at the Public Works machine shop on Hart Street in Montego Bay and that police believed a connection existed between the Marxist-Leninist Young Communist League based in the Allman Town section of Kingston and the Hart Street shop.

Because of events and connections such as these, and because of anticolonial insurgencies occurring outside Jamaica, including the Mau Mau Rebellion in Kenya (1953–60) and the Zanzibar Revolt (January 1964) — events that were seen to influence Rastafarians — Rastafarians became associated with criminality and violence (Nettleford 1970; Simpson 1998). The

Mau Mau Rebellion in particular was cause for concern because it is often cited as providing the impetus for Rastafarians to begin wearing dreadlocks. This insurgency was given a fair amount of coverage in the Jamaican press (see, for example, "The Mau Mau in Kenya" 1954). The Zanzibar Revolt was also a critical source of inspiration for Rastafarians, and at least one Ras claims that the leaders of that revolt, John Okello and Abdul Rahman Mohammed Babu, wore dreadlocks (Ras Maurice Clarke, testimony given to Jake Homiak, 23 January 2005). In other words, there was also an internationalist framework of black revolution within which the government and ordinary Jamaicans interpreted the events at Coral Gardens. And, of course, some Rastafarians themselves also assessed what happened at Coral Gardens in terms of such events. Mortimo Planno's autobiographical essay *The Earth's Most Strangest Man: The Rastafarian* contains a description of what happened at Coral Gardens that includes the following passage: "It was said like in real Mau Mau fashion the Rastafarian hid and attack the police who had summon reinforcement from Montego Bay" (1969).

Despite the fact that Rastafarians' early calls for reparations and repatriation were not generally welcomed — especially not among the ruling classes within Jamaican society — they became foundational ideological tenets of the movement. During the trial after his arrest for sedition in 1934, Robert Hinds, who with Leonard Howell was one of the founders of Rastafari, argued that the 20 million pounds sterling that had been granted to Jamaica after emancipation was supposed to have been earmarked for the repatriation of the former slaves, not to compensate slave owners for their so-called loss of property (Owens 1976: 16; see also Nettleford 1970: 66; Simpson 1998: 225). Repatriation here was seen as a form of reparation. Of course, this kind of accounting for slavery is still current. As recently as 2004, the Rastafarian Nation in Jamaica, a consortium of the Jamaica Reparation Movement, the Ethiopian Orthodox Church, and the UNIA, created an invoice that placed the value of reparations due them at 7.9 trillion Jamaican dollars. This money represented a mere fraction of the US$770 trillion that was put forward at the Reparations Conference in Ghana in 2000 as fair compensation for all of the descendants of Africans who were traded to the New World as slaves. Nevertheless, the funds were to provide the necessary resources for 500,000 Rastafarians to resettle on the African continent (Jackson 2004).

Both Stuart Hall and Randall Robinson, founder and former president of the Trans-Africa Forum, have framed debates about reparations and repatriation in terms of identity. Robinson (2001: 56) argues that the experience of slavery led to a kind of cultural death for African Americans, which in turn has led to an erasure of black presences and achievements and thus to a gnawing set of questions: Who am I? What is my history? What is my culture? For Robinson, the fight for reparations is the only way to reverse the psychological, political, and material consequences of slavery because it is only through the acknowledgment of slavery's legacy that black identities can be reclaimed and black histories can be rewritten. Similarly, Hall, reflecting in a radio interview he conducted with a Rastafarian elder, argues that the quest for reparations and repatriation has been rooted in the refashioning of an identity, again to re-vision Jamaica's history. "The point," he argues, "was not that some people, a few, could only live with themselves and discover their identities by literally going back to Africa . . . but that a whole people symbolically re-engaged with an experience that enabled them to find a language in which they could retell and appropriate their own histories" (Hall 2001: 36–37). For both, a common formulation grounds their understanding of the role of identity in political struggles: to understand our present and imagine our futures, we must know our pasts.

Yet for Rastafarians, the search for identity is not primarily what has grounded their arguments for reparations and repatriation. As several scholars have argued, early Rastafarians did not have the identity problem that characterized other Jamaicans leading up to independence (Nettleford 1970; Norris 1962). They knew they were "African," and they preached about the racist evils of slavery and imperialism, defying the norms of so-called polite society. In fact, it was Rastas, as Barry Chevannes (1990) and Rex Nettleford (1970) both argued long ago, who kick-started Jamaicans into thinking about, and even valuing, their African heritage (see also Bogues 2003). Yet, their assertions of an African identity and their professed allegiance to Haile Selassie were only part of what was seen to challenge the consolidation of Jamaican nationalism in the mid-twentieth century. It was their critique of capitalist development models—a critique that was embodied and lived, not merely stated—that was equally critical in placing them beyond the boundaries of citizenship during that period, making them a threat to the body politic and ultimately causing the government's panicked overreaction to the events at Coral Gardens in 1963.

After the region-wide labor riots in the late 1930s and the subsequent analysis of these riots by the West India Royal Commission, a particular notion of citizenship became hegemonic and was institutionalized through the creation in 1941 of the Office of Colonial Development and Welfare. As I noted in chapter 2, the commission's report argued that one of the causes of the region's labor problems was a "dysfunctional" family structure among poor and working-class black West Indians. For the report's authors, dysfunctional families generated a lack of economic productivity and motivation and, therefore, a lack of ability to participate politically in an engaged and thoughtful way. To move the West Indian colonies toward independence, then, the Office of Colonial Development and Welfare was to see to improvements in housing, education, public health and to land resettlement, and to foster more responsible parenting and sexual restraint. Encouraging the development of respectable wage-laboring households with a male breadwinner at the helm and a female helpmate who managed the domestic sphere was seen as critical to creating citizens who would have a stake in the economic and political systems of an independent nation-state, whose primary economic development strategy, by the late 1950s, would become that of industrialization by invitation. Further, these citizens would accept and profess the nationalist ideology that ultimately became hegemonic—that of creole multiracialism—to move forward as a unified nation.

Rastafarians rejected several aspects of this logic—most notably, that they should profess loyalty to an independent Jamaican state (represented by many Rastafarians as an earthly hell) and that they should involve themselves as wage laborers in a capitalist economy (Price 2003). Their rejection of the modernist model of development placed them outside the boundaries of citizenship as it was defined in the mid-twentieth century. As a result, they suffered continual harassment at the hands of the police and other security forces, both in Jamaica and in the United States. Early leaders were imprisoned for sedition or hospitalized for lunacy (Nettleford 1970); Howell's settlement at Pinnacle was raided consistently between its establishment in 1940 and its ultimate dismantling in 1954, and, of course, in 1963 both civilians and the police followed the order attributed to Bustamante: "Shoot first; ask questions later."

Today, however, the context is much changed. Rasta is known throughout the world largely because of reggae music, Jamaicans' consciousness of an African identity (or, at least, pride in blackness) has become relatively taken for granted (the popularity of bleaching creams notwithstanding[35]), the hegemony of creole multiracial nationalism has weakened (Meeks 1994; Scott 1999; D. Thomas 2004), and respectability is no longer the only measure of citizenship (Bogues 2002). More broadly, the post–Cold War neoliberal moment, while exacerbating inequalities globally and domestically, has also created new spaces through which individuals and groups can claim rights to citizenship. One of these spaces is the language of international human rights, through which claims for reparations have been newly forged.

REPARATIONS AND RECONCILIATIONS

In February 2007, as part of the events and discussions linked to the bicentenary of the abolition of the British slave trade, the Jamaican Parliament began a debate regarding reparations. Mike Henry, the JLP's member of Parliament for Central Clarendon and a longtime supporter of both reparations and Rastafari, argued for the establishment of a committee that would determine both the exact form and the amount of reparations. Citing the precedents of Germany's payments to individual Jews and to the State of Israel after the Second World War and the plans afoot to sue the Japanese government for the systematic murder of Chinese and for the forcing of Korean women into prostitution during that war, Henry contended that reparations would help soothe both the material and the mental legacies of slavery (Campbell 2007; "Henry Bats for Reparation" 2007). Henry was also at the commemoration of the Coral Gardens incident in 2007. There, he asked Rastas for forgiveness as a government representative — indeed, as a representative of the party that was in government in 1963 — and asserted that while it was important to seek reparations from England for the brutality of the slave trade, it was also critical to seek reparations in Jamaica (Hines 2007). Although many Rastafarians were suspicious about the motives behind Henry's support, his reasoning on this topic was well received.

But what would constitute appropriate measures of reparation for the Rastafarians who were directly affected by the aftermath of the events in Coral Gardens? Would it be servicing the national debt or the development of an educational foundation, as it was for so many of those who wrote into the newspapers with their ideas of how reparations money would be best used (see, for example, Barnett 2007; Global Afrikan Congress 2007; Lawton 2007)? Would it be the establishment of a Truth and Reconciliation Commission that would force public acknowledgment of the role of politicians in the establishment of garrison communities (see, for example, Morgan 2007; Rattray 2007)? At the commemoration in 2007, while talking with Icient Iyah and Empress Enid, Junior and I asked what they felt would constitute reparations for what they—individually and as a community of Rases—had experienced. First, despite their skepticism about what an official apology could do for them, they argued that a government apology was necessary. This, of course, echoed the call made by Ras Junior Manning, the organizer of the commemoration, for "an apology in words and actions," itself an attempt to "set the record straight about what really happened in 1963 and present the facts in black and white" (Manning, quoted in Roxborough-Wright 2007). This call was picked up by the daily *Observer*, which printed an editorial on the following day urging Jamaicans to see the Coral Gardens commemoration as an impetus toward "an honest assessment of Rastafari and how as a nation we have treated with the movement" ("Time for Honest Assessment of Rastafari" 2007). The editorial concluded, "A nation now deeply involved in exploring the experience of slavery should do no less."

Beyond the official apology, the elders with whom I spoke argued that land grants would be an appropriate form of reparation. "From I and I have land," Iyah stated, "I and I can solve domestic and financial problems." Enid concurred. "Give Rastas free access to land," she said. "They ought to give us repatriation. But at the same time, we are not leaving here until we get equal rights and justice." When I asked what justice would look like in this particular case, she said, "Repatriate us to our homeland. . . . Repatriate us in Jamaica." In some ways, Enid's comments here seem to reflect a more general trend noted by many observers that after Selassie's passing, some Rastafarians began to de-emphasize the ideological tenet of repatriation to Africa, stressing instead the pursuit of social justice within Jamaica (Barrett 1988; Chevannes 1990; Murrell 1998). To a degree, this observation also reflects the hegemonic position of the Jamaican state on the matter, which has been oriented toward assimilating Rastafarians into an acceptance of Jamaican nationhood (Smith et al. 1960). Although a government-sponsored mission that included two Rastafarians was sent to Africa following the release of the University of the West Indies study in 1960, there has never been sustained formal support at the state level for the project of repatriation. By the late 1970s, repatriation had become somewhat more uncertain as a foundational principle among Rastafarians themselves due to changing conditions in Ethiopia (Yawney 1978). Nevertheless, the Nyabinghi Order never really shied away from its emphasis on repatriation, and Yawney and Homiak have both argued that the globalization of the Rastafari movement has led not only to an intensification of demands for repatriation, but also to a more generally supportive climate for these demands because of the current popularity of the language of international human rights. Their sense is that the contemporary political climate is more conducive than ever to serious consideration of repatriation (Homiak 1985, 2001; Yawney 2001). However, moving toward the goal of repatriation and agitating for social justice within Jamaica are not seen among Rases as mutually exclusive projects, so when people talk about pursuing land, justice, and development within Jamaica, that does not preclude an assumption that repatriation is the ultimate end, both spiritually and physically.

However, there is something more to be said about this emphasis on land within Jamaica, especially in the present, when landownership and farming seem to generate less interest among young Jamaicans. In part, the privileging of landownership evokes the discourse of both missionaries in the immediate post-emancipation period and nationalist elites in the mid-twentieth century, for whom living on the land conjured idealized images of Jamaicans—Diane Austin-Broos's (1992) "Christian Blacks" or Catherine Hall's (1995) "respectable peasants"—who were independent, self-sufficient, and eager to respect the leadership of a moderate middle-class nationalist party. Even those less eager to define leadership in these terms were anxious to sit under their own "vine and fig tree" following the abolition of slavery. These are the populations Mimi Sheller (2000) has called black publics, those peasants who forged a vibrant political culture based on a radical vision of democracy and a critique of unbridled market capitalism.

However, the emphasis on land also reinforces Rastafarians' earlier anti-capitalist critique, their resistance to tethering their futures to the whims of a neoliberal global market that privileges movement, entrepreneurship, and individualism. In part, this is due to their history of continuous forced displacement and harassment at the hands of the Jamaican state. Within this context, landownership became important in relation to establishing communal spaces "over which they exercised a modicum of jurisdictional control." These spaces could not, of course, fully withstand either an outright onslaught or a more clandestine co-optation by the state, but the control Rastafarians could mobilize within them "is embedded in the Rasta ethos of the counter-nation they represent in exile."[36] Incidentally, we should not think of the kind of rooting or grounding that is inherent in the notion of rural retreat as an eschewal of internationalization. Rasta, like other contemporary phenomena, is a globalized movement that takes differ-ent forms in different locations and forges international alliances through various conferences, consultations, and trods. Moreover, nyabinghis and other Rastafarian events are attended not only by Rastafarians near and far but also by international guests and visitors. In other words, Rastafarian Jamaica — whether urban or rural — is also fully globalized, in terms of ad-herents, technology, and outlook. Nevertheless, what is most critical for our purposes here is that Icient Iyah's and Empress Enid's focus on land-based reparations forces a deeper look at the patterns of land distribution after the abolition of slavery and how these patterns contributed to a process of class formation nationally that would continue to structurally marginalize black Jamaicans. By tracking this national process in relation to contempo-rary global shifts, we gain insight into the sorts of futures that are currently being imagined.

THE POLITICAL ECONOMY OF MILLENNIAL CONVICTIONS

In Jamaica, the sector of society that has produced not only Rastafari but also Revivalism and other Afro-Jamaican forms of religious expression is descended from the poorest sector of the post-emancipation peasantry. In his seminal text tracing the roots of Rastafari, Barry Chevannes (1994) outlines the twists and turns of this black peasant class from the period of emancipation through the early twentieth century. Drawing from Gisela Eisner's study of Jamaica's economy from 1830 to 1930 (Eisner 1961), he shows that in the three decades after emancipation, the number of small-holdings (less than forty acres) increased exponentially. In part, this is the result of the financial downturn the landholding class faced after the Sugar Duties Act was passed in 1846, which forced many planters to break up their large estates. But the growth of the post-emancipation peasantry was also due to the formation of free villages by the nonconformist churches at the time. These villages were created by missionaries who bought the pro-vision grounds that planters had begun to sell off, in the hope of forcing former slaves to work under conditions of quasi-slavery, and resold them in small lots to the people. Peasant communities began to thrive — even where peasants were forced to supplement their labor on their own plots by working on nearby plantations — and these communities became the primary counterpoints to the plantation system (Chevannes 1994: 4; see also Besson 2002). Even after the Morant Bay Rebellion in 1865 — the only instance during the nineteenth century of black peasants' taking up arms against the state, resulting in the removal of local government and the establishment of Crown Colony rule — the growth of this peasant class was encouraged by the creation of banks for farmers and the establishment of the Jamaica Agricultural Society. "By 1930," Chevannes (1994: 5) writes, "there were over 180,000 holdings of less than fifty acres each, of which 85 percent were less than five acres."

However, this growth would not be sustained. The lowest stratum of the peasantry, among whom squatting was the primary means of land tenure, began to lose its foothold and by 1961, "holdings of five acres and less had declined by 26 percent" (Chevannes 1994: 5–6). This decline coincided with an increase in the number of larger peasant holdings, a coincidence that highlights a more general process of social differentiation in the post-emancipation period: while the more successful peasants who accumulated land and animals and owned the cottages in which they lived became the backbone of the emergent banana and coffee industries, poorer peasants lost their squatting privileges, were forced into tenant relations with the larger banana estates on which they labored, and became more and more impoverished. The paths followed by more and less successful peasants would diverge even more sharply as some members of the more successful peasantry became teachers, ministers, or civil servants, joining the ranks of the lower middle classes by taking advantage of the new education measures put into place by both churches and a post–Morant Bay colonial government.

Yet although education provided a path to upward social mobility for these peasants, this mobility was not equally available to all Jamaicans. In his study of social mobility between 1943 and 1984, Derek Gordon demonstrated that black Jamaicans as a whole experienced slower upward social mobility than lighter-skinned Jamaicans (Gordon 1991, cited in Chevannes 1994: 7). Moreover, intensifying rural impoverishment encouraged the poorer stratum of black peasants to migrate — both overseas to work in Central America, Cuba, the United States, and Panama (Eisner 1961) and domestically to urban centers throughout Jamaica and, ultimately, to Kingston (Clarke 1975). Between 1921 and 1943, Kingston's population more than doubled, growing again by 86 percent between 1943 and 1960 to nearly a half-million, more or less the same as it is today (Chevannes 1994: 16). Many of these urban migrants—among them many who would come to espouse Rastafarian livity—squatted in western Kingston and the adjacent areas of St. Andrew, creating some of the "ghetto areas" I discussed in chapter 1.

As I have already noted, the argument proffered by several commentators is that these areas—having been armed and mobilized by political leaders throughout the post-independence period and, in many cases, denuded of the basic institutions of social reproduction, such as schools, child-care centers, and health-care clinics—have fostered a "culture of violence." This culturalist discourse regarding the reproduction of violence in Jamaica is akin to that attributed to inner-city areas in the United States and similarly blames the victims of structural marginalization for perpetuating their own marginality. Yet it is worth pointing out that most accounts of the development of garrison (and post-garrison) communities—even those that are sympathetic to a political economic approach and those that tie their creation to processes of postcolonial nation building—do not tend to link their creation and manipulation directly to the history of landlessness and to processes of class formation among black Jamaicans during and after slavery, as I attempted to demonstrate in chapter 1. This is what a reparations framework can foreground. It destabilizes the notion that violence is a cultural attribute and instead emphasizes how poverty and privilege are generated through the societal institutions created as the result of nationalist and other agendas, themselves shaped by global forces.

Of course, these forces—both local and global—also shape how people experience, remember, and mobilize their histories. In other words, Rastafarians highlight the pain and suffering endured by those who were rounded up after the events at Coral Gardens at the annual commemoration to generate support for reparations from the Jamaican government to the Rastafarian community and, now, to reposition themselves in relation to both national and transnational approaches to development and citizenship. This is done through a performative strategy that is apprehended by members of the community as a means of strengthening relations and establishing eldership, a strategy that is also currently directing Rastafarians to consider the idea of reparations in a new light.

ENGAGING BABYLON

The stories that Incient Iyah and Empress Enid and other elder Rases pass on to those who listen—the stories they perform publicly year after year at the annual commemoration—should no longer be the focus of any inquiry into the status of Rastafarians who were persecuted after the Coral Gardens incident in 1963. This is what I was told during the summer of 2008. Enid, herself an extremely forceful performer, told Junior Manning after the commemoration in 2008 that it would be her last appearance on stage because she did not want to keep doing the same thing year after year if nothing changed as a result. And Iyah's "son" Eddie "First Man" Wray said he was not so sure about the ongoing emphasis on the past, the drive to relive these events over and over. Instead, he wanted me to focus on the right now, and on the future, in whatever it was I was writing. He told me this in July. I had gone to Kingston to present preliminary ideas about the meanings of their call for reparations from the Jamaican government at the International Association of Cultural Studies conference in Kingston. Afterward, I traveled with Junior and my family to Montego Bay to spend more time talking with Iyah and Enid. Eddie Wray was at my panel, the third of the day in a series called "Rastafari in the New Millennium." He told me that in talking about potential connections between Rasta and the government within the context of reparations, I had hit a nerve.

This is, of course, because of the early doctrinal resistance to participation in state-centered politics, despite Sam Brown's establishment of a Rastafarian political party in 1961 and more recent efforts by the Rastafarian Centralization Organization to field candidates in local and national elections. But Eddie Wray and many other Rastafarians were now seeking closer alliances with both the Jamaican government and international agencies and organizations. Lest we imagine this strictly as a generational phenomenon, with younger Rastafarians seeking to move beyond the older ways of doing things, the commemoration's organizer, Ras Junior Manning, also argued forcefully at the Coral Gardens commemoration in 2008 that the different branches of Rastafari needed to come together and work with the government to address issues important to the community.[37] "We are establishing a Coral Gardens Agitation Committee," he said, "to meet with government . . . to talk to the leader of this government about our own business." In part, Manning felt this was one way to "make sure that this government is answerable to what happened to Rasta in 1963." But he also entreated the audience, saying that, because this is a new millennium, Rasta is "taking it to a new gear." Eddie Wray concurred, putting the issue within an even broader context. "The reparations argument might be setting us up for a big joke," he cautioned, "because one day the European countries will say, 'But look how much money we've poured into this or that development project or investment. Rasta what? Where were you?'"

For this reason, he said, Rastafarians must engage the government because they are already being engaged by it—for example, through the general consumption tax; because the government sponsored the commemoration in 2008 by subsidizing the fee for the venue; and because Rasta is often mobilized as a defining element of "brand Jamaica." While it once may have seemed radical to disengage from "politricks" and the "shitstem," Wray argued, in today's world, real radicalism requires participating more fully. He maintained that Rasta must hold the Jamaican government accountable to formulate a policy vis-à-vis Rasta, "its own indigenous population," so that Rastafarians are part of any development agenda related to trade or tourism and so they are able to care for themselves and, in particular, for their elders and children.

Something should be said here about the framing of Rasta as Jamaica's indigenous population, since Wray is not the only one to do so. This is not only a bit of rhetorical sleight of hand, since the indigenous populations in Jamaica were largely exterminated by the time the British took the island from Spain in 1655. It is also an attempt to redefine "indigenous" as that which has been created and developed on Jamaican soil, though not necessarily prior to European conquest. In many ways, this is also the thrust behind the term "creole," a conceptual framework that has long defined citizenship and belonging for New World nationalists (see, for example, Brathwaite 1971a; Smith 1956, 1967).[38] Yet there is also something more to this redefinition as it relates to Rastafari. In the introduction to Father Joseph Owens's study *Dread* (1976), Nettleford argues that Rastafari is a "native-born and native-bred concentration of effort, drive, and will to bring about *fundamental transformation of an unjust society if not its total destruction*" (Owens 1976: ix; emphasis added). Nativeness here represents more than mixture, more than creative amalgamation within the context of violent stratification. It is mobilized instead to draw attention to a history of disenfranchisement—both politically and in relation to landownership. Redefining indigeneity in this way, then, gives teeth to the reframing of citizenship that Wray and others are envisioning. To position Rastafarians as "indigenous" is thus not only to emphasize their connection to land and their rejection of the technologies and simulacra that provide toxic structure to the modern condition or to focus on the aspects of their lifestyle that are rooted in a relationship to the natural landscape that few Jamaicans currently maintain. It is also to invert the usual hierarchies, to convince people around the world of the superiority of Rastafarians' lifestyle, which emphasizes what Ras K'admawe K'nife (2008), a lecturer at the University of the West Indies, calls "sustainable deep ecology."

For Wray and his business partners, aligning Rasta with indigeneity further represents a move toward forging connections with two global social movements: the worldwide indigenous rights movement and global environmentalism. They are interested in making these connections by capitalizing on Jamaica's tourism industry to create a more sustainable development model for Rastafari. St. Lucia regulates the percentage of local products that must be used in every tourist property, Wray noted, so why not develop a similar policy in Jamaica regarding the use of products made by Rastafarians? People are "product ready," he said, so developers should be required to invest in them. Moreover, he continued, Rasta has to find ways to take advantage of various European Union initiatives, even when the government is not doing so. As an example, he mentioned that the European Union had been offering money for the development of programs for indigenous populations. Since the money was there, he said, Rasta should have jumped on it, even though protecting indigenous rights was not a priority of the Jamaican government at the time.

As Wray's and others' initiatives demonstrate, it is not only the Jamaican government that certain Rastafarians are seeking to engage. They have also initiated contact with an international community of NGOs, lawyers, and social movements, in part through the formation of the Ethio-Africa Diaspora Union Millennium Council. The organization is conceived as "an interim Rastafari All-Mansion Government," with the purpose of unifying the various mansions of Rastafari and coordinating efforts among Rastafarians to interact with the government and the United Nations in the service of their own development goals (Ethio-Africa Diaspora Union Millennium Council Secretariat 2008). The council, established in June 2007, is registered as an NGO in Jamaica.[39] Among its many activities are three that directly relate to the discussions in these pages.

The first has to do with its efforts to protect the intellectual property of Rastafari. On its establishment, the council invited the World Intellectual Property Organization and a number of lawyers to think through ways to manage Rastafari intellectual property rights as an "indigenous culture" and to stop the exploitation of Rastafari imagery and cultural symbols internationally. Under recommendations from the South African indigenous-rights lawyer Roger Chennells, it is attempting to establish Rastafari trademarks through the Jamaican Intellectual Property Organization to help control the manufacture of products with Rastafarian imagery and to ensure that it is Rastafarians who benefit economically from the commercial use of their icons. Relatedly, the council is currently lobbying the government of Jamaica and working through international organizations (as well as with the Maroon Federation) to develop protections in relation to "indigenous" cultural heritage.

The second has to do, of course, with the council's work toward reparations and repatriation. In its report of the first year's activities, it mentions that the Caribbean Community (CARICOM), the government-to-government organization of Caribbean countries geared toward promoting economic integration and coordinating foreign policy, had been negotiating with the African Union, the government-to-government organization of African countries geared toward promoting integration, unity, and economic development, for the formation of a Sixth Region representing the diaspora. In the belief that Rastafari representation at the African Union is necessary not only to facilitate the goal of repatriation but also to assist African claims for reparations for slavery, the council has been holding ongoing meetings with the South African High Commission, which represents the African Union in Jamaica.

And third, the council has begun to support a number of programs related to cultural heritage and the protection and promotion of Rastafarians's livity, among them the development of a "Rastafarian Indigenous Village." Following on the council's efforts to establish an archive and Rastafari Heritage Centre at Pinnacle, the first Rastafari community founded by Leonard Howell, it is working toward collaborating with the IION (In-

The IION Station family. COURTESY OF MARCO DI FLORO.

digenous Initiatory Circle of Nature) Station Rases on the creation and management of this village, which is located in Montego Bay. Iyah, Wray, and Wray's partner, Arlene, have all been involved in the conceptualization and implementation of the village, which represents an effort to attract so-called intrepid tourists globally who are interested in spending a "day in the life of" — in this case, of Rastafarians. But it was Wray's other business partner, Ras Kanaka, who gave me a postcard describing the village itself. Kanaka had also attended my panel at the university conference and, like Wray, wanted to reason with me further about the future rather than the past and about how Rasta must engage with the government. We spoke together for a long time outside the library in the center of Montego Bay; then he casually handed Junior and me a postcard advertising the Rastafarian Indigenous Village.

On the front of the postcard is a photograph of the IION Station family dressed in coordinating outfits made from crocus bags, with insets of family members communing with nature, drumming, and enjoying the children. Contact information for the organizers appears below the photograph, and on the back, superimposed over a beautiful photograph of a bonfire, is the following description: "The Rastafari Indigenous Village will showcase

Jamaica's natural heritage and the Rastafari way of life, namely our culture, our music, our food and of course our indigenous herbs and spices. The Village will be an illustration of living in harmony." The postcard also lists the various attractions of the village, which is "comprised of homes, a school, a herbal farm, and a organic farm." It states that "there will be a donkey on site used to show the cane milling process," and that one can take a "tour of the property that points out the various fruit trees, herbs and spices, and their traditional uses and the benefits of each." The postcard also lists the "cultural experiences" one might have, including drumming, chanting, and dancing; highlights the river and activities park to enhance physical fitness; and offers a campsite "for those desirous of overnight stays in an indigenous setting" (the option to stay over has since been discontinued). Under the heading "Health–Wellness–Oneness" are the following items: bush baths, balms, cosmic channeling, spiritual healing, clairvoyance, organic foods and products, yoga fitness classes, food demonstrations and recipes, and wellness workshops. Finally, visitors will be able to buy various crafts, herbs, compact discs, handmade clothing, postcards, and items made from plants, as well as watch these crafts being made. Junior cringed when he first saw the postcard. "This," he asked, "is where we have come to?"

It is tempting to give these sorts of tourism-related initiatives a very cynical read. Some elder, and more purist, Rastafarians do, and the council itself recognizes that, while the village might generate substantial revenue for the Rastafari community, it also might "cause significant misunderstanding and misappropriation of Rastafari culture" (Ethio-Africa Diaspora Union Millennium Council Secretariat 2008). Our own training as cultural critics of one variety or another almost demands a certain skepticism here, because these kinds of efforts—whether spearheaded by multilateral organizations such as UNESCO, by nationalist institutions such as the Institute for Puerto Rican Culture or the Jamaica Cultural Development Commission, or by groups like these Rastafarians—reek of a kind of cultural essentialism, the kind that tends to emerge when cultural practices are showcased as part of some sort of "authentic" experience.[40] Culture, in this sense, becomes static, something to perform for insiders and outsiders alike to generate an interest in history and a sense of community (cf. Alexander Craft 2008). The cynicism only compounds when we consider that, although it is likely that there might be travelers who are genuinely interested in learning more about Rastafari, the majority of tourists visiting the Rastafarian Indigenous

Village might expect merely to participate in those aspects of Rastafari they feel they already know: listening to reggae music and smoking weed. But this kind of knee-jerk cynicism is too easy, particularly if we keep in mind that Rastafarians' principles regarding economic development have always been to capitalize on what is available, oriented toward community, and locally occurring. Within the context of Montego Bay, tourism is the only real game in town, so it stands to reason that this would be a privileged realm of economic action by and for Rastas.[41] In other words, we must see their engagement with the tourism industry not as sensational but as continuous with a more general Rastafarian philosophy on development.

When Junior and I first visited the village in November 2008, we asked Wray whether it was true that the first thing visitors asked for was weed. He laughed. He said that it was, which was why the first thing announced to visitors when they arrive is the no smoking policy. The village itself is located on a quiet piece of land on the Montego River that has been cleared and subsequently planted with the trees and locally grown roots, herbs, and flowers that are used for natural remedies and that are also shown to visitors. The village has a ten-year lease for the land in which the terms of the agreement with the owner are outlined, and the IION Station Rases have poured significant funds into the compound to date, outfitting it with a stage, tents, and an altar. Wray, Arlene, and Kanaka imagine that bringing the village to its full vision will cost them ten times the amount they have already invested, as they envision an on-site kitchen, computer stations with wireless transmission, and lodging and bath facilities. Nevertheless, foreigners have already been visiting, and the village, registered as a business, is advertised through the Jamaica Tourist Board as a destination to those who arrive by air and ship. Wray compares his "product" favorably to other tourist venues in Jamaica, and he, Junior, and I all laughed about the fact that Wray is so conversant with the language of tourism, something that seems anathema to older Rastafarian principles. For him and his partners, however, the goal is to develop the village as a business—ultimately one among many—that will enable the community to provide financial support in an organized and ongoing way for the care of elders and children. They consider this to be another form of reparations, and one that vindicates Rasta as prescient in relation to the contemporary focus on sustainability.

The overarching objectives of the village—centralization, coordination, and engagement—are also those of the Millennium Council, yet it is important to note that not all Rastafarians equally support these objectives. The Nyabinghi branch has perhaps been the most prominent and visual proponent of these efforts, and within that group, those who are involved in the activities in and around Montego Bay have been the most active. Nevertheless, because their mobilization in this regard represents such a marked departure from previous positions on citizenship and involvement with the government, it is important to imagine what this departure might signal on a broader scale. If, as Eddie Wray, Junior Manning, and others now argue, Rastafarians must pressure the Jamaican state to develop a formal policy on their behalf, and if certain elements of that policy are geared toward earmarking a percentage of the tourism business to members of the Rastafarian community, then we must view these arguments as calling for another form of reparations, a form that, moreover, vindicates Rasta as early adopters, as it were, of the contemporary global emphasis on sustainability. We must also eschew easy cynicism and instead think about what Rasta's shift from disengagement to engagement means in the contemporary context and, in the process, consider the kinds of engagement that are possible today, compared with those that might have been possible at other moments.

In other words, if during the modernist moment of the mid-twentieth century Rastafarians condemned the state, defined citizenship in relation to Africa, and refused wage labor and instead emphasized self-determination and self-sufficiency through a form of communal living, in the neoliberal era they seek greater recognition from and representation within the Jamaican state. And while they continue to emphasize self-determination and self-sufficiency, the means by which this might be realized have changed. Entrepreneurialism and innovation have become important values that are consistent with current hegemonic neoliberal ideologies (Ebron 2008; Freeman 2007). Of course, this is by no means a unique story, and the sorts of cultural tourism being organized by Rastafarians like Wray and Kanaka precisely represent the "ethno-futures" John and Jean Comaroff (2009: 6) have recently discussed. In this context, like so many others around the world, ethnicity is increasingly being commodified to serve the economic and social interests of ethnic groups themselves. In other words, the self-commodification of ethnicity is becoming a more frequently proposed development strategy through which consumers are invited to partake in cultural spectacle. Lest we imagine this phenomenon as a complete turn from explicit political mobilization, however, we must remember that, like other communities, this group of Rastafarians is also attempting to engage the state by pressuring it, in part through an emphasis on the legal incorporation of cultural difference (Comaroff and Comaroff 2009).[42] They do this not only by working with government agencies but also by developing contacts with multilateral organizations and global social movements through their work on intellectual property rights, environmentalism, and cultural heritage protection. Toward these ends, they are supported by an international team of lawyers and consultants, as well as by social contacts that span the globe.

In terms of the state's perspective on Rastafari, the same kind of harassment and terrorism that was directed toward the community in the early years is no longer as palpable. Yet even as the state is attempting to co-opt Rasta and its symbols to promote its tourism industry (as particular political parties also did in the 1970s to attract grassroots voters [Waters 1985]), new kinds of harassment have emerged, centered mainly on the issue of representation. That is, the Jamaican state wants to promote the image of Rasta in its tourism advertisements, but it wants a cleaned-up version (i.e., Rasta without the ganja), just as in earlier moments Caribbean states wanted to promote the image of the independent peasant but one whose clothes were not too tattered and whose hands were not too dirty. Although there may have been an opening during the period of democratic socialism in the 1970s when Rastafarians might have been supported at the highest levels in their efforts to pursue alternative community development models had they been inclined to engage the state, any contemporary engagement — like other aspects of development — too often must be framed in relation to tourism. This is the vexation of the neoliberal moment, a moment in which the benefits of citizenship are given to those entrepreneurial individuals whose innovation and pluck allow them access to rights formerly imagined as belonging to all members of the national body (Ong 2006).

Now, how might we think about these shifts in relation to reparations? These Rastafarians' engagement with global social movements and their mobilization of the language of international human rights provide a way for them to counter neoliberal claims to inclusivity. At once, those involved in the Coral Gardens commemoration and the Millennium Council demand that long-terrorized groups be recognized and that both their contributions and their suffering be contextualized in relation to ongoing processes of state formation that are carried out locally but often developed transnationally. This vision of reparations still embodies a counter-discourse; it still provides the means by which contemporary inequalities are historicized. For them, the claim for reparations is not just a claim for compensation. Rather, the quantification of redress is a strategy for recognition and an argument for understanding violence as an effect of class formation rather than of culture. Viewing their efforts through the prism of reparations means not only that we historicize notions of citizenship, but also that we mine the archives of testimony and narrative to glean more complex understandings of the relationships between the political economy of development and the elaboration of individual and group subjectivities over time.

Repairing Bodies

Reparations to victims of slavery, the slave trade, and colonialism and their descendants should be in the form of enhanced policies, programmes and measures at the national and international level to be contributed to by States, companies and individuals who benefited materially from these practices, in order to compensate, and repair, the economic, cultural, and political damage which has been inflicted on the affected communities and people, through inter alia, the creation of a special development fund, the improvement of access to international markets of products from developing countries affected by these practices, the cancellation or substantial reduction of their foreign debt and a programme to return art objects, historical goods and documents to the countries of origin.

GROUP OF 21, DRAFT DECLARATION PREPARED FOR THE WORLD CON-
FERENCE AGAINST RACISM, 31 AUGUST–8 SEPTEMBER 2001, PARA. 116

Just before the planes flew through the World Trade Center on 11 September 2001, debates regarding the long-term effects — structural, interpersonal, and psychic — of slavery, colonialism, and other forms of mass terror were gaining some public speed as the result of preparations for and deliberations at the World Conference against Racism, Racial Discrimination, Xenophobia, and Related Intolerance held in Durban, South Africa. The draft declaration from which the epigraph is taken framed these issues, and thus the relationship between the past and the present, in robust terms. Here, damages were portrayed not only as economic in nature, but also as political and cultural; it was not only states but also the companies and individuals who operate in transnational spheres who were being called to account; and redress was imagined on various planes, all of which reflected a deep understanding that geopolitical relations, past and present, are *global* in scope and therefore have *global* implications. We should not be especially surprised that the paragraph was omitted from the final document, and likely would have been even if the United States and Israel had not withdrawn from the conference as charges of racism and Zionism took center stage. However, what its language signals is a growing appreciation for the application of a reparations framework to injustice and to imagining new ways to repair broken relationships between people and new channels through which collectivities might be forged.

While the discussions in Durban occurred at a meta-state level, it is also the case that governments have been attempting to grapple with this framework, partly as the result of these sorts of multilateral initiatives. Indeed, in January 2009, the Jamaican government announced the establishment of a Reparations Commission.[1] This commission, chaired by the anthropologist Barry Chevannes, was charged with developing a position on the issue for the country as a whole and making recommendations that would take into account those that were formulated at the World Conference in 2001 ("Chevannes to Chair Reparations Commission" 2009). The commission was asked to "receive submissions, hear testimony, evaluate research and study, and engage in dialogue with relevant interest groups, legal and academic experts," as well as to "undertake public consultation as necessary" with a view toward elaborating a sense of appropriate reparations from Britain for the transatlantic slave trade and, to a degree, colonialism (Hall 2009). Before his death in March 2010, Junior Manning sat alongside the various scholars and lawyers who were appointed members of the commission. He saw his participation as a chance to engage the *Jamaican* government on the question of reparations to Rastafari and, in particular, for those Rastafarians who were immediately affected by the events at Coral Gardens. What might largely be viewed as a progressive move on the part of the Jamaican government therefore became substantially more complex, for if Manning's entreaties are followed, the commission will not only have to confront how the brutality of the slave trade (and plantation slavery more generally) stunted Jamaica's colonial and postcolonial development, but it will also have to acknowledge that the Jamaican state's own brutality has stunted the development of sectors of its own population.

This would also be the effect of other initiatives that are currently being proposed. For example, in his recent *Envisioning Caribbean Futures* (2007), Brian Meeks has advocated the establishment of a Truth and Reconciliation Commission to bring the political violence that tore Jamaican society apart between 1976 and 1980 into public discussion with a view toward exorcising it:

> The near-civil war moment of 1980 still haunts Jamaican social and political life. The burning out of entire communities—a primitive form of ethnic cleansing, in which the "ethnicities" comprised persons of opposing political affiliation—was perfected in that time. Many families still grieve silently over relatives who were lost because they drank at the wrong bar or wore the wrong colour shirt on a particular day. The blood feuds generated in those violent days have fed into the marrow of urban communities and continue to exist in the saliency of areas and zones of exclusion, long after memory of the era has passed. (Meeks 2007: 117)

Meeks believes that we must "put to bed the ghosts of the past" (Meeks 2007: 117) to move forward as a society, to find ways to diminish the violence that currently plagues the country. He argues that, as in South Africa, a Truth and Reconciliation Commission in Jamaica should be primarily therapeutic and should not seek to prosecute, and he contends that this sort of process would best serve to "break with the past and set the template for truth and honesty in political behaviour in further stages of the new national consensus" (Meeks 2007: 118).

Because the history of political violence in Jamaica is so lengthy and complicated, however, it seems we need to develop a broader perspective on how to think about reconciliation—and, indeed, reparations—especially given the scandal that erupted at the beginning of the summer of 2010 over the extradition request by the U.S. for Christopher "Dudus" Coke, purported leader of the Shower Posse and "don" of Tivoli Gardens. This was a scandal that shook the ruling Jamaica Labour Party to the point that the opposition People's National Party demanded the resignation of Prime Minister Bruce Golding, and that turned Tivoli Gardens into a police state in late May and throughout the better part of June. The extradition request for Coke to stand trial in the United States on charges related to drug trafficking came in August 2009, but the prime minister—who is also the member of Parliament for Tivoli Gardens—was not in a hurry to comply and argued against the extradition on the grounds that the evidence against Dudus was obtained by wiretapping, a practice that is illegal under Jamaican law. In May 2010, after weeks of lying about it, Prime Minister Golding finally admitted in Parliament that he had authorized the services of a U.S. lobbying firm to pressure the U.S. government to change its position on Coke. He agreed to sign the extradition order the next week, which led to the standoff between the security forces that now had to find Dudus and the community members who were bent on protecting him at any cost.

The first few days after the prime minister signed the extradition order were both tense and bloody, with at least seventy people killed as the Jamaican Defense Force and Jamaican Constabulary Force attempted to penetrate the various roadblocks and fires community members had put up to deter them. A curfew was established for Tivoli Gardens, and residents of the community were forced to show passes when leaving or entering. Most movement in or out was effectively stopped, which meant people were unable to work, go to school, shop for food, or go about the ordinary routines of their lives. This continued until 22 June, when Dudus turned himself in, though rumors had been circulating as early as the last week of May that "the Feds" (that is, the U.S. government) had Dudus in custody but that the Jamaican government was keeping quiet about it. Of course, this incident generated immediate promises among politicians to evacuate the "culture of donmanship," as Prime Minister Golding put it, from their political constituencies, a "culture"—or, rather, a set of structural practices—they themselves established and from which they benefited. What locally focused commission could really reconcile this tangled, transnational legacy?

Most human rights workers, and some scholars, have viewed Truth and Reconciliation Commissions as a form of restorative justice, a kind of reparative work oriented toward acknowledging—and ultimately forgiving—past atrocity. The underlying assumption is that, to move forward as a society in the wake of trauma, genocide, or other forms of mass violence, there has to be some kind of bringing to account, some acknowledgment, even, perhaps, an apology. I am interested in these assumptions—as well as in the scale at which they are imagined—and in how they lead to a certain framing of social change and action.

Indeed, both reparations movements and Truth and Reconciliation Commissions have proliferated in recent decades, in part due to the elaboration of an international human rights framework through which instances of mass genocide and some forms of mass trafficking have come to be understood as crimes against humanity. While the development of international standards of right and responsibility has provided critical support for those activists and lawyers involved in exposing the terrors of particular governmental regimes, several scholars have argued persuasively that these commissions serve a liberal democratic status quo by consolidating the norms and institutions of liberal jurisprudence (Grandin and Klubock 2007). This is largely because their battles are fought within the theaters of law and legal rhetoric, theaters that are themselves characterized by processes of political wrangling that result "in inclusions and exclusions and a moral gradation of atrocity" (O'Neill and Hinton 2009: 8). This means that the space of international law, and the sense of international morality that supposedly grounds it, is always already *interested*. Thus, fully apart from the thorny logistical questions raised by reparations movements—How do we identify those to whom reparations are owed? What form should reparations take? Should there be a relationship between reparations programs and other social justice goals?[2]—are a whole host of conceptual issues that shape outcomes and expectations for the future.

One of these issues has to do with how the context of emergent neoliberalism has shaped the parameters of inquiry, especially for Truth and Reconciliation Commissions. If we agree with Greg Grandin and Thomas Klubock that "reconciliation, forgiveness, and political consensus have been understood as the basis for moving forward into an era of market-driven economic progress," and that therefore Truth and Reconciliation Commissions avoid a concept of history that is rooted in "a conflict of interests and ideas within a context of unequal power" (Grandin and Klubock 2007: 5), then we have to concede that they *cannot* address the structural historical processes and political conflicts that gave rise to human rights violations in the first place and therefore are unable to significantly alter material inequalities (McCalpin 2007). They are, in Michel Rolph Trouillot's words, "abortive rituals" (2000). The inability of collective apologies or reconciliation commissions to address the root causes of violence through a more robust structural analysis, Kamari Clarke (2009: 4) tells us, results in a situation "in which violence is increasingly viewed in terms of individual

"3 o'Clock Roadblock," by Hubert Neal Jr. Acrylic on board. COURTESY OF THE ARTIST.

"Dudus Wet Himself," by Hubert Neal Jr. Acrylic on board. COURTESY OF THE ARTIST.

ARTIST'S STATEMENT, HUBERT NEAL JR.

i arrived in jamaica 20 may to do an artist's residency, which is exciting in it's own right. i had no idea it was such a tense time in jamaica. as i tried to figure out what body of work i would produce during my time here, the events surrounding me began to filter in. i decided to do one piece, "the hunt for dudus," and figured that would address the situation

"Garrison Justice 2," by Hubert Neal Jr. Acrylic on board. COURTESY OF THE ARTIST.

"Garrison Justice," by Hubert Neal Jr. Acrylic on board. COURTESY OF THE ARTIST.

and i would paint other things. but from that painting sprang another, and another, and pretty soon i was overflowing with ideas on how i could depict this situation. i realized that my subject was all around me and "the dudus chronicles" was born.

rather than collective guilt and justice is articulated through the achievement of a guilty conviction." One effect of this is that agents of powerful states can endlessly defer culpability by framing their actions in terms of a shameful, though temporary, immorality—an immorality that can be embodied within a single person (or group of people) and that therefore can be relegated to the past. This is a point Nandini Sundar (2004: 148) makes in relation to the killing of Muslims in Gujarat in 2002 and the U.S. invasion of Iraq in 2003. She argues that, contrary to the popular opinion that activism within the sphere of international jurisprudence both reflects and generates an emergent international morality, in fact this morality "becomes part of a self-congratulatory liberal understanding that allows real and ongoing inequalities and injustices to go unchallenged." For Sundar, the focus on morality also allows for the persistence of culturalist explanations for mass violence, and these explanations reproduce the ideology that we can delineate a hierarchy of societies based on their cultural logics. In other words, the framework of international law—an increasingly ubiquitous technology of modern governance—can nonetheless reproduce culturalist approaches to global geopolitical issues, and especially violence.

A second issue has to do with how both reparations movements and Truth and Reconciliation Commissions must rely on the law to support broader projects of community development and empowerment (Barkan 2007), a reliance John Comaroff and Jean Comaroff (2009: 56) have called "lawfare." In chapter 5, for example, we saw how communities might appeal to international bodies to push their own governments for recognition on various levels. But it is also this sort of cultural activism through legal channels that has a tendency to reproduce narrowly defined culturalist frameworks for understanding issues such as violence, because international human rights instruments that are designed to protect minority cultures within particular nation-states can have the effect of essentializing culture, even as they are developed to recognize past injustice and to protect collective rights to land, among other things (Hastrup 2003).

Moreover, while "lawfare" is mobilized within the realm of the transnational, its aims generally tend to target the more modest space of the nation-state, as we also saw in chapter 5.[3] This can have the effect of presenting the past as an aberrant break within a longer trajectory toward greater democracy and inclusion. As Richard Wilson (2003: 370) has pointed out for the South African context, the Truth and Reconciliation Commission sought to construct a new national self in relation to, but discontinuous with, the past of apartheid: "The new national self is one which is forged in the suffering and violence of the past, but no element of that political past has entered into the present. The present political order is presented as purified, decontaminated and disconnected from the old authoritarian order. Truth commission hearings construct a new vision of the national self by inscribing the individual into a new national narrative on person-hood." Because of these limitations, Wilson argues, *truth* can neither serve the process of reconciliation nor guarantee "honesty in [future] political behaviour," to remind us of Meeks's entreaty. And again, this is so, on one hand, because the language of rights can also fall into the same patterns of culturalist thinking that has been used to legitimate violence, and on the other, because violence itself is located at the level of the national and grounded within particular individuals. More broadly, the problem here is that legal language instrumentalizes and so is able neither to apprehend the transnational dimensions of various levels of political, economic, social, and cultural violence affecting populations nor to capture the symbolic and expressive dimensions of violence (Hastrup 2003). What is more, the sorts of grammars mobilized by particular Truth and Reconciliation Commissions delineate the range of "truths" that are permitted. Fiona Ross (2003b: 76) has shown that by framing its inquiries in terms of the violation of human rights, the South African Truth and Reconciliation Commission produced certain kinds of "victims" while ignoring others. In other words, as she argues, "The work of 'rights' frequently performs the same erasure of power [as the state]." In the case she examines, women were made to de-scribe horrifying bodily harm, and they were encouraged to describe their suffering in relation to their roles as wives, sisters, and mothers of activists, but they were not permitted to describe how they might have suffered as a result of their own political activism (Ross 2003a, 2003b; see also Grandin and Klubock 2007; Motsemme 2004).

Of course, despite these various limitations, Truth and Reconciliation Commissions do also work to unearth specific silences within official his-torical records, even as they reproduce a view of democratic process as progressive and perfectible. According to this view, the system generally works; it just must be *extended* to accommodate black folk, other people of color, women, homosexuals, immigrants, religious minorities . . . the list is ever increasing. In this view, what we fail to capture is what Sybille Fischer

(2004: 273–74) would call a complex movement of suppression and denial. The denial, in the context she discusses, is of the centrality of the Haitian Revolution to concepts of modernity and nation building. "The modernity that took shape in the Western Hemisphere (in theoretical discourse as well as in cultural and social institutions) in the course of the nineteenth century contains," she argues, was rooted in "the suppression of a struggle whose aim was to give racial equality and racial liberation the same weight as those political goals that came to dominate nineteenth-century politics and thought — most particularly, those relating to the nation and national sovereignty." In other words, the painstaking disavowal of notions of black self-determination, as well as the transnational dimensions of effort that realized it in the nineteenth century, resulted in a privileging of the persona of the "creole" and the space of the national in the twentieth century. I argue here that a focus on the historical political economy of global geopolitics would bring into view the complex and dynamic imbrications of the national with the global, the regional, and the circum-Atlantic, thereby both defying the fetishism of the space of the nation-state and preventing us from falling into the trap of culturalism. It is this focus that I believe a *reparations framework for thinking* can give, and this is a framework that can also help us to map social change efforts according to different parameters.

NOSTALGIA, ROMANCE, AND VANGUARDS

David Scott's recent rereading of C. L. R. James's *The Black Jacobins* (1989) as tragedy is rooted in his observation that the "old modalities of imagining social change" — nationalism and socialism — "do not serve us in the present," a period he identified as "a time of postcolonial crisis in which old horizons have collapsed or evaporated and new ones have not yet taken shape" (Scott 2004: 168). The sense of movement in the last line I cite here suggests that the present occupies some sort of vacuum in relation to social change, a vacuum waiting to be filled by the next set of struggles that will inspire mass mobilization. I argue that we cannot characterize the horizon as empty; that new futures are constantly being imagined and emplotted, but we will not see them if our vision is oriented only toward the very kinds of mass-based revolutionary movements Scott discusses — movements we could characterize as being masculinist in nature. By arguing this, I mean to echo Imani Tafari-Ama (2006), whose work on sexual politics in downtown Kingston reveals that the symbolic dimensions of authority in the PNP community in which she conducted research are themselves mirrors of how elites manipulate political influence to produce violence in inner-city communities, and that this manipulation relies on a particular embodiment of gender that identifies norms of masculinity with violence and power. Tafari-Ama (2006: 144) argues that, despite the fact that gender issues have been important in some resistance movements throughout Jamaica's history, we must conceptualize "race resistance as a masculinist discourse." Of course, a long trajectory of scholarship has pointed out how national, pan-African, and transnational political movements have not, as Richard Iton (2008: 259) has argued, been "exempt from the masculinist and heterosexist impulses that energize modern arrangements and categories and much of our understanding of the political" (see also Carby 1998; Edmondson 1999a; Lubiano 1998). Indeed, Josie Saldaña-Portillo (2003) has insightfully shown us the complicated symbiosis between revolutionary movements and mid-twentieth-century development discourses, a symbiosis that is rooted in the theory of progress and subjectivity that undergirds these discourses.

In her analysis of why revolutionary movements in Latin America ended up reproducing discourses of development, "often to the detriment of the constituencies these movements sought to liberate through their anti-imperialist struggle," Saldaña-Portillo (2003: 5) locates the problem within their shared theory of human perfectibility, the notion that the subject must "become an agent of transformation in his own right, one who is highly ethical, mobile, progressive, risk-taking, and masculinist, regardless of whether the agent/object of a development strategy is a man or a woman, an adult or a child" (Saldaña-Portillo 2003: 9). In other words, she argues that the revolutionary subject is always already a male subject, and the process of revolutionary change itself is embodied through masculinist modes of subjectivity, however these might be defined from place to place. Now, while many of us (as scholars) may recognize this as a conceptual dilemma, we rarely theorize alternative ways to envision political action *that is already happening on the ground*. If we reorient our gaze away from the tragedy of postcolonial crisis, what sorts of change movements might we see?

Like Veena Das (2007), Fiona Ross has argued that in the face of the spectacular violence of apartheid, the attempt to re-create the ordinary is in itself a project worth examining. "In an ideal everyday," she writes, "facets of life scarcely imaginable under apartheid—the possibilities of living coherent lives unhindered by pass laws and exploitative work conditions, for example, or the cessation of violence, or the non-disruption of efforts to secure valued goals — might be achievable, might even come to be taken for granted" (Ross 2003b: 141). The re-creation of ordinariness, therefore — the development of new though unspectacular ways of moving through everyday life — is in this context something extraordinary. Memory work can also serve this purpose, but here I am not talking about the sort of memory work that happens in normative locations such as Truth and Reconciliation Commissions, or even at memorializations such as the Coral Gardens commemoration. Instead, I am thinking about the sort of work Rosalind Shaw has illuminated in her research about how people are recovering from the devastating violence that characterized Sierra Leone's eleven-year civil war. There, many people were unwilling to testify within a Truth and Reconciliation Commission because they worried about reactivating the past and disrupting processes of reintegration. Instead, many families and communities used public ritual practices — such as plays put on by the youth organization of a Pentecostal church — to reintegrate former combatants. Within these plays, Shaw argues, youth reframed their experiences of violence in relation to the Pentecostal notion of spiritual warfare and to their own fight against the demonic "underworlds" they encountered. In this way, they turned these experiences into a lesson about how to live a Christian life, thereby critiquing not only the government but also all the factions that had displaced and terrorized them. "Memories of war that have shaped the lives of these youth," she argues, "are themselves reshaped through the reconfigured deliverance concept of the Underworld — a concept that, by melding a globalized space of geopolitical evil with a personal memory space of the depths of terror, enables displaced Pentecostal youth to fight both of these in their terms (Shaw 2007: 88). Both of these examples offer significantly different readings of how to understand processes of social change. Importantly, these rereadings are not mobilized through masculinist visions of revolution, development, or transformation but through the institutional spheres of the everyday.

That it is far more difficult to quantify the sorts of transformation that occur within these kinds of spheres is made obvious by Aimee Cox's work with BlackLight, an arts-based social justice project that was started by a group of young women in a shelter in Detroit (Cox 2009). BlackLight emerged as the result of a conflict within the shelter about the proper modes of dress and behavior within the shelter's public spaces. Some of the young women staying there spontaneously expressed their dissatisfaction with the shelter's policies through the language of movement. Because this was such a cathartic experience for them—helping them to see the issues confronting them through a new lens and thus enabling them to think through alternative solutions to their problems—they developed a dance and poetry program within the shelter and eventually began conducting public workshops with other communities. In these workshops, participants first verbally expressed the issues facing their communities, then BlackLight members gave them clay, paint, and music and asked them to represent their issues visually. "With these new artistic tools," Cox (2009: 52) writes, "the young people reconstructed the problems and reimagined potential solutions for their communities through frameworks inspired by their own creativity." Afterward, BlackLight members played these representations back to the participants, as it were, through choreography; they translated the narratives they heard into movement, allowing participants to see their issues in yet another format that they could compare with their own renderings. These comparisons resulted in discussions about the sorts of solutions they might be able to generate.

This kind of process sounded exciting to me as a former dancer who had been involved in this sort of community-based work. And it did to others, too. This is where the problems began. BlackLight became part of youth arts programming in the Detroit branch of a national nonprofit community organization. Its headquarters were moved into the downtown building of the organization, and the administrators of the organization monitored BlackLight's activities, a situation that made the young women feel patronized. In addition, BlackLight was required to provide written reports about their activities in which they were asked to quantify the effects of their work. This presented a problem, because their activities were geared to working through a process of embodiment to generate a change in consciousness. This is a process that is profoundly *internal* and that manifests externally primarily in relation to new decision-making processes and, potentially, new patterns of association. These are not easy phenomena to quantify as measurable indices of social change, especially not in the short term. Nor is it easy to track the effects of these processes beyond the individual participants in the workshops themselves, yet it is likely that someone's internal transformation produces profound effects on those within their networks. Because BlackLight could not find ways to fulfill these expectations, it found it living up to the terms of the arrangement with the nonprofit organization and its stipulations related to funding difficult.

The situation of BlackLight encapsulates the problem with our visions of social change. While we are looking for revolutions, complete transformations in social order that upend previous patterns of dominance and inequality, we are capitulating to the development discourses Saldaña-Portillo warns us about. At the same time, and equally critical, we are blinded to the ongoing forms of self-making and social change work that are occurring within the realms of everyday life and that, not insignificantly, often are being led by women. This is not to argue that we do not need mass movements or charismatic leaders who are able to capture the imagination of populations in ways that motivate them to imagine new futures. Nor do I mean to suggest that women's visions of social change are inherently more radical than men's. However, privileging the mass-mobilization model of transformation leads us always to search for the vanguard and to forget the various ways vanguardism is complicit not only with conservative patterns of control and hierarchy but also with a specific ideology regarding revolutionary change that does not speak to the realities of contemporary Jamaica.[4] We need to shift our gaze.

While this shift requires a close look at what is happening at grassroots level, it also necessitates a more macro-level contextualization. At the moment, in part, it means interrogating the effects of a change in U.S. foreign policy toward the region from the language of development to the language of security, a change that was signaled most clearly in the establishment of the Caribbean Basin Security Initiative, inaugurated at the Summit of the Americas by President Barack Obama in April 2009. The Caribbean Basin Initiative, begun in 1984 under President Ronald Reagan during the prime ministership of Edward Seaga, appears to have grown a new arm, and its purported concern with economic assistance and development is belied by the proposed figures for the 2011 fiscal year budget. President Obama has requested the allocation of nearly $73 million for both military and economic aid, broken down as follows: $37,463,000 for international narcotics control and law enforcement; $18,160,000 for foreign military financing; and $17,000,000 for economic support ("The Caribbean Basin Security Initiative" 2010). In other words, the militarization of security will receive the lion's share of U.S. funding, and the economic and social dimensions of security will remain significantly less elaborated. This sort of policy focus leads to tensions that were on display when Hillary Clinton toured the region in June 2010, ending her trip in Barbados by meeting with CARICOM leaders who were significantly more concerned with economic development than with transnational crime and drug trafficking, despite the fact that, at the time of the meeting Dudus still had not turned himself in to the authorities. The ongoing complaint is that the U.S. government does not seem sufficiently inclined to appreciate the links between security and economic development.

Indeed, looking at the issue of drug trafficking and Caribbean gang violence through a diasporically regional lens gives a better sense of what the dimensions of concern are on the part of the U.S. government, as well as insight into views about how this concern should be managed. I will give several significant examples. In 2006, Shaheed "Roger" Khan, a Guyanese man alleged to be the biggest trafficker of cocaine in that nation, was arrested in Suriname and extradited to the United States with the help of the FBI. Khan is said to be backed by the Phantom Squad, one of the most notorious gangs in Guyana, which also purportedly has links to the government. Khan pleaded guilty to trafficking in 150 kilos of cocaine, witness tampering, and gun running and is now in prison in Brooklyn serving fifteen years ("Shaheed 'Roger' Khan" 2009). In 2008, the U.S. Fourth Fleet, an armada equipped with nuclear aircraft carriers that had been dismantled in 1950, was reactivated. The rationale behind reestablishing the fleet was to build collaboration among maritime security efforts through the region; yet given the history of extensive U.S. military intervention throughout Latin America and the Caribbean during the long twentieth century and the current emphasis on counter-narcotics mobilization, many believe the fleet will provide an offshore base from which to observe, coordinate, and possibly even launch black operations, a role similar naval groups have carried out in the past (Council on Hemispheric Affairs 2008). In October 2009, the controversial Defense Cooperation Agreement was signed by the United States and Colombia, granting the U.S. armed forces access to seven Colombian military bases for the next ten years. Again, the public rationale for the agreement is to support counter-narcotics and counterinsurgency initiatives within Colombia. However, setting the agreement in conjunction with the redeployment of the Fourth Fleet, and with the massive amount of congressional funding for forthcoming military construction at the Colombian bases, leads to speculation that the United States is looking for an opportunity to conduct more general operations within a context in which many Latin American nations are electing left-leaning political leaders.[5]

Finally, and more specific to what went on in Jamaica in the summer of 2010, in May of that same year more than seventy Shower Posse members were rounded up and arrested in Toronto based on information gleaned from a nine-month investigation by the Canadian police in conjunction with U.S. security and intelligence groups. At the time of this writing, twelve of those arrested were likely to be deported back to Jamaica. And an article by Richard Drayton published in the *Guardian* in June 2010 pointed out significant continuities between how Jamaican security forces, with the assistance of those from the United States, were carrying out their search for Dudus inside Tivoli Gardens and how U.S. forces carried out aspects of the wars in Iraq and Afghanistan (Drayton 2010). In the article, Drayton cites a manual on counterinsurgency operations of the U.S. Joint Chiefs of Staff that seems to have been based on a master's thesis submitted by Major Wayne Robinson, a member of the Jamaican armed forces who was studying at the U.S. Marine Corps University. The title of the thesis was "Eradicating Organised Criminal Gangs in Jamaica: Can Lessons Be Learned from a Successful Counterinsurgency?" The manual equates police action against "criminal organizations" with counterinsurgency and describes key tactics and strategies, all of which were being used at the time in Tivoli Gardens.

Outside the region, only the Council on Hemispheric Affairs has joined with local peace management initiatives, academics, grassroots organizations, and feminist groups in Jamaica to argue that the key to solving the problem of the regional drug and arms trade is not a consolidated militarized effort led by the United States but a comprehensive approach to economic and social development in the region in conjunction with some sort of concerted intervention on the demand side. This, of course, is the only viable solution. A militarized approach will only pave the way for new actors to become involved, and it will never provide spaces for self-making outside of gangsterism.

What I have attempted to show throughout this book is that social transformation happens on a variety of levels and works in extraordinarily complex (and sometimes contradictory) ways. We have seen how a changing global political economy of development, despite the various deleterious consequences of neoliberalism, has generated a situation whereby the family is no longer seen as the primary institution through which citizens are able to engage the political and economic life of the nation-state. This opens the potential for citizenship to be defined in less patriarchal and heteronormative terms *should we seek to mobilize around this issue and, by mobilizing, make it more visible.* We have seen how particular sectors of society—Rastas, in this case—have engaged global social movements to organize on many different levels at once, rethinking citizenship in new ways for the new millennium. And we have seen how transnationalism more generally has necessitated a reconceptualization of the space of the nation-state and therefore the scope of its governance. We cannot perceive the potential in any of these changes without taking a long historical view and without letting go of a particular nostalgia regarding the moment(s) of revolution.

Witnessing takes many forms. It is embodied by the humanitarian and human rights workers who tell stories of tragedy and atrocity to move others to action. These are individuals, James Dawes (2007: 3) tells us, who exist in a "unique position of intimacy and distance, connection and alienation," individuals who grapple with the ethics of repeating other people's narratives to generate some sort of political or social action. Witnessing can also be performative, as is the case for those who participate in peace marches or in public theater projects like the spectacles organized by Honor Ford-Smith in Toronto and Kingston. These are marches and performances that index the spatial dimensions of violence by mapping them on the landscape, memorializing victims of gun violence and confronting unsuspecting publics with their own complicity in it. We might also think about the sorts of videotaped testimonies that have accompanied projects to exhume mass graves as a form of performative witnessing. These are testimonies that, Francisco Ferrándiz (2008, paragraph 13) argues, help those who were disappeared during Spain's Civil War to "recover their identity through the spoken words and bodily expression of those who remember them" as the corpses themselves are being made visible. Finally, witnessing can take the shape of Truth and Reconciliation Commissions, which, despite their limitations, do seek to bring to light previously hidden or silenced forms of suffering.

My efforts at witnessing in these pages might be framed in relation to what Glen Loury (2007: 104) has called an "interpretive approach" to reparations, a complexly cyclical engagement with history that can help "establish a common baseline of historical memory—a common narrative, if you like—through which the past injury and its continuing significance can enter into current policy discourse." By advocating an interpretive approach to African American inequality, Loury is rejecting the compensatory model of reparations activism, arguing instead that the ontological basis of race thinking that permeates the Enlightenment's legacy perpetuates racial stigma not as the result of one or another individual's prejudice or ignorance, but because of common-sense systems of value that reproduce notions of black inferiority: "What is required . . . is a commitment on the part of the public, the political elite, the opinion-shaping media, and so on to take responsibility for such situations as the contemporary plight of the urban black poor, and to understand them in a general way as a consequence of an ethnically indefensible past. Such a commitment would, on this view, be open-ended and not contingent on demonstrating any specific lines of causality" (Loury 2007: 105). From his perspective, this is what would provide the most meaningful and enduring form of repair for African Americans in the United States, and it would require a break with the liberal notion of colorblindness as "*the* moral standard in regard to issues of social justice and racial inequality in the United States" (Loury 2007: 100).

What is needed to generate real justice, in other words, is a sustained conversation about history—and about the place of the past in the present—in terms other than those of righteous blame or liberal guilt. This conversation must demand something more robust than memorialization, but it must also envision the future in new ways and on new terms. It must have something more profound than "forgiveness" at stake, for forgiveness—as it is generally imagined—is not reparative and is only sometimes restorative.[6] Its principal focus cannot merely be perfectibility or progress, for as we have seen, these are notions that undergird particular kinds of conservatism in relation to self-making. I end with a polemic. Reparations is *the* framework through which we must view contemporary inequalities. Anything short of it represents a capitulation to the more conservative aspects of multiracial nationalist discourse and to the demands of a so-called postracial cosmopolitan vision of citizenship that threatens to become intractable in the neoliberal era.

Notes

INTRODUCTION

1. See, e.g., Thomas 2002, 2004.
2. For more on how the Caribbean has, untenably, been represented as timeless, see Bronfman 2007; Sheller 2003.
3. With this in mind, Karla Slocum and I have been working on a collaborative project designed to rethink current debates within many U.S. universities regarding both the parameters of disciplinary boundaries and the area studies research paradigms that were institutionalized after the Second World War by taking stock of the contributions of anthropological research within particular regions to the theoretical and ethnographic contours of the discipline as a whole. Our purpose has been to promote cross-regional, transnational, and interdisciplinary dialogue in various venues that explore the role Caribbeanist research has played within the structure and foundations of anthropology in specific places, the topics that have been important to specific Caribbeanist anthropologies, the relationships among these various anthropologies, and the ways these relationships have been rooted in a broader political economy of knowledge production. This project is ongoing and has resulted in a range of publications: see Slocum and Thomas 2003, 2007; Thomas and Slocum 2008.
4. For an evocative discussion of the nuanced distinction between these two frameworks (postcolonial and post–Cold War), see Piot 2010.
5. On the relationships between postcolonial genocide and colonial violence, see Fanon 1963; Mamdani 1996; Mbembe 2001; Stein 2003. On gangs' taking on state functions within the exceptional spaces of many urban areas, see Bourgois 1995; Goldstein 2003; Venkatesh 2002. On fear becoming a way of life, see Green 1999; see also Agamben 1998; Arendt 1951; Mbembe 2003; Taussig 1986. Of course, the

reference to greeting death without surprise is to Scheper-Hughes 1993, and the reference to suffering as an everyday practice is to Das et al. 2001. Excellent analyses of how torture is mapped onto reconfigured bodies can be found in Feldman 1991; Klima 2002; Nelson 1999, 2009; Starn 1999. The focus on landscape can be seen in Caldeira 2000; Silber 2004. On discourses of history in relation to communal violence, see Axel 2000; Daniel 1996; Malkki 1995. On the gendering and racialization of violence, see Bourgois 1995; Sutton 1995; Trotz 2004. Finally, on human rights activism and violence, see Sanford 2004; Silber 2007; Tate 2007.

6. I am thinking here especially of Appadurai 1998; Bourgois 2001; Bourgois and Scheper-Hughes 2004; Farmer 2003; Harrison 1997; Taussig 1992b.

7. On the magic of spectacular violence in relation to state formation, see Comaroff and Comaroff 1999; Coronil 1997; Klima 2002.

8. Richard Iton would call this "apparent state" a "duppy state," referring to the ghost that emerges when the dead are not buried properly. For Iton, the duppy state "marks the potent after life, mocking persistence, and resurgence — rather than the remission — of coloniality: the state that is 'there and not there' at the same time" (Iton 2008: 135).

9. Other scholars would push this origin story back even further. Irene Silverblatt (2004), for example, argues that the Inquisition — as a modern bureaucracy — worked through processes of race thinking to determine the guilt or innocence of "new Christians," and Michel Rolph Trouillot (1995) has argued that contemporary understandings of racial difference actually have their origin in the expulsion of the Moors from Europe in the eleventh century.

10. Exceptions to this general argument are, of course, Trujillo in the Dominican Republic in the mid-twentieth century and both Duvaliers in Haiti. Fidel Castro of Cuba is something of a special case in this regard, as he was, of course, opposed by the U.S. government until his retirement from formal leadership in 2006.

11. Here I am thinking in particular about the insightful work done by M. Jaqui Alexander (1991, 1994, 1997, 2005); Partha Chatterjee (1989); Caren Kaplan, Norma Alarcón, and Minoo Moallem (1999); Aihwa Ong (1990); Andrew Parker, Mary Russo, Doris Sommer, and Patricia Yaeger (1992); Ann Stoler (1989, 2002); and Diana Taylor (1997). For an excellent early review essay on gender and state formation, see Silverblatt 1991. More recent work includes Abu-Lughod 2004; Navaro-Yashin 2002; Rofel 1999.

12. The Caribbeanist literature on transnational migration is enormous. See Slocum and Thomas 2003 for a review and citations.

13. On black Marxisms, see Kelley 1990; Robinson 1983. On research that deals with specific sites of pan-Africanist and internationalist mobilization, see Davies 2007; Edwards 2003; James 1993; McDuffie 2006; Stephens 2005.

1. For a more detailed and extended discussion of this community, see D. Thomas 2004, chap. 3.

2. I thank Christopher Charles for encouraging me to develop this point.

3. An "alias" is a sort of pet name, a public name used on the street. In this chapter, I use real names or aliases for people who have been publicly identified in newspaper reports. For those who have not, I use pseudonyms.

4. For more on the development of political garrisons, see also National Committee on Political Tribalism, "Report," Constitutional Reform Unit, Government of Jamaica, Kingston, 1997. See also Chevannes 1992; Edie 1991; Figueroa and Sives 2002; Stone 1980.

5. In addition, during the 1970s under the government of Michael Manley, the community of Portmore was constructed, in part as an effort to move people out of garrison communities. For an analysis of this process and how it reorganized the spaces of violence, see Horst 2008.

6. See Harrison 1982 for an ethnographic discussion of gangs and area leaders in central Kingston during the late 1970s.

7. The anthropologist Rivke Jaffe of Leiden University is currently conducting research on these questions and explores the ways crime-based systems of urban governance work simultaneously through and against the state. She is particularly interested in how neighborhood dons gain legitimacy through the mobilization of affect, a mobilization often mediated through popular culture.

8. National Committee on Political Tribalism, "Report," 12.

9. Imani Tafari-Ama (2006: 32) points out that guns and ammunition currently enter Jamaica not only from North America and South America but also from Haiti, which, as she writes, "was flooded with guns as a precursor to the U.S. coordinated ousting of democratically elected former Haitian President Jean-Bertrand Aristide in February 2004."

10. In May 2010, government security forces did successfully penetrate Tivoli Gardens in a search for the alleged don of the community, Christopher "Dudus" Coke. This move was prompted by pressure from the U.S. government and the Federal Bureau of Investigation, institutions that were attempting to extradite Coke on drug- and murder-related charges in the United States. The JLP government, led by Bruce Golding, attempted to stall the extradition but eventually, under the shadow of significant corruption charges, was forced to offer Dudus up. At least seventy people were killed as government forces entered the community of Tivoli Gardens in their search, and hundreds more were arrested, searched, and interrogated during the curfew that ensued. Tivoli Gardens residents, for their part, burned down a number of buildings, including two police stations, and established roadblocks throughout the community. Dudus was eventually found, but not in the community, and was extradited to the United States, where he is now on trial. I come back to the issues raised by this event in the coda.

11. This is also an argument made by Igor Kopytoff, whose innovative work on frontiers represented an attempt to think beyond the notion of the "tribe" as the primary means of ethnogenesis and social organization within Africa. He pointed out that many, if not most, African societies were formed through a process of movement from established metropoles to frontier zones. These communities would develop into small polities, perhaps growing through time to become more complex societies. In other words, he argues that rather than accepting the a-historical ideology that "tribes" were the organizing political units within Africa, we must instead view processes of ethnic formation as dynamically responding to the movements and fluxes that were the results of wars, famines, urban and industrial expansion, and imperialism. One of the innovations of Kopytoff's work in relation to Turner's original Frontier Thesis, however, is his argument that constant communication between the metropole and the frontier actually reproduces a valorization of the metropole. As a result, "The frontier may also be a force for culture-historical continuity and conservatism" (Kopytoff 1987: 3).

12. Of course, this is also the argument in Hannah Arendt's seminal *The Origins of Totalitarianism* (1951). However, Arendt stops short of the broader claim Césaire makes, which is that it was not that the specifics of late-nineteenth-century European imperialism uniquely created a situation in which this brutality would be visited on populations "at home," but that imperialism *generally* (and *always*) creates the conditions for fascism by installing brutality at the foundation of state formation.

13. See Brown 2008 for a critique of Patterson's "social death" thesis.

14. Aihwa Ong (2006: 23) critiques Agamben's oft-used formulation about spaces of exception by arguing that he "ignores the possibility of complex negotiations of claims for those without territorialized citizenship." In other words, she suggests that with ethnographic attention to the ways exceptions are produced and to how "bare life" is lived, we might discover various kinds of mobilization that both include and move beyond the state as their target.

15. The anthropologist R. T. Smith (1988: 2) has also argued that the Caribbean was "a region of open frontiers, shifting populations, vast cultural heterogeneity, complex economic relations and unstable political authority. Caribbean history has been turbulent, bringing together peoples from every part of the globe in a swirling vortex of greed, lust and striving reminiscent of the destructive hurricanes that sweep through the region every year."

16. For relatively early critiques and extensions of Turner, see Billington 1971 (1958); Hennessy 1978; Walsh 1981. For later applications of the term to racial experiences and ideologies, see Stephens 1999; Taylor 1998. For Social Darwinism, see Baker 1998.

17. Slotkin (1994) also argues that, although the material conditions of population development changed throughout the nineteenth century, the frontier myth continued to define American nationalist ideology, even throughout the process of industrialization.

18. Examples of this literature include Beckles 1984, 1989; Craton 1978, 1982; Gaspar 1985; Genovese 1979; Mullin 1992; Turner 1982.

2. DEVIANT BODIES

1. It is not only within metropolitan centers that the discourse of the Jamaican culture of violence is mobilized. In early-twentieth-century Cuba, there was general criminalization of black migrants who came to work on the sugar estates (de la Fuente 2000; Giovanetti 2006).

2. See Garraway 2006 for a compelling analysis of the links between violence and sexual promiscuity in early French Saint-Domingue.

3. Baptists and other missionaries were very interested in creating respectable "Christian Blacks" out of the masses of freed people after full emancipation in 1838. They imagined legitimate family formation through marriage as an integral part of a series of reforms that would remake former slaves into a nascent middle class modeled on middle-class Englishmen—in other words, a middle class that embodied the values of independence, thrift, moderation, modesty, and education (Austin-Broos 1992; C. Hall 1995, 2002). If slavery had created "an unnatural phenomenon, male slaves who were entirely dependent on their masters" (Hall 1995: 53), within the missionary communities that were developed after emancipation in Jamaica, black men were to have the opportunity to be *real* men by casting off dependence and taking charge of their now legitimate households. Nevertheless, former slaves maintained their own patterns of family formation.

4. Amy Kaplan (2005: 97–98) has shown how this sort of linkage continued with the shift from expansion across the Western frontier to overseas imperialism by analyzing the new white masculinity that started to be heralded during the 1890s. "The culture at large was in the process of redefining white middle-class masculinity from a republican quality of character based on self-control and social responsibility to a corporeal essence identified with the vigor and prowess of the individual male body," she writes, and thus "in the revitalized male body, geographic distension and overseas conquest figure as a temporal return to origins."

5. Of course, it is also true that biological and cultural racisms work in concert with each other, and that "culture" often serves as a proxy for race in discussions of difference: see, e.g., Austin-Broos 1994; Baker 1998; Michaels 1992; Smedley 1993. I thank Ania Loomba and David Kazanjian for pushing me to clarify this point.

6. For an extended discussion of the context surrounding this study, as well as of the study itself, see Jackson 1990.

7. Despite its extremely pathological view of the black family, the Moynihan report also diverges from a more generally psychological approach and advocates employment of black men as the solution to a host of social ills.

8. This is a view that is also reproduced within the reports of the various riot commissions, particularly those after the Second World War, especially the Report of the National Advisory Commission on Civil Disorders that was established after the

riots throughout the United States in 1968 (otherwise known as the Kerner Commission Report). As Herman (1995: 210) notes, it is this view that strengthened the bond between "psychological authority and governmental pronouncements on race and urban crisis."

9. Outside the Office of Colonial Development and Welfare, other initiatives were developed to promote marriage among the majority of black Jamaicans. In 1944, Lady Huggins, the wife of the governor of Jamaica, initiated the infamous Mass Marriage Movement. Begun in 1944, the movement was an island-wide campaign designed to halt what was seen as alarmingly rampant promiscuity among lower-class Jamaicans by sponsoring the marriages of consensually cohabitating couples and others whose sexual relations seemed to warrant marriage. At its peak in 1946, the movement increased marriage rates in Jamaica from 4.44 per thousand to 5.82 per thousand. But by 1951, the annual marriage rate and illegitimacy ratios had returned to their earlier levels, and by 1955, the Mass Marriage Movement had petered out completely (Smith 1966: xxiii). It is often anecdotally noted that after marrying, many of these couples actually broke up. The failure of this movement was attributed to the erroneous assumption that marriage had the same meaning and value among different social strata, something the body of literature on West Indian family structure sought to address.

10. E.g., Cox 1948; Davis et al. 1941; Dollard 1937; Powdermaker 1939; Warner et al. 1941.

11. A more recent perspective has also developed that returns to Herskovits's position that West Indian family forms are modifications of West African forms (Kerns 1989; Sudarkasa 1988; Sutton 1984). For a cogent review of the literature on the theoretical shifts within studies of West Indian family and kinship practices, see Barrow 1996, 1998a.

12. In this essay, Trotz (2003) also makes the point that within Caribbean societies that are seen to be divided along ethnic lines, populations descended from Africans and Indians were discursively positioned in contradictory ways that also redounded to issues such as land settlement and nationalist strivings.

13. Like the discourse of dysfunction I analyzed earlier, the culture of poverty formulation was also transnational in its genesis and application. See Rosemblatt 2009 for a detailed discussion of the ways Lewis's thesis was picked up in both Mexico and the United States and how it worked to produce notions of difference, hierarchy, and nationalism within both contexts.

14. Of course, Lewis's ideas have been widely criticized. Anthropologists and others have taken issue with his use of the culture concept; with how his data sometimes contradicted his theoretical assertions; with how he contributed to a racialization and sexualization of poor people; and with the sense that, despite his various disclaimers, ultimately the "culture of poverty" thesis has been taken up as a way to blame the poor for their own poverty and marginalization ("Book Review" 1967; Briggs 2002; DiLeonardo 1998; Leacock 1971; Rodman 1971; Valentine 1968). See also Rosemblatt 2009 for a discussion of the reception of Lewis's work among Mexican scholars. While Lewis's solutions for poverty tended to emphasize collec-

tive action and political protest geared toward achieving the rights and responsibilities of true citizenship (Lewis 1965: xlvi, 1), those who took his ideas and ran with them were seen as offering up solutions that emphasized self-help and governmental nonintervention. For a classic argument, and still one of the most provocative, against Moynihan's report, see Spillers 1987.

15. See, e.g., Davies 2007; Edwards 2003; James 1998; Kelley 1990; McDuffie 2006; Robinson 2000; Stephens 2005.

16. But see Yelvington 1999 for a more nuanced discussion on how the question of origins, or of ethnic subjectivity, is dialectally and mutually constituted by the question of class.

17. The notions of acculturation and syncretism and the typology he developed in *The Myth of the Negro Past* were also critiqued by other anthropologists. For example, Sidney Mintz and Richard Price (1992: 9) argued that, instead of identifying particular cultural traits that might link New World blacks to African societies, it would be better to conceptualize these linkages as "unconscious 'grammatical' principles" and to analyze the political economy surrounding peoples' efforts to make their worlds by holding on to particular cultural practices and adapting others to their new circumstances—circumstances within which they were unable to define the terms of their lives.

18. Of course, this is by no means the first example of the national trumping more radical internationalist political agendas. Indeed, this story is as old as that of revolution itself. In her brilliant exploration of the legacies of the Haitian Revolution throughout the region, Sibylle Fischer (2004: 11) also indicates that "Haiti itself had to renounce the transnationalism of its founding ideology in order to ensure the country's survival."

19. Drake has also identified the Cold War as inspiring a move away from internationalism but suggests that it was the *success* of anticolonial movements in Africa that played such a decisive role in turning African Americans away from coordinated political action. He argues that once African countries became nations, the sense of a unity of purpose fractured: "The period of uncomplicated united struggle to secure [African] independence from the white oppressor had ended for each colony as it became a nation. Diaspora blacks had to decide which of various political factions, if any, within the new nations they would support" (Drake 1982: 351). Many black intellectuals rued these changes, E. Franklin Frazier chief among them. While Frazier himself deployed a culturalist frame for viewing African American family life (despite the fact that he also emphasized socio-structural factors in his analysis of African American family organization), he saw in the move away from internationalist anticolonial politics a diminished inclination to critique Western society and culture. He also felt that the turn from an analytic framework that privileged the language of political economy inhibited the elaboration of a model of black modernity that was inspired, at least in part, by African independence (Gaines 2005). Frazier's *Black Bourgeoisie*—written and published in France before it was published in the United States in 1957—articulated as scathing a critique of U.S.

black middle-class intellectual and political leaders as Fanon's *Wretched of the Earth* did of the newly postcolonial political leadership. Both saw in bourgeois nationalism a narrowing of focus and an emphasis on culture and assimilation rather than an impetus toward the radical transformation of the relationships between black people, capitalism, and nation-states.

20. It is also this anti-nationalist sense that pervades the use of "diaspora" within British cultural studies, though here we see the maintenance of explicit attention to class and political economy, at least until the publication of Gilroy's *The Black Atlantic* (1993). This is because within this context, diaspora became a way to identify the relationships between racism and British nationalism.

21. See Gunst 1995 for a detailed history of the development of Jamaican political violence, drug wars, posses, and the transnational crack cocaine trade.

22. See Small 1994 for an analysis of the Yardie phenomenon in Britain.

23. See Davies 1995; Goodwin 1999; Small 1994. On the new "infiltration" of Yardies in Britain, see Burrell 2002: 4; Lockett 2002.

24. I thank Pat Saunders for this insight: Pat Saunders, personal communication, 7 May 2009.

25. See Hall et al. 1978 for an analysis of how "mugging" developed as a discourse of black criminality in Britain.

26. There is, of course, a long history to this kind of discourse within Britain, a discourse that proliferated especially after the report on the Brixton riots written by Sir Leslie Scarman (1981). See also Gilroy 1987. I thank Mary Chamberlain and Faith Smith for directing me to these sources.

27. One might also argue that Lord Scarman was approaching this sort of analysis in his report, as he recognized the existence of a "matriarchal" extended family structure among West Indian immigrants and argued that it had been undermined by social conditions in Britain. Daniel Moynihan comes to a similar conclusion regarding households headed by women, arguing that they only mark pathology because they are not the accepted norm in the United States.

28. This is true not only for European states, many of whose consolidation was the result of imperialist expansion and slavery, but also for "new" states formed in the post–Second World War period as the result of anticolonial movements. See Nagengast 1994 for an early review essay on the topic.

29. Higglers are Jamaican traders—usually working-class women (but see Freeman 2000)—who buy and sell goods in the market and on the street.

30. For an excellent critical analysis of these so-called reforms and the sorts of gendered dynamics they mobilized, see Iton 2008.

3. SPECTACULAR BODIES

1. See, e.g., Beckford 1972; Clarke 1966; Frazier 1966 (1939); Girvan 1975; Herskovits 1941; Patterson 1969; Stone 1973.

2. See also Fischer 2004 for a gripping discussion of how the very objects, events, and

processes we attempt to forget reappear constantly in the present, confounding our efforts to disavow them.

3. We might also think of this as similar to what Antonio Benítez-Rojo (2006) has meant by "repeating islands," the regularities within Caribbean societies and experiences that repeat themselves through time.

4. See Austin-Broos 1984 for a discussion of the importance of "inside" and "outside" as organizing principles within Jamaican society.

5. This is a point also made by Paul Gilroy in the essay "Declaration of Rights" in Gilroy 2010: 78–85.

6. See Allison 2006 for a discussion of other sites from which these fantasies are generated.

7. For an analysis of what is missed in Foucault's *The History of Sexuality* (1990) by not attending to the centrality of French imperialism to notions of gender, race, and sexuality, see Stoler 1995. For an analysis of the links between modernity and racial terror, see Gilroy 1993.

8. I thank Barnor Hesse for this insight. For more on how that which is spectacular destabilizes Debord's notion of the society of the spectacle, see Goldsby 2006; Smolenski and Humphrey 2005; Spillers 1987; Taussig 1986. On how states have mobilized particular forms of spectacular performance in their quest for legitimacy, see Coronil 1997; Piot 2010; Taussig 1997.

9. The literature on national cultures and cultural politics is too vast to list here, but for review essays, see Alonso 1994; Foster 1991; Fox 1990; Glick Schiller 1997; Miller and Yudice 2002; Slocum and Thomas 2003; Yelvington 2001.

10. Elsewhere (D. Thomas 2004) I discuss Jamaica's first cultural policy and comment on the deliberations that ultimately led to the publication of the current policy.

11. See Bolland 1997 and Price 1998 for an elaboration of this argument.

12. Of course, this was also the position taken by the Frankfurt School of theorists.

13. This is not unique to Jamaica. The anthropologist Danilyn Rutherford (1996: 601) has also discussed how residents of Biak, an Indonesian region considered by those in Jakarta to be the "nation's outer edge," use that which is foreign to mark their identity and prestige, much to the chagrin of nationalist cultural producers who instead want to promote "traditional" forms of dance and music. She argues that Biak, rather than being a land "supposedly forgotten by time" (Rutherford 1996: 580), is actually a politically self-conscious frontier shaped by the colonial encounter in which youth construct modern, cosmopolitan subjectivities by privileging foreign (and in this case, Western) materials.

14. I thank Michelle Stephens for reminding me of Foucault's discussion of how genealogies recover the past in opposition to discourses of the present that obscure the past (Foucault 2003).

15. Doris Garraway (2005: 243–44) shows that similar tactics were used in early colonial Saint-Domingue, arguing that "colonists would nail their slaves to a wall or a tree by the ear for a few days before cutting it off" and that runaway slaves "could be subjected to more prolonged rituals of torture, during which their bodies, slashed

by the whip, were periodically rinsed in a searing solution of peppers, salt, and lemon juice. Alternatively, they were quartered, burned at the stake, or fitted with iron collars topped with enormous crossing bars such that they would never again be able to take flight."

16. See Dayan 1998 for a similar discussion of the Black Code in Haiti.

17. Irene Silverblatt (2004) makes a similar argument in relation to Peru in the Inquisition era.

18. The classic work on Afro-Jamaican cultural practices developed during slavery is Brathwaite 1971b, but see also Bilby 2005. When the Jamaica Festival Commission and the National Dance Theatre Company of Jamaica began encouraging research into Afro-Jamaican "folk forms" in the 1960s and 1970s, however, this situation began to change somewhat.

19. Obeah is a local term for magical spirituality, and is generally feared among Jamaicans. An obeahman is a sort of "bush doctor" who might cast spells through the mobilization of animal sacrifice, among other things.

20. Other accounts have her dying by being strangled by her slave lover in her bed.

21. The novel of the same name by the Jamaican author and journalist Herbert G. de Lisser, who was the editor of the *Gleaner* for the better part of the first four decades of the twentieth century, was first published in 1929.

22. I thank Annie Paul and Vanessa Spence for suggesting that I visit Greenwood Great House and the Bettons for patiently enduring my questions.

4. PUBLIC BODIES

1. This is a paradox that has been explored in the literature on transnational migration: see esp. Basch et al. 1994; Glick Schiller and Fouron 2001; Laguerre 2005. As Michel Laguerre (2005: 207) has observed in the Haitian case, diasporic political engagement and activism "establishes a disconnect between the state's fixed boundaries and the nation's flexible territorial expansion." This generates a constant circulation of available political figures between Haiti and its diaspora that is facilitated by a diasporic public sphere that has expanded its reach through new technology.

2. For an analysis of cross-class masculinity, the dual marriage system, and how these aspects of gender relations reproduce patriarchy, see Douglass 1992. For more recent work on Caribbean masculinity, see Reddock 2004.

3. This inscription was subsequently removed because Facey Cooper had not sought copyright permission to use Marley's quote.

4. That a poll was conducted regarding the possibility of removing the statue was not surprising, given that this kind of action has precedent. In 1981, the Jamaican government commissioned the artist Christopher Gonzales to create a statue commemorating the reggae icon Bob Marley. Just before it was unveiled in 1982, Gonzales's statue, which represented Marley emerging from tree roots, was removed because it was "criticized as an inaccurate and an 'inappropriate' representation of the renowned musician both by members of Marley's family and by members of the

public" (Mains 2004: 189). The government then commissioned "a safer and 'more realistic' piece" (Mains 2004: 189) designed by Alvin Marriott to stand outside the National Stadium, and Gonzales's work found a home first at the National Gallery and, later, at the music mogul Chris Blackwell's north coast beach development, Island Village.

5. Constance Sutton reports in the unpublished manuscript "Public Monuments in Post-Colonial Barbados: Sites of Memory, Sites of Contestation" that a similar argument was made about the Emancipation Statue erected in Barbados in 1985. In that instance, the sculptor responded to the criticism by "adding a light wrap around the man's lower torso."

6. Carolyn Cooper (1989, 2004) has been the main proponent of the position that reads dancehall as a form of marronage that destabilizes the social relations that buttress ideologies of morality and respectability in Jamaica.

7. Here, Brooks is drawing from Deborah Willis's and Carla Williams's collection of photography, *The Black Female Body*, to show how black women's bodies themselves are consistently spectacles of exploitation.

8. The male-marginalization thesis was originally put forward by the educator Errol Miller (1986) and has been vociferously discredited by, among others, Barriteau 2003; Chevannes 2001; Robinson 2003. See Lewis 2004 for an important rethinking of the dynamics of crisis in relation to masculinity.

9. By arguing this, I do not mean to suggest that a more global exchange of ideas *began* in the late nineteenth century, as instances of prior cross-territorial interactions between people of African descent are well documented. For example, black Baptists from the Thirteen Colonies were among the thousands of black loyalists and slaves who arrived in Jamaica toward the end of the American Revolution (Pulis 1999), and Haitians were among those advocating for colored Jamaicans' political rights after emancipation (Heuman 1981). What was different about these interactions at the turn of the twentieth century was their scale.

10. Daniel Miller (1994) has advanced a similar argument based on his ethnographic research in Trinidad. He suggests that it is equally plausible to locate reputation in the influences of the colonial power, and particularly in the leisure activities of colonial men—what he calls the "culture of mistresses" (Miller 1994: 263). In this view, he argues, a female-centered search for respectability based on the formation of stable descent groups with long-term ambitions for family development and the cultivation of property are true markers of resistance, given the history of slavery. Although this analytical possibility is seductive, it maintains the problematic assumption that women and men are associated with mutually exclusive spheres of social life.

11. *The Harder They Come* was first a film directed by Perry Henzell (1972) and subsequently a novel by Michael Thelwell that was published by Grove in 1980. *Rockers*— part documentary and part drama—was produced in 1978 by Patrick Hulsey and was directed by Ted Bafaloukos. It was finally distributed in 1980 by New Yorker Films. *Children of Babylon* was directed and produced by Lennie Little-White in

1979 and was distributed by Mediamix and Rainbow Productions. *Shottas* was produced and directed by Cess Silvera in 2001 and was distributed by Sony Entertainment in 2006. *Belly* was released in 1998 by Artisan Entertainment. *Third World Cop* was directed by Chris Browne and released by Island Jamaica Films in 1999. *Rude Boy* was produced by Amsell Entertainment, 3G Films, and Bent Outta Shape Productions and released in 2004 by Lions Gate Entertainment. And *Rollin' with the Nines* was released in 2006 by Flakjacket Films.

12. They include older classics, such as *Blood Posse*, written by Phillip Baker in 1995, as well as more recent offerings, such as Courttia Newland's *The Scholar* (1997, Abacus Press) and more obscure titles like *Yardies: The Making of a Jamaican Posse* (Prince Kofi, Ghetto Life Publishing, 2007).

13. Unlike these nonfictional accounts, however, the books in the *Yardie* trilogy do not tie drug violence to political violence. In fact, while Headley refers occasionally to corrupt police officers who attempt to profit from the drug trade, nowhere in the three novels is it mentioned that these cops are part of a broader system in which politicians are also implicated.

14. For more on media representations of Jamaican Yardies in the United Kingdom, see Murji 1999; Skelton 1998; Small 1998.

15. Sony released the film to DVD in January 2007. The DVD features an introduction by Kymani Marley (who plays the lead actor) and Cess Silvera authenticating the 2006 release as the "official director's cut." They argue that people should throw away their old bootleg versions because "now you get to see *Shottas* crystal clear, all the missing scenes that you was reading. . . . That's done away with." Silvera concludes the introduction by stating: "The director's cut is, like, it's raw, it's unapologetic, you know what I mean, it's like in your face, like this is what the movie was supposed to be like, not the little bootleg thing, the real thing. So right now you have to see *Shottas* in its glory. . . . *Shottas* is official, *Shottas* is here, *Shottas* is the shit."

16. Kevin Jackson, "Spragga Benz and Kymani Marley for Lead Roles in Upcoming Movie, 'Shottas,'" February 2001, available online at http://www.jahworks.org/music/movies/shotta_movie.html (accessed 16 September 2005); Michael Fleming, "Silvera Taking a Shot with 'Shottas' Sequel, Helmer Seeks Legit Hit," 13 April 2005, available online at http://www.variety.com/ (accessed 16 September 2005). An earlier Reuters article has Silvera telling the press that he found a bag full of cash in the airport parking lot when he was retrieving his car after returning from his grandmother's funeral in Jamaica: "Luck, Famous Friends Get Jamaica Crime Film Made," 11 September 2002, available online at http://www.melodymakers.de (accessed 16 September 2005).

17. In Jamaica, Biggs lives with his auntie Pauline.

18. It is important here to note that while Chiquita may have been the fiercest killer in this instance, her ferocity does not signify that she is the "top don." Rather, the power she wields is symbolic of more general ideologies about violence and retribution in Jamaica. For more extensive treatments that might help to ground the

gender implications of this move, and how they articulate with broader gender dynamics within Jamaica, see Barnes 1997; Cooper 1993; Ford-Smith 1997; D. Thomas 2004; Ulysse 1999.

19. Several other scholars have fleshed out the various ways transgressive sexualities have marked the boundaries of citizenship in the Caribbean: see, e.g., Chin 1997; Glave 2005; Gutzmore 2004; Kempadoo 2004; Kempadoo (ed.) 1999; Rosenberg 2004; Silvera 1992; Smith 2011.

20. See Human Rights Watch 2004 for a full discussion of homophobic violence in Jamaica and its effects related to HIV/AIDS awareness and prevention.

21. See the blog "The Unspeakable Truth," available online at http://revaluushan .blogspot.com, for consistently critical and provocative insights into the various dimensions of homophobia in Jamaica.

22. Kezia Page (personal communication, 6 April 2009) makes the excellent point that, while there has always been a pamphlet culture in Jamaica and while forms of popular theater have long created public spaces for debate about community norms, the popular fiction culture is somewhat new. The *Yardie* books therefore might primarily be consumed by a diasporic audience that is dealing with different sorts of racialized pressure.

23. The song I refer to here is "Goggle," which was released on the album *Too Hype* (VP Records, 1997).

24. Released on *Give Me the Reason* (VP Records, 1996).

25. This, of course, is also the main connotation of "respect" among the inner-city African American and Latino communities analyzed by Elijah Anderson (1999) and Philippe Bourgois (1995). Within the United States, the assertion of a need for respect is also formulated within the context of institutionalized inequalities that are both racialized and gendered in ways that disproportionately marginalize young black and Latino men.

26. I thank Faith Smith for pushing me to flesh out this argument.

5. RESURRECTED BODIES

1. *Star*, 11 April 1963, 1; "Two Cultists Held on Murder Charge," "About Five Who Died," "No Cause for Alarm—Sir Alex," "Police Hold 150," all in *Daily Gleaner*, 13 April 1963, 1; "Judah Tells How RJR Reported MoBay Incident," *Daily Gleaner*, 23 April 1963, 2.

2. These two themes—universalism and black nationalism—continue to exist in a sort of dialectical relationship with respect to Rastafari. The universalist position, which foregrounds peace, love, unity, and interracial harmony, is the one that is more easily co-opted by the state (e.g., through the ideology of "One Love" as it is used by the Jamaica Tourist Board). The black nationalist position, on the other hand, maintains a tension with the Jamaican state and, therefore, a more explicitly critical read on state-driven initiatives. I thank Jake Homiak for pushing me to identify this relationship more overtly.

3. "Rastas on Rampage in MoBay—Eight Persons Killed," *Star*, 11 April 1963, 1; "Two Cultists Held on Murder Charge"; "Police Hold 150"; "PM, Security Chief Fly to Scene," *Star*, 11 April 1963, 1; "Police Net 160 Beards," *Star*, 13 April 1963, 12.

4. Typically, collective memory has been seen as a site of resistance to dominant nationalist narratives, but, as Marita Sturken (1997: 7) has pointed out, "Cultural memory may often constitute opposition, but it is not automatically the scene of cultural resistance. . . . There is nothing politically prescribed in cultural memory." More recently, historians have been interested in problematizing the privileged location of memory in the formation of communities that are simultaneously sub-national and part of diasporic formations: see, e.g., Campt 2004.

5. For a similar, though earlier, take on "dread history," see Hill 1983.

6. I thank Jake Homiak for calling my attention to Yawney's important work, especially this conference paper.

7. Nyabinghis are Rastafarian groundations—drumming and chanting ceremonies that can last for up to a week.

8. On the shifts in practice and consciousness from the late 1980s and the new centrality of international trods, see Homiak 1990, 1999. For the critical role of Rastafari in youth pedagogy, see Niaah 2005.

9. The Coral Gardens affair is also briefly mentioned in Owens 1976 and Price 2003 and more elaborately in Williams 2005. Ras Flako also recently released the pamphlet *Icient Wisdom* (2010), which contains transcribed testimonies of many of the elders who personally experienced the persecution of the aftermath of Coral Gardens.

10. On 5 January 1978, while the PNP was in government under the leadership of Michael Manley, fourteen men who were said to be activists in a gang located in a JLP stronghold in Kingston were duped into thinking they would be given guns and military jobs if they cooperated with the government. On the morning of that day, they were picked up by an army ambulance and taken to the military range at Green Bay. They were allegedly given instructions not to move, and when the ambulance drove away, a sniper team opened fire on them. Five died, and the remainder ran into the bushes nearby. The official military report of the incident argued that the men were shot after being surprised by soldiers conducting target practice on the range, but this report was challenged by an official inquiry that nevertheless claimed that the snipers were acting in self-defense. The Manley government disavowed any knowledge of the covert action, but the massacre still stands as one of the worst and most blatant acts of state violence in Jamaica's history. It is memorialized in fictional accounts, such as Perry Henzell's *Power Game* and the film director Storm Saulter's *Better Mus' Come*. A series of survivors' accounts was recently published in the *Jamaica Gleaner* (Sinclair 2008a, 2008b). For additional discussion of the Green Bay Massacre, see Sives 2010: 104–7. For an ethnographic discussion of how residents of central Kingston understood what happened at Green Bay at the time, see Harrison 1982.

11. "Coral Gardens Killings: Inspector Slow in Releasing Ammunition," *Star*, 13 April

1963, 1, 12; "Coral Gardens Murder Trial: Court Hears of Attack on Cottage, Escape in Canefield," *Daily Gleaner*, 19 July 1963, 5.

12. Many, but not all, of the elders, as well as Selbourne Reid, the retired police officer, mentioned that Franklin cultivated ganja on his property and that this was one of the main issues between him and the security forces.

13. Reid, who was born in the rural parish of Portland, remembered that often he was almost brought to tears while watching full crops being trashed but that as a police officer at the time he could not refuse to follow orders.

14. "Coral Gardens Killings: Murder Trial Begins," *Daily Gleaner*, 16 July 1963, 5; "Holy Thursday Killings: Accused Aunt Testifies at Coral Gardens Murder Trial," *Daily Gleaner*, 17 July 1963, 4.

15. The initial newspaper stories reported that six "bearded" men were involved in the events of the day, but on appeal, the third accused man, Leabert Jarrett, was acquitted, the judge having found no concrete evidence of a sixth man: "Jarrett Freed in Coral Gardens Murder Appeal," *Daily Gleaner*, 21 March 1964, 1; "Coral Gardens Murder Appeal: Court Gives Written Reasons for Its Judgment," *Daily Gleaner*, 27 May 1964, 4.

16. "Two Cultists Held on Murder Charge"; "Rastas on Rampage in MoBay"; "Holy Thursday Killings."

17. "Coral Gardens Murder Trial."

18. According to testimony by Constable Victor Nelson, before the police left the station, they were given empty rifles by Inspector Fisher. Another constable suggested that the ammunition cartridges also be distributed so the guns could be loaded before reaching Tryall, but Fisher refused, saying he would distribute the cartridges when he felt they were necessary: "Coral Gardens Murder Trial: Witness Shot Dead the Man Who Was Chopping Inspector," *Daily Gleaner*, 27 July 1963, 4.

19. "Coral Gardens Killings" (13 April 1963); "Coral Gardens Murder Trial: Policemen Dropped Empty Guns, Ran When Macheteman Advanced—Witness," *Daily Gleaner*, 25 July 1963, 5.

20. "Coral Gardens Murder Trial" (27 July 1963).

21. "Coral Gardens Murder Trial: Melbourne Fired at Man Hacking Causewell but Was Speared Down, Chopped Up, Detective Tells Court," *Daily Gleaner*, 26 July 1963, 2; *Daily Gleaner*, 16 July 1963, "Coral Gardens Killings" (16 July 1963); "Coral Gardens Murder Trial: Court Visits Death Scene Today," *Daily Gleaner*, 30 July 1963, 5.

22. "Coral Gardens Murder Trial" (27 July 1963); "Coral Gardens Murder Trial: Behaviour Tantamount to Contempt of Court, Judge Tells Witness," *Daily Gleaner*, 1 August 1963, 4; "Coral Gardens Murder Trial: Bowen's, Larman's Statement Read to the Jury," *Daily Gleaner*, 8 August 1963, 4; "Coral Gardens Murder Trial: Would Have Given Permission for Larman to Give Statement—Doctor," *Daily Gleaner*, 9 August 1963, 4; "Defense Opens at Coral Gardens Murder Trial," *Daily Gleaner*, 15 August 1963, 4.

23. Beresford Hay and David Muirhead appeared for Bowen. Hay subsequently taught

at the the University of the West Indies Law School, and Muirhead later became the Jamaican High Commissioner in London. Carl Rattray appeared for Larman. Rattray later became the president of the Court of Appeal in Jamaica and helped to found the Dispute Resolution Foundation in 1984. Hewart Henriques appeared for Jarrett. He later became active in politics for the JLP, running for member of Parliament for St. James Northwestern, which includes Rose Hall, in 1972, and for the Parish Council's general elections in 1969 (he did not win either race). The director of public prosecutions was the Hon. W. H. Swaby, and he was assisted by Crown Counsel Churchill Raymond. Much later, Swaby became a member of the Privy Council of Jamaica, and Raymond was the first ombudsman for public utilities in Jamaica.

24. "Jarrett Freed in Coral Gardens Murder Appeal"; "Coral Gardens Murder Appeal" (, 27 May 1964); "Two Hanged for Coral Gardens Murders," *Daily Gleaner*, 2 December 1964, 2.

25. "Police Hold 150"; "Police Net 160 Beards."

26. "Coral Gardens: PM Defends Right to Call Army," *Daily Gleaner*, 5 May 1963, 2.

27. "Rastas Shaving 'Locks': Drive against Ganja Opens in East," *Star*, 19 April 1963, 12.

28. The tourism industry emerged in Port Antonio, Portland, during the 1890s as the result of the development of the banana industry under the auspices of the United Fruit Company. At the end of the Second World War, Montego Bay became the center of the trade because of the passage, in 1944, of the Hotels Aid Law, which waived customs duties and provided other concessions for the construction of resort hotels and because, unlike Port Antonio, Montego Bay had an airstrip, which provided easier access to overseas territories. The shift to Montego Bay paralleled another one — that from high-end tourism to mass tourism. Jamaica was the leader among Anglophone Caribbean countries in establishing mass tourism, and by 1962 the industry had been reorganized to accommodate a summer season geared toward mass tourists and a winter season to maintain wealthier ones. For more on the development and transformation of the tourism industry in Jamaica, see Taylor 1993.

29. I have not been able to locate a report of any such investigation.

30. The study was prompted by a desire on the part of Rastafarians to generate a more informed public face for their movement in the aftermath of the Claudius Henry Rebellion in 1959–60 and was ultimately published in twelve installments in the *Daily Gleaner* (Smith et al. 1960). For critiques of the study, see Hill 1983; Niaah 2005.

31. We are collaborating with members of the Coral Gardens Agitation Committee and the Millennium Council on a film that documents the experiences of the surviving elders.

32. In *The Promised Key*, Leonard Howell (Maragh 2007 [1935]) introduces "Babylon" as another name for Rome.

33. See Price 2009 for discussions by Rastafarian elders of their early experiences in the faith.

34. For more on Claudius Henry, see Bogues 2003; Chevannes 1976; Meeks 2000; Nettleford 1970.

35. See Brown-Glaude 2007 for an important perspective on the popularity of skin-bleaching creams.

36. Both quotes are from personal e-mail communication with Jake Homiak, 24 November 2008.

37. This is an allusion to the biblical statement, "In my father's house there are many mansions." Within Rastafari, the best-known groupings are the Nyabinghi Order, the Twelve Tribes, and the Boboshanti. The call for centralization, however, seems to contradict one of the organizing principles of the movement: heterogeneity.

38. I thank Melanie Newton for influencing my thinking here.

39. The objectives of the council are "(1) To ensure effective governance and co-operation between all the Houses and Mansions that make up the Rastafari nation in Jamaica, as well as worldwide, in order that it shall represent the Rastafari nation of the world, in a united Theocratic Government; (2) To advocate and negotiate with appropriate bodies in order to further the interests of the Rastafari communities, in matters of Repatriation, Reparations, Cultural Heritage projects, Human Rights and Welfare, Intellectual Property and the like; (3) To secure, protect and manage the intellectual property of the Rastafari community worldwide, for the benefit of the Rastafari community worldwide; (4) To provide support and empowerment to all Rastafari members and Rastafari mansions and organizations in the practice and furtherance of their living faith; (5) To form productive working alliances with all organizations that are able to assist the Millennium Council with the fulfillment of its objectives; (6) To serve as a communication, resource and information centre for all Rastafari communities, in Jamaica, the Caribbean, the United States of America, Africa, Europe, worldwide; (7) To raise and manage funds in order to better achieve all the Millennium Council's objectives and serve the Rastafari nation" (Ethio-Africa Diaspora Union Millennium Council Secretariat 2008).

40. On UNESCO's World Heritage Sites, see Wang 2007; on the Institute for Puerto Rican Culture, see Davila 1997; on the Jamaica Cultural Development Commission, see D. Thomas 2004.

41. I thank Anthony Bogues for reminding me of this crucial point.

42. See also Ebron 2008 for an important discussion of how black style and black politics have become conjoined and what this has meant for transnational black politics and the reception of black popular culture.

CODA

Epigraph: Group of 21, draft declaration prepared for the World Conference against Racism, 31 August–8 September 2001, available online at http://www.racism.gov.za/substance/confdoc/decldraft189b.htm.

1. It is perhaps ironic that after the Jamaican government embarked on this initia-

tive, the British government set aside £600,000 toward research by the University College, London, into who benefited from the slave trade and how money accrued from the slave trade was spent. See "Britain to Track Slave Trade Money," *Jamaica Gleaner*, 2 August 2009, available online at http://www.jamaica-gleaner.com (accessed 2 August 2009).

2. These are the questions many of the authors grapple with in Miller and Kumar 2007, and are questions that more generally pervade the literature on reparations movements.

3. In fact, as Kamari Clarke (2009: xii) points out, one of the advantages of the International Criminal Court, among other multilateral justice frameworks, is that it "protest[s] against national sovereignty, which was represented as stunting human progress."

4. Anthony Bogues has made a similar argument about the dominant historiographical assessments of the workers' rebellions in Jamaica of 1938 (and across the Caribbean throughout the second half of the 1930s). He notes that the leftist analyses of these rebellions (Ken Post's and Don Robotham's in particular) were too wedded to strict Marxist analysis and categorization that they failed to take account of the "*ideas of those who participated in the uprising*" (Bogues 2010: 85). By focusing on the classical goals of revolution as defined by Marx, these scholars and popular educators could only frame the workers' rebellions in terms of what they lacked (supposedly, leadership, ideology, and arms). Instead, Bogues argues, we must take into account the imaginative frame within which these rebellions occurred, a frame that can be gleaned only by taking seriously a locally developed historical consciousness that emphasized respect for black people, better wages, and land. That these are still among Jamaicans' primary concerns should be clear from the analyses presented throughout these pages.

5. I thank Alissa Trotz for pushing me to develop these arguments and for the work she shared on Roger Khan.

6. Jacques Derrida (2009: 59) has argued that forgiveness always invokes a sovereign power; that the power to forgive always results from the ability to enact sovereignty. For him, therefore, the goal should be to imagine forgiveness without power, to conceptualize forgiveness as "unconditional but without sovereignty."

References

Abraham, Carolyn, and Peter Hum. 1994. "A Piece of the Action." *Ottawa Citizen*, 24 July, A4.

Abrahams-Clivio, Tara. 2005. "Let's Renounce the Title of Murder Capital." *Jamaica Observer*, 20 October. Available at http://www.jamaicaobserver.com (accessed 20 October 2005).

Abu-Lughod, Lila. 2004. *Dramas of Nationhood: The Politics of Television in Egypt*. Chicago: University of Chicago Press.

Agamben, Giorgio. 1998. *Homo Sacer: Sovereign Power and Bare Life*. Stanford, Calif.: Stanford University Press.

Alexander, M. Jacqui. 1991. "Redefining Morality: The Postcolonial State and the Sexual Offences Bill of Trinidad and Tobago." *Third World Women and the Politics of Feminism*, ed. Chandra T. Mohanty, Ann Russo, and Lourdes Torres, 133–52. Bloomington: Indiana University Press.

———. 1994. "Not Just (Any) Body Can Be a Citizen: The Politics of Law, Sexuality, and Postcoloniality in Trinidad and Tobago and the Bahamas." *Feminist Review* 48: 5–23.

———. 1997. "Erotic Autonomy as a Politics of Decolonization: An Anatomy of Feminist and State Practice in the Bahamas Tourist Economy." *Feminist Genealogies, Colonial Legacies, Democratic Futures*, ed. Chandra T. Mohanty and M. Jacqui Alexander, 63–100. New York: Routledge.

———. 2005. *Pedagogies of Crossing: Meditations on Feminism, Sexual Politics, Memory, and the Sacred*. Durham: Duke University Press.

Alexander Craft, Renee. 2008. "'Los gringos vienen!' (The Gringos Are Coming!): Female Respectability and the Politics of Congo Tourist Presentations in Portobelo, Panama." *Transforming Anthropology* 16(1): 20–31.

Allison, Anne. 2006. *Millennial Monsters: Japanese Toys and the Global Imagination.* Berkeley: University of California Press.

Alonso, Ana Maria. 1994. "The Politics of Space, Time, and Substance: State Formation, Nationalism, and Ethnicity." *Annual Review of Anthropology* 23:379–405.

Althusser, Louis. 2001. *Lenin and Philosophy and Other Essays.* New York: Monthly Review Press.

"A National Security Strategy for Jamaica." 2006. *Sunday Gleaner.* Available at http://www.jamaica-gleaner.com/gleaner/20060507/news/news5.html (accessed 2 October 2006).

Anderson, Elijah. 1999. *Code of the Street: Decency, Violence, and the Moral Life of the Inner City.* New York: W. W. Norton.

Appadurai, Arjun. 1990. "Disjuncture and Difference in the Global Cultural Economy." *Public Culture* 2(2): 1–24.

———. 1998. "Dead Certainty: Ethnic Violence in the Era of Globalization." *Public Culture* 10(2): 225–47.

———. 2002. "Deep Democracy: Urban Governmentality and the Horizon of Politics." *Public Culture* 14(1): 21–47.

———. 2006. *Fear of Small Numbers: An Essay on the Geography of Anger.* Durham: Duke University Press.

Appleby, Timothy. 1992a. "The Jamaica Connection." *Globe and Mail,* 10 July.

———. 1992b. "The Jamaica Connection." *Globe and Mail,* 31 July.

Arendt, Hannah. 1951. *The Origins of Totalitarianism.* New York: Harcourt and Brace.

Aretxaga, Begoña. 2003. "Maddening States." *Annual Review of Anthropology* 32:393–410.

Armstrong, Chris. 1994. "Win or Lose." *Globe and Mail,* 13 August.

Austin-Broos, Diane. 1984. *Urban Life in Kingston, Jamaica: The Culture and Class Ideology of Two Neighborhoods.* New York: Gordon and Breach.

———. 1992. "Redefining the Moral Order: Interpretations of Christianity in Post-Emancipation Jamaica." *The Meaning of Freedom: Economics, Politics, and Culture after Slavery,* ed. Frank McGlynn and Seymour Drescher, 221–44. Pittsburgh: University of Pittsburgh Press.

———. 1994. "Race/Class: Jamaica's Discourse of Heritable Identity." *New West Indian Guide* 68(3–4): 213–33.

———. 1997. *Jamaica Genesis: Religion and the Politics of Moral Order.* Chicago: University of Chicago Press.

———. 2005. "The Politics of Moral Order: A Brief Anatomy of Racing." *Social Analysis* 49(2): 182–90.

Axel, Brian Keith. 2000. *The Nation's Tortured Body: Violence, Representation, and the Formation of a Sikh "Diaspora."* Durham: Duke University Press.

Baker, Lee D. 1998. *From Savage to Negro: Anthropology and the Construction of Race, 1896–1954.* Berkeley: University of California Press.

Baker, Phillip. 1995. *Blood Posse.* New York: St. Martin's Press.

Barkan, Elazar. 2007. "Introduction: Reparation: A Moral and Political Dilemma."

Reparations: Interdisciplinary Inquiries, ed. Jon Miller and Rahul Kumar, 1–19. Oxford: Oxford University Press.

Barnes, Natasha. 1997. "Face of the Nation: Race, Nationalisms, and Identities in Jamaican Beauty Pageants." *Daughters of Caliban: Caribbean Women in the Twentieth Century*, ed. Consuelo Lopez Springfield, 285–306. Bloomington: Indiana University Press.

Barnett, Courtenay. 2007. "Reparations and Globalization." *Daily Observer*, 1 January. Available at http://www.jamaicaobserver.com (accessed 1 January 2007).

Barrett, Leonard E. 1988. *The Rastafarians*, rev. ed. Boston: Beacon Press.

Barriteau, Eudine. 2003. "Requiem for the Male Marginalization Thesis in the Caribbean: Death of a Non-Theory." *Confronting Power, Theorizing Gender: Interdisciplinary Perspectives in the Caribbean*, ed. Eudine Barriteau, 324–55. Mona: University of the West Indies Press.

Barrow, Christine. 1996. *Family in the Caribbean: Themes and Perspectives*. Kingston: Ian Randle.

———. 1998a. "Introduction and Overview: Caribbean Gender Ideologies." *Caribbean Portraits: Essays on Gender Ideologies and Identities*, ed. Christine Barrow, xi–xxxviii. Kingston: Ian Randle.

———. 1998b. "Caribbean Masculinity and Family: Revisiting 'Marginality' and 'Reputation.'" *Caribbean Portraits: Essays on Gender Ideologies and Identities*, ed. Christine Barrow, 339–58. Kingston: Ian Randle.

Basch, Linda, Nina Glick Schiller, and Cristina Szanton-Blanc. 1994. *Nations Unbound: Transnational Projects, Postcolonial Predicaments, and Deterritorialized Nation-States*. Langhorne, Pa.: Gordon and Breach.

Baucom, Ian. 2005. *Specters of the Atlantic: Finance Capital, Slavery, and the Philosophy of History*. Durham: Duke University Press.

Beckford, George L. 1972. *Persistent Poverty: Underdevelopment in Plantation Economies of the Third World*. New York: Oxford University Press.

Beckles, Hilary. 1984. *Black Rebellion in Barbados: The Struggle against Slavery, 1627–1838*. Bridgetown: Antilles.

———. 1989. *Natural Rebels: A Social History of Enslaved Black Women in Barbados*. New Brunswick: Rutgers University Press.

Benedict, Ruth. 1934. *Patterns of Culture*. New York: Houghton Mifflin.

Benítez-Rojo, Antonio. 1997. *The Repeating Island: The Caribbean and the Postmodern Perspective*. Durham: Duke University Press.

Benjamin, Walter. 1999. *The Arcades Project*. Cambridge: Harvard University Press.

Besson, Jean. 1993. "Reputation and Respectability Reconsidered: A New Perspective on Afro-Caribbean Peasant Women." *Women and Change in the Caribbean*, ed. Janet H. Momsen, 15–37. London: James Currey.

———. 2002. *Martha Brae's Two Histories: European Expansion and Caribbean Culture-Building in Jamaica*. Chapel Hill: University of North Carolina Press.

Best, Lloyd, and Kari Levitt. 1969. "Externally Propelled Industrialisation and Growth in the Caribbean: Selected Essays, Volumes I, II, III, and IV." Unpublished ms., McGill Center for Developing Area Studies, Montreal.

Biehl, João. 2005. *Vita: Life in a Zone of Social Abandonment*. Berkeley: University of California Press.

Bilby, Kenneth M. 2005. *True Born Maroons*. Gainesville: University Press of Florida.

Billington, Ray Allen. 1971 [1958]. *The American Frontier Thesis: Attack and Defense*. Washington: American Historical Association.

Biondi, Martha. 2003. "The Rise of the Reparations Movement." *Radical History Review* 87:5–18.

Black, Clinton. 1966. *Tales of Old Jamaica*. Kingston: Longman Jamaica.

Blaine, Betty Ann. 2005. "Death and the Death of Outrage." *Jamaica Observer*, 11 October. Available at http://www.jamaicaobserver.com (accessed 11 October 2005).

Blake, Duane. 2003. *Shower Posse: The Most Notorious Criminal Organization*. New York: Diamond.

Blake, Judith. 1961. *Family Structure in Jamaica: The Social Context of Reproduction*. Glencoe, Ill.: Free Press.

Blue Falcon. 2003. "Education, not Sterilisation." Letter to the editor, *Jamaica Gleaner* August 2. Available at http://www.jamaica-gleaner.com (accessed 28 November 2003).

Bogues, Anthony. 2002. "Politics, Nation and PostColony: Caribbean Inflections." *Small Axe* 11:1–30.

———. 2003. *Black Heretics, Black Prophets: Radical Political Intellectuals*. New York: Routledge.

———. 2005. "The Politics of Power and Violence: Rethinking the Political in the Caribbean." Paper presented at Yale University, 11 November.

———. 2006. "Power, Violence, and the Jamaican 'Shotta Don.'" *NACLA Report on the Americas* 39(6): 21–26, 62.

———. 2010. "History, Decolonization, and the Making of Revolution: Reflections on Writing the Popular History of the Jamaican Events of 1938." *Interventions* 12(1): 76–87.

Bolland, O. Nigel. 1997. *Struggles for Freedom: Essays on Slavery, Colonialism and Culture in the Caribbean and Central America*. Kingston: Ian Randle Press.

"Book Review: The Children of Sanchez, Pedro Martinez, and La Vida by Oscar Lewis." 1967. *Current Anthropology* 8(5): 480–500.

Bourdieu, Pierre. 1984. *Distinction: A Social Critique of the Judgment of Taste*. Cambridge: Harvard University Press.

Bourgois, Philippe. 1995. *In Search of Respect: Selling Crack in El Barrio*. New York: Cambridge University Press.

———. 2001. "The Power of Violence in War and Peace: Post Cold-War Lessons from El Salvador." *Ethnography* 2:5–34.

Bourgois, Philippe, and Nancy Scheper-Hughes, eds. 2004. *Violence in War and Peace: An Anthology*. Malden, Mass.: Wiley-Blackwell.

Brathwaite, Edward. 1971a. *The Development of Creole Society in Jamaica, 1770–1820*. Oxford: Clarendon.

———. 1971b. *Folk Culture of the Slaves in Jamaica*. London: New Beacon.

Breckenridge, Carol. 1989. "The Aesthetics and Politics of Colonial Collecting: India at World Fairs." *Comparative Studies in Society and History* 32(2): 195–215.

Briggs, Laura. 2002. *Reproducing Empire: Race, Sex, Science, and U.S. Imperialism in Puerto Rico*. Berkeley: University of California Press.

Brodkin, Karen. 2000. "Global Capitalism: What's Race Got to Do with It?" *American Ethnologist* 27(2): 237–56.

Bronfman, Alejandra. 2007. *On the Move: The Caribbean since 1989*. London: Zed.

Brooks, Daphne A. 2006. *Bodies in Dissent: Spectacular Performances of Race and Freedom, 1850–1910*. Durham: Duke University Press.

Brown, Vincent. 2006. "Spiritual Terror and Sacred Authority in Jamaican Slave Society." *New Studies in American Slavery*, ed. Edward E. Baptist and Stephanie M. H. Camp, 179–210. Athens: University of Georgia Press.

———. 2008. *The Reaper's Garden: Death and Power in the World of Atlantic Slavery*. Cambridge: Harvard University Press.

Brown-Glaude, Winnifred. 2007. "The Fact of Blackness? The Problem of the Bleached Body in Contemporary Jamaica." *Small Axe* 11(3): 34–51.

Burnard, Trevor. 2003. *Mastery, Tyranny, and Desire: Thomas Thistlewood and his Slaves in the Afro-Jamaican World*. Chapel Hill: University of North Carolina Press.

Burns, Christopher. 2003. "What's the Fuss about?" Letter to the editor, *Jamaica Observer*, 11 August. Available at http://www.jamaicaobserver.com (accessed 28 November 2003).

Burrell, Ian. 2002. "On the Street: The Yardie Threat." *Independent*, 12 April, 4.

———. 2004. *Precarious Life: The Powers of Mourning and Violence*. New York: Verso.

Caldeira, Teresa. 2000. *City of Walls: Crime, Segregation, and Citizenship in São Paulo*. Berkeley: University of California Press.

Campbell, Edmond. 2007. "Henry Wants Committee 'to Quantify the Reparation.'" *Jamaica Gleaner*, 14 February. Available at www.jamaica-gleaner.com (accessed 1 April 2007).

Campbell, John. 2003. "Replace the Statues or Cover the Nakedness." Letter to the editor, *Jamaica Observer*, 16 August. Available http://jamaicaobserver.com (accessed 28 November 2003).

Campt, Tina M. 2004. *Other Germans: Black Germans and the Politics of Race, Gender, and Memory in the Third Reich*. Ann Arbor: University of Michigan Press.

Carby, Hazel. 1998. *Race Men*. Cambridge: Harvard University Press.

"The Caribbean Basin Security Initiative: What Is It?" 2010. *Just the Facts: A Civilian's Guide to U.S. Defense and Security Assistance to Latin America and the Caribbean*, blog, 4 February. Available at http://justf.org/blog (accessed 13 July 2010).

Carnegie, Charles. 2002. *Postnationalism Prefigured: Caribbean Borderlands*. New Brunswick: Rutgers University Press.

Central Intelligence Agency. 2010. *The World Factbook, Jamaica*. Available at www.cia

.gov/library/publications/the-world-factbook/geos/jm.html (accessed 8 February 2010).

Césaire, Aimé. 2000 [1955]. *Discourse on Colonialism*. New York: New York University Press.

Chamberlain, Mary. 2006. *Family Love in the Diaspora*. New Brunswick, N.J.: Transaction.

Chambers, Marva. 2003. "'Redemption Song' Is Picture Perfect." Letter to the editor, *Jamaica Gleaner*, 7 August. Available at http://www.jamaica-gleaner.com (accessed 28 November 2003).

Charles, Christopher. 2002. "Garrison Communities as Counter Societies: The Case of the 1998 Zeeks' Riot in Jamaica." *Ideaz* 1(1): 29–43.

Chatterjee, Partha. 1989. "Colonialism, Nationalism, and Colonized Women: The Contest in India." *American Ethnologist* 16(4): 622–33.

Chevannes, Barry. 1976. "The Repairer of the Breach: Reverend Claudius Henry and Jamaican Society." *Ethnicity in the Americas*, ed. Frances Henry, 263–89. The Hague: Mouton.

————. 1990. "Healing the Nation: Rastafari Exorcism of the Ideology of Racism in Jamaica." *Caribbean Quarterly* 36(1–2): 59–84.

————. 1992. "The Formation of Garrison Communities." Paper presented at Grassroots Development and the State of the Nation symposium in honor of Carl Stone, University of the West Indies, Mona, 16–17 November.

————. 1994. *Rastafari: Roots and Ideology*. Syracuse: Syracuse University Press.

————. 2001. *Learning to Be a Man: Culture, Socialization and Gender Identity in Five Caribbean Communities*. Mona: University of the West Indies Press.

"Chevannes to Chair Reparations Commission." 2009. *Daily Observer*, 23 January. Available at http://www.jamaicaobserver.com (accessed 23 January 2009).

Chin, Timothy. 1997. "'Bullers' and 'Battymen': Contesting Homophobia in Black Popular Culture and Contemporary Caribbean Literature." *Callaloo* 20(2): 127–41.

Chuckman, John. 2006. "City at Risk." Available at http://chuckman.blog.ca/?tag= guns (accessed 2 October 2006).

Churchville, Victoria. 1988. "Elusive Jamaican Drug Gangs Frustrate Police." *Washington Post*, 13 February, A1.

Clarke, Colin. 1975. *Kingston, Jamaica: Urban Development and Social Change, 1692–1962*. Berkeley: University of California Press.

Clarke, Edith. 1966 [1957]. *My Mother Who Fathered Me: A Study of the Family in Three Selected Communities in Jamaica*. London: George Allen and Unwin.

Clarke, Kamari. 2009. *Fictions of Justice: The International Criminal Court and the Challenge of Legal Pluralism in Sub-Saharan Africa*. New York: Cambridge University Press.

Clarke, Kamari M., and Deborah A. Thomas, eds. 2006. *Globalization and Race: Transformations in the Cultural Production of Blackness*. Durham: Duke University Press.

Cohen, Cathy. 2004. "Deviance as Resistance: A New Research Agenda for the Study of Black Politics." *Du Bois Review* 1(1): 27–45.

Cohen, S. 1988. "Jamaican Posses are the U.S.'s New Outlaws." *Herald,* 21 January.

Collins, Loretta. 2001. "Ragamuffin Cultural Studies: X-Press Novels' Yardies and Cop Killers Put Britain on Trial." *Small Axe* 9:70–96.

Comaroff, Jean, and John Comaroff. 1999. "Occult Economies and the Violence of Abstraction: Notes from the South African Postcolony." *American Ethnologist* 26(2): 279–303.

———. 2009. *Ethnicity, Inc.* Chicago: University of Chicago Press.

Comaroff, John L. 2009. "The Ends of Anthropology (Again)." Paper presented at the University of Pennsylvania, 2 December.

Connerton, Paul. 1989. *How Societies Remember.* New York: Cambridge University Press.

Cooper, Carolyn. 1989. "Slackness Hiding from Culture: Erotic Play in the Dancehall." *Jamaica Journal* 22(4): 12–31.

———. 1993. *Noises in the Blood: Orality, Gender, and the "Vulgar" Body of Jamaican Popular Culture.* London: Macmillan.

———. 2004. *Sound Clash: Jamaican Dancehall Culture at Large.* New York: Palgrave Macmillan.

Cooper, Carolyn, and Alison Donnell. 2004. "Jamaican Popular Culture: Introduction." *Interventions* 6(1): 1–17.

Coronil, Fernando. 1997. *The Magical State: Nature, Money, and Modernity in Venezuela.* Chicago: University of Chicago Press.

Cox, Aimee. 2009. "The BlackLight Project and Public Scholarship: Young Black Women Perform against and through the Boundaries of Anthropology." *Transforming Anthropology* 17(1): 51–64.

Cox, Oliver. 1948. *Caste, Class, and Race: A Study in Social Dynamics.* Garden City, N.Y.: Doubleday.

Council on Hemispheric Affairs. 2008. "Washington Revives the Fourth Fleet: The Return of U.S. Gun Boat Diplomacy to Latin America," 2 June. Available at http://www.coha.org (accessed 4 June 2010).

Craton, Michael. 1978. *Searching for the Invisible Man: Slaves and Plantation Life in Jamaica.* Cambridge: Harvard University Press.

———. 1982. *Testing the Chains: Resistance to Slavery in the British West Indies.* Ithaca: Cornell University Press.

Daniel, E. Valentine. 1996. *Charred Lullabies: Chapters in an Anthropography of Violence.* Princeton: Princeton University Press.

Da Silva, Denise Ferreira. 2009. "No-Bodies: Law, Raciality, and Violence." *Griffith Law Review* 18(2): 212–36.

Das, Veena. 2007. *Life and Words: Violence and the Descent into the Ordinary.* Berkeley: University of California Press.

Das, Veena, Arthur Kleinman, Margaret Lock, Mamphela Ramphele, and Pamela Reynolds, eds. 2001. *Remaking a World: Violence, Social Suffering, and Recovery.* Berkeley: University of California Press.

Davenport, Justin. 2001. "Yardies at War, Part One." *Evening Standard,* 10 September, 10–11.

Davies, Carole Boyce. 2007. *Left of Karl Marx: The Political Life of Black Communist Claudia Jones*. Durham: Duke University Press.

Davies, Nick. 1995. "The Yard's Yardie." *Guardian*, 6 November, T2.

Davila, Arlene. 1997. *Sponsored Identities: Cultural Politics in Puerto Rico*. Philadelphia: Temple University Press.

Davis, Alison, Burleigh B. Gardner, and Mary R. Gardner. 1941. *Deep South: A Social Anthropological Study of Caste and Class*. Chicago: University of Chicago Press.

Davis, Stephen, and Geordie Grieg. 1987. "Spectrum: Yardies Spark New Gangster Fear in Britain." *Sunday Times*, 25 October.

Dawes, James. 2007. *That the World May Know: Bearing Witness to Atrocity*. Cambridge: Harvard University Press.

Dayan, Joan. 1998. *Haiti, History, and the Gods*. Berkeley: University of California Press.

"Dead 'Don' Dug Up, Shot." 2004. *Jamaica Observer*, 1 June. Available at http://www.jamaicaobserver.com (accessed 1 June 2004).

Debord, Guy. 1967. *The Society of the Spectacle*. Detroit: Black and Red, 1977. Available at http://www.marxists.org/reference/archive/debord/society.htm.

———. 2007 (1987). *Comments on the Society of the Spectacle*. New York: Verso.

De la Fuente, Alejandro. 2000. *A Nation for All: Race, Inequality and Politics in Twentieth-Century Cuba*. Chapel Hill: University of North Carolina Press.

Delavante, Marilyn. 2003. "Appreciate the Beauty of the Human Form." Letter to the editor, *Jamaica Gleaner*, 11 August. Available at http://www.jamaica-gleaner.com (accessed 28 November 2003).

"Dennis Marshall's Seven Days." 1963. *Public Opinion*, 11 May, 1.

Derrida, Jacques. 2009. *On Cosmopolitanism and Forgiveness*. New York: Routledge.

Diamond, Macka. 2007. *Bun' Him!!!*. St. Catherine, Jamaica: Page TurnER Publications.

DiLeonardo, Micaela. 1998. *Exotics at Home: Anthropologies, Others, American Modernity*. Chicago: University of Chicago Press.

Dirks, Robert, and Virginia Kerns. 1976. "Mating Patterns and Adaptive Change in Rum Bay, 1823–1970." *Social and Economic Studies* 25(1): 34–54.

Dollard, John. 1937. *Caste and Class in a Southern Town*. New Haven: Yale University Press.

Douglass, Lisa. 1992. *The Power of Sentiment: Love, Hierarchy, and the Jamaican Family Elite*. Boulder: Westview.

Drake, St. Clair. 1975. "The Black Diaspora in Pan-African Perspective." *Black Scholar* 7 (September): 2–14.

———. 1982. "Diaspora Studies and Pan-Africanism." *Global Dimensions of the African Diaspora*, ed. Joseph E. Harris, 341–402. Washington: Howard University Press.

Drayton, Richard. 2010. "From Kabul to Kingston: Army Tactics in Jamaica Resemble Those Used in Afghanistan—and It's No Mere Coincidence." *Guardian*, 14 June. Available at http://www.guardian.co.uk (accessed 14 June 2010).

Ebron, Paulla. 2008. "Strike a Pose: Capitalism's Black Identity." *Recharting the Black

Atlantic: Modern Cultures, Local Communities, Global Connections, ed. Annalisa Oboe and Anna Scacchi, 319–36. New York: Routledge.

Edie, Carlene. 1991. *Democracy by Default: Dependency and Clientelism in Jamaica.* Boulder: Lynne Rienner.

Edmondson, Belinda. 1999a. *Making Men: Gender, Literary Authority, and Women's Writing in Caribbean Narrative.* Durham: Duke University Press.

———. 1999b. "Trinidad Romance: The Invention of Jamaican Carnival." *Caribbean Romances: The Politics of Regional Representation*, ed. Belinda Edmondson, 56–75. Charlottesville: University Press of Virginia.

Edwards, Brent. 2001. "The Uses of Diaspora." *Social Text* 19(1): 45–73.

———. 2003. *The Practice of Diaspora: Literature, Translation, and the Rise of Black Internationalism.* Cambridge: Harvard University Press.

Edwards, Pauline. 2001. *Trench Town, Concrete Jungle: Kill or Be Killed.* London: self-published.

Egerton, Douglas R. 2003. "A Peculiar Mark of Infamy: Dismemberment, Burial, and Rebelliousness in Slave Societies." *Mortal Remains: Death in Early America*, ed. Nancy Isenberg and Andrew Burstein, 149–60. Philadelphia: University of Pennsylvania Press.

Eisner, Gisela. 1961. *Jamaica, 1830–1930: A Study in Economic Growth.* Westport: Greenwood.

Ellison, James. 2009. "Governmentality and the Family: Neoliberal Choices and Emergent Kin Relations in Southern Ethiopia." *American Anthropologist* 111(1): 81–92.

Ethio-Africa Diaspora Union Millennium Council Secretariat. 2008. "Millennium Council Report." Available at http://www.assatashakur.org/forum/afrikan-world-news/34505-ethio-africa-diaspora-union-millennium-council-report.html (accessed 28 January 2009).

Evans-Pritchard, E. E. 1940. *The Nuer: A Description of the Modes of Livelihood and Political Institution of a Nilotic People.* Oxford: Clarendon Press.

"The Eye of the Beholder." 2003. Editorial, *Jamaica Gleaner*, 6 August. Available at http://www.jamaica-gleaner.com (accessed 28 November 2003).

Eyre, L. Alan. 1984. "Political Violence and Urban Geography in Kingston, Jamaica." *Geographical Review* 74: 24–37.

———. 1986. "The Effects of Political Terrorism on the Residential Location of the Poor in the Kingston Urban Region, Jamaica, West Indies." *Urban Geography* 7(3): 227–42.

Falloon, Dew. 2003. "What about the Men?" Letter to the editor, *Jamaica Gleaner*, 31 July. Available at http://www.jamaica-gleaner.com (accessed 28 November 2003).

Fanon, Frantz. 1963. *The Wretched of the Earth.* New York: Grove.

Farmer, Paul. 2003. *Pathologies of Power: Health, Human Rights, and the New War on the Poor.* Berkeley: University of California Press.

Farquhar, Judith, and Qicheng Zhang. 2005. "Biopolitical Beijing: Pleasure, Sovereignty, and Self-Cultivation in China's Capital." *Cultural Anthropology* 20(3): 303–27.

Farred, Grant. 2001. "The Postcolonial Chickens Come Home to Roost: How *Yardie* Has Created a New Postcolonial Subaltern." *South Atlantic Quarterly* 100(1): 287–305.

———. 2003. *What's My Name? Black Vernacular Intellectuals*. Minneapolis: University of Minnesota Press.

Feldman, Allen. 1991. *Formations of Violence: The Narrative of the Body and Political Terror in Northern Ireland*. Chicago: University of Chicago Press.

Ferguson, James. 2006. *Global Shadows: Africa in the Neoliberal World Order*. Durham: Duke University Press.

Ferguson, James, and Akhil Gupta. 2002. "Spatializing States: Toward an Ethnography of Neoliberal Governmentality." *American Ethnologist* 29(4): 981–1002.

Ferguson, Roderick A. 2004. "Nightmares of the Heteronormative: *Go Tell It on the Mountain* versus *An American Dilemma*." *Aberrations in Black: Toward a Queer of Color Critique*, 82–109. Minneapolis: University of Minnesota Press.

Ferrándiz, Francisco. 2008. "Digital Memory: The Visual Recording of Mass Grave Exhumations in Contemporary Spain." *Forum: Qualitative Social Research* 9(3): art. 35. Available at http://www.qualitative-research.net.

———. 2009. "Open Veins: Spirits of Violence and Grief in Venezuela." *Ethnography* 19(1): 39–61.

Figueroa, Mark, and Amanda Sives. 2002. "Homogenous Voting, Electoral Manipulation, and the Garrison Process in Post-Independence Jamaica." *Journal of Commonwealth and Comparative Politics* 40(1): 81–108.

Fineman, Martha. 1995. *The Neutered Mother, the Sexual Family, and Other Twentieth Century Tragedies*. New York: Routledge.

Fischer, Sibylle. 2004. *Modernity Disavowed: Haiti and the Cultures of Slavery in the Age of Revolution*. Durham: Duke University Press.

Forbes, Curdella. 2006. "X Press Publications: Pop Culture, 'Pop Lit,' and Caribbean Literary Criticism: An Essay of Provocation." *Anthurium: A Caribbean Studies Journal* 4(1). Available at http://anthurium.miami.edu.

Ford-Smith, Honor. 1997. "Ring Ding in a Tight Corner: Sistren, Collective Democracy, and the Organization of Cultural Production." *Feminist Genealogies, Colonial Legacies, Democratic Futures*, ed. Chandra T. Mohanty and M. Jacqui Alexander, 213–58. New York: Routledge.

Foster, Robert. 1991. "Making National Cultures in the Global Ecumene." *Annual Review of Anthropology* 20:235–60.

Foucault, Michel. 1990. *The History of Sexuality, Volume 1*. New York: Vintage.

———. 1991. "On Governmentality." *The Foucault Effect: Studies in Governmentality*, ed. Graham Burchell, Colin Gordon, and Peter Miller, 87–104. London: Harvester/Wheatsheaf.

———. 2003. *Society Must Be Defended*. New York: Picador.

Fox, Richard, ed. 1990. *Nationalist Ideologies and the Production of National Cultures.* Washington: American Anthropological Association.

Frazier, E. Franklin. 1957. *Black Bourgeoisie.* Glencoe, Ill.: Free Press.

———. 1966 [1939]. *The Negro Family in the United States.* Chicago: University of Chicago Press.

Frederickson, George. 1999. "Reform and Revolution in American and South African Freedom Struggles." *Crossing Boundaries: Comparative History of Black People in Diaspora,* ed. Darlene Clark Hine and Jacqueline McLeod, 71–84. Bloomington: Indiana University Press.

Freeman, Carla. 2000. *High Tech and High Heels in the Global Economy: Women, Work, and Pink-Collar Identities in the Caribbean.* Durham: Duke University Press.

———. 2007. "The 'Reputation' of Neoliberalism." *American Ethnologist* 34(2): 252–67.

Friedman, Jonathan, ed. 2003. *Globalization, the State, and Violence.* Walnut Creek, Calif.: Alta Mira.

Gaines, Kevin. 1996. *Uplifting the Race: Black Leadership, Politics and Culture in the Twentieth Century.* Chapel Hill: University of North Carolina Press.

———. 2005. "E. Franklin Frazier's Revenge: Anticolonialism, Nonalignment, and Black Intellectuals' Critiques of Western Culture." *American Literary History* 17(3): 506–29.

Gallimore, Patrick. 2003. "Nude, but Not Rude." Letter to the editor, *Jamaica Gleaner,* 6 August. Available at http://www.jamaica-gleaner.com (accessed 28 November 2003).

Gardner, D. 1988. "The Yardies Are Coming!" *Telegraph,* 14 January.

Garraway, Doris. 2006. *The Libertine Colony: Creolization in the Early French Caribbean.* Durham: Duke University Press.

Garvey, Bruce. 2005. "Jamaica's 'Born fi Dead' Culture." *National Post,* 27 October.

Gaspar, David Barry. 1985. *Bondmen and Rebels: A Study of Master–Slave Relations in Antigua, with Implications for Colonial British America.* Baltimore: Johns Hopkins University Press.

Gennep, Arnold van. 1960. *The Ritual Process.* Chicago: University of Chicago Press.

Genovese, Eugene. 1979. *From Rebellion to Revolution: Afro-American Slave Revolts in the Making of the Modern World.* Baton Rouge: Louisiana State University Press.

Gillis, John. 1994. "Memory and Identity: The History of a Relationship." *Commemorations: The Politics of National Identity,* ed. John Gillis, 3–24. Princeton: Princeton University Press.

Gillis, John, ed. 1994. *Commemorations: The Politics of National Identity.* Princeton: Princeton University Press.

Gilroy, Paul. 1987. *There Ain't No Black in the Union Jack: The Cultural Politics of Race and Nation.* Chicago: University of Chicago Press.

———. 1993. *The Black Atlantic: Modernity and Double Consciousness.* Cambridge: Harvard University Press.

———. 2000. *Against Race: Imagining Political Culture Beyond the Color Line*. Cambridge: Harvard University Press.

———. 2006. *Postcolonial Melancholia*. New York: Columbia University Press.

———. 2010. *Darker than Blue: On the Moral Economies of Black Atlantic Culture*. Cambridge: Harvard University Press.

Giovanetti, Jorge. 2006. "The Elusive Organization of 'Identity': Race, Religion, and Empire among Caribbean Migrants in Cuba." *Small Axe* 19(1): 1–27.

Girvan, Norman. 1975. "Aspects of the Political Economy of Race in the Caribbean and the Americas: A Preliminary Interpretation," Atlanta, Institute of the Black World Occasional Paper. Reprinted as an ISER Working Paper, 1976.

Glave, Thomas. 2005. *Words to Our Now: Imagination and Dissent*. Minneapolis: University of Minnesota Press.

Glazer, Nathan, and Daniel Moynihan. 1963. *Beyond the Melting Pot: The Negroes, Puerto Ricans, Jews, Italians, and Irish of New York City*. Cambridge: MIT Press.

Glick-Schiller, Nina. 1997. "Cultural Politics and the Politics of Culture." *Identities* 4(1): 1–7.

Glick Schiller, Nina, and Georges Fouron. 2001. *Georges Woke Up Laughing: Long Distance Nationalism and the Search for Home*. Durham: Duke University Press.

Global Afrikan Congress. 2007. "Give Descendants of Slaves Their Due." *Daily Observer*, 3 February. Available at http://www.jamaicaobserver.com (accessed 3 February 2007).

Goldsby, Jacqueline. 2006. *A Spectacular Secret: Lynching in American Life and Literature*. Chicago: University of Chicago Press.

Goldstein, Daniel. 2004. *The Spectacular City: Violence and Performance in Urban Bolivia*. Durham: Duke University Press.

Goldstein, Donna. 2003. *Laughter Out of Place: Race, Class, Violence, and Sexuality in a Rio Shantytown*. Berkeley: University of California Press.

Goldstein, Lorrie. 2006. "Stop Blaming Jamaicans for Gun Crime." *Toronto Sun*, 7 May. Available at http://www.torontosun.com (accessed 2 October 2006).

Goodwin, Jo-Ann. 1999. "War on the Yardies." *Daily Mail*, 25 September, 18.

Gould, Eliga. 2003. "Zones of Law, Zones of Violence: The Legal Geography of the British Atlantic, circa 1772." *William and Mary Quarterly* 60(3): 471–510.

Gonzalez, Nancie. 1970. "Towards a Definition of Matrifocality." *Afro-American Anthropology: Comparative Perspectives*, ed. Norman Whitten and John Szwed, 231–44. New York: Free Press.

Gordon, Derek. 1991. "Race, Class, and Social Mobility in Jamaica." *Garvey: His Work and Impact*, ed. Rupert Lewis and Patrick Bryan, 265–82. Trenton: Africa World Press.

Graham, Narda. 2004. "Whose Monument?: The Battle to Define, Interpret, and Claim Emancipation." *Small Axe* 8(2): 170–78.

Grandin, Greg, and Thomas Miller Klubock. 2007. "Editors' Introduction." *Radical History Review* 97:1–10.

Gray, Obika. 1991. *Radicalism and Social Change in Jamaica, 1960–1972*. Knoxville: University of Tennessee Press.

———. 2004. *Demeaned but Empowered: The Social Power of the Urban Poor in Jamaica*. Kingston: University of the West Indies Press.

Green, Linda. 1999. *Fear as a Way of Life*. New York: Columbia University Press.

Greenfield, Sidney. 1966. *English Rustics in Black Skin: A Study of Modern Family Forms in a Pre-Industrialized Society*. New Haven: College and University Press.

Gregory, Steven. 2006. *The Devil behind the Mirror: Globalization and Politics in the Dominican Republic*. Berkeley: University of California Press.

Grewal, Inderpal. 2005. *Transnational America: Feminisms, Diasporas, Transnationalisms*. Durham: Duke University Press.

Gunst, Laurie. 1995. *Born fi' Dead: A Journey through the Jamaican Posse Underworld*. New York: Henry Holt.

Gutzmore, Cecil. 2004. "Casting the First Stone! Policing of Homo/Sexuality in Jamaican Popular Culture." *Interventions* 6(1): 118–34.

Halbwachs, Maurice. 1992. *On Collective Memory*. Chicago: University of Chicago Press.

Hall, Arthur. 2009. "Commission Set up to Review Reparations." *Jamaica Gleaner*, 23 January. Available at http://www.jamaica-gleaner.com (accessed 23 January 2009).

Hall, Catherine. 1995. "Gender Politics and Imperial Politics: Rethinking the Histories of Empire." *Engendering History: Caribbean Women in Historical Perspective*, ed. Verene Shepherd, Bridget Brereton, and Barbara Bailey, 48–59. Kingston: Ian Randle.

———. 2002. *Civilising Subjects: Metropole and Colony in the English Imagination, 1830–1867*. Chicago: University of Chicago Press.

Hall, Douglas. 1989. *In Miserable Slavery: Thomas Thistlewood in Jamaica, 1750–86*. Mona: University of the West Indies Press.

Hall, Stuart. 2001. "Negotiating Caribbean Identities." *New Caribbean Thought: A Reader*, ed. Brian Meeks and Folke Lindahl, 24–39. Mona: University of the West Indies Press.

Hall, Stuart, Chas Critcher, Tony Jefferson, John N. Clarke, and Brian Roberts. 1978. *Policing the Crisis: Mugging, the State, and Law and Order*. London: Macmillan.

Hanchard, Michael. 2008. "Black Memory versus State Memory: Notes toward a Method." *Small Axe* 12(2): 45–62.

Hansen, Thomas Blom. 2001. "Governance and State Mythologies in Mumbai." *States of Imagination: Ethnographic Explorations of the Postcolonial State*, ed. Thomas Blom Hansen and Finn Stepputat, 221–54. Durham: Duke University Press.

Harold, Gywneth. 2003. "Redemption Song—Symbol of Freedom?" *Jamaica Observer*, 10 August. Available at http://www.jamaicaobserver.com (accessed 28 November 2003).

Harrington, Michael. 1981 [1962]. *The Other America: Poverty in the United States*. New York: Penguin.

Harriott, Anthony. 1996. "The Changing Social Organization of Crime and Criminals in Jamaica." *Caribbean Quarterly* 42(2–3): 61–81.

———. 2004. "The Jamaican Crime Problem: New Developments and New Challenges for Public Policy." *Understanding Crime in Jamaica: New Challenges for Public Policy*, 1–12. Mona: University of the West Indies Press.

Harrison, Faye. 1982. "Semiproletarianization and the Structure of Socioeconomic and Political Relations in a Jamaican Slum." Ph.D. diss., Stanford University, Stanford, Calif.

———. 1988. "The Politics of Social Outlawry in Urban Jamaica." *Urban Anthropology* 17(2–3): 259–77.

———. 1997. "The Gendered Politics and Violence of Structural Adjustment: A View from Jamaica." *Situated Lives: Gender and Culture in Everyday Life*, ed. Louise Lamphere, Helena Ragone, and Patricia Zavella. New York: Routledge.

Hartman, Saidiya. 1997. *Scenes of Subjection: Terror, Slavery, and Self-Making in Nineteenth Century America*. New York: Oxford University Press.

———. 2008. *Lose Your Mother: A Journey along the Atlantic Slave Route*. New York: Farrar, Straus, and Giroux.

Hastrup, Kirsten. 2003. "Violence, Suffering, and Human Rights: Anthropological Reflections." *Anthropological Theory* 3(3): 309–23.

Headley, Bernard. 2002. *A Spade Is Still a Spade: Essays on Crime and the Politics of Jamaica*. Kingston: LMH.

Headley, Victor. 1993. *Yardie*. London: Pan.

———. 1994. *Excess*. London: Pan.

———. 1995. *Yush!*. London: Pan.

Hennessy, Alistair. 1978. *The Frontier in Latin American History*. Albuquerque: University of New Mexico Press.

Hennessey, Martin, Richard Holliday, and William Lowther. 1993. "The Yardie Crack Wars." *Sunday Mail*, 6 June, 8–9.

"Henry Bats for Reparation." 2007. *Sunday Gleaner*, 11 February.

Herman, Ellen. 1995. *The Romance of American Psychology: Political Culture in the Age of Experts*. Berkeley: University of California Press.

Herskovits, Melville. 1941. *The Myth of the Negro Past*. New York: Harper.

Hesse, Barnor. 1999. "Reviewing the Western Spectacle: Reflexive Globalization through the Black Diaspora." *Global Futures: Migration, Environment, and Globalization*, ed. Avtar Brah, Mary J. Hickman, and Máirtín Mac an Ghaill, 122–43. London: Macmillan.

Heuman, Gad. 1981. *Between Black and White: Race, Politics, and the Free Coloureds in Jamaica, 1792–1865*. Westport: Greenwood.

Higginbotham, Evelyn Brooks. 1993. *Righteous Discontent: The Women's Movement in the Black Baptist Church, 1880–1920*. Cambridge: Harvard University Press.

Higman, Barry. 1976. *Slave Population and Economy in Jamaica, 1807–1834*. Cambridge: Cambridge University Press.

———. 1984. *Slave Populations of the British Caribbean, 1807–1834*. Baltimore: Johns Hopkins University Press.

Hill, Robert. 1983. "Leonard P. Howell and Millenarian Visions in Early Rastafari." *Jamaica Journal* 16(1): 24–39.

Hines, Horace. 2007. "'Forgive I,' Henry Pleads to Rastas: MP Expresses Remorse for 'Coral Gardens Incident.' *Jamaica Observer*, 9 April. Available at http://www.jamaicaobserver.com (accessed 9 April 2007).

Hintzen, Percy. 1997. "Reproducing Domination Identity and Legitimacy Constructs in the West Indies." *Social Identities* 3(1): 42–75.

Hirsch, Marianne, and Valerie Smith. 2002. "Feminism and Cultural Memory: An Introduction." *Signs* 28(1): 1–19.

Ho Lung, Richard. 1998. *Diary of a Ghetto Priest*. Kingston: Missionaries of the Poor.

Holt, Thomas. 2000. *The Problem of Race in the 21st Century*. Cambridge: Harvard University Press.

Holston, James. 2008. *Insurgent Citizenship: Disjunctions of Democracy and Modernity*. Princeton: Princeton University Press.

———. 2009. "Insurgent Citizenship in an Era of Global Urban Peripheries." *City and Society* 21(2): 245–67.

Homiak, John P. 1985. "The 'Ancients of Days' Seated Black: Eldership, Oral Tradition, and Ritual in Rastafarian Culture." Ph.D. diss., Brandeis University, Waltham, Massachusetts.

———. 1990. "From Yard to Nation: Rastafari and the Politics of Eldership at Home and Abroad." *Ay Bobo: African-Caribbean Religions*, ed. Manfred Kremser, 49–76. Vienna: Institut für Völkerkunde, Universität Wien.

———. 1999. "Movements of Jah People: From Soundscapes to Mediascape." *Religion, Diaspora, and Cultural Identity: A Reader in the Anglophone Caribbean*, ed. John W. Pulis, 87–123. London: Gordon and Breach.

———. 2001. "'Never Trade a Continent for an Island': Rastafari Diasporic Practice, Globalisation, and the African Renaissance." *A United States of Africa?*, ed. Eddy Maloka, 186–232. Pretoria: Africa Institute of South Africa.

Hornsby, Stephen. 2005. *British Atlantic, American Frontier: Spaces of Power in Early Modern British America*. Hanover, N.H.: University Press of New England.

Horst, Heather. 2008. "Planning to Forget: Mobility and Violence in Urban Jamaica." *Social Anthropology* 16(1): 51–62.

Human Rights Watch. 2004. "Hated to Death: Homophobic, Violence and Jamaica's HIV/AIDS Epidemic." Report, vol. 16, no. 6 (B).

Iton, Richard. 2008. *In Search of the Black Fantastic: Politics and Popular Culture in the Post-Civil Rights Era*. New York: Oxford University Press.

Jackson, Celia. 2003. "Redemption Song Bigger but Not Better." Letter to the editor, *Jamaica Gleaner*, 5 August. Available at http://www.jamaica-gleaner.com (accessed 28 November 2003).

Jackson, John. 2005. *Real Black: Adventures in Racial Sincerity*. Chicago: University of Chicago Press.

Jackson, Steven. 2004. "Rastas Want J$7.9 Trillion in Reparation." *Daily Observer*, 7 September. Available at http://www.jamaicaobserver.com (accessed 1 April 2007).

Jackson, Walter A. 1990. *Gunnar Myrdal and America's Conscience: Social Engineering and Racial Liberalism, 1938–1987*. Chapel Hill: University of North Carolina Press.

Jaffe, Rivke. 2009. "'They Ain't Gonna See Us Fall': Affect, Popular Culture, and Criminal Governance in Urban Jamaica." Paper presented at the annual meetings of the American Anthropological Association, Philadelphia, 4 December.

James, C. L. R. 1989. *The Black Jacobins: Toussaint L'Ouverture and the San Domingo Revolution*. New York: Vintage.

———. 1993. *American Civilization*, ed. Anna Grimshaw and Keith Hart. Cambridge: Blackwell.

James, Winston. 1998. *Holding Aloft the Banner of Ethiopia: Caribbean Radicalism in Early Twentieth Century America*. New York: Verso.

Jan van Dyck, Frank. 1995. "Sociological Means: Colonial Reactions to the Radicalization of Rastafari in Jamaica, 1956–1959." *New West Indian Guide* 69(1–2): 67–101.

Jones, LeRoi. 1963. *Blues People*. Edinburgh: Payback Press.

Kaplan, Amy. 2005. *The Anarchy of Empire in the Making of U.S. Culture*. Cambridge: Harvard University Press.

Kaplan, Caren, Norma Alarcón, and Minoo Moallem, eds. 1999. *Between Woman and Nation: Nationalisms, Transnational Feminisms, and the State*. Durham: Duke University Press.

Kelley, Robin D. G. 1990. *Hammer and Hoe: Alabama Communists during the Great Depression*. Chapel Hill: University of North Carolina Press.

Kelly, C. 2003. "Baring Our All." Letter to the editor, *Jamaica Gleaner*, 9 August. Available at http://www.jamaica-gleaner.com (accessed 28 November 2004).

Kempadoo, Kamala. 2004. *Sexing the Caribbean: Gender, Race, and Sexual Labor*. New York: Routledge.

Kempadoo, Kamala, ed. 1999. *Sun, Sex and Gold: Tourism and Sex Work in the Caribbean*. Oxford: Rowman and Littlefield.

Kerns, Virginia. 1989. *Women and the Ancestors: Black Carib Kinship and Ritual*. Chicago: University of Illinois Press.

Kerr, Madeline. 1952. *Personality and Conflict in Jamaica*. Liverpool: Liverpool University Press.

Khan, Aisha. 2001. "Journey to the Center of the Earth: The Caribbean as Master Symbol." *Cultural Anthropology* 16(3):271–302.

———. 2004. *Callaloo Nation: Metaphors of Race and Religious Identity among South Asians in Trinidad*. Durham: Duke University Press.

Klima, Alan. 2002. *The Funeral Casino: Meditation, Massacre, and Exchange with the Dead in Thailand*. Princeton: Princeton University Press.

K'nife, K'admawe. 2008. "Rastafari: An Ethic for Sustainable Development. Insights from Deep Ecology." Paper presented at the International Association of Cultural Studies conference, University of the West Indies, Kingston, 6 July.

Kopytoff, Igor. 1987. "The Internal African Frontier: The Making of African Political Culture." *The African Frontier: The Reproduction of Traditional African Societies*, ed. Igor Kopytoff, 3–84. Bloomington: Indiana University Press.

Lacey, Terry. 1977. *Violence and Politics in Jamaica, 1960–1970*. Manchester: Manchester University Press.

Laguerre, Michel. 2005. "Homeland Political Crisis, the Virtual Diasporic Public Sphere, and Diasporic Politics." *Journal of Latin American Anthropology* 10(1): 206–25.

Lamming, George. 1992. *The Pleasures of Exile*. Ann Arbor: University of Michigan Press.

Lawton, Carol. 2007. "Letter of the Day—Reparation Money to Reduce National Debt." *Jamaica Gleaner*, 29 March. Available at www.jamaica-gleaner.com (accessed 29 March 2007).

Leacock, Eleanor, ed. 1971. *The Culture of Poverty: A Critique*. New York: Simon and Schuster.

Levy, Horace. 1995. "Urban Poverty and Violence in Jamaica." Report on research, Center for Population, Community, and Social Change, Department of Sociology and Social Work, University of the West Indies, Mona.

Lewis, Linden. 2004. "Caribbean Masculinity at the *Fin de Siècle*." *Interrogating Caribbean Masculinities: Theoretical and Empirical Analyses*, ed. Rhoda Reddock, 244–66. Kingston: University of the West Indies Press.

Lewis, Oscar. 1965. *La Vida: A Puerto Rican Family in the Culture of Poverty—San Juan and New York*. New York: Random House.

———. 1975 [1959]. *Five Families: Mexican Case Studies in the Culture of Poverty*. New York: Basic Books.

Lewis, R. Anthony, and Robert Carr. 2009. "Gender, Sexuality, and Exclusion in Sketching the Outlines of the Jamaican Popular Nationalist Project." *Caribbean Review of Gender Studies* 1(3): 1–23.

Lewis, Rupert. 1998. "Marcus Garvey and the Early Rastafarians: Continuity and Discontinuity." *Chanting Down Babylon: The Rastafari Reader*, ed. Nathaniel Samuel Murrell, William David Spencer, and Adrian Anthony McFarlane, 145–58. Philadelphia: Temple University Press.

Lockett, Jon. 2002. "Britain on Yardie Gangs War Alert." *Daily Star*, 27 October, 16.

Loomba, Ania. 2007. "Periodization, Race, and Global Contact." *Journal of Medieval and Early Modern Studies* 37(3): 595–620.

Lorey, David, and William Beezley, ed. 2002. *Genocide, Collective Violence, and Popular Memory: The Politics of Remembrance in the Twentieth Century*. Wilmington, Del.: Scholarly Resources.

Loury, Glen. 2007. "Transgenerational Justice—Conpensatory versus Interpretative Approaches." *Reparations: Interdisciplinary Inquiries*, ed. Jon Miller and Rahul Kumar, 87–113. New York: Oxford University Press.

Lowe, Lisa. 2006. "Intimacies of Four Continents." In *Haunted By Empire: Geogra-*

phies of Intimacy in North American History, ed. Ann Laura Stoler, 191–212. Durham: Duke University Press.

Lubiano, Wahneema. 1998. "Black Nationalism and Black Common Sense: Policing Ourselves and Others." *The House that Race Built*, ed. Wahneema Lubiano, 232–52. New York: Vintage.

MacLeod, Robert. 1989. "Suspect in Shooting Linked to Drug Gang from New York City." *Globe and Mail*, 21 February.

Mahmood, Saba. 2004. *The Politics of Piety: The Islamic Revival and the Feminist Subject*. Princeton: Princeton University Press.

Maingot, Anthony P., and Wilfredo Lozano. 2005. *The United States and the Caribbean: Transforming Hegemony and Sovereignty*. New York: Routledge.

Mains, Susan. 2004. "Monumentally Caribbean: Borders, Bodies, and Redemptive City Spaces." *Small Axe* 8(2): 179–98.

Malkki, Liisa. 1995. *Purity and Exile: Violence, Memory, and National Cosmology among Hutu Refugees in Tanzania*. Chicago: University of Chicago Press.

Mamdani, Mahmood. 1996. *Citizen and Subject: Contemporary Africa and the Legacy of Late Colonialism*. Princeton: Princeton University Press.

———. 2001. *When Victims Become Killers: Colonialism, Nativism, and the Genocide in Rwanda*. Princeton: Princeton University Press.

Maragh, G. G. (Leonard Howell). 2007 [1935]. *The Promised Key*. N.p.: Forgotten Books.

Marcus, Anthony. 2005. "The Culture of Poverty Revisited: Bringing Back the Working Class." *Anthropologica* 47:35–52.

Mascoll, Philip, 1990. "Murderous Posses Gain Metro Foothold." *Toronto Star*, 25 February, A1.

Matthews, Kimmo. 2011. "Good news on crime — Police report drop in all major crimes." *Jamaica Gleaner*, 25 January 2011. Available at http://www.jamaicaobserver.com (accessed 25 January 2011).

Mau, James. 1968. *Social Change and Images of the Future: A Study of the Pursuit of Progress in Jamaica*. Cambridge, Mass.: Schenkman.

"The Mau Mau in Kenya: A Nightmare, Only It's Real." 1954. *Jamaica Gleaner*, 23 July, 8.

Maxwell, John. 1963a. "Living in a Burning House." *Public Opinion*, 20 April, 4.

———. 1963b. "Oh, It's Hard to Be Poor." *Public Opinion*, 8 June, 4.

———. 1963c. "Peace and Love?" *Public Opinion*, 27 April, 4.

———. 1963d. "Rule by Panic." *Public Opinion*, 20 April, 1.

Mbembe, Achille. 2001. *On the Postcolony*. Berkeley: University of California Press.

———. 2003. "Necropolitics." *Public Culture* 15(1): 11–40.

———. 2006. "On the Postcolony: A Brief Response to Critics." *African Identities* 4(2): 143–78.

McCalpin, Jermaine. 2007. "For the Sake of the Future?: Restorative Justice, Forgiveness, and Reconciliation in Deeply Divided Societies." *Proteus* (Fall).

McDuffie, Erik. 2006. "'[She] Devoted Twenty Minutes Condemning All Other Forms of Government but the Soviet': Black Women Radicals in the Garvey Movement and in the Left during the 1920s." *Diasporic Africa: A Reader*, ed. Michael Gomez, 219–50. New York: New York University Press.

Mead, Margaret. 1935. *Sex and Temperament in Three Primitive Societies*. New York: W. Morrow.

Meeks, Brian. 1994. "The Political Moment in Jamaica: the Dimensions of Hegemonic Dissolution." *Radical Caribbean: From Black Power to Abu Bakr*, 123–143. Mona: University Press of the West Indies.

———. 2000. *Narratives of Resistance: Jamaica, Trinidad, the Caribbean*. Mona: University of the West Indies Press.

———. 2007. *Envisioning Caribbean Futures: Jamaican Perspectives*. Kingston: University of the West Indies Press.

Michaels, Walter Benn. 1992. "Race into Culture: A Critical Genealogy of Cultural Identity." *Critical Inquiry* 18(4): 655–85.

Mignolo, Walter. 2000. *Local Histories / Global Designs: Coloniality, Subaltern Knowledges, and Border Thinking*. Princeton: Princeton University Press.

Miller, Daniel. 1991. "Absolute Freedom in Trinidad." *Man* (new series) 26: 323–41.

———. 1994. *Modernity, an Ethnographic Approach: Dualism and Mass Consumption in Trinidad*. New York: Berg.

Miller, Errol. 1997. *The Marginalization of the Black Male: Insights from the Development of the Teaching Profession*. Kingston: Canoe Press.

Miller, Jon, and Rahul Kumar, eds. 2007. *Reparations: Interdisciplinary Inquiries*. Oxford: Oxford University Press.

Miller, Toby, and George Yudice. 2002. *Cultural Policy*. Thousand Oaks, Calif.: Sage.

Mills, Claude. 2003. "'Renude' Controversy." *Jamaica Gleaner*, 2 August. Available at http://www.jamaica-gleaner.com (accessed 28 November 2003).

Ministry of Education, Youth, and Culture. 2003. *Towards Jamaica, the Cultural Superstate: The National Cultural Policy of Jamaica*. Kingston: Division of Culture.

Mintz, Sidney. 1989. *Caribbean Transformations*. New York: Columbia University Press.

———. 1996. "Enduring Substances, Trying Theories: The Caribbean Region as Oikoumene." *Journal of the Royal Anthropological Institute* 2(2): 289–312.

Mintz, Sidney, and Richard Price. 1992. *The Birth of African-American Culture: An Anthropological Perspective*. Boston: Beacon.

Mitchell, Timothy. 1991. *Colonising Egypt*. Berkeley: University of California Press.

Morgan, Henley. 2007. "Reparation for Garrison Victims." *Daily Observer*, 22 March. Available at http://www.jamaicaobserver.com (accessed 22 March 2007).

Morganthau, Tom, et al. 1988. "The Drug Gangs." *Newsweek*, 28 March, 20–27.

Morss, Susan Buck. 2000. "Hegel and Haiti." *Critical Inquiry* 26(4): 821–65.

Motsemme, Nthabiseng. 2004. "The Mute Always Speak: On Women's Silences at the Truth and Reconciliation Commission." *Current Sociology* 52(5): 909–32.

"MP Suggests Virginity Tests." 2003. *Jamaica Observer*, 30 July. Available at http://www.jamaicaobserver.com (accessed 28 November 2003).

Mullin, Michael. 1992. *Africa in America: Slave Acculturation and Resistance in the American South and the British Caribbean, 1736–1831*. Urbana: University of Illinois Press.

Murji, Karim. 1999. "Wild Life: Constructions and Representations of Yardies." *Making Trouble: Cultural Constructions of Crime, Deviance, and Control*, ed. Jeff Ferrell and Neil Websdale, 179–201. Hawthorne, N.Y.: Aldine de Gruyter.

Murrell, Nathaniel. 1998. "Introduction: The Rastafari Phenomenon." *Chanting Down Babylon: The Rastafari Reader*, ed. Nathaniel Samuel Murrell, William David Spencer, and Adrian Anthony McFarlane, 1–19. Philadelphia: Temple University Press.

Myrdal, Gunnar. 1944. *An American Dilemma: The Negro Problem and Modern Democracy*. New York: Harper.

Nagengast, Carole. 1994. "Violence, Terror, and the Crisis of the State." *Annual Review of Anthropology* 23: 109–36.

National Task Force on Crime. 1993. *Report*. Kingston: Gleaner Company.

Navaro-Yashin, Yael. 2002. *Faces of the State: Secularism and Public Life in Turkey*. Princeton: Princeton University Press.

Nelson, Diane. 1999. *A Finger in the Wound: Body Politics in Quincentennial Guatemala*. Berkeley: University of California Press.

———. 2009. *Reckoning: The Ends of War in Guatemala*. Durham: Duke University Press.

Neptune, Harvey. 2007. *Caliban and the Yankees: Trinidad and the United States Occupation*. Chapel Hill: University of North Carolina Press.

Nettleford, Rex. 1970. *Mirror, Mirror: Identity, Race, and Protest in Jamaica*. Kingston: William Collins and Sangster.

Newland, Courttia. 1997. *The Scholar*. New York: Abacus Press.

Niaah, Jalani. 2005. "Sensitive Scholarship: A Review of Rastafari Literature(s)." *Caribbean Quarterly* 51(3–4): 11–34.

Niaah, Sonjah Stanley. 2004. "Making Space: Kingston's Dancehall Culture and Its Philosophy of Boundaryless." *African Identities* 2(2): 117–32.

Nordstrom, Carolyn. 2004. *Shadows of War: Violence, Power, and International Profiteering in the Twenty-First Century*. Berkeley: University of California Press.

———. 2007. *Global Outlaws: Crime, Money, and Power in the Contemporary World*. Berkeley: University of California Press.

Norris, Katrin. 1962. *Jamaica: The Search for an Identity*. London: Oxford University Press.

Observer Reporter. 2003. "Let the Statue Stay, Majority Say." *Jamaica Observer*, 26 September. Available at http://www.jamaicaobserver.com (accessed 28 November 2003).

Olick, Jeffrey K., ed. 2003. *States of Memory: Continuities, Conflicts, and Transformations in National Retrospection*. Durham: Duke University Press.

O'Neill, Kevin, and Alexander Hinton. 2009. "Genocide, Truth, Memory, and Representation: An Introduction." *Genocide: Truth, Memory and Representation*, ed. Alexander Hinton and Kevin O'Neill, 1–26. Durham: Duke University Press.

Ong, Aiwha. 1990. "State versus Islam: Malay Families, Women's Bodies, and the Body Politic in Malaysia." *American Ethnologist* 17(2): 258–76.

———. 2006. *Neoliberalism as Exception: Mutations in Citizenship and Sovereignty*. Durham: Duke University Press.

Owens, Joseph. 1976. *Dread: The Rastafarians of Jamaica*. Kingston: Heinemann Educational.

Page, Kezia. 2006. "'What If He Did Not Have a Sister [Who Lived in the United States]?': Jamaica Kincaid's *My Brother* as Remittance Text." *Small Axe* 10(3): 37–53.

Pandey, Gyanendra. 2006. *Routine Violence: Nations, Fragments, Histories*. Stanford: Stanford University Press.

Parker, Andrew, Mary Russo, Doris Sommer, and Patricia Yaeger. 1992. *Nationalisms and Sexualities*. New York: Routledge.

Paton, Diana. 2004. *No Bond but the Law: Punishment, Race, and Gender in Jamaican State Formation, 1780–1870*. Durham: Duke University Press.

Patterson, Orlando. 1967. *An Absence of Ruins*. London: Hutchinson.

———. 1969. *The Sociology of Slavery: An Analysis of the Origins, Development, and Structure of Negro Slave Society in Jamaica*. Rutherford, N.J.: Farleigh Dickinson University Press.

———. 1982. *Slavery and Social Death: A Comparative Study*. Cambridge: Harvard University Press.

Patterson, Thomas. 2001. *A Social History of Anthropology in the United States*. New York: Berg.

Patterson, Tiffany, and Robin D. G. Kelley. 2000. "Unfinished Migrations: Reflections on the African Diaspora and the Making of the Modern World." *African Studies Review* 43(1): 11–45.

Paul, Annie. 2004. "Emancipating Ourselves . . . in 'Post-Slave Societies of the New World.'" *Axis* 7 (June): 122–35.

Pettersburgh, Fitz Balintine. 2003 [1926]. *The Royal Parchment Scroll of Black Supremacy*. Chicago: Miguel Lorne.

Piot, Charles. 2010. *Nostalgia for the Future: West Africa after the Cold War*. Chicago: University of Chicago Press.

Planno, Mortimo. 1963a. "Rastafari." Letter to the editor *Public Opinion*, 20 April, 2.

———. 1963b. "Rastafari," Letter to the editor, *Public Opinion*, 4 May, 2.

———. 1969. *The Earth's Most Strangest Man: The Rastafarian*. Comitas Institute for Anthropological Study. Available at http://www.cifas.us/new/caribbean/most_strangest.html.

Povinelli, Elizabeth. 2006. *The Empire of Love: Toward a Theory of Intimacy, Genealogy and Carnality*. Durham: Duke University Press.

Powdermaker, Hortense. 1939. *After Freedom: A Cultural Study in the Deep South*. New York: Viking.

Price, Charles Reavis. 2003. "Social Change and the Development and Co-optation of a Black Antisystemic Identity: The Case of Rastafarians in Jamaica." *Identity* 3(1): 9–27.

———. 2009. *Becoming Rasta: Origins of Rastafari Identity in Jamaica*. New York: New York University Press.

Price, Richard. 1985. "An Absence of Ruins? Seeking Caribbean Historical Consciousness." *Caribbean Review* 14(3): 24–30.

———. 1998. *The Convict and the Colonel*. Boston: Beacon.

———. 2007. *Travels with Tooy: History, Memory, and the African American Imagination*. Berkeley: University of California Press.

Prince Kofi. 2007. *Yardies: The Making of a Jamaican Posse*. New York: Ghetto Life Publishing.

Pulis, John W. 1999. "Bridging Troubled Waters: Moses Baker, George Liele, and the African American Diaspora to Jamaica." *Moving On: Black Loyalists in the Afro-Atlantic World*, ed. John Pulis, 183–221. New York: Garland.

Puri, Shalini. 2004. *The Caribbean Postcolonial: Social Equality, Post-nationalism, and Cultural Hybridity*. New York: Palgrave MacMillan.

Putnam, Lara. 2002. *The Company They Kept: Migrants and the Politics of Gender in Caribbean Costa Rica, 1870–1960*. Chapel Hill: University of North Carolina Press.

———. 2007. "Parenthood at the End of Empire: Great Britain and Its Caribbean Colonies, 1910–1940." Paper presented at the Latin American Labor History Conference, Duke University, Durham, N.C., 4–5 May.

———. 2008. "Civic Maternalism, Paternal Obligation, and Fraternal Love in the British Caribbean, 1910–1940." Paper presented at Caribbean Studies Panel, Conference on Latin American History Annual Meeting, Washington, D.C., 4 January.

———. Forthcoming. "'Children of the Dispersion': Circum-Caribbean Migration and the Varieties of Race Consciousness in the Early Twentieth Century." *Caribbean Migrations: Transnationalisms and Diasporas*, ed. Hyacinth Simpson. Newcastle upon Tyne: Cambridge Scholars.

Rabinow, Paul. 2008. *Marking Time: On the Anthropology of the Contemporary*. Princeton: Princeton University Press.

Ramos-Zayas, Ana Yolanda. 2003. *National Performances: The Politics of Class, Race, and Space in Puerto Rican Chicago*. Chicago: University of Chicago Press.

Rankine, D. 2003. "Castrate the Men." Letter to the editor, *Jamaica Observer*, 7 August. Available at http://www.jamaicaobserver.com (accessed 28 November 2003).

Ras Flako. 2010. *Icient Wisdom: Coral Gardens Atrocity, 1963*. Montego Bay: Wisemind.

Rattray, Garth. 2007. "Reparations Here at Home." *Jamaica Gleaner*, 12 March. Available at http://www.jamaica-gleaner.com (accessed 12 March 2007).

Reddock, Rhoda. 1994. *Women, Labour, and Politics in Trinidad and Tobago: A History*. London: Zed.

Reddock, Rhoda, ed. 2004. *Interrogating Caribbean Masculinities: Theoretical and Empirical Analyses*. Mona: University of the West Indies Press.

Redfield, Robert. 2005. "Doctors, Borders, and Life in Crisis." *Cultural Anthropology* 29(3): 328–61.

Reid, Selbourne A. 2009. *Rastafarian Uprising at Coral Gardens, Jamaica*. Longwood, Fla.: Xulon Press.

Renda, Mary. 2000. *Taking Haiti: Military Occupation and the Culture of U.S. Imperialism, 1915–1940*. Chapel Hill: University of North Carolina Press.

Richards, Shirley P. 2003. "Is It an Appropriate Message?" Letter to the editor, *Jamaica Gleaner*, 19 August.

Rivers, Eugene. 2005. "The Sins of the Fathers Are Visited on Black Youth." *Globe and Mail*, 2 December, A23.

Roach, Joseph. 1996. *Cities of the Dead: Circum-Atlantic Performance*. New York: Columbia University Press.

Roberts, Dorothy. 1998. *Killing the Black Body: Race, Reproduction, and the Meaning of Liberty*. New York: Vintage.

Robinson, Cedric. 1983. *Black Marxism: The Making of the Black Radical Tradition*. Chapel Hill: University of North Carolina Press.

Robinson, Randall. 2001. *The Debt: What America Owes to Blacks*. New York: Plume.

Robinson, Tracy. 2003. "Beyond the Bill of Rights: Sexing the Citizen." *Confronting Power, Theorizing Gender: Interdisciplinary Perspectives in the Caribbean*, ed. Eudine Barriteau, 231–61. Mona: University of the West Indies Press.

Robotham, Don. 1980. "Pluralism as an Ideology." *Social and Economic Studies* 29: 69–89.

———. 2000. "Blackening the Jamaican Nation: The Travails of a Black Bourgeoisie in a Globalized World." *Identities* 7(1): 1–37.

Rodman, Hyman. 1959. "On Understanding Lower-Class Behavior." *Social and Economic Studies* 8(4): 441–50.

———. 1971. *Lower-Class Families: The Culture of Poverty in Negro Trinidad*. New York: Oxford University Press.

Roering, Johanna. 2007. "No One Cares about Piccadilly Circus in the Ghetto: Representations of Space in Black British Pulp Fiction." *Territorial Terrors: Contested Spaces in Colonial and Postcolonial Writing*, ed. Gerhard Stilz, 213–26. Würzburg: Verlag Königshausen and Neumann.

Rofel, Lisa. 1999. *Other Modernities: Gendered Yearnings in China after Socialism*. Berkeley: University of California Press.

Roitman, Janet. 1998. "The Garrison-entrepôt." *Cahiers d'études africaines* 38, 150–52 (2–4): 297–329.

———. 2005. *Fiscal Disobedience: An Anthropology of Economic Regulation in Central Africa*. Princeton: Princeton University Press.

Roorda, Eric. 1998. *The Dictator Next Door: The Good Neighbor Policy and the Trujillo Regime in the Dominican Republic, 1930–1945*. Durham: Duke University Press.

Rosemblatt, Karin Alejandra. 2009. "Other Americas: Transnationalism, Scholarship, and the Culture of Poverty in Mexico and the United States." *Hispanic American Historical Review* 89(4): 603–41.

Rosenberg, Leah. 2004. "Caribbean Models for Modernism in the Work of Claude McKay and Jean Rhys." *Modernism/Modernity* 11(2): 219–38.

Ross, Fiona. 2003a. *Bearing Witness: Women and the Truth and Reconciliation Commission in South Africa*. London: Pluto.

———. 2003b. "On Having Voice and Being Heard: Some After-Effects of Testifying before the South African Truth and Reconciliation Commission." *Anthropological Theory* 3(3): 325–41.

Roxborough-Wright, Pat. 2007. "Rastafarians Demand Apology for Coral Gardens Incident." *Jamaica Observer*, 1 April. Available at http://www.jamaicaobserver.com (accessed 1 April 2007).

Rubenstein, Hymie. 1980. "Conjugal Behavior and Parental Role Flexibility in an Afro-Caribbean Village." *Canadian Review of Sociology and Anthropology* 17(4): 331–37.

———. 1983. "Caribbean Family and Household Organization: Some Conceptual Clarifications." *Journal of Comparative Family Studies* 14(3): 283–98.

Rutherford, Danilyn. 1996. "Of Birds and Gifts: Reviving Tradition on an Indonesian Frontier." *Cultural Anthropology* 11(4): 577–616.

Rydell, Robert. 1987. *All the World's a Fair: Visions of Empire at American International Expositions, 1876–1916*. Chicago: University of Chicago Press.

Saldaña-Portillo, María Josefina. 2003. *The Revolutionary Imagination in the Americas and the Age of Development*. Durham: Duke University Press.

Sanford, Victoria. 2004. *Buried Secrets: Truth and Human Rights in Guatemala*. New York: Palgrave Macmillan.

Sassen, Saskia. 1991. *The Global City: New York, London, Tokyo*. Princeton: Princeton University Press.

———. 2000. *Globalization and Its Discontents: Essays on the New Mobility of People and Money*. New York: New Press.

Saunders, Patricia. 2003. "Is Not Everything Good to Eat, Good to Talk: Sexual Economy and Dancehall Music in the Global Marketplace." *Small Axe* 7(1): 95–115.

Scarman, Baron Leslie. 1981. *The Scarman Report: The Brixton Disorders, 10–12 April 1981*. Harmondsworth: Penguin Books.

Scheper-Hughes, Nancy. 1993. *Death without Weeping: The Violence of Everyday Life in Brazil*. Berkeley: University of California Press.

Scott, David. 1997. "The 'Culture of Violence' Fallacy." *Small Axe* 1(2): 140–47.

———. 1999a. "The Archaeology of Black Memory: An Interview with Robert A. Hill." *Small Axe* 3(1): 80–150.

———. 1999b. *Refashioning Futures: Criticism after Postcoloniality*. Princeton: Princeton University Press.

———. 2004. *Conscripts of Modernity: The Tragedy of Colonial Enlightenment*. Durham: Duke University Press.

———. 2008. "Introduction: On the Archaeologies of Black Memory." *Small Axe* 12(2): v–xvi.

"Shaheed 'Roger' Khan: Drugs, Dirty Money, and the Death Squad." 2009. *Stabroek News*, 20 August. Available at http://www.stabroeknews.com (accessed 4 June 2010).

Shaw, Rosalind. 2007. "Displacing Violence: Making Pentecostal Memory in Postwar Sierra Leone." *Cultural Anthropology* 22(1): 66–93.

Sheller, Mimi. 2000. *Democracy after Slavery: Black Publics and Peasant Radicalism in Haiti and Jamaica*. Gainesville: University Press of Florida.

———. 2003. *Consuming the Caribbean: From Arawaks to Zombies*. New York: Routledge.

———. Forthcoming. *Citizenship from Below*. Durham: Duke University Press.

Silber, Irina Carlota. 2004. "Commemorating the Past in Post-War El Salvador." *Memory and the Impact of Political Transformation in Public Space*, ed. Daniel J. Walkowitz and Lisa Maya Knauer, pp. 211–232. Durham: Duke University Press.

———. 2007. "Local Capacity Building in 'Dysfunctional' Times: Internationals, Revolutionaries, and Activism in Postwar El Salvador." *Women's Studies Quarterly* 35(3–4): 167–84.

Silvera, Makeda. 1992. "Man-Royals and Sodomites: Some Thoughts on the Invisibility of Afro-Caribbean Lesbians." *Feminist Studies* 18(3): 521–32.

Silverblatt, Irene. 1991. "Interpreting Women in States: New Feminist Ethnohistories." In *Gender at the Crossroads of Knowledge: Feminist Anthropology in the Postmodern Era*, ed. Micaela di Leonardo, 140–71. Berkeley: University of California Press.

———. 2004. *Modern Inquisitions: Peru and the Colonial Origins of the Civilized World*. Durham: Duke University Press.

Simey, Thomas S. 1946. *Welfare and Planning in the West Indies*. Oxford: Clarendon.

Simpson, George Eaton. 1998. "Personal Reflections on Rastafari in West Kingston in the Early 1950s." *Chanting Down Babylon: The Rastafari Reader*, ed. Nathaniel Samuel Murrell, William David Spencer, and Adrian Anthony McFarlane, 217–28. Philadelphia: Temple University Press.

Sinclair, Glenroy. 2005a. "Eight Murdered in Twenty-Four Hours—Homicides Hurtle to Record Figure." *Jamaica Gleaner*, 4 November. Available at http://www.jamaica-gleaner.com (accessed 4 November 2005).

———. 2005b. "Gunmen Murder Six Women in Four Days—One Hundred and Nineteen since January." *Jamaica Gleaner*, 29 September. Available at http://www.jamaica-gleaner.com (accessed 2 October 2006).

———. 2005c. "Thugs Torch Family of Four—Ten-Year-Old's Wail Dies in Blaze." *Jamaica Gleaner*, 6 October. Available at http://www.jamaica-gleaner.com (accessed 6 October 2005).

———. 2007. "Fire for bullets—Gunmen hunt children with firebombs." *Jamaica Gleaner*, 10 October. Available at http://jamaica-gleaner.com (accessed 10 October 2007).

———. 2008a. "Green Bay Survivors Remember—Thirty Years after Killings,"

Jamaica Gleaner, 6 January. Available at http://www.jamaica-gleaner.com (accessed 13 March 2009).

———. 2008b. "Green Bay Survivors Remember 30 Years after the Massacre." *Sunday Gleaner*, 13 January. Available at http://www.jamaica-gleaner.com (accessed 25 February 2009).

Sinclair, Glenroy, and Dionne Rose. 2007. "Slaughter! Reprisal killings claim seven in east Kingston." *Jamaica Gleaner*, 6 October. Available at http://jamaica-gleaner.com (accessed 6 October 2007).

Sives, Amanda. 2002. "Changing Patrons, from Politician to Drug Don: Clientelism in Downtown Kingston, Jamaica." *Latin American Perspectives* 29(5): 66–89.

———. 2003. "The Historical Roots of Violence in Jamaica: The Hearne Report." *Understanding Crime in Jamaica: New Challenges for Public Policy*, ed. Anthony Harriott, 49–62. Mona: University of the West Indies Press.

———. 2010. *Elections, Violence, and the Democratic Process in Jamaica, 1944–2007.* Kingston: Ian Randle.

Skelton, Tracey. 1998. "Doing Violence / Doing Harm: British Media Representations of Jamaican Yardies." *Small Axe* 1(3): 27–48.

Slocum, Karla. 2006. *Free Trade and Freedom: Neoliberalism, Place, and Nation in the Caribbean.* Ann Arbor: University of Michigan Press.

Slocum, Karla, and Deborah A. Thomas. 2003. "Rethinking Global and Area Studies: Insights from Caribbeanist Anthropology." *American Anthropologist* 105(3): 553–65.

———. 2007. "Locality in Today's Global Caribbean: Shifting Economies of Nation, Race, and Development." *Identities* 14(1–2): 1–18.

Slotkin, Richard. 1973. *Regeneration through Violence: The Mythology of the American Frontier, 1600–1860.* Norman: University of Oklahoma Press.

———. 1994. *The Fatal Environment: The Myth of the Frontier in the Age of Industrialization, 1800–1890.* New York: Harper Perennial.

Small, Geoff. 1994. *Ruthless: The Global Rise of the Yardies.* London: Little Brown.

———. 1998. "Do They Mean Us?: A Reflection on the Making of the Yardie Myth in Britain." *Small Axe* 3:13–26.

Smalling, Ricardo. 2003. "Nudity as Symbol." Letter to the Editor, *Jamaica Gleaner*, 9 August. Available at http://www.jamaica-gleaner.com (accessed 28 November 2003).

Smedley, Audrey. 1993. *Race in North America: Origin and Evolution of a Worldview.* Boulder: Westview.

Smikle, Dwight. 2003. "Respect Each Other's Opinion." Letter to the editor, *Jamaica Gleaner*, 7 August. Available at http://www.jamaica-gleaner.com (accessed 28 November 2003).

Smith, Faith. 2006. "Commentary on 'Public Bodies: . . .'" *Journal of Latin American and Caribbean Anthropology* 11(1): 37–42.

Smith, Faith, ed. 2011. *Sex and the Citizen: Interrogating the Caribbean.* Charlottesville: University of Virginia Press.

Smith, Lloyd. 2003. "The Naked Truth." *Jamaica Observer*, 12 August. Available at http://www.jamaicaobserver.com (accessed 28 November 2003).

Smith, M. G. 1965. *The Plural Society in the British West Indies*. Berkeley: University of California Press.

———. 1966. "Introduction." *My Mother Who Fathered Me: A Study of the Family in Three Selected Communities in Jamaica*, ed. Edith Clarke, i–xliv. London: George Allen and Unwin.

Smith, M. G., Roy Augier, and Rex Nettleford. 1960. *The Rastafari Movement in Kingston, Jamaica*. Mona: Institute for Social and Economic Research, University College of the West Indies.

Smith, R. T. 1956. *The Negro Family in British Guiana*. London: Routledge and Kegan Paul.

———. 1967. "Social Stratification, Cultural Pluralism, and Integration in West Indian Societies." *Caribbean Integration: Papers on Social, Political, and Economic Integration*, 226–58. Rio Pedras: Institute of Caribbean Studies.

———. 1988. *Kinship and Class in the West Indies*. Cambridge: Cambridge University Press.

Smolenski, John, and Thomas J. Humphrey, eds. 2005. *New World Orders: Violence, Sanction, and Authority in the Colonial Americas*. Philadelphia: University of Pennsylvania Press.

Spillers, Hortense. 1987. "Mama's Baby, Papa's Maybe: An American Grammar Book." *Diacritics* 17(2): 65–81.

Stack, Carol. 1974. *All our Kin: Strategies for Survival in a Black Community*. New York: Basic Books.

Starn, Orin. 1991. "Missing the Revolution: Anthropologists and the War in Peru." *Cultural Anthropology* 6(1): 63–91.

———. 1999. *Nightwatch: The Politics of Protest in the Andes*. Durham: Duke University Press.

Stein, Rebecca. 2003. "Of Cafés and Colonialism: Israeli Leisure and the Question of Palestine (Again)." *Theory and Event* 6(3).

Stephens, Gregory. 1999. *On Racial Frontiers: The New Culture of Frederick Douglass, Ralph Ellison, and Bob Marley*. Cambridge: Cambridge University Press.

Stephens, Michelle. 2005. *Black Empire: The Masculine Global Imaginary of Caribbean Intellectuals in the United States, 1914–1962*. Durham: Duke University Press.

———. 2009. "What Is This *Black* in Black Diaspora?" *Small Axe* 29:26–38.

Stoler, Ann. 1989. "Making Empire Respectable: The Politics of Race and Sexual Morality in 20th Century Colonial Cultures." *American Ethnologist* 16(4): 634–60.

———. 1995. *Race and the Education of Desire: Foucault's History of Sexuality and the Colonial Order of Things*. Durham: Duke University Press.

———. 2002. *Carnal Knowledge and Imperial Power: Race and the Intimate in Colonial Rule*. Berkeley: University of California Press.

Stone, Carl. 1983. *Democracy and Clientelism in Jamaica*. New Brunswick: Transaction.

———. 1986. *Class, State, and Democracy in Jamaica*. New York: Praeger.

———. 1988. "Crime and Violence: Socio-Political Implications." *Crime and Violence: Causes and Solutions,* ed. Peter Phillips and Judith Wedderburn, 19–48. Mona: Department of Government, University of the West Indies.

Strangeways, Sam. 2010. "Bermuda's Per Capita Homicide Rate Was More than Five Times London's Rate in 2009." *Bermuda Royal Gazette,* 8 February. Available at http://www.royalgazette.com (accessed 8 February 2010).

Statistical Institute of Jamaica. 2009. *Labour Market and Earnings.* Kingston: Statistical Institute of Jamaica. Available at http://statinja.gov.jm/Unemployment RatesByAgeGroup.aspx (accessed 8 February 2010).

Sturken, Marita. 1997. *Tangled Memories: The Vietnam War, the AIDS Epidemic, and the Politics of Remembering.* Berkeley: University of California Press.

Stycos, J. Mayone, and Kurt Back. 1964. *The Control of Human Fertility in Jamaica.* Ithaca: Cornell University Press.

Sudarkasa, Niara. 1988. "African and Afro-American Family Structure." *Anthropology for the Nineties,* ed. Johnnetta Cole, 182–210. New York: Free Press.

Sundar, Nandini. 2004. "Toward an Anthropology of Culpability." *American Ethnologist* 31(2): 145–63.

Sutton, Constance. 1974. "Cultural Duality in the Caribbean." *Caribbean Studies* 14(2): 96–101.

———. 1984. "Africans in the Diaspora: Changing Continuities in West Indian and West African Sex/Gender Systems." Paper presented at New Perspectives on Caribbean Studies: Toward the 21st Century conference, 29 August.

Sutton, Constance, ed. 1995. *Feminism, Nationalism, and Militarism.* Arlington, Va.: Association for Feminist Anthropology, American Anthropological Association.

Sydial, Sylbourne. 2003. "Are Our Leaders Bankrupt of Vision and Ideas?" Letter to the editor, *Jamaica Observer,* 21 August. Available at http://www.jamaicaobserver.com (accessed 28 November 2003).

Tafari-Ama, Imani. 2006. *Blood, Bullets and Bodies: Sexual Politics below Jamaica's Poverty Line.* Kingston: Multi Media Communications.

Tate, Winnifred. 2007. *Counting the Dead: The Culture and Politics of Human Rights Activism in Colombia.* Berkeley: University of California Press.

Taussig, Michael. 1986. *Shamanism, Colonialism, and the Wild Man: A Study in Terror and Healing.* Chicago: University of Chicago Press.

———. 1992a. "Maleficium: State Fetishism." *The Nervous System,* 111–40. New York: Routledge.

———. 1992b. "Culture of Terror—Space of Death: Roger Casement's Putumayo Report and the Explanation of Torture." *Colonialism and Culture,* ed. Nicholas Dirks, 135–74. Ann Arbor: University of Michigan Press.

———. 1997. *The Magic of the State.* New York: Routledge.

Taylor, Diana. 1997. *Disappearing Acts: Spectacles of Gender and Nationalism in Argentina's "Dirty War."* Durham: Duke University Press.

———. 2003. *The Archive and the Repertoire: Performing Cultural Memory in the Americas.* Durham: Duke University Press.

Taylor, Frank. 1993. *To Hell with Paradise: A History of the Jamaican Tourism Industry.* Pittsburgh: University of Pittsburgh Press.

Taylor, Quintard. 1998. *In Search of the Racial Frontier: African Americans in the American West, 1528–1990.* New York: W. W. Norton.

Thomas, Antonnette. 2003. "Nudity Is Not Emancipation." Letter to the editor, *Jamaica Gleaner*, 18 August. Available at http://www.jamaica-gleaner.com (accessed 28 November 2003).

Thomas, Deborah A. 2002. "Democratizing Dance: Institutional Transformation and Hegemonic Re-Ordering in Postcolonial Jamaica." *Cultural Anthropology* 17(4): 512–50.

———. 2004. *Modern Blackness: Nationalism, Globalization, and the Politics of Culture in Jamaica.* Durham: Duke University Press.

———. 2005. "Development, 'Culture,' and the Promise of Modern Progress." *Social and Economic Studies* 54(3): 97–125.

Thomas, Deborah A., and Kamari M. Clarke. 2006. "Introduction: Globalization and the Transformations of Race." *Globalization and Race: Transformations in the Cultural Production of Blackness*, ed. Kamari M. Clarke and Deborah A. Thomas. Durham: Duke University Press.

Thomas, Deborah A., and Karla Slocum. 2008. "Caribbean Studies, Anthropology, and U.S. Academic Realignments." *Souls* 10(2): 123–37.

Thomas, Phyllis. 2004. "Reversing the Culture of Violence in Jamaica." *Sunday Gleaner*, 2 May. Available at http://jamaica-gleaner.com (accessed 2 October 2006).

"Time for Honest Assessment of Rastafari." 2007. Editorial, *Jamaica Observer*, 2 April. Available at http://www.jamaicaobserver.com (accessed 2 April 2007).

"Tony Blair's 'Sorrow' over Slave Trade." 2006. *Daily Mail*, ed., 26 November. Available at http://www.dailymail.co.uk (accessed 2 November 2007).

Treaster, Joseph B. 1988. "Jamaica's Gangs Take Root in U.S." *New York Times*, 13 November, sec. 1, 15.

Trotz, D. Alissa. 2003. "Behind the Banner of Culture?: Gender, 'Race' and the Family in Guyana." *New West Indian Guide* 77(1–2): 5–29.

———. 2004. "Between Despair and Hope: Women and Violence in Contemporary Guyana." *Small Axe* 8(1): 1–20.

Trouillot, Michel Rolph. 1992. "The Caribbean: An Open Frontier." *Annual Review of Anthropology* 21:19–42.

———. 1995. *Silencing the Past: Power and the Production of History.* Boston: Beacon.

———. 2000. "Abortive Rituals: Historical Apologies in the Global Era." *Interventions* 2(2): 171–86.

———. 2001. "The Anthropology of the State in the Age of Globalization: Close Encounters of the Deceptive Kind." *Current Anthropology* 42(1): 125–38.

———. 2002. "The Otherwise Modern: Caribbean Lessons from the Savage Slot." *Critically Modern: Alternatives, Alterities, Anthropologies*, ed. Bruce Knauft, 220–37. Bloomington: Indiana University Press.

Tsing, Anna. 2005. *Friction: An Ethnography of Global Connection*. Princeton: Princeton University Press.

"Tubal Ligation Proposal Causes a Stir in House." 2003. *Jamaica Gleaner*, 30 July. Available at http://www.jamaica-gleaner.com (accessed 28 November 2003).

Turner, Frederick Jackson. 1963. *The Frontier in American History*. New York: Holt.

Turner, Mary. 1982. *Slaves and Missionaries: The Disintegration of Jamaican Slave Society, 1787–1834*. Urbana: University of Illinois Press.

Turner, Victor. 1969. *The Ritual Process: Structure and Anti-Structure*. Chicago: Aldine.

———. 1974. *Dramas, Fields, and Metaphors: Symbolic Action in Human Society*. Ithaca: Cornell University Press.

Ulysse, Gina. 1999. "Uptown Ladies and Downtown Women: Female Representations of Class and Color in Jamaica." *Representations of Blackness and the Performance of Identities*, ed. Jean Rahier, 147–72. New Haven: Greenwood.

United Nations Office on Drugs and Crime and Latin American and Caribbean Region of the World Bank. 2007. *Crime, Violence, and Development: Trends, Costs, and Policy Options in the Caribbean*. Report no. 37820, Washington.

Uribe, Maria Victoria. 2004. "Dismembering and Expelling: Semantics of Political Terror in Colombia." *Public Culture* 16(1): 79–95.

U.S. Department of Labor. 1965. *The Negro Family: The Case for National Action*. Washington: U.S. Department of Labor.

Valentine, Charles. 1968. *Culture and Poverty: Critique and Counter-Proposals*. Chicago: University of Chicago Press.

Venkatesh, Sudhir Alladi. 2002. *American Project: The Rise and Fall of a Modern Ghetto*. Cambridge: Harvard University Press.

Verdery, Katherine. 2000. *The Political Lives of Dead Bodies: Reburial and Postsocialist Change*. New York: Columbia University Press.

Von Eschen, Penny M. 1997. *Race against Empire: Black Americans and Anticolonialism, 1937–1957*. Ithaca: Cornell University Press.

Wagley, Charles. 1957. "Plantation-America: A Culture Sphere." *Caribbean Studies: A Symposium*, ed. Vera Rubin, 3–13. Mona: Institute of Social and Economic Research, University College of the West Indies.

Walker, Karyl. 2004a. "Jacks Hills Erupts as Gangs Clash." *Jamaica Observer*, 10 December. Available at http://www.jamaicaobserver.com (accessed 10 December 2004).

———. 2004b. "Teen Gangs in Deadly Battle for Control of Jacks Hill Community." *Jamaica Observer*, 13 June. Available at http://www.jamaicaobserver.com (accessed 13 June 2004).

Walsh, Margaret. 1981. *The American Frontier Revisited*. Atlantic Highlands, N.J.: Humanities.

Wang, Yu. 2007. *Naturalizing Ethnicity, Culturalizing Landscape: The Politics of World Heritage in China*. Ph.D. dissertation, Department of Cultural Anthropology, Duke University.

Warner, Lloyd, Buford Junker, and Walter Adams. 1941. *Color and Human Nature:*

Negro Personality Development in a Northern City. Washington: American Council on Education.

Waters, Anita. 1985. *Race, Class, and Political Symbols: Rastafari and Reggae in Jamaican Politics.* New Brunswick, N.J.: Transaction Books.

Watkins-Owens, Irma. 1996. *Blood Relations: Caribbean Immigrants and the Harlem Community, 1900–1930.* Bloomington: Indiana University Press.

Whitehead, Neil. 2004. "Introduction: Cultures, Conflicts, and the Poetics of Violent Practice." *Violence,* ed. Neil Whitehead, 3–24. Santa Fe: School of American Research Press.

"Why Jamaican Men Rape." 2006. *Sunday Gleaner,* 19 March. Available at http://www.jamaica-gleaner.com (accessed 19 March 2006).

Williams, Brackette. 1996. "Introduction: Mannish Women and Gender after the Act." *Women Out of Place: The Gender of Agency and the Race of Nationality,* ed. Brackette Williams, 1–33, 129–58. New York: Routledge.

Williams, Joan. 1997. "A Squandered Legacy." *Daily Observer,* 4 August, 6.

Williams, Prince Elijah. 2005. *Book of Memory: A Rastafari Testimony,* ed. Michael Kuelker. St. Louis, Mo.: CaribSound.

Willis, Deborah, and Carla Williams. 2002. *The Black Female Body: A Photographic History.* Philadelphia: Temple University Press.

Wilson, Cedric. 2005. "Broken Windows and Young Minds." *Sunday Gleaner,* 16 October. Available at http://www.jamaica-gleaner.com (accessed 16 October 2005).

Wilson, Peter. 1973. *Crab Antics: The Social Anthropology of English-Speaking Negro Societies of the Caribbean.* New Haven: Yale University Press.

Wilson, Richard A. 2003. "Anthropological Studies of National Reconciliation Processes." *Anthropological Theory* 3(3): 367–87.

Wintour, Patrick, and Vikram Dodd. 2007. "Blair Blames Spate of Murders on Black Culture." *Guardian,* 12 April. Available at http://www.guardian.co (accessed 19 July 2007).

Witter, George. 2003. "Still in 'Chains.'" Letter to the editor, *Jamaica Gleaner,* 12 August. Available at http://www.jamaica-gleaner.com (accessed 28 November 2003).

Wynter, Sylvia. 2003. "Un-settling the Coloniality of Being/Power/Truth/Freedom: Towards the Human, after Man, Its Overrepresentation." *New Centennial Review* 3(3): 257–338.

Yawney, Carole. 1978. "Lions in Babylon: The Rastafarians of Jamaica as a Visionary Movement." Ph.D. diss., McGill University, Montreal.

———. 2001. "Exodus: Rastafari, Repatriation, and the African Renaissance." *A United States of Africa?,* ed. Eddy Maloka, 131–85. Pretoria: Africa Institute of South Africa.

Yelvington, Kevin. 1995. *Producing Power: Ethnicity, Gender, and Class in a Caribbean Workplace.* Philadelphia: Temple University Press.

———. 1999. "The War in Ethiopia and Trinidad, 1935–1936." *The Colonial Caribbean in Transition: Essays on Postemancipation Social and Cultural History,* ed. Bridget Brereton and Kevin A. Yelvington, 189–225. Gainesville: University Press of Florida.

————. 2001. "The Anthropology of Afro-Latin America and the Caribbean." *Annual Review of Anthropology* 30:227–260.

————. 2006a. "Introduction." *Afro-Atlantic Dialogues: Anthropology in the Diaspora*, ed. Kevin A. Yelvington, 3–32. Santa Fe: School of American Research Press.

————. 2006b. "The Invention of Africa in Latin America and the Caribbean: Political Discourse and Anthropological Praxis, 1920–1940." *Afro-Atlantic Dialogues: Anthropology in the Diaspora*, ed. Kevin Yelvington, 35–82. Santa Fe: School of American Research Press.

Young, Kevin. 2003. "Conceptions of Morality." Letter to the editor, *Jamaica Gleaner*, 8 August. Available at http://www.jamaica-gleaner.com (accessed 28 November 2003).

Žižek, Slavoj. 2002. *Welcome to the Desert of the Real*. New York: Verso.

Index

Page numbers in italics refer to illustrations.

Counterculture of modernity, 120
Cox, Aimee, 232–33
Crack trade, 70, 235. *See also* Drug trade
Creolization, 102–3, 132, 167, 204, 212
Crime. *See* Drug trade; Murder rates;
  Violence; Weapons trade
Crisis talk, 19–20, 128–29
Culture, 4, 18, 146, 176; authenticity and,
  99–101; citizenship and, 15, 20–21, 43,
  126, 131–32, 140, 170; idealist theory
  of, 60; national policy, 19, 90, 97–105;
  of poverty, 56, 65–66, 69, 83, 84, 244
  n. 14; of violence, 54–56, 70–79, 83,
  210
Culture (band), 119

Dancehall culture, 19, 28, 82, 135, 138, 139,
  146–47, 153–54, 157–58
Dancehall Queen (film), 147
Das, Veena, 26, 43, 110, 177
Dayan, Joan, 112
Death and dying practices, 50, 106
Debord, Guy, 91–93, 105, 123
Delavante, Marilyn, 134
Delgado, Junior, 118
Detective character, 122
Diamond, Macka, 126, 146, 154, 157, 165.
  See also *Bun' Him!!!*
Diaspora, 56, 67, 128; community for-
  mation and, 69, 142; effects of, 20, 21;
  historical reconstruction and, 178;
  identity and, 10; political engagement
  and, 141–42, 245 n. 19, 248 n. 1; scholar-
  ship on, 16, 17, 68–69, 84–85; social
  divisions and, 143; as term, 16, 18, 246
  n. 20; transnationalism and, 3–4, 16, 57,
  74, 85, 126, 153; violence and, 55, 74
DiGenova, Joseph E., 70
Discrimination: of black Britons, 76; in
  Canada, 73; global, 101; institutional, 6;
  against Jamaicans, 55, 79, 141–42, 170
Drake, St. Clair, 67
Drug trade, 73, 152; authority and, 42;

crack trade, 70, 235; ganja trade, 37,
  192; posses, 150; rivalries in, 149; solution to, 236; violence and, 24, 35, 42, 55,
  70–72, 74, 235; wealth in, 124; weapons
  trade and, 37, 71, 88, 96, 124, 147
"Dudus Wet Himself" (Neal painting),
  226
Dysfunction discourse, 56

Edwards, Brent, 67, 84
Egerton, Douglas, 106
Ellis, Vincent, 196–97
Emancipation Day, 20, 112, 129, 194
Emancipation Park (New Kingston), 129
Enid, Empress, 194, 195–96, 206, 208, 211
Ethio-Africa Diaspora Union Millennium
  Council, 213–14
Ethiopian Orthodox Church, 202
Ethnic difference and violence, 9, 10, 109,
  111, 223
Exclusion, 8, 79, 102, 174, 223. *See also*
  Belonging

Facey Cooper, Laura, 129–31. *See also*
  "Redemption Song"
Family formation, 58, 62–65, 83; African
  American, 61; black, 7, 57–60, 84; dys-
  functional, 18, 75–77; gender roles in,
  19; missionaries on, 243 n. 3; neoliber-
  alism on, 82; racialized difference and,
  64, 79; role models and, 105; slavery
  and, 7; social position and, 127; state
  and, 59–60, 79, 131
Fanon, Frantz, 8
Farred, Grant, 152–53
Fascism, 44
Femininity, policing, 166, 170–71
Ferguson, James, 17–18, 44
Fineman, Martha, 140
Fisher, John, 186
Forbes, Curdella, 152
Ford-Smith, Honor, 237
Forgiveness, 110, 205, 225, 238

Foucault, Michel, 59–60
Fowler, Edward, 186, 188
Franklin, Rudolph, 180–88
Frazier, E. Franklin, 61, 63, 68
Freedmen's Bureau, 59
Freeman, Carla, 83
Frontiers, 40–51; cultures of, 27; move-
　ment to, 242 n. 11

Galley, Pa, 184–85
Gangs, 36; branding by, 74; genealogies
　and, 34; political, 3, 35, 37, 96; state
　functions by, 8; war mobilization, 26.
　See also Posses
Gangster character, 20, 122–23, 147. *See*
　also under titles of specific works
Ganja, 37, 192
Garbarino, Steve, 146–47
Garraway, Doris, 108
Garrell, Sidney, 201
Garrison communities, 3, 35–37, 43, 206,
　210
"Garrison Justice" and "Garrison Jus-
　tice 2" (Neal paintings), 227
Garvey, Marcus, 130, 141
Gender, 64, 163; ideologies, 80; norms of,
　15, 19, 20, 56, 168; relations of, 145, 162;
　roles of, 63; spectacular punishments
　and, 108; value systems and, 144–45
Genealogies, 34; performance, 89; slavery
　and, 49, 93; violence and, 27, 29, 32,
　106, 123
Gilroy, Paul, 75–76, 120
Golding, Bruce, 223–24
Goldstein, Daniel, 109–10
Gould, Eliga, 106
Governance entities, 6–7, 16–17
"Governmentality" (Foucault), 59–60
Graham, Narda, 136
Gray, Obika, 13, 94–95, 96
Great houses, 114–15, *116–17*
Greenwood Great House, 114–15; arti-
　facts of terror at, 115, *116–17*

Grewal, Inderpal, 126
Grosset, Noel, 186
Gupta, Akhil, 17–18
Gutzmore, Cecil, 168

Haitian Revolution, 107, 122, 230
Halbwachs, Maurice, 176
Hale, Owen, 184–85, 186, 188
Hall, Stuart, 202–3
Hanchard, Michael, 178
Hansen, Thomas, 9
Harder They Come, The (film), 147
Harrison, Faye, 38
Hay-Webster, Sharon, 80
Headley, Victor, 126, 146, 147, 150–53, 162.
　See also *Yardie* trilogy
Hegel, G. W. F., 7
Henriques, Hewart, 197
Henry, Mike, 205
Herman, Ellen, 61
Heroin trade, 73
Herskovits, Melville, 63, 67–68
Hesse, Barnor, 93
Heteropatriarchy. *See* Patriarchy
Hewitt, Joyce, 80
Higgs, Joe, 119
Hinds, Robert, 202
Hintzen, Percy, 132
Holston, James, 33
Homophobia, 168
Homosexuality, 127, 164
Howell, Leonard, 202, 204, 214
Hugh, Bernadette, 201

Identity: creolization and, 102–3; dias-
　pora and, 10; inherited, 78–79; Jamai-
　can national, 12, 78, 102–3, 132–33, 167;
　reparations and, 203
IION (Indigenous Initiatory Circle of
　Nature) Station, 214–16, *215*, 217
Immigration and Naturalization Service,
　U.S. (INS), 70, 71
Imperialism: democracy and, 5; as ob-

Violence (*continued*)
57, 79; genealogies and, 29, 32, 34; guns and, 150, 237; imperial, 12; roots of, in slavery, 19; sexual, 58, 80, 127, 163–64; sovereignty and, 43; spatial effects of, 26; spatial logic to, 54; spectacular, 19, 89–91, 93, 120, 124, 231; by state, 8, 20, 174, 252 n. 10; structural, 24

Virginity testing, 80, 82

Von Eschen, Penny, 68

vp Records, 154

Wailing Souls (band), 119

Waldron, Barry, 184

Waldron, Clifton, 184

Waldron, Lloyd (Felix), 185–86, 187

Walker, Karyl, 34–35

Weapons trade, 124, 152; drug trade and, 37, 71, 88, 96, 147; inner-city communities and, 35, 38; solution to, 236; transnational, 74

Wedderburn, Junior "Gabu," 193–94, 199

Welfare reforms, 84

West, William D., 70

West India Royal Commission, 62, 203

"What is Slackness?" (song), 169

Whiteness, 131, 143

White Witch of Rose Hall, 113–14

Wild 2 Nite (album), 154

Williams, Corporal, 186

Williams, Hype, 126, 159, 161. See also *Belly*

Williams, Prince Elijah, 181–82, 197–99

Wilson, Cedric, 54

Wilson, Peter, 143–45

Wilson, Richard, 228–29

Witnessing, 107, 237–38

Witter, George, 136

Women, 64, 80, 82; family formation and, 63; representation of, 163; on respectability, 144–45, 249 n. 10; sterilization of, 81

Women's Bureau, 82

Women's Inc., 80

Women's Media Watch, 80

World Bank, 2, 36

World Conference against Racism, Racial Discrimination, Xenophobia, and Related Intolerance, 221–22

World Trade Center attacks (2001), 92

Wray, Eddie "First Man," 211, 212–13, 215, 217–18

X Press, 150

Yardies. *See* Posses

Yardie trilogy (Headley), 20, 126, 153, 162–63; criticism of, 150–52; *Excess* story line, 148, 164–65; *Yardie* story line, 147; *Yush!* story line, 149

Yawney, Carole, 179

Young, Kevin, 136

Zanzibar Revolt (1964), 202

Zionism, 8, 222

Žižek, Slavoj, 92

Deborah A. Thomas is professor of anthropology at the University of Pennsylvania. She is the author of *Modern Blackness: Nationalism, Globalization, and the Politics of Culture in Jamaica* (Duke, 2004) and the editor, with Kamari Clarke, of *Globalization and Race: Transformations in the Cultural Production of Blackness* (Duke, 2006).

Library of Congress Cataloging-in-Publication Data
Thomas, Deborah A., 1966–
Exceptional violence : embodied citizenship in
transnational Jamaica / Deborah A. Thomas.
p. cm.
Includes bibliographical references and index.
ISBN 978-0-8223-5068-2 (cloth : alk. paper)
ISBN 978-0-8223-5086-6 (pbk. : alk. paper)
1. Violent crimes—Jamaica. 2. Social classes—Jamaica.
3. Slavery—Jamaica—History. 4. Reparations for historical
injustices—Jamaica. I. Title.
F1874.T466 2011
364.15097292—dc22   2011015703